SCHLESWIG-HOLSTEIN
1815–48

SCHLESWIG–HOLSTEIN, GENERAL MAP

Schleswig-Holstein
1815–48

A STUDY IN
NATIONAL CONFLICT

by

W. CARR
Lecturer in Modern History
in the University of Sheffield

MANCHESTER
UNIVERSITY PRESS

Published by the University of Manchester at
The University Press
316–324 Oxford Road, Manchester 13

Printed in Great Britain by Butler & Tanner Ltd, Frome and London

Preface

THE fortunes of war made me familiar with Schleswig-Holstein and prompted me in the first place to inquire into the growth of German nationalism in this historic corner of Germany. But the present work is not concerned solely with German nationalism; Schleswig is one of those frontier regions where rival nationalisms contended for power in the nineteenth century. It is the conflict between the German and Danish nationalities which forms the central theme of this book. It was readily assumed in the early nineteenth century that liberalism and nationalism were compatible and complementary concepts. The history of Schleswig and of other frontier regions seems to show that there is a point beyond which nationalism can easily become an illiberal force. Once that point had been reached in Schleswig in the late 1840's the mutual trust between German and Dane on which the *Helstat* had rested for generations was destroyed, and an armed conflict broke out on the eve of the 1848 revolution.

The first chapter on the origins of German nationalism does not pretend to be more than a survey of the intellectual and economic forces making for unification. It is intended to assist the general reader who may be unfamiliar with the complexities of the subject. Similarly, a final chapter has been added which summarizes the main developments in Schleswig-Holstein between 1848 and 1864 and carries the story on to the point when it assumed major international importance.

A word of explanation is called for on the use of personal and place-names in the text. When referring to the kingdom of Denmark proper, the Danish name has been used, i.e. King Frederik, not Frederick, and Roskilde, not Roeskilde—but it would have been unduly pedantic to have preferred the Danish København to the well-established English name Copenhagen. In the case of Germany and of Holstein German personal and place-names have generally been used. Schleswig, however, presents a more difficult problem in view of its national division. The Germans call it Schleswig, the Danes call it Slesvig or Sønderjylland whilst Palmerston preferred the Anglicized form Sleswick. I have used the German name Schleswig, but this does not, I trust, imply uncritical acceptance of the claims of the German nationality. In an attempt to do justice to both German and Dane—as far as this is possible—and for the sake of uniformity, I have used the Danish name for all places in Schleswig which lie north of the Flensburg–Tønder line, i.e. roughly the line of the present frontier between Germany and Denmark, and the German name for places in Schleswig lying south of this frontier. It seemed more sensible to use the Danish names Tønder and Haderslev as these towns have been called since the plebiscite of 1920 returned them to Denmark, rather than the old German names Tondern and Hadersleben. Equally there seemed little point in writing Slesvig and Egernførde—as some Danish writers do—instead of Schleswig and Eckernförde when these towns have been indisputably German for centuries.

Finally, I wish to acknowledge my indebtedness to the Research Fund Committee of the University of Sheffield without whose generous financial assistance the long periods of research entailed by this project in London and in Kiel as well as the publication of the present volume would not have been possible. I am also grateful for helpful suggestions and encouragement given me by the head of the Department of Medieval and Modern History at Sheffield University, Professor G. R. Potter.

W. CARR

Contents

The following abbreviations have been used in the footnotes and bibliography:

A.A.Z.	*Augsburger Allgemeine Zeitung*
D.M.	*Danske Magazin*
H.T.	*Historisk Tidsskrift*
K.B.	*Kieler Blätter*
K.K.B.	*Kieler Korrespondenz Blatt*
L.A.S.	Landesarchiv Schleswig
N.K.B.	*Neuen Kieler Blätter*
P.A.	Primkenauer Archiv
P.R.O.	Public Records Office
S.A.	*Sønderjydske Aarbøger*
St.Z.	*Ständezeitung*
U.B.	Universitätsbibliothek, Kiel
Z.	*Zeitschrift der Gesellschaft für Schleswig-Holsteinische Geschichte*

Note

The German term 'Schleswig-Holsteiner' referring to those who live in the duchies has been translated as 'people' or 'inhabitants'. Where the term Schleswig-Holsteiner has been used in the text it refers to those people who supported the political movement seeking partial or complete independence for the duchies.

I

The origins of German nationalism

NATIONALISM, one of the dynamic, formative forces of the nineteenth and twentieth centuries, was a sentiment alien to the eighteenth century. There were no signs of German national feeling in the ramshackle Holy Roman Empire at this time. Loyalty to the Emperor was to all intents and purposes non-existent; his authority was restricted to the hereditary possessions in Austria. The dominant feature of the German political landscape was the existence of over three hundred states, great and small, all virtually independent since the Treaty of Westphalia in 1648.

The rulers of these states had absolute powers; they slavishly imitated the methods of government and the court life of the 'grand monarch' Louis XIV. In some ways these rulers were more powerful at the close of the eighteenth century than they had ever been before. It is true that absolutism had been tempered somewhat by the spirit of the *Aufklärung*—but it had also been strengthened by this spirit. The second half of the eighteenth century was a period of economic change in Europe; war had stimulated a demand for wheat, new techniques were improving productivity in the countryside, trade was expanding and towns were growing in size. The social pattern was beginning to alter, the rigidity of the seventeenth century was breaking down and the middle class was at last beginning to assume some social significance. But this did not lead to any alteration in the internal balance of power in Germany, partly because in a pre-industrial society the middle class is too small and weak to offer effective resistance to rulers, and partly because many rulers were prepared to accommodate themselves to this changing pattern. They made some effort to modernize the state, loosening the feudal ties restricting trade and industry, alleviating the hardship of the peasant and beginning the removal of the more irksome feudal jurisdictions. In this way rulers were able to preserve their absolute monopoly of political power. The middle-class officials and merchants, grateful for favours received, were strengthened in their loyalty. They accepted exclusion from affairs of state and made little attempt to create a politically conscious public opinion. In general they preferred to philosophize about education and dabble in literature rather than in politics.

The *Aufklärung*, which came to Germany from England and France, had helped to mellow and preserve absolutism. It also produced a great cultural renaissance in Germany, an unparalleled outpouring of the genius of the German people in poetry, philosophy and music. This was the age of classical humanism between 1780 and 1830 when the names of Goethe, Schiller, Lessing, Kant and Beethoven made Germany the intellectual centre of Europe for about sixty years. The new humanism was the product of a revolt against the ossified categories of the eighteenth century. The German humanists were contemptuous of the stifling etiquette and servility of the small courts and resentful of the slavish imitation of French styles. They turned away in disgust to the study of classical antiquity, where they discovered in Greek man—or thought they had discovered—the prototype of the autonomous, self-reliant and fully-developed individual they sought to emulate. The central tenet of the new humanism was the belief that it was the supreme goal of society to assist the individual to develop his personality through the harmonious cultivation of all his potentialities.

The revolt of the new humanists against the dominance of French literary styles led them, inevitably, to a new appreciation of their national past so neglected by eighteenth-century historians. J. von Herder, one of the great figures of classical humanism, played a major part in the rediscovery of Germany's past. Von Herder found a whole world beyond the superficial analysis of the eighteenth century, a world where the infinite variety and depth of the differences between individuals and peoples enriched the tapestry of human existence. Von Herder was the first to realize that civilization was national rather than universal in its manifestations; men became creative forces only as members of a national community with roots reaching back to a remote past. They expressed themselves through the medium of a folk language and in folk-lore; these were manifestations of a folk-spirit (or *Volksgeist*) to which von Herder was the first to attach great significance.

Von Herder was, in fact, the first to develop a philosophy of national culture. But neither von Herder nor his fellow humanists were nationalists properly so-called. The *Aufklärung* in Germany was a middle-class renaissance; the humanists naturally shared the values and attitudes of the social group to which they belonged. The eighteenth century was the age of patriotic societies founded by the middle class to further their material and cultural advancement. But 'patriotism' and 'national spirit' were equated in the middle-class mind not with nationalism but with civic virtue and obedience to lawful authority. In general the *Aufklärung* was hostile to national idiosyncrasies, for it was believed that what divided men was far less important than that which united them; all men were endowed with reason, a common humanity embraced them all irrespective of national divisions. Von Herder always condemned national pride, regarding all peoples as equal and all subject to the universal laws of humanity. The notion that nations might be beyond the operation of the moral law he rejected as 'a remnant of the madness and stupidity of the barbarians'.[1] *Weltbürgertum* was the educational ideal for the educated man; as H. Voss, a Schleswig-Holstein poet, remarked, '*Ein edler Geist klebt nicht am Staube; ihn engt kein Vaterland.*'[2]

All the same, there were some signs of national sentiment in Germany in the second half of the eighteenth century. The Seven Years War, for example, stimulated pride in the martial deeds of

[1] K. S. Pinson, *Modern Germany, its history and civilisation*, New York, 1954, p. 16.

[2] P. von Hedemann-Heespern, *Die Herzogtümer Schleswig-Holstein und die Neuzeit*, p. 586.

Prussia far beyond the frontiers of that kingdom. When poets like J. Klopstock praised Frederick the Great and attacked the French there were unmistakable national undertones in their writing. But it was not modern nationalism because it lacked political connotations. A people is only nationally conscious in the modern sense of the word when emotional awareness of their nationality moves them to seek a political framework; that is, when they seek to identify the concept of nation with that of the state. This may take the form of a conscious act of will by the people concerned; this is the liberal path to nationhood, a path which predicates political change, because only when the old relationship between ruler and subject has been superseded by a nation of free citizens will the people be able to express their conscious desire for nationhood. The ground in Germany was unfavourable for this theory; there were no signs of political discontent at the close of the eighteenth century because, as indicated above, the pre-industrial middle class was perfectly satisfied with the existing structure of government.

There was, however, another path to nationhood, the conservative path. This did not predicate political change because conservatives maintained that a nation came into being not in response to the will of the people, but as a result of a slow, organic process, a movement of blind, primeval forces over which man had little if any control; this implied that nationalism was quite compatible with an autocratic society. By and large Germany took the conservative rather than the liberal path in her advance to nationhood.

The connection between nationalism and conservatism received its first indelible expression in German Romanticism. Romanticism, like the *Aufklärung*, was part of a broader European movement; but nowhere did it exert a more profound influence than in Germany, where it affected most branches of human activity, science as well as the arts, economics as well as politics. The Romantics originated as a literary circle in the 1790's, including such figures as A. W. Schlegel, A. Müller and J. G. Fichte. Romanticism represented a reaction against the *Aufklärung*. The new humanists, although believing in the autonomous development of the individual, had always been guided and restrained by reason. Not so the Romantics; they delved deep down into the irrational springs of human conduct. Enthusiasm, feeling and imagination were their criteria, not reason. The Romantics were anti-French partly because they were in revolt against the *Aufklärung*, and partly because the French were in occupation of a large area of Germany.

At first, like the humanists of the older generation, the Romantics evinced no interest in politics. So disgusted were they with the sorry spectacle of Germany weak and divided at the beginning of the nineteenth century, that they turned away from real life and immersed themselves in the rich cultural heritage of Germany. '*Deutsches Reich und deutsche Nation sind zweierlei Dinge*,' commented Schiller in a revealing phrase.[1] This revulsion from politics had a curious and vitally important result for Germany. The national sentiment latent in Romanticism found expression in a purely cultural concept of nationalism—the *Kulturnation* or *Kulturgemeinschaft*. The Romantics came readily to believe that Germany had a special mission to represent humanity in the modern world much as the Greeks had represented it in the ancient world. Natural pride in the great intellectual achievements of their fellow countrymen was soon transformed into a belief in the superiority of the Germans. The Romantics were convinced that the German people were the true embodiment of universal ideas and were destined to educate a race of intellectual supermen. Schlegel and Novalis agreed with Schiller that Germany served humanity best by disengaging the national concept from politics; it was Germany's mission to lead the world to true universality. In effect the Romantics transformed the universally oriented culture of the Enlightenment into a German national culture with an expansionist mission. The close links which they forged between national and supranational concepts were not severed until the middle of the nineteenth century. The result was that German intellectuals in the first half of the century were never conscious of any real antithesis between the national idea and the service of

[1] *Deutsche Literatur. Reihe Politische Dichtung.* Bd. 2. *Fremdherrschaft und Befreiung 1795–1815*, Leipzig, 1932, p. 18.

humanity. In F. Meinecke's apt phrase they considered it 'un-German to think only of Germany'.[1]

The early years of the nineteenth century saw great changes in Germany. There were territorial changes which drastically reduced the number of states and completely destroyed the old Empire. Even more important were the changes caused by the impact of the French Revolution on the structure of German society. The French armies brought with them new techniques of government and the Code Napoleon. In the areas directly under their control they emancipated the serfs, freed trade and abolished feudal jurisdictions. Those princes, few in number, who had survived the territorial changes were transformed into modern rulers, and the middle class was liberated from the accumulated lumber of centuries of feudalism. But this did not lead to any alteration in the relationship between ruler and subject; this pre-industrial middle class was a passive recipient of benefits bestowed on it from above by the French and by their satellite princes. Napoleon was a popular figure in Germany; statesmen and middle-class writers regarded him as the regenerator of Germany. Hegel sang his praises; Goethe never went out without wearing the cross of the French Legion of Honour and always referred to Napoleon as 'my emperor'. Outside the circle of the Romantics the dissolution of the Empire in 1806 aroused little comment and no misgiving. The Confederation of the Rhine was generally regarded as a more viable and socially progressive political form. When Austria and Prussia went to war with the French the conflict did not arouse much interest in other parts of Germany.

Only after 1808 was there a reaction against French domination. In Germany, as elsewhere in Europe, there was bitter resentment at the ever-increasing burden of taxation, the hardship of Napoleon's interminable wars and his interference in the internal affairs of many German states; the result was a recrudescence of national sentiment deeply influenced by the writings of the Romantics.

The contribution of the Romantics to the development of

[1] F. Meinecke, *Weltbürgertum und Nationalstaat. Studien zur Genesis des deutschen Nationalstaates*, p. 59.

German nationalism was twofold. In the first place they taught Germany to look back to the Middle Ages for the prototype of a truly national society. This was an accidental by-product of their interest in history. Depressed by the political weakness of Germany, they turned to history for consolation and rediscovered the Middle Ages, a period dismissed by the eighteenth century as 'barbaric' and 'gothic'; they were fascinated by what they found —or imagined they had found—in the history of medieval Germany. They saw Germany by candlelight and in the shadow of ruined Rhineland castles, conjuring up a fantastic picture of a patriarchal society unspoilt by the rational spirit of the Enlightenment or by modern capitalism. They were enthusiastic collectors of medieval folk-lore and folk songs because they considered medieval culture a truly popular culture, a manifestation of the *Volksgeist*. It was also a truly national culture; national characteristics were never so pronounced and pure as in the days of the 'German' knighthood and the 'German' guilds. For this reason the Romantics elevated the political structure of medieval Germany into an absolute binding for all time; the resurrection of the old 'German' estates of the Middle Ages seemed the form of government best suited to a nationally conscious Germany. This longing for a return to the patriarchal and corporate society of the Middle Ages exerted a profound influence upon liberal as well as conservative thought in the first three decades of the nineteenth century.

Secondly, the Romantics stumbled on a new concept of the state; this was perhaps their most important contribution to German nationalism. The eighteenth century had conceived of the state as a static entity, the conscious creation of isolated individuals co-operating for purely utilitarian purposes. Although the Romantics were individualists, paradoxically enough this led them to recognize the need for community and fellowship with others because the personality of the individual was moulded by the culture and traditions of the society to which he belonged. The Romantics were reinforced in their views by their study of medieval history. This made them familiar with the concept of society as a corporate entity, a secular counterpart to the Mystical

Body of Christ, in which all members were bound indissolubly to each other, and where each had a function to perform for the greater good of the corporate whole. The state, too, was a corporate body and a historic personality. After the Church the state was the most important association to which the individual belonged for it was the function of the state to harmonize the interests of the individual with those of humanity. This brought the Romantics face to face with the latent power of the state which Müller described as 'the totality of all human concerns'.[1]

Romantics like Müller and Fichte were prepared to subscribe to the belief that the state lay outside the moral law. But this was an exceptional attitude. Most Romantics were as cosmopolitan as the humanists of the *Aufklärung*. Even Fichte, who did identify the state with the nation, cared little whether there was one or many German states; his interest in the power of the state was inspired solely by a desire to see Germany fulfilling her mission of leading all the peoples of Europe towards a humanitarian goal; for, as indicated above, all the Romantics believed ardently in the German cultural mission; Müller believed that all that was great and enduring in European institutions was German and L. T. Kosegarten described Germany as the focal point of all higher culture.

Because they were cosmopolitans the Romantics were interested in a united Europe. This union would be based not on any utilitarian concept of common interest but on a religious foundation. The Romantics were full of admiration for the Catholic Church because in the shadow of the medieval church national cultures had evolved as part of a harmonious pattern. The popularity of Austria with the Romantics was due largely to the fact that it was a prototype of the unity they longed for—the diverse peoples ruled by the Habsburgs were bound together in one political entity by common loyalties, dynastic and religious. Obviously the Romantics overestimated those elements which European states have in common and grossly underestimated the power which a nation state can generate in its struggle for complete autonomy. But the religious idealism of the Romantics did ensure that their

[1] Pinson, *op. cit.*, p. 64.

dynamic concept of the state was firmly anchored to a moral foundation and did not degenerate into mere deification of the *Machtstaat.* Half a century was to elapse before the Romantics' concept of the state was shorn of its religious connotations and came into its own when Prussia encompassed the unification of Germany.

The year 1813 has a special place in the history of German nationalism. The War of Liberation released a flood of national sentiment reaching down to the masses of the people for the first time. This nationalism was characterized by bitter hatred of the French, glorification of war and dreams of German domination in Europe. For E. Arndt, one of the pamphleteers of the day, nationalism was a great religious experience which would cleanse Germany and build a fatherland 'in which every Frenchman was an enemy'.[1] In his poem, *Was ist des deutschen Vaterland?* Arndt declared that the frontiers of the new fatherland would extend:

so weit die deutsche Zunge klingt
und Gott im Himmel Lieder singt.[2]

'*Das ganze Deutschland*' included not only Austria, Prussia and Bavaria but also Pomerania, Styria and Switzerland. F. Jahn, '*Turnvater Jahn*', an even more influential figure, thought that *Grossdeutschland* included not only Switzerland but the Low Countries and Denmark, the *Nordreich* as he called it. Jahn pinned his hope to the youth of Germany believing it was destined to shake off the detestable influence of the French and create a united Germany by harnessing the deep-rooted, mystical force of the people to the national cause; Jahn coined the word *Volkstum* to describe this force. To prepare the youth of Germany for the battle against the French, Jahn founded gymnastic societies, the *Turnerschaften*, and helped to raise a volunteer corps in 1813. The symbolic significance of these volunteers far outweighed their military value. Hatred of the enemy reached a climax in the writings of H. von Kleist who managed to combine hatred of the French, the Romans and the Christians with the glorification of

[1] H. Kohn, *The Mind of Germany, the education of a nation*, London, 1961, p. 78.
[2] *Deutsche Literatur, op. cit.*, p. 136.

war and exaltation of the values of ancient pagan Germany—in von Kleist the National Socialists had a worthy forerunner.

The enthusiasm generated by the War of Liberation did not last long. The Germans were satisfied with the end of French domination; for the most part they welcomed the return of the old dynasties, symbols of order and authority after the change and turmoil of the French Revolution. The princes quickly restored the old order with all its extravagance, inefficiency and aristocratic pretension although the economic and administrative changes effected by the revolution remained undisturbed. Anti-French feeling quickly subsided. Only in the student societies, the *Burschenschaften*, did the exaggerated nationalism of 1813 linger on for a few years. The *Burschenschaften*, originally founded in the 1790's to reform student morals, were reformed in 1815 under the influence of F. Jahn. The students decked themselves in the black, red and gold colours symbolical of the struggle out of the black night of slavery, through the red blood of battle to the golden day of liberty. The political importance of the *Burschenschaften* has been much overrated; they played little part in politics much preferring to enthuse in private about the Christian German past of their country and avoid the use of French words. On the other hand it is significant that most of those Germans who attained positions of pre-eminence in the nationalist movement in later years, had their first experience of national feeling in the *Burschenschaften*.

Most Germans evinced little interest in the Congress of Vienna, being content to leave the future of Germany to the princes and the Great Powers. Speculation about Germany was confined to a small minority of intellectuals, writers and academicians, who lived in high hopes that the Congress would give institutional form to the spirit of 1813. They had no very clear idea of what they wanted. Nationalism and supranationalism was inextricably intertwined in their thinking. This was evident in the fairly general desire for the restoration of the Holy Roman Empire under the Habsburgs; it was evident in the political writings of men like K. Freiherr vom Stein, the embodiment of German patriotism during the War of Liberation. Vom Stein wanted a new German Empire consisting of a North German and South German federation; yet he readily agreed with A. von Gneisenau that England should be given Northwest Germany as a barrier against French expansion. Stein undoubtedly conceived of the nation in political terms but he clearly did not subordinate the state to the nation for, like most of his contemporaries, he was primarily concerned with the freedom of the individual; the nation was merely the medium through which the individual expressed himself. W. von Humboldt was almost alone in his view that a powerful German state was indispensable if the German nation was to maintain its position in Europe and give adequate expression to the national character of the German people.

The intellectuals were quickly disillusioned by the Vienna Congress. The old empire was not restored; instead Germany became a loose confederation of thirty-nine sovereign states, the imperial knights and the ecclesiastical states disappeared for ever and only four imperial cities survived; everywhere *Kleinstaaterei* had triumphed. The intellectuals were condemned to the role of disgruntled spectators lacking popular support. It was now clear how naïve had been their fond hope that the Great Powers would be as anxious as they were to make Germany great once more. There was one gleam of hope; clause thirteen of the constitution of the German Confederation held out the prospect of constitutions in the various states; the intellectuals now concentrated on the task of persuading the princes to grant constitutional liberties to their subjects, consoling themselves with the thought that constitutions were an essential medium for the expression of national sentiment at local level.

The liberal intellectuals had little success in their self-imposed task. In Schleswig-Holstein and Württemberg they were associated with the local aristocracy in attempts to revive the old medieval estates, fondly believing that paternally-minded rulers would rejoice at the chance of sharing power with the aristocracy and the upper middle class. They were quite wrong; there was no future for the *Ständestaat*; new administrative techniques had enhanced the power of the German princes. They were not inclined to share power with an aristocracy already overtaken by the tide of history. Nor were the liberals—few in numbers and unwilling to seek popular support—ever very clear about the role they expected their own class to play in these estates. Some South German states did receive constitutions; Nassau in 1814, Saxe-Weimar in 1816, Baden, Bavaria and Württemberg between 1818 and 1819. But this was by the free choice of their rulers. The assemblies established in these states were purely consultative in nature and elected on a highly illiberal franchise; effective power still resided with the ruler—not that the liberals wanted much more than this. In any case the limited interest aroused by the constitutional agitation soon declined; in 1817 an economic depression brought the post-war boom to an end; in 1819, following the murder of Kotzebue, the Carlsbad decrees ushered in a period of political reaction when the *Burschenschaften* were dissolved and schools and universities were closely supervised.

Romanticism remained the dominant cultural force in Germany throughout the 1820's and 1830's. It shaped the pattern of historical writing; in the works of R. Niebuhr and L. von Ranke the pragmatical approach of the eighteenth century historians was superseded by a deeper sense of the individuality of historical events and the wealth and variety of national history. In the field of jurisprudence the Romantic historical school of K. von Savigny held sway, superseding the older eighteenth century concept of natural law. German styles of architecture were deeply influenced by the Romantics. Finally, Romanticism supplied the princes with a useful philosophy of reaction in the works of K. L. Haller and J. F. Stahl, both of whom emphasized the supreme importance of order, tradition, religion and authority in society.

Romanticism was not without rivals. French ideas were beginning to make some impact in Germany especially in the Rhineland and in the south and west in those states possessing constitutions. The chamber of deputies in Baden became a school for parliamentary life in Germany; the political writings of K. von Rotteck and K. T. Welcker, members of that chamber, exerted great influence on liberal thought. After 1830 French influence was on the increase; the old paternalistic pattern of government started to crumble under the impact of the July revolution and the Polish revolt of 1831; there were disturbances in several of the smaller states and constitutional concessions were made by the rulers to appease the people. The death of Goethe in 1832 marked the end of a literary epoch; a new school of writers and journalists known as Young Germany emerged in the 1830's. This school, which included H. Laube, F. Freiligrath, H. Börne and H. Heine, had its counterparts in other countries. It was in revolt against the excesses of Romanticism, preferring sober, realistic prose to the exaggerated and fanciful poetry of the Romantics. These young men of lower middle class origins were the standard-bearers of rationalism and liberalism; if they did not enjoy a wide following in Germany, at least their angry iconoclasm had a profoundly disturbing effect on accepted standards. They recognized that Romanticism had been the ally of reaction, paralysing the will of the German people for political change. They looked with favour upon French and Belgian political development; 'Paris is the new Jerusalem', wrote Heine, 'and the Rhine is the Jordan which divides the land of freedom from the land of the philistines.'[1] Young Germany contemptuously dismissed the belief of the older generation that a constitution was the product of agreement between a benevolent prince and his grateful people. These angry young men declared war on the princely houses, insisting that constitutions were wrung out of reluctant princes only by the determination of the people—at last the Germans had found a political theory which destroyed the traditional relationship between ruler and subject.

The 1830's were characterized by this new and radical spirit. The Hambach festival in 1832 was a very different gathering from the Wartburg festival in 1817; in place of a vague longing for the return of a fictitious Christian German past, there were demands for the creation of a *Rechtsstaat* safeguarding personal liberties such as the French and Belgians already enjoyed. The German princes were alarmed by the strident tone of the Hambach festival and even more by the abortive rising in Frankfurt in 1833 when a few young men attempted to seize the arsenal and arm the people.

[1] Pinson, *op. cit.*, p. 70.

Prompted by Metternich, the Federal Diet intensified its anti-liberal measures, imposing a ban on the writings of Young Germany. This conflict between the princes and the radicals retarded the growth of nationalism because the radicals fraternized with Polish, Italian and French liberals, regarding them all as allies in the struggle against the common enemy absolutism. Nationalism, on the other hand, was a retrograde force; A. Ruge, the Young Hegelian philosopher, considered a return of the spirit of 1813 'a dangerous reaction against reason and liberty'.[1] G. Kühne wrote in 1831 that the unity of Germany was to be sought not in external forms but rather in the world of German art and science.[2] Laube, writing the first part of *Junges Europa* in 1833, prophesied the disappearance of nationalities and the establishment of a world republic to serve humanity.[3]

Five years later, writing the second part of this work, Laube had abandoned the world republic and declared his allegiance to the national cause.[4] This was a typical conversion, due in large measure to the success of the *Deutscher Zollverein*. In the 1830's industrialization had begun to affect parts of Germany; a textile industry was growing up in Saxony and Silesia and a flourishing iron industry in the Ruhr. But these were only tentative beginnings; one of the most serious obstacles to economic expansion was the existence of customs barriers between the various states and between the provinces in those states. Prussia was concerned about this problem on account of widespread smuggling across her straggling frontiers. She decided in 1818 that the best way of stamping out smuggling was to abolish all internal customs barriers. This soon led to the negotiation of customs agreements with Prussia's neighbours, all anxious to share in the benefits of a uniform customs code. For a time in the 1820's three customs unions struggled for supremacy in Germany. Eventually the Prussian union secured the mastery. On 1 January 1834 the *Deutscher Zollverein* came into being, sweeping away all customs barriers between eighteen states with a total population of over

[1] Pinson, *op. cit.*, p. 74.
[2] K. Lamprecht, *Deutsche Geschichte*, Berlin, 1920–2, vol. 10, p. 508.
[3] *Ibid.*, p. 483.
[4] *Ibid.*, pp. 484–5.

twenty-three millions. This was an event of tremendous significance, the importance of which can hardly be overemphasized. The *Zollverein* led to an immediate and substantial increase in the volume of trade; it encouraged the growth of industry and improved communications; in 1835 the first section of the German railway system was laid. So great was the economic success of the *Zollverein* that in the course of the next twenty years the other German states joined in. The *Zollverein* was an object lesson for all Germans, an impressive tribute to the benefits which unification could bestow on a people. It did not fail to make a profound impression on all German liberals:

Denn ihr habt ein Band gewunden
Um das deutsche Vaterland
Und die Herzen hat verbunden
Mehr als unser Bund dies Band

wrote H. von Fallersleben of the *Zollverein* in 1840.[1] The result was that by the end of the 1830's German liberals were generally agreed that national unification was an overriding necessity. This did not weaken their interest in political change; on the contrary it reinforced their arguments, for without political freedom how could the German people give adequate expression to their desire for nationhood?

While the liberals were returning to a political concept of nationhood largely under the impact of economic change, a rather different interpretation was being worked out in conservative circles in Prussia. This interpretation merits special mention. Conservatives naturally clung longer than liberals to the non-political *Kulturnation* because they feared that the liberal demand for a single German state representing the whole German people would endanger the political and social privileges conservatives enjoyed in the existing states. The conservatives rationalized their fears by rejecting the liberal view of the nation as the product of the conscious will of the national group, and reaffirming their belief in the Romantic view of the nation as the product of evolutionary processes beyond human control. Normally this view leads to political

[1] *Deutsche Literatur, op. cit.*, Bd. 3. *Um Einheit und Freiheit 1815–48*, Leipzig, 1936, p. 132.

quietism. But in the course of the 1830's a new political concept was hammered out by conservative writers in the columns of the *Berliner Politischen Wochenblätter*. These conservatives argued that a unitary state was not essential for the attainment of national unification; on the contrary, this erroneous French idea did violence to the conservative thesis that the unique feature of the German fatherland was diversity not unity. The various German states were all legitimate political manifestations of a common cultural pattern and as such ought to be preserved—confederation, not federation, was the only solution of the German problem acceptable to conservatives. They also argued that Prussia was a 'German nation' invested with that autonomous personality which liberals were only prepared to confer on a unitary state. This was a development of crucial importance for German nationalism. Conservatives were still frightened, in the pre-March period, of the latent power of the state and insisted on anchoring it to a firm moral foundation; but in the 1860's, when these moral restraints had worn thin and when liberals were beginning to appreciate the importance of power, the conservative concept of Prussia as an autonomous personality and as the pre-eminent German nation came into its own and was accepted by many liberals.

The year 1840 witnessed a new upsurge of national sentiment in Germany reminiscent of the War of Liberation. Once again it took the form of anti-French feeling. In the summer there were threatening military preparations in France and demands for the restoration of the Rhineland; the German answer came in the words of N. Becker's poem, '*Die sollen ihn nicht haben, den freien deutschen Rhein*'. The desire for unification was now uppermost in the German mind and remained there throughout the 1840's. In the autumn Friedrich Wilhelm IV came to the Prussian throne; the accession of this unHohenzollern ruler fired the liberals with hope of constitutional liberties in the near future. These events determined the pattern of the 1840's. National liberalism became the dominant political posture; the demand for German unification was married to a moderate liberal belief in constitutional monarchy. Allied with this was a growing conviction, especially among liberals in North Germany, that Prussia had a decisive role to play in the unification of Germany. True, many liberals were intensely suspicious of autocratic Prussia but they confidently expected that Prussia would abandon her particularism and liberalize herself once she had assumed leadership of the unification movement.

National liberalism grew steadily in strength and popularity in this decade because at last a politically conscious public opinion was being formed in Germany. This was due in part to the general improvement in communications and the introduction of new printing techniques which created a popular press capable of arousing and sustaining public interest in affairs of state. This was a development of crucial importance; in 1837 when seven Göttingen professors had been dismissed for refusing to take an oath of allegiance to the king of Hanover, the protests were few and isolated; but when the Danish monarch issued his open letter in 1846 it aroused a great storm of protest in all parts of Germany.

The growth of political consciousness in the middle class was also a reflection of the continuing economic expansion of Germany. The *Zollverein* grew in strength throughout the 1840's. A railway network had begun to spread out all over Germany; over 3,000 kilometres of line had been laid by 1849, a development which gave a direct stimulus to the expansion of heavy industry. Economic expansion broadened the basis of the middle class; commercial and industrial elements grew in importance and supported the intellectuals in their demand for political change. Economic expansion was breaking down provincial barriers, drawing the merchants and industrialists closer together and equalizing their interests. This made them increasingly conscious of the fact that further expansion was impeded by the political division of Germany, by the remnants of feudalism and by the absolutist system of government in most states. As the decade moved to a close amidst mounting tension, the German middle class as a whole believed that unification and liberal government was an infallible formula which would ensure a glorious future for the German people.

The story of the failure of the national liberals to realize these ideals during the revolution of 1848–9 cannot be retold here. It is sufficient to say that the failure had a devastating effect on German liberalism and important results on the evolution of German nationalism. It is fair to say that the national liberals had over-estimated the persuasive power of ideas and underestimated the importance of physical force—whether there was any alternative in 1848–9 is another matter. The error was reversed in the 1850's and 1860's; German liberals began to despise ideas and over-estimate the importance of the power factor. 'The German nation', wrote J. Froebel, one-time radical member of the Frankfurt Parliament, in 1859, 'is sick of principles and doctrines, literary existence and theoretical greatness. What it wants is power, power, power and whoever gives it power to him will it give honour, more honour than he can imagine.' [1] The result was that when liberalism revived again in the early 1860's, carried forward on a wave of economic expansion, it was preoccupied with considerations of power; the links between nationalism and supranationalism were finally severed and the conservative concept of the *Machtstaat* finally won general acceptance.

The intellectual content of the national liberalism of the 1860's is reflected in the writings of the political professors, writers like H. von Sybel, J. G. Droysen and H. von Treitschke, who mobilized public opinion behind Prussia. These men were deeply influenced by Hegelian philosophy; from Hegel they derived their concept of the state as a corporate personality and organism —an idea which Hegel in his turn had borrowed from the Romantics. In common with Hegel and the Prussian conservatives, the political professors saw in Prussia the embodiment of this autonomous personality. Unification could be achieved only through the power of the Prussian state and to that end all other considerations had to be subordinated. If they were obliged to choose between liberty and unity, the political professors unhesitatingly chose the latter. They were, it is true, still interested in obtaining a constitution but 'one in keeping with the German *Volksgeist*'—which meant that they were able to settle for much less than responsible government in 1867. They were still anxious

[1] *New Cambridge Modern History*, vol. 10, Cambridge, 1960, p. 504.

to safeguard personal liberties but they put the nation state before the individual—for only in a mighty and powerful state could a worthwhile culture flourish and in Germany that meant only in Prussia. History for them was not a painful search for truth but an avowed propaganda weapon. Von Sybel shifted the centre of German history to Prussia; Droysen continued this tradition in his *Geschichte der preussischen Politik*, a history which eulogized the Prussian state, gloried in its martial spirit and lavished praise on the Great Elector and Frederick the Great on the improbable grounds that they had served the German national idea. Austria, on the other hand, was depicted as unprogressive and an obstacle to unification. It was significant that Droysen had no hesitation in spurning the idea of a concert of powers; he boldly asserted that the state marked out for pre-eminence had a moral right to grasp the leadership. His only yardstick was the national self-interest of Prussia. This was the logical implication of the conservative concept of the state as an autonomous personality—the supranational colouration had worn off at last.

Thus when Otto von Bismarck-Schönhausen became minister president of Prussia in September 1862 the intellectual climate was already favourable for a display of *Realpolitik*—a word which significantly enough was first used in the 1850's. The liberals protested at first; after all the constitutional conflict in Prussia made the minister president the enemy of liberalism. But, as Bismarck calculated, the liberals were prepared in the final instance to forgive his illiberality once unification had been achieved. 'We thought that by our agitation we could transform Germany. But the tremendous events which we have witnessed have taught us how frail these premises were on which . . . we have built our national liberal policy in the last years. Almost all the elements of our political system have been shown erroneous by the facts themselves. It would be difficult for us to accept this new insight if it were accompanied by our misfortune. But we have experienced a miracle almost without parallel. The victory of our principles would have brought us misery, whereas the defeat of our principles has brought us boundless salvation. Truly, we could not be conscientious, altruistic and pure if we did not respond to such a celestial blessing by sincere self-criticism and by the unshakeable determination to start life anew with unassuming dedication and faithful obedience to the great revelation which this year has brought us.'[1] These words written in 1866 by H. Baumgarten, a South German historian and former opponent of Bismarck, are a fitting comment on the revolution in liberal thinking brought about by the marriage between the national liberal desire for unification and the *Realpolitik* of Bismarck.

[1] H. Kohn, *op. cit.*, p. 159.

II

Schleswig-Holstein at the turn of the century

At the beginning of the nineteenth century Schleswig and Holstein, the two small duchies lying north of the river Elbe and south of the river Kongeaa,[1] bridgehead between Germany and Scandinavia, had been formally associated with Denmark for three and a half centuries. Their history had been a troubled one since the historic day in March 1460 when Christian of Oldenburg, king of Denmark, was elected duke of Schleswig and count of Holstein at Ribe by the Schleswig-Holstein *Ritterschaft* or nobility. The association with Denmark was at this time dynastic only, for the *Ritterschaft* was powerful enough to insist upon the retention of its privileged position. King Christian was obliged to affirm solemnly that he was ruler by election and not by hereditary right, that only his male heirs would be eligible for election, that the close association between the duchies must remain unimpaired, that only residents could be appointed to high office in the duchies and, finally, that the local estates would be consulted before taxes were levied or war was waged.

As the medieval period drew to a close and the feudal nobility declined in strength, it would not have been surprising had Christian's successors transformed personal union between the duchies and the Danish crown into a much closer political union, in the manner of the English, Swedish and Spanish monarchs in the sixteenth century. This did not happen for in the late sixteenth century the brothers of the reigning monarch partitioned the duchies like a private estate, and entrenched themselves in various parts of the duchies as rival authorities to the crown. It took the crown the greater part of two centuries to combat these

[1] German Königsau.

centrifugal tendencies and reassert its authority over all parts of the duchies. This was by no means an easy task, for in the seventeenth century the private feud between the crown and the house of Holstein-Gottorp, the most powerful of these rivals, assumed international importance affecting the whole of Northern Europe. Sweden, the traditional enemy of Denmark, was seeking control of the Sound and gave support to the dukes of Holstein-Gottorp. This involved Denmark in three serious wars in the course of the century. When Denmark recovered the Gottorp parts of Schleswig in 1721 it was only by courtesy of France and Great Britain when the Swedish star was on the wane. Denmark had to wait another half century before securing the Gottorp possessions in Holstein, because the Holstein-Gottorps found a new ally in Russia and married into the Romanov family. Not until 1773 did Denmark regain these possessions for a cash payment and the surrender of the counties of Oldenburg and Delmenhorst, and only then because Catherine the Great was more interested in expanding her empire at the expense of Poland and Turkey than in upholding the Holstein-Gottorp claims.

The strenuous exertions of the preceding century and a half exhausted the Danish crown. Consequently the task of integrating the duchies into the Danish kingdom was postponed to a later date. The formal reunion was effected in time for the duchies to benefit from a spate of progressive legislation at the close of the century, but no determined exploitation of the political victory of 1773 was ever possible. When King Christian VIII made a serious attempt to centralize and reform the *Helstat*[1] in the 1840's it was too late; national antagonisms had already begun to tear the state asunder. But largely because the Danish crown had never been free from political distractions since the late sixteenth century, the duchies were able to retain their distinctive social and political structure despite the long association with Denmark.

Another contributory factor was their geographical remoteness. Bounded by the North Sea on the west, the duchies were separated from Copenhagen by the Baltic Sea, while several deep

[1] Name given to Denmark, the duchies and colonial possessions overseas; German *Gesamtstaat*.

fiords along the east coast made travel difficult between Germany and Scandinavia. In the centre of the duchies inhospitable and weatherbeaten moorland discouraged contact between the storm-tossed east and west coasts. Communications, never good in this sparsely populated area,[1] almost ceased during the worst of the winter weather. Not until 1830 was the first metalled road built, to be followed in 1844 by the first railway between Kiel and Altona. For most of the year the only reliable link between the duchies and Copenhagen was by sailing ship, replaced by steamship in the 1840's.

As a result of their distinctive historical experiences the duchies differed from Denmark in several respects. In Denmark the power of the crown had been unlimited in theory since 1665, when the weakness of the aristocracy and the inexperience of the middle class enabled King Frederik III to obtain absolute power under the *Kongelov*[2] which remained in force until 1849. In the eighteenth century the power of the crown had been limited in practice by dependence upon a considerable bureaucratic apparatus and tempered by the spirit of the Enlightenment. But in the seventeenth century Danish absolutism was the most effective in Christendom. The nobility was reduced in status, the remnants of elective machinery lingering on from medieval days were swept away and *Amter*[3] and towns alike were brought under royal control. Typical of the measures designed to secure uniformity was the *Dansk Lov* of 1683, which established the equality of all before the law and replaced the jumble of local customs and jurisdictions by a single coherent legal code.

In sharp contrast to this, the pattern of society in the duchies was still characterized by multifarious and virile local traditions, the product of centuries of historical growth. A classic example of this local particularism was to be found in the narrow strip of marshland running along the east coast from the Elbe estuary in a

[1] The population of Schleswig-Holstein was 604,085 in 1803, and had increased to 773,783 by 1835.

[2] Lex Regia.

[3] The *Amt* was the primary administrative subdivision analogous to the English county.

northerly direction through Ditmarschen, Eiderstedt and Nordfriesland to the present frontier between Denmark and Germany. Here lived the Frisians, clinging tenaciously to their extensive financial and judicial privileges exercised by all property-owning members of the community. In effect they practised self-government in local affairs under their own officials, for in this society of independent and often well-to-do farmers, with their proud motto '*lever duad as slaav*',[1] royal officials had a purely supervisory function.

In most of Schleswig, especially in the north, and in Holstein—with the exception of the east—the small farmers, who formed the backbone of the community, did not enjoy the very considerable privileges of the Frisians. But even so they owned over seventy-five per cent of the land and for that reason attached great importance to property-owning as a sign of personal maturity and a guarantee of independence. They had some share in the administration; they appointed minor parish officials, especially the *Kirchenspielvogt* or *Sognefoged*,[2] and they elected assessors—*Gerichtsbeisitzer* or *Sandemaend*[3]—to the lower courts or *Dingegerichte* which were presided over by the *Hardesvogt* or *Herredsfoged*.[4] The people were subject to the patriarchal control of the royal officials, the *Amtmann* and his assistants, whose powers, mainly financial and judicial, varied greatly in different parts of the duchies. Towns were few in number, strung out along the east coast and accounting for only twenty-two per cent of the population in 1845. They differed from Danish towns in that the Hamburg and Lübeck models, on which their administration was based, allowed the citizens to elect members to the *Bürgerversammlung* and excluded royal influence from their affairs.

Only in east Holstein and in the southeastern corner of Schleswig were the people less privileged. This was the home of the

[1] 'Death before slavery.'
[2] Beadle.
[3] Assessors, often unlettered men, had to decide whether cases should be referred to higher courts.
[4] An important official appointed by the *Amtmann* to supervise all communal officials.

thirty-nine families who formed the *Schleswig-Holsteinische Ritterschaft*.[1] Together with the *non-recepti*,[2] the *Ritterschaft* owned twenty-five per cent of the land in the duchies. Although the privileges of the *Ritterschaft* were confirmed by successive monarchs, its great days of political power in the sixteenth century had ended long ago. Its right to elect the duke had long been in abeyance and as no *Landtag* had been called since 1721, its right of attendance in that body had little significance. By the end of the eighteenth century the privileges possessed no political significance, applying almost exclusively to private estates, where the condition of *Ritterschaft* tenants, compared with the rest of the duchies, was most backward. In these aristocratic republics the landowners were absolute monarchs; they exercised full financial and judicial powers over their tenants and controlled church and school alike. Long after the liberation of the serfs in 1805, the landowners continued to exercise very considerable economic and administrative power over their tenants, a fact which helps to explain why this part of the duchies was least affected by political development in the first half of the nineteenth century.

The economy of the duchies was overwhelmingly agrarian like that of Denmark. But there were important differences. The duchies formed a separate unit for customs purposes. They possessed their own coinage and since 1788 had their own bank at Altona with authority to issue notes. Their finances were sounder than those of Denmark which suffered from persistent inflation after 1750. Because economic conditions were generally superior to those in the Danish countryside, the North Schleswig farmer considered himself superior to his neighbour in Nørrejylland, although the reforms of the 1780's had improved conditions north of the Kongeaa.

These economic differences were accentuated when a rise in wheat prices and the introduction of new agrarian techniques led to an increase in productivity in the second half of the eighteenth

[1] The corporate body of the Schleswig-Holstein nobility was founded in the thirteenth century. Its members owned 64 of 133 estates in Holstein and 30 of 116 estates in Schleswig in 1800.

[2] Landowners who were not members of the *Ritterschaft*.

century. The duchies were unable to dispose of this new economic surplus in Denmark; they found the new markets they needed in England where the demand for wheat was growing under the stimulus of industrialization. As the duchies normally disposed of their produce via Hamburg, their ties with this great port grew steadily stronger after the Napoleonic wars. The fact that neither Flensburg nor Altona was ever able to break the grip of Hamburg over the duchies' trade in the early nineteenth century was not without considerable political significance.

There were considerable differences between the legal system in the duchies and in Denmark. The *Dansk Lov* applied to all parts of Denmark, but south of the Kongeaa a multi-coloured and chaotic tangle of local jurisdictions still existed well into the nineteenth century. In Holstein, a member of the Holy Roman Empire since 1476, the Saxon law of 1218 applied to rural areas and the Lübeck law of 1586 in most towns. But in Schleswig, originally a Danish fief and never a member of the Empire or of the German Confederation, the *Jydske Lov* of 1241, translated into Low German in 1486, applied in most rural areas. In the towns various legal codes were in force with the Jutish enclaves around Ribe adding further to the complex picture. In fact the only uniform division common to the duchies was that of the parish. It was indeed a lawyer's paradise which reminded J. G. Droysen in 1841 of the chaotic conditions in the Holy Roman Empire in 1700.

Such was Schleswig-Holstein on the threshold of a new century, a rather remote and secluded world, parochial in its interests, indifferent to a changing world beyond the Elbe and Kongeaa, steeped in the history of the past and clinging tenaciously to its old traditions and privileges. Later in the nineteenth century, when German nationalism became a dynamic force, the semi-autonomy enjoyed by the duchies was used by nationalists to justify their demands for the severance of all ties with Denmark and the establishment of a completely independent Schleswig-Holstein. That lay in the distant future. At the beginning of the nineteenth century no one suspected that the semi-autonomy enjoyed by the duchies might one day prove incompatible with the continued existence of the *Helstat.* The positive forces holding

Danes, Germans and Norwegians together were infinitely more powerful than the negative forces making for disruption, a balance which lasted well into the nineteenth century. Two forces in particular, the pre-eminent position of Germans in the *Helstat* and the loyalty which the duchies felt towards the crown, acted as a powerful cement preserving the association.

Germans had played an important part in the *Helstat* since the sixteenth century when the Holstein nobility obtained dominant influence at the Danish court. After a decline in influence in the early seventeenth century, the importance of the Germans increased again with the creation of a new nobility to replace the old nobility hostile to the *Kongelov*. In the eighteenth century German influence was very considerable because, in order to revivify Denmark after the intellectual and economic exhaustion caused by the seventeenth century wars, the crown encouraged the entry of German artists, administrators and workmen in increasing numbers after 1720.

The Germans possessed considerable political influence in the *Helstat* at the beginning of the nineteenth century. In the duchies there were some three thousand five hundred civil servants and nine thousand teachers and church officers. The teachers in country districts, poorly paid as always, and the minor officials were largely Danish. But the important officials, the *Amtmann* and his assistants, the pastors and the officials of the intermediate authorities for Schleswig-Holstein in Glückstadt and in Gottorp were invariably Germans.[1] In Copenhagen about sixty Germans from the duchies occupied key positions in the administrative machine, especially in the *Deutsche Kanzlei* which supervised the administration, police, church and schools in the duchies and was virtually independent of the other government colleges.[2] The finances of the duchies were dealt with by other colleges, but even in the *Rentekammer* and *Finanzkollegium* special treatment was

[1] Even in the Danish-speaking *Amter* of Åbenraa and Sønderborg 112 German pastors were appointed between 1795 and 1848 but only 33 Danish pastors.

[2] Between 400 and 450 officials were employed in government departments in Copenhagen. J. Paulsen, *Tyske Embedsmaend i København*, etc., p. 48.

accorded to Schleswig-Holstein. Moreover in the *Statsraad*[1] certain German families, especially the Reventlows, Schimmelmanns and Bernstorffs, exerted great influence on the formulation of policy.

The career of the Bernstorffs illustrates the profound influence exerted by Germans and the prestige which they conferred upon the *Helstat* in the late eighteenth century. Born in Mecklenburg, J. H. Bernstorff became chief minister in 1750, a post he held for twenty years while his nephew, A. P. Bernstorff, was president of the *Deutsche Kanzlei* from 1773 and chief minister between 1784 and 1797. Indifferent to nationality in the fashion of the eighteenth century, these cultured cosmopolitans fostered the growth of German influence in the administrative machine during their forty years of power. They aroused the *Ritterschaft* out of its lethargy, encouraging it to play an active role in the affairs of state. With the assistance of the Bernstorffs the Holstein family of Reventlow attained political prominence; Count Detlev Reventlow became A. P. Bernstorff's personal adviser on Schleswig-Holstein; Detlev's eldest son, Fritz, was appointed Danish ambassador to Great Britain and later to Sweden and his younger son, Cai, was appointed Danish ambassador to Spain. Cai married Bernstorff's daughter and eventually succeeded him as president of the *Deutsche Kanzlei* in 1797.

Although the Bernstorffs were responsible for the negotiations leading to the formal reunion of the Gottorp parts of Holstein with Denmark in 1773, they were always careful to respect the semi-autonomous position of the duchies—'administrative Schleswig-Holsteinism' as it is sometimes called. This caution was inspired in some measure by a partiality for the *Ritterschaft*—A. P. Bernstorff was flattered to have been nominated a member of this most exclusive club. But caution was also deliberate policy because the Bernstorffs appreciated that there was a considerable tradition of hostility towards the crown in the former Gottorp territories, around Kiel, Bordesholm and Neumünster in the duchy of Holstein and in the *Amter* of Åbenraa, Løgumkloster,

[1] The Council of State composed of heads of administrative colleges and other advisers presided over by the king; German *Staatsrat*.

Tønder, Husum and Gottorp in the duchy of Schleswig. Kiel, for example, had been the centre of the Holstein-Gottorp government until its dissolution in 1774 when Glückstadt became the seat of the *Holsteinische Landesregierung*. Some Danish historians consider that memories of the Gottorp period were not without influence on later developments; they point out that Dahlmann's mother had Gottorp connections and that the towns of Kiel, Åbenraa and Schleswig were all prominent centres of Schleswig-Holsteinism in the nineteenth century.

German cultural influence in the *Helstat* was as strong as French influence had been in Germany in the early eighteenth century. German cultural values were accepted in high society and at court, German words of command were used in the army and many German classicists studied in Copenhagen. For Herder the *Helstat* was the 'Danish end of Germany' [1] and when Klopstock was invited to Denmark by King Frederik V in 1751 he was at once lionized by polite society in Copenhagen. Yet neither the Danish middle class nor the Danish farmers were much affected by German culture which remained essentially the preserve of the upper classes in Copenhagen. German cultural values went unchallenged simply because the old humanism associated with the Danish nobility declined with it in the seventeenth century, and the Danish middle class was not strong enough, economically and socially, to exert much influence on the cultural life of Denmark. True, L. Holberg's Danish comedies did much to raise the standard of the language in the 1720's, laying the basis of a new theatre and a new literature. But his appeals for the creation of a popular Danish culture fell on deaf ears.

The German cultural renaissance in the late eighteenth century soon evoked a response from young Danish writers, especially J. H. Wessel, H. F. Ewald and J. Baggersen. Their interest was aroused in Denmark's past history and a new patriotic sentiment began to emerge in their writings. But there was no hostility to German cultural values. Ewald's family, for example, came from

[1] P. Koopman, *Deutsch und Dänisch um die Wende des achtzehnten Jahrhunderts*, etc., p. 16.

Tønder; he had been educated at the Schleswig *Domschule*, moving to Copenhagen in 1760, where he came under the influence of German writers especially that of Klopstock. It was in the shadow of the dominant German culture that these young Danish writers created an indigenous culture. One may speak of 'cultural unity' in the *Helstat* in the sense that German and Danish intellectuals showed a mutual respect for each other's cultural heritage and were influenced by it. This cultural cross-fertilization was an important factor restraining the national animosity between German and Dane, of which there were some signs at the beginning of the nineteenth century.

Since King Christian VII's illness the court had ceased to be the cultural centre of the *Helstat*. That role was now assumed by the Copenhagen residences of the Bernstorffs and of H. E. Schimmelmann, a Pomeranian financial wizard who made a fortune during the Silesian war and at the request of J. H. Bernstorff reorganized Denmark's finances, ending up as a Danish count famed for fabulous balls and dinner parties. In Holstein a number of cultural Meccas arose in the late eighteenth century. Klopstock, expelled from Copenhagen by Struensee in 1770, had taken up his abode in Hamburg. Many members of a famous literary circle, the Göttingen *Hainbund*, were now resident in Holstein; Count Fritz Reventlow in Emkendorf, Count Cai Reventlow in Altenhof, Count C. Stolberg in Tremsbüttel, H. Boie in Meldorf, J. Voss in Eutin and A. Hennings in Plön, all of whom raised the cultural level in Holstein, although in no sense of the word did they create a genuinely popular culture.

The aristocratic Romanticism of Emkendorf had a very limited appeal in the duchies where most officials, teachers and pastors were enthusiastic disciples of the Enlightenment. They were rationalists, interested in all manner of material and moral advancement, but they carefully avoided all political issues. Although they disliked the social pretension of aristocracy, they were not attracted on that account by the political experiments in France. They remained staunchly loyal to their king because they believed that absolute monarchy was more likely to bring about the material and moral changes they considered desirable, than either aristocracy-ridden oligarchies or revolutionary republics with their dangerous democratic connotations.

Loyalty to the person of the sovereign, Frederik VI, regent since 1784 and king since 1808, and pride in the *Helstat* were widely diffused and characteristic political attitudes both in the duchies and in Denmark. Perhaps it was instinctive and irrational loyalty, a natural by-product of political immaturity, but it was undoubtedly a deep and genuine sentiment shared by all classes of the population. No less strong was the sense of loyalty to the *Helstat*. German as well as Dane was indignant when Sir Hyde Parker attacked Copenhagen in 1801; Professor Weber of Kiel echoed the feelings of all King Frederik's German subjects when he wrote, '*Erhoben steht unsere Nationalehre . . . mit edlem Stolze fühlt dies jeder brave Däne . . . denn auch wir sind brave Dänen.*' [1] The threats to the *Helstat* in 1801 and 1807 and the experiences of the war years deepened these loyal sentiments. The people made considerable material sacrifices for their king-duke, accepting war against their best customer Great Britain and remaining faithful to the French alliance to the bitter end. Indeed, the bombardment of Copenhagen in 1807 aroused in many of them a positive desire for revenge on Great Britain. This deeply ingrained sentiment of loyalty to the crown helped the duchies to withstand the storms of 1813–14, and to celebrate the coronation and silver wedding anniversary of '*den ejegode Frederik*' [2] as fervently as ever in 1815.

The inhabitants of the duchies were influenced by other loyalties operating at different levels in society and in varying degrees of intensity. They were unswerving in their loyalty to crown and *Helstat* but had an equally deep-rooted attachment to their native soil. In this geographically remote region, with a population proud of their traditions but somewhat restricted in their mental horizons and suspicious of all change, local loyalties assumed a very real significance. Thus the people of Flensburg, Kiel and Husum regarded themselves primarily as 'Flensburger', 'Kieler' and 'Husumer' and only in a secondary sense as 'Holsteiner' or, in the

[1] *Blätter für Polizei und Kultur. Jahrgang 1801*, Tübingen. *Schleswig-holsteinische Chronik*, 4, p. 6.

[2] 'Frederik the well-beloved.'

case of Schleswig, as '*dansk Holsteiner*'.[1] Most people did not think of themselves as 'Schleswig-Holsteiner' at the beginning of the nineteenth century. Only the *Ritterschaft* and the German officials functioning as corporate entities in both duchies were conscious of any community between Schleswig and Holstein.

The world outside the *Helstat* did not greatly concern the duchies. Only in the rarified and exotic atmosphere of Emkendorf was there much speculation about the political fate of Germany in the first decade of the new century. The vast majority of people were quite uninterested in such matters and perfectly content to look upon Denmark as their only fatherland. However, in one respect the duchies were conscious of some affinity with Germany—educated people in Schleswig-Holstein displayed a lively interest in the cultural renaissance in Germany in the second half of the eighteenth century. They began to call themselves 'German' and spoke with pride of 'our German fatherland'; but only in a cultural sense; they did not cease for a moment to be loyal 'Danes'.

Peace and prosperity in the late eighteenth century strengthened the universal sentiment of loyalty to the crown. A. P. Bernstorff's successful foreign policy increased the prestige and wealth of the *Helstat* very considerably giving German and Dane alike legitimate cause for pride in the *Danebrog*.[2] Economically, increased agrarian productivity and expanding markets raised wheat prices to a high level where they remained for decades. Between 1780 and 1814 an important series of reforms helped to stabilize social conditions in the *Helstat*, doing much to remove those causes of discontent which had led to revolution and the destruction of the monarchy in France. A. P. Bernstorff and his associates, men permeated with the cosmopolitan, humanitarian ideals of the Enlightenment, were largely responsible for the peaceful demolition of medieval economic and social conditions which had depressed the farming class in Denmark and in certain parts of the duchies. The liberation of the serfs in 1805 was the most important of these reforms, leading to changes in the system of land tenure of con-

[1] The name Holstein was also applied to Schleswig from the fifteenth century onwards and superseded Sønderjylland, the old Danish name for Schleswig.

[2] Flag of the *Helstat* since 1776.

siderable benefit to small farmers. Other reforms secured civil rights for farmers, established training colleges and new schools, modernized police arrangements in the towns and instituted a poor relief system. The success of these reforms, which applied to the duchies as well as to Denmark, was a major factor behind the consistent support given to the crown by the middle class. The instinctive loyalty of the middle class was reinforced with the positive quality of gratitude for favours received. The effective political power of the crown remained unbroken precisely because its willingness to modernize the economic and social structure of the state had removed possible causes of antagonism between subject and ruler before they acquired a more dangerous political significance. A satisfied middle class, prosperous economic conditions, tolerable social conditions and a settled international background made the closing years of the eighteenth century a veritable Golden Age for the *Helstat*.

Yet the storm clouds were gathering over the *Helstat* even in the eighteenth century. It began with the reaction against J. F. Struensee's brief dictatorship. The Altona doctor, confidant of King Christian VII, lover of the queen and rationalist dictator, had alienated court circles by the rapidity and nature of his innovations and had finally been removed from power by a court conspiracy in 1772.

In the decade which followed his downfall the chief minister, Ove Guldberg, introduced measures to prevent future misuse of royal power by political adventurers. The most important measure was the *Indigenatengesetz* of 1776 which excluded foreigners from high office in the *Helstat* and made it impossible in the future for men like Struensee, born in Saxony, or the Bernstorffs from Mecklenburg to hold office. But it did not, of course, exclude the Holstein nobility from high office. Other measures included a directive in 1773 requiring the use of Danish in all official correspondence in Denmark with the exception of the *Deutsche Kanzlei*. In the same year Danish was introduced into the army.

It was not Danish national feeling which motivated Guldberg's policy. An enthusiast for the Enlightenment, his patriotism was inspired by devotion to the crown and his main aim was to safeguard the absolute power of the monarchy against German adventurers. A member of the Danish middle class, Guldberg shared its traditional hostility to the German nobility who held over half the high official positions in the *Helstat*. He and the small group of like-minded Danish officials who implemented his policy were anti-German because they resented German political influence in Copenhagen. Occasionally this anti-German feeling was shared by wider circles of the population, as, for example, in 1772 when P. Suhm condemned Struensee's contemptuous attitude towards the Danish language and urged the king to speak only that tongue;[1] Struensee had spoken only German and had regarded Danish as a dialect fit only for the lower classes, an aspect of his policy which had aroused popular feeling against him in Copenhagen where his downfall was the object of much rejoicing.

Guldberg's anti-German feeling inspired his attempts to replace German officials with men from the Danish middle class, in the hope that Denmark could return to the pristine splendour of 1660 when middle class and crown had co-operated against the nobility. His preference for the Danish language was due solely to a conviction that it was an effective means of preserving the power of the crown and of excluding foreign influence.

At the close of the eighteenth century a struggle was being waged behind the scenes in Copenhagen between the associates of Guldberg and the friends of A. P. Bernstorff, with the person of the young crown prince as the prize. In 1784 Prince Frederik made himself regent, superseding his mentally sick father, King Christian VII, and bringing Bernstorff back to office. For the next fifteen years he restrained the Guldberg group and by inaugurating the period of reforms increased his own power and prestige.

But after Bernstorff's death in 1797 the determined efforts of the regent to strengthen the *Helstat* led to renewed tension between German and Danish officials. The darkening international scene necessitated heavy expenditure on armaments if Denmark was to defend her neutrality. The need for increased financial contribu-

[1] J. Krumm, *Der schleswig-holsteinische dänische Gesamtstaat des achtzehnten Jahrhunderts*, p. 79.

tions from his subjects reinforced Frederik's natural inclination to centralize the *Helstat,* destroy all medieval remnants in the administration and create a uniform and efficient system. This development was accelerated after 1807 when Denmark finally abandoned her neutrality and became the faithful ally of France.

In the past there had been no serious difference of opinion between the German and Danish officials in Copenhagen despite the resignation of the president of the *Deutsche Kanzlei,* Count Cai Reventlow, in 1802 in protest against the introduction into the duchies of a new taxation system which adversely affected the privileged financial position of the *Ritterschaft.* Few German officials were interested in the preservation of *Ritterschaft* privileges; the great majority remained completely loyal to the crown until well in the 1840's, finding *Helstatsførelse*[1] quite compatible with 'administrative Schleswig-Holsteinism'. They preserved their German in church and in the family circle, but were on the best of terms with their Danish colleagues, even sharing to some extent in the Danish cultural heritage.

It was the dissolution of the Holy Roman Empire in 1806 which caused the first serious dispute between German and Dane in the *Statsraad.* Prussia had requested Denmark to allow Holstein, technically an independent state, to enter a North German Confederation. Frederik, however, was determined to annex Holstein and establish a unitary state, a dream cherished for many years. But he faced considerable opposition from German members of the *Statsraad.* The Duke of Augustenburg resigned in protest against Frederik's proposal that the female succession be introduced into Holstein. The foreign minister, Christian Bernstorff, and his brother Joachim, director of the foreign office, opposed the use of the word 'province' instead of 'duchy' in the patent of incorporation as well as the new title of *Schleswig-Holsteinische Kanzlei* in place of the old *Deutsche Kanzlei.*[2] The finance minister, E. Schimmelmann, considered incorporation a dangerous step

[1] Pride in the *Helstat.*

[2] A. Friis, 'Aktstykker og Breve vedrørende Holstens Indlemmelse i Danmark i Aaret 1806', *D.M.* 5 R VI, 1905, p. 44, J. F. Bernstorff to C. Bernstorff, 16 September 1806.

liable to alienate the duchies and bluntly refused to sign the patent.[1]

The regent was not deterred by the opposition of his German advisers. Holstein was annexed and measures were announced to bring the administration of Holstein into line with that of Denmark. In 1806 a commission was appointed to consider the introduction of the *Dansk Lov* into Holstein but the outbreak of war prevented the implementation of its findings. Many orders were issued concerning the use of Danish. Frederik did not, as he told F. Guldberg, attach much importance to language as a symbol of patriotism;[2] but, like Joseph II, he believed that the use of one administrative language was a convenient means of securing uniformity. In 1807 an order required all ordinances in Holstein to be issued in Danish as well as in German in order to encourage the use of Danish. In 1809 all official appointments had to be made in Danish as well as German. In 1810 a rescript proposed the introduction of Danish in the administration, churches and schools wherever Danish was spoken, a proposal which was never implemented owing to the doubts of Frederik's advisers about its practicability.[3] In 1811 and 1812 all candidates for official positions were required to possess a knowledge of Danish, and in 1811 a chair of Danish literature was founded at Kiel university. F. H. Guldberg, son of Ove Guldberg and tutor to the crown princess at Kiel from 1805 to 1810, sought continually to encourage the duchies to become Danish in spirit and language. In 1806 he urged them to become Danes 'so that they might amount to something', and in 1807 he prophesied that the name of the German people would disappear from history. He bluntly refused to call the people of Schleswig-Holstein his brothers until such time as they acquired a knowledge of the Danish language.

Guldberg was primarily concerned with the creation of a unitary state; all the same his remarks were prompted in some

[1] A Friis, *Holstens Indlemmelse i Danmark i aaret 1806*, etc., p. 87.

[2] K. Fabricius, *Sønderjyllands Historie*, IV, p. 56.

[3] K. Fabricius examines the history of the rescript in *Festskrift til H. P. Hanssen*, S. A. Åbenraa, 1932, and in *D.M.* 6 R VI; he disproves the generally accepted view of C. F. Allen that German officials deliberately sabotaged the king's plans.

measure by the first stirrings of Danish national sentiment in the early years of the new century. The middle class had been enriched by commercial activity and was assuming some social importance in Copenhagen; it was no coincidence that the Golden Age of Danish literature began around 1800. Interest in the rich heritage of Denmark's past was aroused in part by the influence of the German Romantics on Danish writers. This interest was deepened by an indigenous national sentiment which grew up in Denmark during the war years. King Frederik, as the regent had become in 1808, was little affected by national feeling; but Guldberg, a man of the middle class, shared this new-found pride in Denmark; this was a sentiment which merged imperceptibly into his views on the need for a unitary state.

The attempts to centralize the state came to an abrupt end with the Danish defeat in 1813. But the effect of these attempts on the balance of power inside the *Helstat* was decisive. By 1813 German political influence in Copenhagen had been considerably reduced. The *Statsraad* was no longer the preserve of the Holstein nobility; King Frederik, irritated by the opposition of the German members in 1806, naturally preferred to appoint middle-class Danes rather than German noblemen to that body. Danes like J. Møsting, president of the *Schleswig-holsteinische Kanzlei*, and F. J. Kaas, president of the *Dänische Kanzlei* since 1804, were more dependent on the crown than grand seigneurs like the Bernstorffs, Schimmelmanns and Reventlows had ever been. After A. P. Bernstorff's death there were few German officials of outstanding ability left in Copenhagen and their social and political influence was beginning to decline. The ablest of them, Count Cai Reventlow, resigned in 1802, followed by the Bernstorff brothers in 1810. After 1803 Frederik governed his dominions from Kiel and after 1808 called no further meetings of the *Statsraad*, thus depriving his German advisers of any considerable influence on policy. With the resignation of E. Schimmelmann[1] and Count C. Reventlow in 1813 the influence of the German nobility in the *Statsraad* came practically to an end. Not until 1831, when Count Konrad

[1] Schimmelmann remained a member of the *Statsraad* despite his resignation; from 1824–31 he was in charge of the foreign office.

Rantzau-Breitenberg was appointed to the *Statsraad*, did a native of Holstein again sit in that body.

Most people in Schleswig-Holstein had been quite unaffected in their daily lives by the incorporation of Holstein and by the attempts to introduce Danish law and language into that duchy. Indeed many of these measures were warmly welcomed by the rationalist-minded German middle class; only a few German officials, some members of the *Ritterschaft* and academicians like F. C. Dahlmann regarded the measures as evidence of a plot to 'danize' Holstein. But it was a vociferous minority; there were many critical references to Denmark in pamphlets appearing in 1813 and 1814, some of them suggesting that the 'danization' policy even justified the separation of the duchies from Denmark.[1] The accusations died hard; years later U. J. Lornsen referred, in his pamphlet, to the tactless remarks of F. Guldberg,[2] and as late as 1845 attention was still being drawn to them in the German press.[3] These criticisms of Danish policy were grossly exaggerated and did not affect the loyalty with which the overwhelming majority of German officials continued to serve the crown. Indeed it was only when a grave economic and financial crisis overwhelmed the duchies at the end of the war, that the dissatisfaction of the few with Danish policy began to assume a certain transient notoriety. Yet even that was an ominous portent of the approach of a new age, as K. T. Welcker suspected when he remarked in 1816 that 'the times of the Bernstorffs have passed and will never return'.[4]

[1] E.g. A. W. Schlegel, *Betrachtungen über die Politik der dänischen Regierung*, 1813, pp. 42–3.

[2] U. J. Lornsen, *Über das Verfassungswerk in Schleswig-Holstein*, p. 10.

[3] *A.A.Z.*, 1845, no. 297.

[4] O. Brandt, *Geistesleben und Politik in Schleswig-Holstein um die Wende des achtzehnten Jahrhunderts*, p. 418.

III

The origins of Schleswig-Holsteinism

1813 and 1814 were critical years for the *Helstat*. The economic stability and the peaceful international background which had enabled the *Helstat* to prosper in the golden and tranquil years of the late eighteenth century, disappeared during the war years. When the war ended in defeat for Denmark and her ally France, the future was dark and uncertain for the *Helstat*, foreign troops were in occupation of the duchies and the country was in the grip of a severe economic and financial crisis.

At the beginning of the nineteenth century the *Helstat* had enjoyed a period of unrivalled prosperity. In the second half of the eighteenth century numerous wars had stimulated a demand for Norwegian timber and for sugar, tea and tobacco from the West Indies. The Napoleonic wars greatly increased this demand and, as Great Britain was unable to maintain her maritime supremacy in the carrying trade, Denmark earned rich rewards by remaining neutral and supplying all the belligerents. It was short-lived prosperity. After 1807 when she became the ally of France, the great days of Danish commercial prosperity were over.

The volume of Danish trade was immediately reduced by the loss of British markets and by the loss of many ships which fell into the hands of the British navy. A fall in the price of wheat was inevitable; after 1809 this led in its turn to a fall in the price of land. The terms of trade moved decisively against the *Helstat*. Imports became increasingly expensive but agrarian exports continued to fall in price. It is true that there was still a good deal of licensed trade supplemented by smuggling and privateering, but this was insufficient to reverse the steady decline for which the Continental system was partly to blame. The decline was accelerated in

1811 when France annexed Hamburg and Lübeck, paralysing Danish trade with Northwest Germany and the Hansa towns.

By this time the financial situation in Denmark was critical. Deficits had been usual for many years as no serious attempt had ever been made to balance income and expenditure. Inflation was a persistent feature of the economy even in the eighteenth century; the note issue was regularly increased without adequate silver reserves. The situation was seriously aggravated by heavy wartime expenditure on armaments at a time when the decline in trade was reducing the revenue receipts. By 1812 continual depreciation of the currency brought Denmark to the verge of national bankruptcy.

The duchies suffered from the general decline in agrarian prices and the contraction of markets; but because they possessed their own coinage and note issue they had avoided financial instability. Then in December 1812 the Danish government[1] suspended payments by the Altona bank and removed its silver reserves under cover of a rumour that an invasion of the mouth of the Elbe was imminent. In January 1813 the Danes declared their intention of establishing a *Rigsbank*[2] to replace all existing banking institutes, and of issuing a new paper currency to replace all others in circulation. To obtain solid reserves for the new bank, a capital levy of six per cent was imposed on all property.

The rescript of 1813 embodying these decisions was an honest if belated attempt to stabilize the *Helstat's* finances. It failed simply because the new note issue still lacked adequate silver backing and continued to depreciate. But in the duchies the rescript aroused a great storm of protest. In the first place, there was bitter resentment at the cavalier fashion in which the special financial position of the duchies had been ignored in Copenhagen; this was a first fruit of the change in the balance of political power in the *Statsraad* from which German influence had been temporarily eliminated; Danish officials naturally enough saw no reason why the duchies should be exempted from sacrifices made for the common good

[1] I.e. the high officials in Copenhagen, both German and Danish, who, as members of the *Statsraad*, helped in the formulation of policy.

[2] National Bank.

of the *Helstat*. Secondly, the duchies were shaken out of their complacency by the disastrous economic consequences of the rescript. Overnight the duchies' credit was ruined because Hamburg, on which their economy depended, would not accept the new blue notes or lend more money to them, especially as the government insisted that the capital levy have priority over all debts. Because its publication coincided with the annual Kiel fair where most debts were settled, the rescript caused an immediate dislocation of trade, capital began to flow back to Hamburg, prices quadrupled as the new money continued to depreciate, the number of bankruptcies increased sharply, landowners were unable to pay their tax arrears and officials' salaries were drastically cut. In July the government relented, allowing the old currency to remain in circulation, a concession of great assistance to the duchies. But the capital levy remained a major source of discontent to landowners for many years, especially as it was believed that the duchies were bearing an unfair proportion of the debt to the *Rigsbank*.

The hardship caused by the rescript was real and widespread in the duchies and coincided with the government's reluctant admission in the spring of 1813 that Napoleon had suffered a decisive defeat in Russia. At last the *Helstat* paid the price of the French alliance. In the autumn Holstein was invaded by Swedes, Russians and Germans whose presence in the duchies during the hard 'Cossack winter' of 1813–14 added a further burden to the overstrained economy.[1]

The very existence of the *Helstat* lay in the balance in these months. Several pamphleteers commended the partition of the state to their readers.[2] Vom Stein, influential adviser to the Tsar, suggested to Britain that Norway be given to Sweden, Nørrejylland to England and Holstein to Prussia.[3] In the duchies the

[1] The present writer has a German friend whose great-grandparents, on their return from Haderslev church in 1814, discovered that the Cossacks had eaten their wedding breakfast.

[2] E.g. *Das Herzogtum Holstein unter dänische Herrschaft. Ein Beitrag zur Zeitgeschichte*, Germania, 1814.

[3] A. Thurau, *Die Anfänge eines deutschen nationalpolitischen Bewusstseins in Schleswig-Holstein*, p. 67.

greatest danger emanated from Swedish headquarters in Kiel, where Prince Bernadotte, encouraged by his friendly reception in the old Gottorp capital, cultivated anti-Danish feeling in the hope of securing the duchies as well as Norway as his reward for fighting Napoleon. So great were the fears of partition that the members of the commission appointed by the king to take over the duchies after the Peace of Kiel, suggested in May 1814 that Holstein be given a constitution to prevent its separation from the *Helstat*.

But widespread discontent and uncertainty had not shaken the basic loyalty of the duchies to the crown. When Bernadotte issued a proclamation in January 1814, summoning the old estates of Jylland and the duchies to Kiel to elect him king of Cimbria, the response was entirely negative. There was no desire for separation from Denmark among the masses of the people. Whatever pro-German sympathy there had been quickly disappeared when the allied armies appeared in the duchies. The misbehaviour of German occupation soldiers convinced the law-abiding people of Schleswig-Holstein that they still had good reason for gratitude to the crown which had preserved them so long from the evil effects of war. As the year advanced, the duchies were favourably impressed with the considerable efforts the government made to alleviate the economic hardship of the duchies; direct and indirect taxation was reduced, compensation was paid to the worst-affected areas and the interest rate on the capital levy was reduced. By the end of 1814 the Cossacks had withdrawn and the economy was at last recovering. Better harvests and improved marketing prospects were reflected in higher prices for wheat and butter. Improved material conditions combined with a traditional suspicion of foreigners proved a most effective reinforcement of the instinctive loyalty of the people to crown and *Helstat* in 1814.

The great upsurge of national feeling in Germany in 1813 had aroused little interest in the duchies even in the midst of their material hardship. Only at Kiel university had a small handful of professors and teachers, among them F. C. Dahlmann, K. T. Welcker and F. H. Hegewisch, followed the course of the War of Liberation with rapt attention. Though few in numbers and isolated in a small, sleepy university town on the periphery of the

German academic world, these intellectuals occupy an honoured place in the history of Schleswig-Holstein. For it was here in the so-called Kiel Circle and especially in the writings of the leading member, F. C. Dahlmann, that the theory of Schleswig-Holsteinism originated.

Dahlmann towered above his academic colleagues by virtue of his powerful personality rather than his academic attainments. Like most teachers at Kiel university he was not a native of Schleswig-Holstein but had been born in Wismar in 1785 when that part of Germany was under Swedish rule. He had connections with Holstein on his mother's side. His maternal grandfather, two uncles and a cousin held important offices in Danish service. Indeed it was only through the intervention of his influential uncle, F. C. Jensen, a member of the *Schleswig-holsteinische Kanzlei*, former secretary of the permanent deputation of the *Ritterschaft* and a professor at Kiel university, that Dahlmann obtained a lectureship at the university in 1812. A year later he was appointed professor of history, a post which he held for the next sixteen years.

Although Dahlmann had become a citizen of the *Helstat* in 1811 while lecturing in Copenhagen, his student experiences in Germany between 1807 and 1809 were the real turning-point in his life. It was there that he became nationally conscious for the first time, made painfully aware, like so many young Germans, of the impotence of Germany after the end of the Empire in 1806. In 1808 he made the acquaintance of the nationalist poet H. von Kleist in Dresden, and travelled with him to Bohemia in a vain and romantic attempt to transform the war between Austria and France into a general German uprising. Disillusioned by the Austrian defeat and anxious to obtain an academic post as quickly as possible, Dahlmann returned to the *Helstat*. But he had not lost his faith in Germany. Reading Swedish newspapers in the Kiel *Harmonie*, he learnt of the retreat from Moscow and followed the events of 1813 with passionate interest and a mounting sense of indignation at the French alliance, which prevented the duchies participating in the War of Liberation.

In the months that followed the signature of the Peace of Kiel by

Denmark in January 1814, there was eager speculation in academic circles about the political future of Germany. Dahlmann shared the hopes and illusions of most intellectuals as his first political essay indicates. If the sacrifices of the war were not to be in vain, he wrote, Germany must be given a new political framework in place of the loose, moribund ties of the old Empire. Like most of his contemporaries, Dahlmann did not think that it was the task of the German people to effect this change. Their role was purely passive. It was for the German princes and the Great Powers to create a strong German state so that 'the flame which had consumed the enemies of Europe could be preserved as a holy fire burning in the hearts of all Germans'.[1] As all Germans were related by blood ties this state would be based on the old primitive tribal divisions of Saxons, Franks, Swabians and Bavarians. Holstein, inhabited by Lower Saxons, would certainly be part of the new Germany as it had been part of the old Empire. It is significant that even in 1814, before his association with the *Ritterschaft*, Dahlmann already claimed that Schleswig was a German land bound by common ties and fortunes, by language and national character to Holstein. If not absolutely essential, it was at least highly desirable that Schleswig be included in the new Germany.[2]

Dahlmann was bitterly anti-French like most of his contemporaries, yet like them he remained essentially cosmopolitan in outlook. He rejected the contention that the presence of foreign princes on German soil was prejudicial to the interests of Germany. On the contrary; it had a beneficial effect in as much as it provided a basis for a true European union free from that narrow-minded, xenophobic nationalism which he and his colleague Falck thoroughly detested.[3] In a passage reminiscent of Schiller, Dahlmann referred to Germany as the cultural heart of Europe and meeting place for the cultural contributions of all European peoples.[4] He was a staunch believer in the *Helstat* and, although strongly critical of Danish policy after 1806, deprecated ill-feeling

[1] C. Varrentrap (ed.), *Über die letzten Schicksale der deutschen Untertänen Dänemarks*, etc., Z. 17, p. 10. Known as the *Erstlingsschrift*.

[2] *Ibid.*, p. 51. [3] *Ibid.*, p. 52. [4] *Ibid.*, p. 50.

between German and Dane. Denmark would, in his opinion, become a natural ally for Germany once she lost Norway. He sincerely hoped that Denmark would receive territory in Germany to compensate her for this loss, and in that event Schleswig, the bridge between the Danish and German way of life, could enter the new Germany. As late as 1844 Dahlmann favoured an alliance between Scandinavia and Germany and deplored hatred between German and Dane who had so much in common.[1] His associate K. Welcker shared these cosmopolitan views, speaking of different nations enriching and completing the portrait of humanity by preserving their own national characteristics.[2] Like Dahlmann, he considered love of fatherland quite compatible with the continued presence of foreign troops on German soil.[3] In short, the exclusive nationalism of a later age was far removed from the minds of the Kiel intellectuals. Germany still tended to be an intellectual rather than a territorial concept. 'The true fatherland is above', wrote Berger, '. . . it is an eternal spiritual verity of which no material power can rob us.' [4]

The German intellectuals failed to exert any decisive influence on the settlement drawn up at the Vienna Congress. After 1815 a few of them interested themselves in attempts to obtain constitutions in some German states; for as Welcker remarked in the *Kieler Blätter*, 'our national aspirations will now have to become more or less provincial . . . so that in general the Germans will have to seek that which is good and true in the special circumstances of their own locality'.[5] They had not far to look in Schleswig-Holstein; in the renewed dispute between *Ritterschaft* and crown over the payment of tax arrears the intellectuals at Kiel university discovered a local dispute capable of sustaining their demands for a constitution for the duchies.

The members of the *Ritterschaft* had long since lost their predominant political influence. They retained, in the form of privileges, certain rights over their tenants, the right to hold local courts and the right of placing unmarried daughters in any of the

[1] A. Springer, *Friedrich Christoph Dahlmann*, II, pp. 141–2. Cf. Chapter XI.
[2] *K.B.*, I, p. 28.
[3] *Ibid.*, p. 32.
[4] *K.B.*, II, p. 37.
[5] *Ibid.*, p. 37.

four secularized convents in the duchies. As a class the members of the *Ritterschaft* enjoyed exemption from stamp duty and a limited exemption from customs duty. Their financial contribution (known as the ordinary contribution and paid since 1690 in place of various tributes in kind and money) enjoyed preferential treatment; it could not be increased and was not paid on their *Hoffelder*.[1] Should the crown require 'extraordinary contributions' in wartime, the *Ritterschaft* could, in theory, insist upon the calling of a *Landtag* to exercise its right of consent to taxation according to the 1460 Charter. In practice, when the crown imposed additional taxation in the eighteenth century the *Ritterschaft* paid up, hiding behind the euphemistic phrase 'voluntary contributions' to save face. In 1775 the *Ritterschaft* had been allowed to establish a permanent deputation or committee to regulate the internal affairs of this most exclusive corporation.

At the turn of the century the *Ritterschaft* was involved in a conflict with the government. As part of its attempt to modernize the *Helstat* and defray mounting defence expenditure, the government introduced a new land tax into the duchies in 1802, based on the Danish model and abolishing the exemption of the *Hoffelder*. Under the energetic leadership of Count Fritz Reventlow of Emkendorf, some members of the Holstein *Ritterschaft* challenged the government's action, maintaining that these changes required the formal consent of the *Ritterschaft*. But by 1804 resistance to the government had ended as the imminent dissolution of the Empire made appeals to the Imperial court hopeless.

This obscure dispute has attracted more attention than it deserves because an eminent German historian once advanced the theory that Schleswig-Holsteinism originated not in the Kiel Circle but in this obscure *Ritterschaft* dispute. He argued that national sentiment had been the inspiration behind this dispute, and that Count Fritz Reventlow, the *Ritterschaft* leader since 1790, was a German nationalist of sorts and the forerunner of F. C. Dahlmann.[2]

This is no longer regarded as a tenable theory; certainly the

[1] Land retained by the owner for personal use.
[2] Brandt, *Geistesleben und Politik*, *op. cit.*

Emkendorf Circle, a literary group associated with Reventlow's country home near Kiel, was deeply steeped in political Romanticism.[1] Reventlow and his wife, Julia, the Stolberg brothers, Christian and Friedrich, and Christian's wife, Luise, were all bitterly hostile to the French Revolution and to the spirit of the Enlightenment. They attributed these evils to religious indifference for Emkendorf had a local reputation as a centre of orthodox Lutheranism.[2] These aristocrats denounced the absolutism of the old rulers and clamoured for a restoration of the old medieval estates. They were bitter opponents of Napoleon, were unrestrained in their delight at his downfall and displayed a lively interest in the political future of Germany after 1806.

Possibly Reventlow and his friends helped to keep alive memories of the financial power once exercised by the *Ritterschaft* in the *Landtag*. But it is extremely doubtful, to say the least, whether these aristocrats had any clear concept of the German nation as a political entity. Despite bitter anti-Danish and anti-French talk, there was no sign at Emkendorf of any realization that a strong German state was essential to give tangible expression to these nationalist undertones. Like Dahlmann, Reventlow believed in the *Helstat*; he hoped that Denmark would receive Hamburg and Lübeck to compensate her for the loss of Norway. At bottom it was not German national feeling but defence of class privilege which really inspired the oppositional attitude of Reventlow and his associates. True, they referred frequently to their '*teutsche Verfassung*'—but they were thinking only of their own privileges. Their Danish opponents had argued that *Ritterschaft* privileges were revocable at will by the crown; by emphasizing the 'German' character of these privileges, Reventlow and his friends were simply trying to establish the point that aristocratic privileges were as sacrosanct as the power of the crown itself.

The members of the *Ritterschaft*, like all landowners, were affected adversely by the economic crisis of 1813. Land had been

[1] In the 1950's refugees lived in one half of this crumbling edifice and the owner of the *Kieler Nachrichten* in the other.

[2] '*Fromm wie ein Reventlow*' as the local idiom put it.

depreciating in value for some time, taxation arrears had accumulated and the exactions of occupation forces pressed heavily upon them. So at the end of the war the *Ritterschaft* was again involved in a dispute with the government which firmly insisted upon prompt payment of tax arrears under threat of military execution. Under the shadow of this threat Count Adam Moltke, a prominent member of the *Ritterschaft*, was sent to Vienna to plead for leniency with the king.

The petition drafted by Fritz Reventlow and Adam Moltke and handed by the latter to the king requested that a *Landtag* 'suited to our times' be called in Holstein. The experience of other countries, it was argued, proved that a constitution could restore credit ruined by the *Rigsbank* project. In May, when the king returned from the Congress of Vienna, he was presented with a second petition requesting a constitution for both duchies. These demands were not surprising for constitutions were the universal panacea recommended in the pamphlets circulating in 1814 and 1815. But with the exception of a very few enlightened aristocrats like Adam Moltke, the *Ritterschaft* had not been suddenly converted to liberal views. It was merely that a constitution appeared a useful tactical weapon to employ against the crown.

The association of the Kiel Circle with this financial dispute was immensely important because the resultant cross-fertilization laid the basis of the Schleswig-Holstein movement of the nineteenth century. The association began with Dahlmann's election to the post of secretary of the permanent deputation of the *Ritterschaft* in July 1815 as a result of considerable efforts made on his behalf by Fritz Reventlow. The most important result of the association was the infusion of a national political content into a purely financial wrangle. The 'administrative Schleswig-Holsteinism' of the eighteenth century represented the instinctive reaction of particularist-minded officials anxious to preserve the anomalous administrative and financial position of the duchies inside the *Helstat*. The essential tenet of nineteenth century Schleswig-Holsteinism was the conviction that the national character of the duchies justified a demand for political independence and close association with Germany. Dahlmann is rightly regarded as the father of Schleswig-Holsteinism for he worked out the essentials of a political framework for the duchies designed to give full expression to their allegedly German character.

Dahlmann claimed that Schleswig as well as Holstein was German in character. Schleswig he believed to be '*urdeutsch*', inhabited originally by Angles and Saxons, and subsequently invaded by Danes. He did not deny that it had been a Danish fief, that it had the same succession as Denmark or that some Danish and Frisian was spoken there. But the duchy was largely German-speaking and, most important of all, its institutions were German. In Bohemia and Silesia as well as in Schleswig it was generally believed by Germans that historical processes and the presence of a German-speaking upper class had stamped an indelible German character on the legal and administrative superstructure of these regions. It was the German spoken in church, school and court, the language of officials, pastors, lawyers and merchants rather than the Czech, Polish or Danish spoken by at least some of the inhabitants, which constituted in German eyes the most important criterion for determining national character in the early nineteenth century.

It was essential, Dahlmann maintained, that the duchies be given a constitution so that the German customs, language and way of life of their inhabitants, 'of all the German tribes . . . the most free since ancient times', be given adequate political expression.[1] A nationality, as Welcker remarked, had to have a firm foundation in a constitution.[2] A. Moltke, somewhat naïvely, believed that the *Ritterschaft's* demand for a constitution was not motivated solely by economic considerations but by the realization that all branches of the German people needed constitutions to awaken in them a sense of their solidarity. Only then would Germany cease to be 'an unholy chessboard on which the other peoples of Europe find full scope for a display of their arrogant power'.[3]

Dahlmann's conviction that the duchies needed a constitution was reinforced by his experiences in Kiel between 1812 and 1814.

[1] *K.B.*, I, p. 245. [2] *Ibid.*, p. 31.
[3] A. Moltke, *Ansichten bei den Ansichten*, Kiel, 1816, p. 41.

He saw in Danish policy after 1806 evidence of a design to incorporate the duchies in Denmark. Discontented with the rescript of 1813 which had severely reduced the purchasing power of professorial salaries, Dahlmann wrote his first political essay in which he demanded the resurrection of the old medieval constitution to defend the duchies against Danish aggression. He detested the Danish alliance with 'the enemy of the world',[1] rejoiced at the entry of allied soldiers into Holstein and welcomed A. W. Schlegel, anti-Danish pamphleteer in Swedish pay, into the Kiel Circle. There are few signs of these anti-Danish sentiments after 1815 when, as befitted a *Ritterschaft* official, he concerned himself with the defence of its class interests. Economic considerations naturally loomed large in the *Ritterschaft* petitions which he drafted. Only occasionally, as in the final petition to the German Confederation in 1822, did he allow a national note to intrude by pointing out that, much as the Germans were prepared to live on brotherly terms with the Danes, they were not prepared to be assimilated by them.[2] It was really a matter of tactics as he remarked in later years; the alleviation of the *Ritterschaft's* financial difficulties happened to coincide with German national aspirations.[3] But of course most members of the *Ritterschaft* were concerned only with the former, and even N. Falck, one of his closest associates in the Kiel Circle, was unmoved by national considerations.

Dahlmann's interest in constitutional development was not inspired by a belief in the Rights of Man. Like most Germans he heartily detested the French, 'a perjured, godless, avaricious people and all their works'.[4] Being a classical philologist by training and a historian by profession and inclination, Dahlmann delved back into the historical past of the duchies to justify his demand for a constitution. He soon found what he was looking for in the dispute between *Ritterschaft* and crown; he had long been familiar with the historical background, partly through the collection of

[1] Varrentrap, *op. cit.*, p. 21.

[2] *Denkschrift der Prälaten und Ritterschaft des Herzogtums Holstein enthaltend die Darstellung ihrer in anerkannter Wirksamkeit bestehenden landständischen Verfassung insbesondere ihrer Steurgerechtsame*, Frankfurt, 1822, p. 133.

[3] Springer, *op. cit.*, I, p. 138.

[4] *Ibid.*, p. 467.

privileges compiled by his uncle F. Jensen in 1797, and partly because he, C. H. Pfaff and F. H. Hegewisch had been frequent visitors to Emkendorf.

Dahlmann's major premise was that the essentials of the concessions made to the estates by Christian of Oldenburg in 1460 were contained in the *Ritterschaft* privileges. These privileges had been confirmed by successive monarchs, most recently by King Christian VII in 1773. In particular Dahlmann argued that the right of the medieval estates to consent to taxation had not died with that body, but had been preserved in the various attenuated financial privileges still enjoyed by the *Ritterschaft*. It was an ingenious argument, attractive to the legal mind, but of doubtful validity in view of the obvious decline in the fortunes of the *Ritterschaft*.

Not that Dahlmann adhered rigidly to the letter of the old documents—far from it. He reinterpreted them liberally, extracting from them 'general principles' calculated to appeal to a much wider audience than the aristocratic *Ritterschaft*. Thus, as early as 1814, Dahlmann maintained that, according to the 1460 charter, the duchies had the status of an independent state. In his *Erstlingsschrift*, written the same year, Dahlmann implied that the legal and administrative system of the duchies should be separated from Denmark and he maintained that the duchies and Denmark had only the king in common.[1] The word state was not used in this essay, but personal union between independent states was clearly in Dahlmann's mind. In 1820 Dahlmann explained why he could not use the word 'Dane' to describe an inhabitant of Schleswig-Holstein; 'I have never felt that kind of patriotism and do not wish to feel it. I cannot understand why any inhabitant of the duchies should wish to call himself a Dane. . . . Schleswig-Holstein is no fatherland for an intelligent Dane, but for those of us who live in Schleswig-Holstein it is the most important country. History, as well as our instincts, leads us to this conclusion.'[2] During this lecture Dahlmann at last admitted that a constitution for the duchies meant a considerable degree of separation from Denmark.

[1] Varrentrapp, *op. cit.*, pp. 53–4. [2] Springer, *op. cit.*, I, pp. 74–5.

A common constitution for Schleswig-Holstein was just not practical politics as Dahlmann soon discovered. If the king chose to implement clause thirteen of the federal constitution, Holstein, being a member of the German Confederation, would receive a constitution. But Schleswig, being outside the Confederation, could not expect similar treatment. The difficulty arose in an acute form when the king appointed a commission in 1816 to draft a constitution for Holstein only. A moment of crucial importance had arrived for Schleswig-Holsteinism. Dahlmann was determined that the claims of Schleswig to have a constitution should not be overlooked. In defence of these claims he produced a new and ingenious legal argument which became the stock in trade of generations of German nationalists. In the *Ritterschaft* petition of October 1816 he drew attention for the first time to a somewhat obscure sentence in the 1460 charter: '*lauen wy . . . dat se bliven ewich tosamende ungedelt.*' [1] He maintained that this amounted to a royal recognition of the inseparability of the duchies; this was the most important of the *Ritterschaft* privileges for by implication it contained the essentials of all the concessions made to the duchies by Christian of Oldenburg. In effect Dahlmann was trying to summarize all the historical arguments for the autonomous political life of the two German duchies in one brief sentence. The implication of this sentence, Dahlmann maintained, was that the duchies formed a single state in personal union with Denmark. Therefore Schleswig was fully entitled to share in any constitution given to Holstein.

An additional proof was afforded in his opinion by the existence of the *Ritterschaft* as a corporate body whose members lived in both duchies, possessed a permanent deputation and enjoyed privileges confirmed over the centuries. The *nexus socialis* of the *Ritterschaft*, confirmed in 1732, was a living link with the old documents and a symbol of the inseparability of the duchies. The *Ritterschaft* privileges, including the alleged right of consent to taxation, applied to both duchies; therefore a constitution enabling

[1] N. Falck, *Sammlung der wichtigsten Urkunden*, etc., p. 20. 'We allow them to remain always together undivided.' In fact it only meant that neither duchy would be partitioned in favour of sons of the younger line.

the *Ritterschaft* to exercise its political privileges once more must also extend to both duchies.

What kind of constitution did Dahlmann and his friends have in mind? The Kiel intellectuals were typical of the first generation of German liberals in sharing the conservative admiration for the *Ständestaat*[1] as a political ideal. Dahlmann did not look to France for inspiration but to medieval Germany, declaring in 1815 that the liberal mission was merely to restore what the eighteenth century had mistakenly despised as gothic and barbarian.[2] Constitutions were not manufactured; they were the product of organic growth. A new representative assembly for the duchies would be based not on abstract principles but on the old medieval estates, product of centuries of historical growth, embodying the organic view of society in which all conservatives believed. Each estate, concluded Dahlmann, would be restored to its rightful place in a modern setting like a precious jewel purified from the grime of centuries. This was an unrealistic political theory, for the princes, whose power had increased enormously by the adoption of Napoleonic administrative methods, were most unlikely to restore political power to the nobility and clergy. But it proved an attractive theory in the immediate post-Congress period in as much as it satisfied the historical sense and national sentiment of these liberal intellectuals. It conferred respectability upon their activities, enabling them to defend constitutions as a natural product of social evolution and not as detestable French innovations.[3] Because the theory postulated social harmony as the basis of constitutions, it facilitated co-operation between the nobility and the upper middle class; in Württemberg, for example, these classes joined forces in 1815 to demand the restoration of the ancient

[1] A society in which political representation was based on corporate bodies arranged in hierarchical order.

[2] Varrentrapp, *F. C. Dahlmanns Kleine Schriften und Reden, Ein Wort über Verfassung*, p. 27.

[3] It is significant that the Kiel Circle was especially interested in the history of North Friesland because the tradition of local independence in this part of the duchies approximated most closely to their own political ideals; Dahlmann praised the North Frisians for preserving those 'common freedoms' which the Germans lost elsewhere a thousand years ago. *K.B.*, V, 1818, p. 182.

estates, a development commented upon favourably by Pfaff in the *Kieler Blätter*.[1]

For most members of the *Ritterschaft* constitutional questions were of secondary importance. The maintenance of their financial privileges remained the *raison d'être* of their dispute with the crown. Dahlmann, however, saw in their privileges nothing more than a convenient weapon for forcing a constitution out of a reluctant government desperately in need of ready cash. In later years he was prepared to admit frankly that the government had much right on its side in this dispute.[2] But unlike many middle class people in Schleswig-Holstein at this time, Dahlmann felt no animosity towards aristocracy. He was perfectly willing to concede an important role to the *Ritterschaft* in a new estates while insisting that other social groups be properly represented. Like most liberals of his generation he was never very clear about the role he expected the middle class to play. Perhaps it was his detestation of France which blinded him to the historical significance of the French Revolution; for it was this event—and not attempts to resurrect a pseudo-medieval social structure—which made the new century the era of the middle class.

These early liberals were anything but radical in their views. Dahlmann agreed with Hegewisch that their objective was 'not bloody conflict but a battle of the intellects waged in a legislative chamber'.[3] It would never do to pay attention to the disorderly clamour of the masses who ignorantly pursued their own immediate interests. The art of constitution making, wrote Dahlmann, was to render articulate the better part of the people as exemplified by the upper middle class readers of the *Kieler Blätter*.[4] He was sharply critical both of the French constitution of 1791 and the Spanish constitution of 1812 because, in his opinion, they restricted unduly the power of the executive. Certainly the king must not be able to do everything he wanted but he must not be compelled to do anything he did not want to do.[5] Constitutional

[1] *K.B.*, I, p. 201. [2] O. Scheel, *Der junge Dahlmann*, p. 47.
[3] W. Klüver, *Franz Hermann Hegewisch*, p. 417.
[4] Springer, *op. cit.*, I, p. 90.
[5] Varrentrapp, *F. C. Dahlmanns Kleine Schriften und Reden*, *op. cit.*, p. 19.

monarchy of the British variety was his ideal, leaving considerable residual power with the crown while bestowing real but limited power on the propertied and commercial classes and intellectuals in a two-chamber legislature. He and his associates—especially 'Sir Francis' Hegewisch—were ardent Anglophiles. Like many North German liberals they were full of admiration for the English parliamentary system, which they believed to be a perfect product of a truly organic society where all estates, middle-class merchants as well as noblemen, lived in social harmony and played a part in political life.

There can be no doubt about the importance of Dahlmann's contribution to the theory of Schleswig-Holsteinism. With the assistance of his friend Falck he had quarried out of the history of the duchies all the essential features of the German nationalist case in Schleswig-Holstein. It was Dahlmann who invented the major arguments used by German nationalists throughout the nineteenth century, namely that the duchies must remain 'for ever undivided' and that they had a right to an independent political existence. It is true that Dahlmann did not insist upon the inclusion of Schleswig in the German Confederation; nevertheless he considered this to be the logical conclusion of his premises and a highly desirable development. 'Even if the people of Schleswig have never been in the German Confederation', he remarked in 1815, 'they belong to it through their brothers, the people of Holstein, to whom they have extended the hand of friendship over the centuries and with whom they are most intimately united in their constitution, their liberties and their rights. May they grasp each other's hands more firmly still.' [1]

Dahlmann did not confine his activities to the study and lecture hall; like the political professors of a later age he believed political action to be an essential concomitant of historical research, and he played a not inconsiderable role in the leisurely and gentlemanly political agitation of the post-war years.

His attempts to win the support of the upper middle class for a constitution met with modest success between 1815 and 1818. It was largely at his instigation that the *Kieler Blätter* was first

[1] *Ibid.*, pp. 6–7.

published in 1815. This was a new type of periodical with a definite political bias, which undoubtedly helped to break down some of the apathy lingering on from the eighteenth century and aroused interest in constitutional questions. It is significant in this respect that an unprecedented number of pamphlets for those days, sixteen in all, were written between 1815 and 1817, some in support but most sharply critical of the *Ritterschaft* case.

Dahlmann had his most spectacular political success in the towns of Schleswig in the winter of 1816–17. He was personally responsible for petitions to the crown in support of a constitution from ten towns in Schleswig. In some cases, as in Haderlev, the petitioners wanted union with Holstein; in others, as in Flensburg, they asked only for a constitution similar to that promised Holstein. Rural areas were generally unaffected, with the exception of Kiel and district which petitioned in 1818. To some extent Gottorp sentiment lingering on in the Schleswig towns, Åbenraa, Schleswig and Sønderborg, may explain the interest of their officials in petitioning the crown. It is perhaps significant that petitions from these towns emphasized political rather than economic considerations. But other petitions were influenced in varying degrees by a variety of factors; the problem of financial arrears; a desire for a trade revival—which constitutions were confidently expected to produce; fear of competition from Holstein if that duchy obtained a constitution and Schleswig did not; some consciousness of liberal constitutional ideas and, finally, some hazy recollections of the traditional ties between the duchies.

Despite the literary and political endeavours of the Kiel intellectuals, the duchies did not receive a constitution. Several factors contributed to this outcome. Most important of all, the appeal of the agitation was strictly limited; the great landowners and the gentlemen of Kiel had nothing to offer the people. There was no question of mass support—had it been forthcoming it would have been most unwelcome. The middle class was, for the most part, quite out of sympathy with the agitation. The officials, pastors and lawyers remained loyal to the crown, remembering with gratitude the material favours bestowed on them in recent years. Even the few who were sympathetically disposed towards political change, were agreed that the outmoded privileges of the aristocracy were a totally inadequate basis for a modern constitution. In any case it seemed obvious enough that the *Ritterschaft* was only interested in securing preferential financial treatment at the expense of the rest of the community. These suspicions were increased in January 1817 when the *Ritterschaft* refused to pay its arrears unless its ancient right of consent to taxation was recognized. The *Ritterschaft* had been persuaded to defend its special privileges in this defiant fashion by Dahlmann, who was fully aware that 'this daring step' would probably alienate public opinion.[1] But he could see no other way of keeping the agitation alive; for once the king confirmed the *Ritterschaft* privileges in August 1816 these aristocrats rapidly lost all interest in politics. All they now wanted was a financial settlement with the crown. By the end of 1818 even their leader, Fritz Reventlow, was reconciled with the king, turning up a year later in Berlin as Danish ambassador. Like other Holstein noblemen, he realized that continued opposition merely excluded him from lucrative posts in the king's service. Only with the greatest reluctance did the *Ritterschaft* agree in 1818 to appeal to the German Confederation.

Even if the *Ritterschaft* case had been convincing, the political atmosphere was unconducive to a favourable outcome after the murder of A. von Kotzebue. By 1820 press censorship, supervision of universities and suppression of the *Burschenschaften* ushered in a period of illiberalism. These measures applied to Holstein where the *Kieler Blätter* ceased publication, and Kiel university, driving force behind the constitutional agitation, was subjected to supervision, though admittedly mild compared with most German states.

The changing political climate coincided with a disastrous postwar economic crisis. This proved a decisive combination. Between 1814 and 1818 the agrarian produce of the duchies commanded high prices. But prices began to decline in 1818 owing to overproduction and to serious marketing difficulties caused by the English Corn Laws and the imposition of a duty on grain entering Norway. Land fell in price, bankruptcies increased in number, and

[1] Springer, *op. cit.*, pp. 142–3.

for the remainder of the 1820's those who had been interested in politics were far too preoccupied with the economic depression to bother about the final outcome of the *Ritterschaft* dispute. In March 1822 the *Ritterschaft* had appealed to the Confederation on the basis of article fifty-six of the *Schlussacte* of 1820. In November 1823 the Federal Diet rejected the argument that the old medieval constitution was still in force in both duchies. The Diet pointed out that it had no competence to interfere in Schleswig and commended the *Ritterschaft* to the king who would no doubt consider its representations when he implemented clause thirteen for Holstein. The verdict aroused no interest in the duchies. By this time even the royal commission of 1816 had ceased its deliberations without protest and was not summoned again until the late 1820's.

If the general public soon forgot the Kiel Circle the university did not, for it was here that the intellectuals exerted their greatest influence. The university was a focal point in the intellectual life of the duchies where all aspirants for official posts were required to spend four *Semester*.[1] It was here that many of them came under the spell of Dahlmann and accepted the essentials of Schleswig-Holsteinism. In an agrarian society where officials enjoyed an exaggerated importance, this was a development of the utmost significance, as Dahlmann recognized in his final address before leaving Kiel in 1829; 'Many thousands of them, the younger half of the official class, are sympathetic to my political ideas,' he remarked.[2]

No less important was the influence exerted on these young men by the Kiel *Burschenschaft*. This student society did much to awaken in them that sympathy for Germany which had been repressed and inhibited for so long by the French alliance and by a sense of loyalty to the crown. At the time of the War of Liberation it was well known that the professors were 'German' and the students 'Danish'.[3] In fact the students preferred to celebrate the rearguard action fought by retreating Danish soldiers against advancing allied armies at Sehestedt, rather than the Leipzig victory.

[1] I.e. two years. [2] Springer, *op. cit.*, p. 263.
[3] *Ibid.*, p. 463, Julia Hegewisch to Grete Hensler, 25 July 1815.

When Dahlmann delivered a public lecture to commemorate the allied victory at Waterloo, students from Schleswig hissed those passages in the speech where Dahlmann emphasized the intimate nature of the ties between the duchies; after this the students ceased to attend his lectures. It was a native of Württemberg, K. T. Welcker, who effected a significant change in the students' attitude between 1816 and 1817, so much so that some twenty students attended the Wartburg festival. By 1817 they were celebrating Waterloo Day and in 1818 sent representatives to the Jena *Burschentag* held to establish an *allgemeine deutsche Burschenschaft.*

Admittedly the national sentiment of the *Burschenschaften* amounted to little more than a naïve nebulous *Deutschtümelei*, coupled with a praiseworthy attempt to reform student morals. Very few *Burschenschaftler* played any active part in politics and no one in Kiel where the *Burschenschaft* was always particularist in outlook and much more moderate than its German counterparts. Nevertheless a whole generation of students obtained through the *Burschenschaften* the first inkling of a German national political concept going beyond the *Kulturgemeinschaft* to which they had always professed loyalty.

For many young men like W. H. Beseler, T. Olshausen and U. J. Lornsen, all of whom played significant roles in the political life of Schleswig-Holstein in later years, this experience was of decisive importance. 'It will only take a few more years', observed Lornsen with prophetic insight in 1832, 'and then all the offices of state, all the most influential positions in the nation will be in the hands of this generation. It is therefore quite obvious that the trend of events now and in the future will depend upon their attitude. But as anyone knows who belongs to this generation, their supreme ideal is the unification of Germany and all their political activities are directed to this end like radii converging on the centre of a circle. They are clear and determined about the goal of their political activity . . . their unfaltering vision is not blurred by feudal ideas of loyalty and devotion to the princes of the Confederation. They are not fainthearted like the philistines who admire and praise other countries sacrificing everything for freedom and independence, but who express horror the moment they are expected to act in like manner and make similar sacrifices for their fatherland. They know that no European nation has suffered such political ignominy as the Germans when one considers what the German nation used to be, what it is now and what it could become and must become.' [1]

[1] V. Pauls, *Uwe Jens Lornsens Briefe an Franz Hermann Hegewisch*, pp. 132–3, 30 July 1832.

IV

Schleswig: the ethnographical background

TODAY the political frontier between Denmark and Germany coincides, more or less, with the ethnic frontier between German and Dane. But throughout history the political frontiers of the Kongeaa,[1] Elbe and Eider have rarely if ever been ethnographical frontiers. This fact assumed no political significance for the *Helstat* until the era of national conflict dawned in the 1840's. Ever since, the fluid ethnographical situation in the area between Kongeaa and Eider—especially in Central Schleswig—has been an essential feature of the contest between German and Dane for possession of Schleswig. It was indeed a 'moving' frontier because the relative stability of the present frontier is the result of a thousand-year process, which has gradually moved the frontier northwards from the Eider river.

It is impossible to say with certainty whether Schleswig was inhabited originally by North or South Germans before the *Völkerwanderung*. It is, however, beyond dispute that by 800 Danish was spoken as far south as the line of the Dannevirke and Schlei estuary. The land between the Schlei and the Eider was covered until about 1000 with uninhabitable forest, marking the northern boundary of the Saxon march founded by the emperor Charlemagne in 811 to absorb the shock of Danish tribal raids on the periphery of his empire.

The Eider soon ceased to be the ethnographical frontier between German and Dane. German cultural, economic and political influences from the neighbouring county of Holstein (as the Saxon march was now known) spread north of the Eider into the land known by 1340 as the duchy of Schleswig. Germanization,

[1] German Königsau.

as this development is called, was part of a natural and dynamic process by which German influence was extended along the northern, southeastern and eastern frontiers of the Holy Roman Empire. German knights, priests, merchants, and artisans were the standard-bearers of German culture and trade east of the Oder and north of the Schlei.

By the fourteenth century the area between Eider and Schlei had been colonized and almost completely germanized under the patronage of the Holstein aristocracy, which supplanted the native aristocracy north of the Schlei, secured its estates and occupied official positions in the duchy. This penetration was facilitated by the fact that the Schauenburg counts of Holstein secured Schleswig as a fief in 1375 after a century of conflict with the Danish rulers in which the counts had proved their superior military ability.

Geographical factors dictated the speed and direction of the germanization process. The most speedy advance was made along the east coast and through Angeln; it was marked by a line of towns, Schleswig, Eckernförde, Flensburg, Åbenraa and Haderslev, centres of German influence which dominated the surrounding countryside. Slower progress was made along the west coast and least progress of all in the barren moorland of Central Schleswig.

The Reformation gave a tremendous impetus to the spread of German influence; services in the vernacular played a considerable part in the new liturgy, so that Low German, already the language of administration, diplomacy and commerce, became the language of the Church in large areas of Central Schleswig and in the whole of South Schleswig. The use of German in church, more than any other factor, increased its importance as a spoken language and conferred upon it additional prestige by associating it with the most solemn occasions in the lives of the people.

The rapid advance made by Low German in the sixteenth century was not sustained. In the middle of the seventeenth century High German, the new literary language, became the administrative and legal tongue and by the end of the century had been introduced into the churches south of a line from Flensburg to Tønder. The change-over to High German was facilitated by the foundation of the university at Kiel by Duke Christian Albert in 1665. However, High German remained a literary language almost as difficult for ordinary people to master as a foreign tongue. It lacked the incomparable advantages of Low German which, because it had been both a written and spoken language, had spread widely in Schleswig, producing a genuinely popular culture to which the rich treasures enshrined in the Schleswig churches of this period are a striking testimony.

Low German remained the language of the schools for at least a century after the introduction of High German in the churches; it was widely used in the homes of the aristocracy as late as the early nineteenth century. But it had been reduced to the status of a mere dialect without significance as an official or cultural medium. Consequently its use declined in the seventeenth century in the towns of Tønder, Haderslev and Åbenraa and in parts of Tønder and Åbenraa *Amter*. Simultaneously, in those parts of Schleswig where Danish was still known, its use as a popular language increased.[1]

The complexity of the ethnographical position in Schleswig in the early nineteenth century is such that, in the interests of clarity, it is convenient to consider separately the three major geographical divisions of the duchy, viz. North, South and Central Schleswig.

North Schleswig is bounded by the river Kongeaa in the north and in the south by a line running south of Tønder and north of Flensburg following the boundary line between Slogs (or Slux) *Herred* and Karr (or Kaer) *Harde*.[2] Some historians would extend the southern boundary to include most of Karr *Harde* as well as the northern part of Vis *Harde* in Flensburg *Amt*. The Danish islands of Als and Aerø are also included in this first geographical division.

[1] V. Pauls, 'Nationale Spannungen im Herzogtum Schleswig während des achtzehnten Jahrhunderts' in *Festschrift zu Otto Becker*, 1954, points out that the Danish-speaking population in Central Schleswig understood enough Low German to follow sermons in that language, but found High German as difficult to understand as High Danish.

[2] *Amter* in Schleswig were subdivided into *Herreder* (Danish) or *Harden* (German). In this work the terms are used with reference to the present frontier, e.g. Karr *Harde* but Slogs *Herred*.

The overwhelming majority of the 100,000 inhabitants of North Schleswig spoke a Danish dialect, sometimes called Jutish for it was also spoken in Nørrejylland and stood in the same relationship to High Danish as the Austrian and Swiss dialects stand to High German. Danish was spoken in the rural churches and schools. Important exceptions to this general rule were the rural churches in the vicinity of Kristiansfeld, Haderslev, Åbenraa, Sønderborg and Tønder and in an area between Ladelund and Medelby where German and Danish were used on alternate Sundays.[1] Until the eighteenth century Danish had been used in the lower courts; but between 1770 and 1820 it was replaced by High German, though Danish was still used for drafting wills, contracts and mortgages in Haderslev and Sønderborg *Amter*.

In the North Schleswig towns, a by-product of the germanization process, the position was more complex. Commercial and cultural life in these towns was largely dominated by a German upper class of officials, lawyers and merchants, and much German was used in the schools and churches. But there was a considerable Danish element in these towns where Danish was used more frequently as Low German declined in importance. In Haderslev, for example, in 1843 there were 986 families liable to taxation. Of these 189 spoke only German, 90 spoke Danish and German while 651 spoke only Danish.[2] In the schools German was the medium of instruction and the order requiring some instruction in Danish was inadequately implemented. But in the churches much Danish was used; at Løgumkloster German was used only on every third Sunday, at Norborg every fourth Sunday; at Tønder Danish was used exclusively in some churches, while alternating with German in others: at Åbenraa the church authorities petitioned in 1822 for the exclusive use of Danish.

Danish was widely spoken by the small farmers forming the overwhelming majority of the population. Nevertheless, the superstructure of North Schleswig was German; High German was spoken by the small minority of officials and lawyers; it was

[1] See language maps, pp. 321–2.

[2] A. Sach, *Das Herzogtum Schleswig in seiner ethnographischen und nationalen Entwicklung*, III, Abteilung, p. 304.

the language of the administration and of the high courts; it was used in some of the lower courts, and all royal proclamations and directives from Gottorp castle were issued in High German although accompanied by an unsigned Danish translation.

Little need be said about the second area, South Schleswig, bounded in the south by the Eider and in the north by a line running from Husum to Schleswig, following the Schlei estuary to the sea. This area had been almost completely germanized by the close of the fourteenth century. Low German was spoken by the 100,000 inhabitants and was the medium of instruction in school although High German was used in the churches and in the administration.

In the third area, Central Schleswig, bounded in the north by the Flensburg-Tønder line and in the south by the Husum-Schlei line and including the Frisian islands off the west coast, the ethnographical position was most complex and has given rise to considerable controversy in the last century and a half. Unlike North and South Schleswig, Central Schleswig did not form a homogeneous ethnographical unit, despite the use of German in the administration, the courts, the churches and in many schools. It was generally believed that the Schlei estuary, separating Central from South Schleswig, coincided with the ethnographical frontier between German and Dane—a belief which Falck saw confirmed in the difference in customs and style of architecture on the northern shore.[1] But beyond that, very great ignorance prevailed even in official circles about Central Schleswig. J. O. Spies, an influential official in the *Schleswig-holsteinische Kanzlei*, affirmed in 1810 that the language spoken there was either Frisian (which was partly correct) or else a mixture of Danish, Frisian, German and English (which was certainly incorrect).[2]

The situation in Central Schleswig was, however, completely transformed in the early nineteenth century by a renewal of the germanization process. After a long pause in the seventeenth and eighteenth centuries, conditions again favoured a forward surge

[1] *K.B.*, II, p. 128 n.

[2] J. Spies, 'Betaekning om Udførelsen af Kong Frederik VI's Reskript', *D.M.* 6 r VI København, 1933, p. 383.

of German influence which continued throughout the century and had by 1936 moved the ethnographical frontier between German and Dane from the Schlei-Husum line to approximately the Flensburg-Tønder line. Even in the 1840's the ethnographical frontier had moved an appreciable distance north of the Schlei especially in Angeln.

There were two major reasons for this development; educational advance and economic change. Since the close of the eighteenth century there had been considerable improvements in educational facilities, largely as a result of the work of J. G. Adler, superintendent of churches in Schleswig between 1792 and 1834. Adler did much to raise standards and to enforce the 1814 law introducing compulsory education for all children between the ages of seven and fourteen. He reorganized the schools system, establishing grammar schools in Husum, Flensburg, Schleswig and Haderslev, five others in Holstein and some *Realschulen*[1] in other towns. Adler wanted German and Danish to enjoy parity of esteem in the schools; in practice, however, all but two schools in Haderslev used German as the medium of instruction. Nor was the directive requiring these schools to give some instruction in Danish satisfactorily implemented. In rural areas Adler established *Landschulen*[2] where Danish or German was used as a medium of instruction depending on the district.

The establishment of these schools was made possible by the availability of trained teachers supplied by training colleges opened in Kiel in 1781 and in Tønder in 1786. It was of decisive importance that these colleges were German institutions, because the teachers could instruct in High German as well as Low German; it was at last possible to introduce the former into schools where the latter had been entrenched for generations. The authorities desired to spread a knowledge of High German not for national reasons, but primarily to improve the religious knowledge of the children which depended upon a knowledge of the High German catechism. This new development could be ex-

[1] Technical schools teaching mathematics and natural science (Danish *Borgerskolen*).

[2] Village schools.

pected in the fullness of time to end the alienation of the people from the official language, because for the first time since the sixteenth century the language of the schools would be brought into line with that of the church and the administration. In this way educational reforms, inspired by the spirit of the Enlightenment, did much to recover the ground German had lost in Schleswig in the preceding two centuries.

The increased use of High German in the schools is not inconsistent with a revival of Low German in the 1790's along the west coast of Schleswig and in Angeln. Some pastors realized that it was in their interests to discourage the use of non-German dialects in Central Schleswig, whether Frisian, Danish or Anglisch, and to encourage the use of Low German as a stepping stone to a knowledge of High German. So Low German once again became a vehicle for the germanization of Schleswig as in medieval times, although some doubts were expressed on the German side about the advisability of encouraging the use of dialects.[1]

Economic considerations also contributed greatly to the spread of the German language. As indicated earlier, wars and the needs of an expanding population had caused a general rise in the price of agrarian produce in the second half of the eighteenth century. As productivity increased and foreign markets expanded, the farming community in Schleswig-Holstein found it increasingly useful to possess a knowledge of German in order to obtain the best prices for their wheat and cattle at Husum market or in Hamburg.

The complexity of the ethnographical position in Central Schleswig makes it necessary, for the purpose of analysis, to subdivide the area further into three districts: the west coast, Angeln and the central district.

The west coast, lying between Tønder in the north and Husum in the south, included most of Bredstedt *Amt*, part of Husum *Amt* and Boking and Wieding *Harden* in Tønder *Amt*. This was the home of 25,000 Frisians, whose ancestors had settled in the area by the year 1000, and whose language bears a closer affinity to Old English than to German. The Frisians were soon subjected to

[1] Fabricius, *op. cit.*, pp. 117–18.

German influences; Low German spread quickly among them, especially on the mainland, because there was no Frisian literary language to rival Low German in medieval times and because Frisian was sharply divided into various dialects. But although High German was introduced into the churches in the seventeenth century, a knowledge of Low German persisted along this coast especially where the inhabitants came into contact with the towns of Husum and Bredstedt. A certain amount of Danish was spoken on the west coast, but German and Frisian were the media of instruction in the schools. In the 1840's the ethnographical frontier began to move northwards with the increased use of Low German by young people in parishes such as Viol and Olderup. This was largely due to the impact of the Schleswig-Holstein movement on North Friesland. The young national liberals of the 1840's were uninterested in the preservation of the historical conditions which so delighted the Kiel Circle in the 1820's. They were hostile to the Frisian dialect, recognizing in it one of the mainstays of local particularism. They agreed with Mügge that this dialect 'will and must decline because it has never become a literary language, it has never attained any significance in the sciences or in human intercourse and cultural development'.[1] The germanization process continued throughout the nineteenth century and beyond so that by 1951 only 20,000 of the 60,000 Frisians on the west coast still used Frisian at home.

The second district, Angeln, is bounded on the west by a line joining Schleswig and Flensburg, on the south by the broad estuary of the Schlei, and in the north by Flensburg fiord. The ethnographical character of Angeln has been the subject of considerable dispute. Some Danes claim that Danish was spoken as far south as the Schlei, while their German opponents maintain that, on the contrary, Danish was a forgotten language in Angeln when the nineteenth century began. The facts justify neither claim.

Low German was still in common use in Angeln at the turn of the century, partly because of commercial ties with the south—especially with the town of Schleswig—and partly because the

[1] T. Mügge, *Streifzüge in Schleswig-Holstein*, Frankfurt, 1846, p. 288.

close proximity of a German cultural centre, Gottorp, had enabled Low German to survive the change to High German in the seventeenth and eighteenth centuries. German was, of course, used in church and school throughout Angeln. But there is no doubt that a curious Danish dialect called Anglisch was widely spoken, especially by the older inhabitants who knew little or no Low German.

After 1800 there was a marked increase in the use of Low German particularly in South Angeln. Parents were encouraged by the pastors—influential figures in the rural areas—to speak Low German with their children and so facilitate their progress at school. The result was that by 1850 South Angeln had been thoroughly germanized; only a very few old people still spoke Anglisch.

In North Angeln the germanization process was retarded largely because Flensburg and the Danish side of the fiord exerted a considerable influence on the area. It is true that by 1840 many young people spoke Low German, but even as late as 1846 a majority in Husby spoke Anglisch. The Germans were confident that Anglisch would disappear in time because it lacked cultural depth. Nevetheless, children who had to learn Low German in school continued to regard this Danish dialect as the language of adult life.[1] Not until the 1850's did Low German become predominant in Angeln and only then as a by-product of the ill-advised *Sprachrescripte*.[2]

The central area between Angeln and the west coast includes Karr *Harde* (Tønder *Amt*), Vis and Ugle *Harden* (Flensburg *Amt*) and Arnis *Harde* (Schleswig *Amt*). In this moorland country, sparsely populated and relatively inaccessible, a knowledge of Danish lingered longest. In Karr *Harde* Danish was spoken extensively despite the use of German in most churches and schools.[3] In

[1] Young people before 1848 used to remark that only children learnt German, but when one was grown up one spoke Danish and smoked a pipe. Sach, *op. cit.*, p. 423.

[2] Language regulations introduced into Central Schleswig in 1851.

[3] When the 1810 Rescript was under discussion both J. Spies and J. G. Adler favoured the introduction of Danish into the churches and schools of this *Harde*, Fabricius, *op. cit.*, pp. 59–61.

Vis and Ugle *Harden* there was certainly less knowledge of spoken German than in North Angeln. Only in Arnis *Harde* was German spoken extensively owing to the proximity of Schleswig town.

Finally, in Flensburg, the most important town in Schleswig with 13,000 inhabitants, Danish was spoken extensively, although the rich and influential merchant and shipowning class spoke German; German was also used in the schools and in three of the four churches. Danish influence was, however, strong because Flensburg's prosperity depended on her trade with Denmark and the West Indies. Indeed many of the German-speaking merchants were strong opponents of Schleswig-Holsteinism in the 1840's because it ran counter to their economic interests. For that reason they gave active support to projects such as the railway between Flensburg and Husum, a line linking the west and east coasts which might have captured the trade of Central Schleswig for Flensburg and reduced the influence of their great rival Hamburg.

It is impossible to estimate with any accuracy the numbers of those speaking German and Danish in Schleswig in the first half of the nineteenth century.[1] Contemporary estimates vary a great deal because both Germans and Danes claimed an individual as their national if he spoke both languages, as many did especially in Central Schleswig.

Statistics relating to the use of High German and High Danish in church services in the 1830's indicate that out of a population of 330,000 between 204,000 and 208,000 used High German in church (Biernatzki 217,000); between 104,000 and 110,000 used Danish (Biernatzki 25,000) and between 19,000 and 23,000 used High German and Danish alternately in church (Biernatzki 25,000). This analysis would lead one to suppose that approximately twice as much German as Danish was spoken in the duchy.[2]

But the assumption that the language used in church coincided with the distribution of language spoken in daily life was unjustified, although quite in keeping with the German belief that the

[1] Appendix A.

[2] Biernatzki's figures are not comparable with the other estimates as the population had increased by 30,000 by 1849.

German character of the superstructure should determine the national character of Schleswig. This assumption was made by the Schleswig estates in 1840 when the committee reporting on the language rescript accepted Geertz's statistics for the use of German and Danish in church and school as a true representation of the ethnographical position.[1] One member of the estates even argued that as only seven of the seventeen members representing the small farmers spoke Danish, one should assume that the Danish language was restricted to the area north of the Flensburg–Tønder line.[2]

But if the popular use of language is taken as a criterion, a different picture emerges. German was probably spoken by between 120,000 and 128,000 people (Biernatzki 133,000), Danish by between 144,000 and 145,000 people (Biernatzki 123,000) and Frisian by 26,000 people. Estimates for the areas in Central Schleswig, where no language clearly predominated, vary between 47,000 and 60,000 (Biernatzki 75,000). Thus it was not at all unreasonable for Danish members of the Schleswig estates to claim that half the duchy spoke Danish.

Not until the close of the 1830's did the ethnographical position in Schleswig assume any considerable political significance. But some fleeting interest was aroused by this question in academic circles immediately after the Peace of Kiel. For the discerning there was already food for thought in the attitudes adopted by German and Danish writers on this occasion.

The controversy was sparked off by Pastor K. Aagaard's pamphlet describing the position of the Danish language in Schleswig.[3] He drew attention to the use of German in church and school in parts of Schleswig where German was not spoken by the inhabitants. Racial strife was far from the mind of this conscientious North Schleswig pastor. He was as critical of Danes who despised German as he was of German officials who lived in Danish-speaking areas, but were unable to speak Danish as well as

[1] *St. Z.*, Schleswig, 1840, II, *Beilagenheft*, pp. 296–7.

[2] *Ibid.*, 1842, pp. 2042–4.

[3] *Beskrivelse over Torning Lehn. Et Bidrag til Kundskab om Hertugdømmet Slesvig*, København, 1815.

their own tongue. But Aagaard was the first Dane to suggest that Danish be used in the law-courts of North Schleswig as well as in those parts of Central Schleswig where Danish was spoken. The pamphlet attracted attention in Denmark where, after the loss of Norway, there was a growing realization of the enhanced importance of the duchies to the *Helstat*. In 1816 Danish academicians offered a prize for the best essay describing the extent to which Danish was spoken in Schleswig, the reasons for its replacement by German, and, most significant of all, asking for suggestions for making Schleswig a Danish-speaking province once more.

The German reaction was equally portentous. The *Kieler Blätter* denounced the competition as the by-product of a diseased nationalism contemptuous of other languages.[1] It alleged that the competition had aroused great resentment in the duchies, where it had evoked bitter memories of the 'danization' policy before 1813. To drive the point home Falck published a denunciation of that policy written by Hegewisch's father in 1809.[2] The Germans were particularly alarmed by the implied challenge to the German superstructure of Central Schleswig. To defend the German position, the *Kieler Blätter* published an essay written by Pastor E. Kruse of Neumünster for the recent competition.[3] Kruse admitted frankly that Danish was spoken as far south as Husum. The sting lay in the tail of his essay where he maintained that, as both Germans and Danes attached great importance to the use of German in their churches, changes in the superstructure of Central Schleswig were inadvisable.

Even Falck, most fair-minded of Germans, was equally opposed to change in Central Schleswig, although perfectly prepared to see Danish introduced into the courts and administration where it was already used in church and school (i.e. in North Schleswig). He did not deny that Danish was still spoken in some parts of Central Schleswig, though he added that at least some German was spoken there as well. But—and this was the more serious

[1] *K.B.*, II, p. 139. [2] *Ibid.*, pp. 87–102.

[3] *Über das Verhältnis der dänischen Sprache zur deutschen in dem Herzogtum Schleswig*, *Kieler Blätter*, V, pp. 1–39.

argument—the position of German, both as a religious language and a cultural medium, made change undesirable and indeed positively harmful to the people.[1] It was significant that he did not even think it necessary to teach Danish to Germans attending grammar schools in North Schleswig towns. No doubt a knowledge of Danish was useful but, in his opinion, it would never replace German as the leading language in the duchies.[2] This controversy soon died away and two decades elapsed before these matters were discussed again. But during the preliminary skirmish there were already ominous signs of a fundamental difference of approach to the language question by Germans and Danes.

[1] *K.B.*, II, p. 132.

[2] *Ibid.*, p. 124.

V

Uwe Jens Lornsen

SCHLESWIG-HOLSTEIN slumbered peacefully throughout the 1820's. The people were recovering slowly from the effects of the post-war economic depression. They remained as deeply attached as ever to their local traditions; any fleeting interest they had shown in the German nation and in political questions evaporated after 1818. The spirit of these tranquil years was personified by Nikolaus Falck rather than by Dahlmann; the latter retired to his study after the failure of the agitation for a constitution and, bored with the monotony of Kiel life, finally left for a chair at Göttingen in 1829.

Falck, unlike Dahlmann, was a typical native of Schleswig-Holstein with deep roots in the duchies. Son of a Danish-speaking Emmerslev farmer, he was educated at Haderslev Latin school, studied law with distinction at Kiel university, and spent three years in the *Schleswig-holsteinische Kanzlei* in Copenhagen before returning to Kiel where he spent the remainder of his life at the university as professor of law.

Like most natives of Schleswig-Holstein, Falck never regarded the German nation as more than a cultural concept. Schleswig-Holstein remained his fatherland in a deeper and more intimate sense than it could ever have been for outsiders like Dahlmann. Falck's affection for Schleswig-Holstein was not, however, an exclusive loyalty; in common with most people in Schleswig-Holstein he had a very real affection for the *Helstat*. 'The expression fatherland', he wrote in a revealing passage, 'should never be so narrowly construed that it excludes other parts of the Danish monarchy.' [1] Here he parted company with Dahlmann who, although he admired the *Helstat*, never felt, or wished to feel, any affection for it.

[1] *Sammlung zur näheren Kunde des Vaterlandes*, etc., I, Altona, 1819, p. 11.

It is true that during the post-war constitutional agitation Falck had been an active polemical writer. He had denounced the so-called 'danization' policy of the government before 1813. When Dahlmann was silenced by the authorities in 1816, it was Falck who wrote a classic exposition of the thesis that Schleswig had been an independent state since 1658 and had therefore never been subject to the absolutism of the *Kongelov*;[1] he maintained in the *Kieler Blätter* that the association between the duchies and Denmark should be no closer than that between Poland and Saxony, Britain and Hanover or Austria and Hungary.[2] In short, Falck believed that autonomy for the duchies was perfectly compatible with loyalty to the *Helstat*. It was also quite in keeping with the phlegmatic temperament of the people of Schleswig-Holstein that Falck should have been averse to any kind of precipitate political action aimed at securing this autonomous status for the duchies; the appeal to the Confederation offended his deep sense of loyalty to the crown. Nor did Dahlmann's partiality for the aristocracy commend itself to a native of North Schleswig whose sympathies lay instinctively with small farmers, not with great landowners. After the disintegration of the alliance between the Kiel Circle and the Holstein aristocracy, Falck went his own way; in 1820 in collaboration with F. Carstens he founded the *Staatsbürgerliches Magazin*, a journal which soon appealed to a considerable middle-class audience. Falck gauged the political climate of this decade correctly; he avoided those contentious political issues in which the *Kieler Blätter* had specialized; as he wrote in the first number of the new journal, it was as useful and worthy an exercise to spread a knowledge of the fatherland and of right principles and commonsense opinions about affairs in the fatherland, as it was to engage in practical activities.[3] Falck was mainly interested in improving the standard of the administration, correcting abuses and creating well-informed citizens who would take an intelligent interest in their locality. In short, he remained an

[1] *Das Herzogtum Schleswig in seinem gegenwärtigen Verhältniss zu dem Königreich Dänemark und zu dem Herzogtum Holstein.*

[2] *K.B.*, II, p. 84.

[3] *Staatsbürgerliches Magazin*, etc., I, 1821, *Vorwort*, p. 2.

eighteenth-century rationalist for whom patriotism was a compound of dynastic loyalty, love of the locality and a belief in progress.

During this decade Germans were beginning to appreciate more deeply the historical roots of their community. Historical and legal studies were rapidly assuming a dominant position in the hierarchy of the sciences with the accumulation and more critical use of source material, a development especially associated with a young Frisian historian, R. Niebuhr. Serious historical writing had begun at last and in Schleswig-Holstein, with its multi-coloured pattern of local jurisdictions and eventful past, there lay a fruitful field for historical research. Falck, an erudite legal historian and dispassionate scholar, brought the fruits of his work—and that of other local historians—to the notice of the readers of *Staatsbürgerliches Magazin*. These historical essays were intended not only to inform and edify in the eighteenth-century tradition, but also to foster local pride in the '*engere Heimat*', Schleswig-Holstein, and to spread a knowledge of the *Landesrechte*.[1] His audience was a receptive one; his enthusiasm for the past and veneration for positive law readily commended itself to the people of Schleswig-Holstein, who were steeped in tradition, consciously proud of their heritage and stubbornly convinced of the eternal validity of their social and political milieu. This was probably the most important development in the 1820's. For only when the people of Schleswig-Holstein were conscious at a local level of their German past, could they share in the richer outpouring of the German spirit at a national level two decades later. Ironically enough Falck, who sowed the seed, did not approve of the

[1] The term *Landesrechte* originally meant the statutory law in force in Schleswig-Holstein. But during the quarrel between the *Ritterschaft* and the crown in 1803 the *Ritterschaft* privileges had been referred to as the *Landesprivilegien*; at first the Kiel Circle used *Landesprivilegien* and *Landesrechte* as synonymous terms. But in his 1816 pamphlet Falck differentiated between the special privileges of the *Ritterschaft* and the more general privileges or rights of the duchies, i.e. the right of the duchies to close union with each other and their right to a common constitution. Falck suggested the term *Landesfreiheiten* to describe these general rights, fearing that the word *Privilegien* would offend the middle class. Dahlmann agreed but preferred the term *Landesrechte* which gradually came into general usage to describe these rights.

harvest. He remained what he had always been, a local patriot inherently suspicious of the great world south of the Elbe and out of sympathy with the nationalism of the 1840's. But Falck completely dominated the intellectual life of the duchies in the 1820's and early 1830's. It is a tribute to the conservative influence he exerted over a generation of students—as well as over a wider public outside the university—that the young liberals of the 1830's formulated their political programme in terms of the old *Landesrechte* and not, like their Danish colleagues, on the basis of the Rights of Man.

At first it did not look as if the year 1830 would disturb the peaceful parochial life of the duchies in the preceding decade. Disastrous storms in the spring and bad harvests in the summer caused prices to fall; the great cholera epidemic sweeping through Europe added to this material hardship, completely absorbing the attention of the people. The duchies were silent spectators of the widespread unrest following the July revolution. By September Germany was affected, with disturbances in Brunswick, Hessen, Saxony and Hanover. The Federal Diet, unnerved by the sudden proximity of revolution, hurriedly encouraged member-states to grant their subjects constitutions. At last alarming rumours reached Copenhagen of disturbances in Hamburg. Late in September the apprehension of the government increased still further on receipt of a report that the Austrian ambassador in Frankfurt was advising his Danish colleague to recommend constitutional change in Holstein.

But it was soon apparent that conditions in the duchies hardly justified these fears, and once Metternich had informed the Danish government that, in his opinion, there was no need to grant Holstein a constitution, the danger seemed to have passed.

The government had played with the idea of giving Holstein a constitution ever since the appointment of a royal commission in 1816. On that occasion three years of deliberation had ended in deadlock owing to fundamental disagreement between *Ritterschaft* members and the more liberal-minded royal officials. Then in 1823 the king of Prussia set up provincial estates, and Metternich expressed the hope that the Danish monarch would consider the time opportune for similar generosity in respect of Holstein. Another commission was appointed; this time the king actually approved the recommendations that a high court of appeal and a provincial government with limited powers be established for Holstein and Lauenburg, and that the judicial and administrative functions of government be separated in Holstein. But, as always, the inertia of the bureaucratic apparatus of government prevented the implementation of these recommendations. King Frederik was temperamentally averse to making up his mind and would no doubt have continued to equivocate, had not the Lornsen episode finally convinced him that further delay was impossible.

The closing weeks of 1830 were dominated in the duchies by the figure of Uwe Jens Lornsen. A Frisian, born on the island of Sylt in 1793, son of one of the sea captains for which that coastline was famous, Lornsen was educated in Tønder and Schleswig, studied law at Kiel university in 1816, and moved to Jena in 1818. Now in his mid-twenties, Lornsen was profoundly affected by the effervescent idealism of the Jena *Burschenschaft*, and swore passionately to dedicate his whole life to the struggle for freedom.[1] Contemptuous of the people of Schleswig-Holstein because they preferred the social round of cards and wine to politics, Lornsen toyed with the idea of emigrating to the United States, a land which attracted him because it lacked a privileged aristocracy.[2] For some time he thought of fighting for freedom with the German Legion in Greece, but strong paternal opposition finally dissuaded him. At last, having passed his examinations, he obtained a post in the *Schleswig-holsteinische Kanzlei* in Copenhagen in 1821. He proved himself an able and energetic administrator and was soon promoted to a senior post. But he did not cease to indulge his political interests; he was a leading light in the group of young German officials who met regularly to discuss the details of a constitution for the duchies; their draft was modelled on the Norwegian constitution of 1814 and established personal union

[1] W. Jessen, *Uwe Jens Lornsens Briefe an seinen Vater*, pp. 58–9, 16 March 1819, p. 61, 10 May 1819.

[2] *Ibid.*, p. 50, 27 April 1818.

between the duchies and Denmark similar to that existing between Norway and Sweden.

By 1830 Lornsen was thoroughly dissatisfied with life in Copenhagen. It was typical of the young German officials that they regarded the Venice of the North with growing indifference not to say hostility—an attitude in marked contrast to the older generation of official whose *Helstatsførelse* remained unshaken. Depressed and restless after an illness, Lornsen's thoughts turned to his native island, Sylt, where he obtained the post of *Landvogt* in August 1830. Amid congenial surroundings, with more leisure to indulge his tastes, he intended, so he told his cousin, to prepare himself intellectually for the stirring times which were imminent.[1] In company with other young officials in Copenhagen, he was profoundly stirred by the events of that summer. Encouraged by a visit from his old friend, Professor A. L. Michelsen of Kiel university, he decided that the time had arrived to strike a blow for freedom and sailed to Kiel. He arrived on 2 October. 'Have you petitioned yet?' he asked Michelsen eagerly as he stepped onto the quay.[2] As yet there had been only vague talk of a petition, for much as the leaders of public opinion, Falck and Hegewisch, desired administrative reforms, congenital fear of radicalism and fervent loyalty to the crown paralysed their political will. News of the disturbances in Germany merely confirmed their belief that the moment was inopportune.

Lornsen, with characteristic impetuosity and energy, set about his self-appointed task of organizing petitions to obtain a constitution for Schleswig-Holstein. He undertook a whirlwind tour of eleven Schleswig towns to persuade their leading citizens to send representatives to a meeting in Kiel on All Saints Day. At this meeting a petition to the crown would be signed and copies taken back by the representatives for signature in town and country. But, after visiting Flensburg, Lornsen suddenly changed his plans, abandoned the rest of the tour and cancelled the Kiel meeting, feeling that each town should be responsible for its own

[1] A. Scharff, *Uwe Jens Lornsen. Politische Briefe*, pp. 14–16, to J. Bleiken, 12 Aug. 1830.

[2] K. Jansen, *Uwe Jens Lornsen*, etc., p. 202.

petition. He returned to Kiel and started to draft a memorandum outlining the case for a constitution. Meanwhile, a student friend, Georg Hanssen, had agreed to canvass support in the eastern half of Holstein and, quite unaware that Lornsen had changed his plans, arrived in Kiel accompanied by a group of interested citizens. So the meeting was held, as originally planned, and Lornsen was persuaded to address the assembled company. His speech, based on the memorandum, was enthusiastically received. The meeting agreed to publish ten thousand copies of the speech as a pamphlet[1] and distribute these to leading citizens throughout the duchies, with urgent requests to organize petitions immediately.

The pamphlets were distributed on 5 November, but the flood of petitions expected by Lornsen failed to materialize. The burly, blond-haired Frisian undoubtedly made a deep impression on all who met him. Nevertheless, very few of the middle-class people to whom he appealed were prepared to give him their unreserved support. To some extent they were repelled by his iconoclastic and irreverent attitude—although this appealed naturally to the young and it is significant that the students at Kiel university, emerging at last from their parochial feuds, were his most ardent supporters. The landed classes, on the other hand, fearful of social unrest and offended by Lornsen's contempt for the *Landesrechte*, quickly denounced him as a dangerous demagogue. Even the influential older generation, the officials and academicians, led in Kiel by Falck, Hegewisch, Balemann and Wiese, had grave misgivings about his radical methods, much as they desired a constitution. Dahlmann, while approving the pamphlet, did not approve of its wide distribution. 'It is not necessary at all that there be a general feeling that a constitution is needed', he wrote. 'It is sufficient that it is needed and that a number of people are conscious of this need.'[2] Falck, most law-abiding and influential of these older liberals, as Lornsen dubbed them, withdrew from the meeting on 1 November; he was deeply shocked by Lornsen's intransigent language and alarmed by radical suggestions that

[1] Uwe Jens Lornsen, *Über das Verfassungswerk in Schleswig-Holstein.*

[2] M. Liepmann, *Von Kieler Professoren. Briefe aus drei Jahrhunderten*, etc., p. 135, to Hegewisch, 10 Dec. 1830.

representations to the crown take the form of monster petitions bearing thousands of signatures collected in both duchies. He and G. L. Balemann exerted their influence on the side of legality and caution throughout November, being instrumental in persuading the citizens of Kiel to petition the *Magistrat* on 5 November and not the crown, as Lornsen wished.[1]

There is no doubt that Lornsen's pamphlet aroused great interest in the duchies. It was generally assumed that a high official would not have committed himself in print unless he was certain of government approval. Moreover it was rumoured at this time that the Confederation was pressing Denmark to grant Holstein a constitution, and it was supposed that the king would welcome petitions to save his face. This view was encouraged by Lornsen, who may have known about the reports from Frankfurt in September. Within a few days petitions were drafted by interested groups in several towns. But by now the king was scandalized by the 'shameful and malicious' pamphlet,[2] and the *Kanzlei* lumbered into action, ordering Lornsen to proceed to Sylt and assume his official duties immediately. In obedience to this command Lornsen left Kiel on 8 November, but dallied on the way in Schleswig, Flensburg and Tønder to hurry on the petitions. In Tønder, foolishly but characteristically, he informed the *Amtmann* of his intention to continue these activities on the island of Sylt, remarks which were reported back to Copenhagen and were not without influence upon the final decision of the *Statsraad* on 16 November to order his arrest.[3] This was followed, a few days later, by instructions to local authorities to prevent the circulation of petitions.

The decisive event was undoubtedly the royal proclamation on 16 November, warning the people against mischief-makers but promising constitutional change at a more appropriate moment. At times of crisis the king never appealed in vain to his subjects'

[1] *Ibid.*, p. 141, Falck to Rosenvinge, 21 Jan. 1831. Cf. P. Richter, *Aus der Schleswig-Holsteinischen Verfassungs und Verwaltungsgeschichte*, pp. 586–8, Falck to Jensen, 9 Nov. 1830.

[2] K. Jansen, *Zur Lornsenschen Bewegung*, Z 24 p. 198, King Frederik to Höpp.

[3] L.A.S. 399 Michelsen 101, von Krogh to King Frederik, 13 Nov. 1830.

sense of loyalty. This judicious mixture of blandishments and threats was followed on 22 November by the *Ritterschaft's* declaration of loyalty to the crown. This clinched the matter. The Establishment had spoken. Lornsen was isolated, 'a commander without an army', and was taken into custody on 23 November charged with subversive activity. When Kiel *Magistrat* met on 26 November it decided, unanimously and in a spirit of dutiful devotion, not to petition the crown. Significantly, there was not a single protest from the 251 Kiel citizens who had petitioned the *Magistrat*. It was the same in Flensburg and in other towns, so that in the end only Sylt petitioned. The crisis was over; 'Thank God', wrote the king on 30 November, 'everything has quietened down again.' [1]

The prison gates closed behind Lornsen, but the memory of his brief and tempestuous intervention could never be effaced. His slim little pamphlet occupies a place of special honour as the first polemical writing to enjoy any considerable circulation in the duchies. Its attraction lay not in the originality of his analysis, but in the lucidity of the language, the simplicity and boldness of the style and the freshness and vigour with which he expounded his views. He demanded administrative and constitutional reform simply because his personal experience as a high official had convinced him that the existing system was gravely defective. Modernization of the cumbersome bureaucratic machine was urgently necessary in the interests of efficiency. In like manner he demanded a constitution for the severely practical reason that it was an essential prerequisite for a thoroughgoing reform of the *Helstat's* chaotic finances. There was no reference to the *Landesrechte*, for Lornsen was averse to the pretensions of the *Ritterschaft* and attached no constitutional significance to its quarrels with the crown. History for Lornsen was never more than a colourful trapping with which it was sometimes expedient to clothe arguments based primarily on reason and experience. 'We are not concerned about past history,' he exclaimed irritably to an acquaintance in October 1830, 'we want every age to determine

[1] Jansen, *Zur Lornsenschen Bewegung*, Z 24 p. 200, King Frederik to Höpp, 30 Nov. 1830.

its own standards.'[1] Precisely because his pamphlet was free of the tortuous legal intricacies so dear to historians like Dahlmann and Falck, his arguments gained enormously in clarity and popularity.

Lornsen's constitutional proposals were influenced by personal admiration for the Norwegian constitution and by his knowledge, as a senior official, of schemes for administrative reform current in the 1820's. He proposed that financial and legislative power be conferred on a two chamber legislature, although he reserved a veto power to the crown. He envisaged a considerable measure of decentralization of the administrative machine, to be effected by removing from Copenhagen those colleges administering the duchies' affairs—for he was convinced that officials living in the capital city soon lost touch with local conditions. He proposed that two new colleges be established, one in Kiel and one in Schleswig, and that a *Statsraad* be set up in Kiel to replace the *Schleswig-holsteinische Kanzlei*. The king would be expected to spend part of each year in the duchies. Finally, to separate administrative from judicial functions—a most necessary reform—he proposed the creation of a high court of appeal for the duchies in Schleswig. These reforms, by separating the duchies' administration from that of Denmark, would, he hoped, place relations between both halves of the *Helstat* on a sounder and more enduring basis. 'Let us go forward to face the future,' he wrote, 'hand in hand like brothers, with the king at our head, each developing freely and independently of the other, with only the king and the foe in common.'[2] Like Dahlmann sixteen years previously, Lornsen had concluded that the duchies should be completely independent, associated with Denmark only by dynastic ties.

It has been argued that liberal opinion and personal experience, rather than national sentiment, led him to this conclusion.[3] It is true that the War of Liberation left the twenty-year-old Frisian

[1] Fabricius and J. Lomholt-Thomsen, *Flensborgeren, Professor Christian Paulsens Dagbøger*, p. 173, 14 Nov.

[2] U. J. Lornsen, *op. cit.*, p. 11.

[3] V. Pauls, *Uwe Jens Lornsen und die Schleswig-Holsteinische Bewegung*, Z 60.

unmoved and that as a student he was uninterested in the constitutional agitation conducted by Dahlmann. But his days at Jena as a *Burschenschaftler* represent indisputably the turning-point in his life. Without these experiences, giving a new meaning and purpose to his life, he would, on his own admission, have 'drifted about miserably like a ship without sails or rudder'.[1] The *Burschenschaft* ideals—love of justice, love of fatherland and love of freedom—remained his guiding star inspiring his interest in politics. The political unification of Germany was, he told Hegewisch, the inspiration of all those young men who left German universities in the years after 1813; their interest in constitutional liberties in individual states was merely a means to this goal.[2] In 1837, a few months before his death, writing to Heinrich von Gagern, an old friend from the Jena days who later became president of the Frankfurt Parliament, Lornsen composed his own epitaph; 'Twenty years ago, dear Gagern, we committed ourselves to the service of Germany and freedom. We have both kept our promise by our deeds and in the sacrifices we have made for the cause.'[3]

The burning patriotism which inspired Dahlmann's 'Waterloo' speech was certainly absent from Lornsen's pamphlet. But Lornsen probably knew enough about local conditions to understand that the sober reflections of a high official, related to the practical needs of the duchies, were more likely to attract support than flamboyant references to a German fatherland for which few people in Schleswig-Holstein would move a finger. For this reason when Lornsen insisted that Schleswig share fully in the new constitution, he did not make use of the argument that Schleswig was German, as Dahlmann had done; Lornsen simply maintained that any division of the 'beautiful fatherland Schleswig-Holstein' was 'unthinkable'.[4]

But at times the fiery *Burschenschaftler* of old appeared as in the

[1] Jessen, *op. cit.*, p. 61, 10 May 1819.

[2] V. Pauls, *U. J. Lornsens Briefe an Franz Hermann Hegewisch*, p. 128, 30 July 1832.

[3] A. Scharff, *Uwe Jens Lornsens Brief an Heinrich von Gagern vom 16 September 1837*, Z 79 p. 289.

[4] U. J. Lornsen, *op. cit.*, pp. 3–4.

passage where he implied that administrative autonomy would safeguard the duchies against any repetition of recent Danish attempts at assimilation, and would make Schleswig-Holstein 'the most prosperous province in Germany'. 'Germany, the most powerful and noblest nation in Europe, has allowed little peoples to insult her and scoff at her from time immemorial because of her disunity.'[1] But the time had come, announced Lornsen proudly, when the Germans would reject unreasonable demands and the Danes must therefore abandon their attempts to assimilate the duchies. Personal recollections of unfriendly relations in Copenhagen between young German officials and their Danish colleagues no doubt gave added point to these comments.

This does not mean that Lornsen was an enemy of the *Helstat*. True, he was conscious of the parallel with Belgium, which broke away from alien Holland in November; one sentence in his pamphlet—'we are on the eve of great events'—had been copied from the writings of de Potter, the Belgian revolutionary, a fact which greatly alarmed the king.[2] But Lornsen was not seeking to sever all connections between the duchies and Denmark. Writing to Otto Moltke on 5 November, Lornsen reiterated his conviction that political change was imperative precisely because 'in the event of the king's death delay could lead to anarchy and, as great events are in the making, to the separation of both halves of the state'.[3] Like Dahlmann and Falck, Lornsen wanted to preserve the *Helstat*, but his acute sense of power realities told him that its continued existence was only possible if Germans and Danes co-operated as equal partners and respected each other's independence.

The most profound differences between Lornsen and the older liberals, Dahlmann, Falck and Hegewisch, lay in the realm of political theory. The medieval *Ständestaat*, political ideal of conservative academicians, was quite alien to Lornsen's temperament and background. On the Frisian island of Sylt, with its sturdy tradition of local autonomy, as well as in Copenhagen, there was

[1] *Ibid.*, pp. 10–11.
[2] Jansen, *Zur Lornsenschen Bewegung*, Z 24 p. 198, King Frederik to Höpp, 9 Nov. 1830.
[3] Scharff, *op. cit.*, p. 19.

a deeply rooted aversion to privileged aristocracy. Lornsen wished to see political power in the hands of the middle class for, as he remarked with prophetic insight, 'the opinion of this class, in which is vested physical and intellectual power, will alone rule the world; everything which comes into conflict with the opinions of this class will prove to be fruitless opposition'.[1] Unlike the older liberals, Lornsen extended the term middle class to include the small farmers and craftsmen as well as merchants and officials.

He did not share Dahlmann's vituperative hatred of the French and he bitterly disliked England, whose institutions had been idolized by Dahlmann and Hegewisch. The English, in Lornsen's opinion, were a cold, egotistical, irreligious people interested only in money and power. Their character was inimical to freedom and deserving of hatred. Their foreign policy was dictated solely by commercial interests. They were unwilling to lift a finger on behalf of other peoples; they had given little assistance to the Greeks (the heroes of his youth) and, if it suited their interests, they would keep Portugal in 'eternal barbarism'. The only thing he could find in their favour—somewhat illogically—was their successful struggle against despotism in the seventeenth century.[2]

Most important of all, Lornsen rejected the conservative belief of the older generation that constitutions were the product of co-operation and agreement between ruler and people. Endowed with a greater sense of political reality and in tune with the spirit of the rising middle class, he insisted that constitutions had to be forced out of reluctant rulers. 'How often have I argued', he wrote to Hegewisch, 'that absolutely nothing is to be expected from the good will of rulers but that everything is to be gained by fear.'[3] Force was absolutely essential in this struggle for power, expediency alone dictating what use was made of it. Indeed revolution might be the only road to success, for in what country had freedom ever taken root unless the ground was well fertilized by heavy showers of blood? What irritated Lornsen beyond measure was the reverence of the Germans for their rulers—a

[1] U. J. Lornsen, *op. cit.*, p. 13.
[2] Jessen, *op. cit.*, pp. 90–1, June 1822. V. Pauls, *op. cit.*, p. 74, March 1832.
[3] Pauls, *op. cit.*, p. 182, 16 Nov. 1832.

quality in which the people of Schleswig-Holstein excelled—and the docility with which they tolerated despotism. Only when the patience of the Germans was finally exhausted could much be hoped for, he commented bitterly to Hegewisch.[1]

Despite this, Lornsen was never an extreme radical. He preferred constitutional monarchy to a republic, feeling that a head of state should be above politics. In his own model constitution the crown had a veto and the power of the executive was considerable because mob rule, the nightmare of all middle-class politicians, was as abhorrent to him as to Dahlmann. Socially, Lornsen was very much a man of the middle class; like the Danish liberal, Orla Lehmann, Lornsen felt more at home in the company of officials. He was firmly convinced that it was his mission in life to convert the middle class—but not the lower classes—to the liberal philosophy.

Danish historians often regard Lornsen's 'New Schleswig-Holsteinism', rather than Dahlmann's agitation, as the real beginning of the Schleswig-Holstein movement in the nineteenth century. There is much to be said for this view. It cannot, of course, be denied that there is continuity between Lornsen and Dahlmann in as much as they both worked for an independent Schleswig-Holstein, only associated with Denmark by dynastic ties. Admittedly Lornsen at first paid no attention to the *Landesrechte*, believing that they afforded no positive basis for his demands. Indeed, he never ceased to maintain that his case would still stand with or without historical proofs.[2] Historical study, however, convinced him later on of his tactical error. Falck and Dahlmann had made poor use of their material, he complained to Hegewisch; 'They did not draw the sword but fought with it in the scabbard.'[3] With characteristic enthusiasm the amateur historian threw himself into the task of preparing a popular history to repair their sin of omission. The result was *Die Unionsverfassung Dänemarks und Schleswig-Holsteins*. Lornsen claimed that this work, which was published after his death, would provide complete historical justification for the independence of the

[1] *Ibid.*, p. 137, 30 July 1832.
[2] *Ibid.*, p. 23, June or July 1831.
[3] *Ibid.*, p. 234, 15 Sept. 1833.

duchies. In the process he established historical continuity between his activities and those of the Kiel Circle.

Yet in a broader sense the Danes are surely right. Lornsen's appearance in the duchies marked the opening of a new era in their history. This was the northern spring; the ice-floes were breaking up at last and those new forces which moulded the history of the coming decades were liberated and set in motion by him. Hegewisch was not wrong in maintaining that all the progressive steps taken in Schleswig-Holstein and Denmark after 1830 were the result of the initial impulse from his strong hand.[1] His ability to express the essentials of the demand for administrative and constitutional change in bold clear terms intelligible to the layman, fired the imagination of young liberals. He became the idol of the students, who were his most enthusiastic supporters in 1830. Georg Hanssen, a member of the student society *Germania*, toured East Holstein for him; the former Kiel student Theodor Olshausen, editor of the new liberal paper *Kieler Korrespondenz Blatt*, worked for him in Kiel and Wilhelm Beseler, prominent national liberal in the 1840's, supported him in Schleswig. The growth of public opinion, life blood of a vigorous liberal movement, was accelerated by the Lornsen episode. A brisk controversy in pamphlet form developed between 1830 and 1832; at last a political press appeared, sure signs that interest in public affairs, however limited in extent, was at last stirring north of the Elbe. The greatest achievement of all came in 1831. On 31 May Lornsen was sentenced to twelve months' imprisonment and forfeited his post—largely because of his own obstinacy and desire for political martyrdom. It was a hollow victory for the Establishment for, three days previously, on 28 May, a new law establishing provincial estates was promulgated. It is true that there had been a distinct possibility of a constitution for Holstein before Lornsen arrived in Kiel. What is certain is that his intervention ensured a constitution for both duchies by the end of November. The appearance of a representative body of sorts transformed the political scene by providing a focal point for the

[1] A. Scharff, *Uwe Jens Lornsens Vermächtnis. Studien zu Lornsen und seinem Freundeskreis*, Z 74/75 p. 362.

aspirations of young liberals, as subsequent chapters will show. Lornsen deserves the title of 'the first Schleswig-Holsteiner'; this does not mean that he contributed greatly to the theory of Schleswig-Holsteinism—Dahlmann's claim to be the 'father of Schleswig-Holsteinism' is safe enough. But this self-confident young Frisian spanned the gulf between the quiet years of the 1820's and the turbulence of the 1840's; he stood on the threshold of a new era, the embodiment of those radical political qualities which made the nineteenth century the era of the middle class.

Reference has been made above to Lornsen's acute sense of political realism. This is well illustrated in the fascinating political correspondence with Hegewisch between 1830 and 1837. Lornsen took no active part in politics after 1830, but busied himself with his book and with schemes for the unification of Germany; he was greatly heartened in 1832 by P. Pfizer's *Briefwechsel zweier Deutschen*, a book which took the Germans to task for ignoring the problem of unification and dissipating their energies in wrangles about political theory. Unlike the men of 1813, Lornsen had no illusions about the Great Powers. It was not in the commercial interests of Great Britain nor in the power interests of France, who wanted the Rhineland, to unify Germany. Only Germans could perform this task. The greatest obstacle to unification was the loyalty of the Germans towards princely houses; 'thirty-six million people should not be bound hand and foot to permit thirty-four princely families the luxury of ruling themselves', he wrote indignantly.[1] It reflected contemporary thinking that Lornsen was already looking to Prussia in 1832 as the state destined to lead Germany to unification and defend the Rhineland against France. He foresaw the exclusion of Austria from Germany, the assumption of the crown of Imperial Germany by the king of Prussia, and the creation of a federal Germany in which the princes would have jurisdiction only over local affairs. He predicted war between Prussia and France although he thought Prussia would lose and then seek compensation by annexing the Mecklenburgs and Schleswig-Holstein. This would enable Prussia to dominate North Germany and put back the cause of freedom

[1] Pauls, *op. cit.*, pp. 131–2, 30 July 1832.

by half a century—for Lornsen, like all North German liberals, was alienated by Prussian illiberality which he attributed to Russian connections and the preponderance of Slav over German elements. It was because he understood that Prussian power was essential for unification that he continued to hope that Prussia would square the circle by liberalizing herself—by revolution if need be. But, in a pessimistic and perceptive moment, he revealed his fear that she would wait until she could obtain Germany on her own terms, and still remain an autocratic power.[1]

What effect would German unification have on the duchies? At times Lornsen hinted at a status 'still better' than personal union; he blamed the backwardness of the duchies—compared with other German states—on the Danish connection and observed that Norway was happy only when she separated from the 'plague blister' Denmark.[2] He was also worried by reports that the Danes were interested in a Scandinavian union; if a new Calmar union embracing Denmark, Norway and Sweden came into being this, in his opinion, would be the signal for the breakaway of the duchies, for the connection would be untenable with one partner looking northwards and the other southwards. But, generally speaking, Lornsen was not anxious to repudiate the connection with Denmark, if only for tactical reasons. Conclusive proof of this is afforded by the letter to Heinrich von Gagern written in 1837 after the completion of *Die Unionsverfassung*. In this letter Lornsen maintained that once the duchies' independence had been recognized, continued association with Denmark would be possible and 'in the present state of civilization' this was even preferable to complete independence under their own prince (to which they were entitled), because of the baneful influence princely houses exerted in small states.[3]

The most remarkable feature of the correspondence is the revelation of Lornsen's acute insight into the probable course of development in the *Helstat*. Signs of Danish interest in Schleswig soon convinced him that the duchy was destined to become the

[1] Pauls, *op. cit.*, p. 162, 30 Sept. 1832.
[2] *Ibid.*, p. 21, June or July 1831.
[3] Scharff, *Uwe Jens Lornsens Brief an Heinrich von Gagern*, Z 79 p. 297.

object of a power political conflict between German and Dane. In fact Lornsen had stumbled on the important truth that liberalism and nationalism were antithetical and not complementary forces as contemporaries erroneously supposed them to be. Nor were these forces equal to each other. Lornsen was quick to realize that nationalism would prove itself the more potent force and would obtain full recognition only at the expense of liberalism. He foresaw that Danish liberals, who co-operated happily with the Germans in the common struggle against absolutism, would sooner or later subordinate their liberal convictions to the needs of national security, which meant the incorporation of Schleswig in Denmark. 'We must never lose sight of the fact', he wrote to Balemann, 'that we have two opponents, absolutism and Danism.' [1]

During the controversy which followed the appearance of Lornsen's pamphlet, attention had been drawn to the unique legal position of Schleswig. Some of Lornsen's opponents maintained that, in addition to legal differences between the duchies, there were also linguistic differences which made a common constitution quite impossible. In 1832 an important pamphlet, written by Professor C. Paulsen of Kiel university, introduced this new national note into the controversy; the pamphlet contained the first detailed account of the Danish-speaking inhabitants of Schleswig and it emphasized that the Danish they spoke, and not the German spoken by officials, should determine the national character of the duchy.[2] Lornsen was probably seriously alarmed by this argument because there were many more Danish-speaking people in Schleswig in the 1830's than was the case two decades later. He may well have feared that if the Danes suddenly decided to annex Schleswig this would throw the Germans into great confusion, because ever since Denmark regained the Gottorp parts of Schleswig in 1721 the legal position of the duchy had been far from clear. By this time Lornsen was firmly convinced that the Danes intended to seize Schleswig, allowing Holstein to go its own way. He had to admit, reluctantly, that there was little written evidence to substantiate his suspicions but thought the Danish intention

[1] Jansen, *op. cit.*, p. 413, 2 Dec. 1834.

[2] See p. 105.

clear enough. In ten years, he wrote with prophetic insight in 1835, the idea will seem perfectly natural to the Danes however remote the thought may seem at present.[1]

Anxious as always to preserve the *Helstat*, Lornsen thought at first that the Danes would realize the need for unity, in view of the impending conflict between Scandinavia and Germany and would abandon their designs on Schleswig in return for the cession of the Danish-speaking *Amter* of Haderslev, Åbenraa and Løgumkloster. Later on he thought the duchies, like good chess-players, must conceal their ultimate desire for independence, because full personal union would not be conceded by the Danes without a struggle, as it would automatically prevent them detaching Schleswig from Holstein. Lornsen admitted that the struggle against absolutism made some co-operation with the Danes necessary in order to secure freedom of the press and publicity of proceedings in the estates. As a temporary measure, he was even prepared to work out the details of a common estates for the entire *Helstat*. Then later, when the liberal movement was firmly established or when the duchies felt strong enough, they could face the inevitable fight with Denmark to obtain full personal union. But by 1835 he had rejected these complicated tactics as too risky and henceforth insisted that the duchies must seek only personal union.[2] His book, completed in 1837, was intended to prove the right of the duchies to form the independent state of Schleswig-Holstein under their own prince and to define the details of personal union between this state and Denmark. He hoped that his book would make the Danes realize the futility of trying to obtain Schleswig or, if the worst happened, strengthen the duchies' resistance to such designs, by giving them a clear appreciation of the rectitude of their case.

Lornsen had sailed for Brazil in 1834 in search of a cure for an ailment from which he had imagined himself to be suffering for several years. In 1837, after finishing his book, he was filled with longing for his native Sylt and sailed for Europe. He spent several months in Switzerland seeking a publisher in vain. By the winter of 1837 he had abandoned his intention of returning home, was

[1] Pauls, *op. cit.*, p. 249, 15 May 1835. [2] *Ibid.*, pp. 250–3, 4 July 1835.

living the life of a recluse, and finally succumbed to those fits of depression and morbid hallucinations to which he had been subject for years. On a dark winter's evening in February 1838 he shot himself on the shores of lake Geneva while of unsound mind.

His death was mourned by liberals in Kiel and Copenhagen, for Danes and Germans alike were conscious of his services to the liberal movement. They shared his enthusiasm for freedom but they lacked his prophetic insight into the Schleswig problem. Little did they imagine that when the tenth anniversary of his death was commemorated in 1848, co-operation between German and Dane would be a thing of the distant past, rival nationalisms would tear Schleswig asunder and within a very few weeks German and Dane would be locked in mortal combat for possession of the duchy.

VI

The new constitution, the Danish awakening and the language question

It is extremely doubtful whether the king would have promised his subjects a constitution in November 1830, had it not been for the Lornsen affair. Even when the promise had been given, nothing might have come of it in view of the king's chronic aversion to action. King Frederik was greatly alarmed at this time by the restless spirit of German radicalism and impressed by the determined reaction of the German princes. Left to his own devices King Frederik would probably have postponed any reform. It was his advisers who would not let him do this. O. Moltke, Danish president of the *Schleswig-holsteinische Kanzlei*, P. C. Höpp, a native of Flensburg and influential member of the *Kanzlei*, and A. S. Ørsted, a member of the *Dänische Kanzlei*, were all perceptive enough to see that the quiet years of the 1820's had gone for ever. They realized that some concession to the spirit of the age was unavoidable if the king wished to remain an absolute ruler. Their view prevailed. In the end the king instructed the officials of the *Schleswig-holsteinische Kanzlei* and the *Dänische Kanzlei* to draw up a draft constitution based partly on the findings of the Holstein commission of 1818, and partly on the Prussian constitution of 1823. When the constitution emerged in its final form three years later, Lornsen shrewdly commented that all liberals owed a deep debt of gratitude to the responsible high officials in Copenhagen for the successful outcome of the agitation of 1830.[1]

The influence of the Prussian model was evident in the new constitution. Four provincial estates were established, two for Denmark and two for the duchies. The estates for Nørrejylland

[1] Jansen, *op. cit.*, p. 412, to Balemann, 2 Dec. 1834.

and the Ostifterne were to meet in Viborg and Roskilde respectively and the estates for Schleswig and Holstein in Schleswig and Itzehoe respectively. Curiously enough in November 1830 King Frederik would have agreed to united estates for the duchies, for he had been completely unnerved by alarmist reports from the *Statthalter*, that senile dabbler in the occult Prince Karl of Hesse, and from the young Duke of Augustenburg. O. Moltke was gravely perturbed at this turn of events, because he feared that a common constitution would strengthen the association between the duchies and lead ultimately to the disruption of the *Helstat*.[1] However, when more reassuring reports began to arrive, the king's fears abated; O. Moltke and P. C. Höpp finally persuaded him to agree to separate estates for the duchies and for Denmark as well in order to ensure absolute equality of treatment for both halves of the *Helstat*.[2]

The estates were more 'liberal' in complexion than their Prussian counterpart simply because these middle-class officials in the *Schleswig-holsteinische* and *Dänische Kanzlei* disliked the social privilege enjoyed by members of the Schleswig-Holstein *Ritterschaft* and regarded them as potential trouble-makers. The landowners who dominated the Prussian estates were traditionally the most loyal supporters of the crown. This could not be said of the *Ritterschaft* in view of its tradition of opposition to the crown in the last thirty years. If these aristocratic landowners were allowed to dominate the estates of Schleswig and Holstein, might they not revive old quarrels and exacerbate the relations between the duchies and Denmark? So the high officials reasoned; to avoid this danger generous representation was given to the urban middle class and small farmers. It was felt, not without justification, that these classes, traditionally loyal to the crown, hostile to aristocracy and amenable to pressure from pastors and officials, could be relied upon to give consistent support to the government. The *Ritterschaft* was allotted only four representatives in the estates in grudging recognition of its corporate character. It did not constitute a

[1] Jansen, *Zur Lornsenschen Bewegung*, Z 24 p. 207, O. Moltke to Höpp, 13 Nov. 1830.

[2] *Ibid.*, p. 211, O. Moltke to Höpp, 20 Nov. 1830.

separate college for electoral purposes, but had to combine with other landowners in the election of five members to the Schleswig and nine members to the Holstein estates. The *Ritterschaft* was in a permanent minority; twelve of the forty-four members in the Holstein estates represented the towns, seventeen the small farmers, one the university and two the clergy. In the Schleswig estates fifteen of the forty-eight members represented the towns, sixteen the small farmers, one the university and two the clergy. Although members were elected in medieval fashion in separate colleges (viz. great landowners, small farmers and towns), they did not meet as separate estates, as the *Ritterschaft* requested, but in one assembly reaching decisions by majority vote.

The estates had purely advisory functions because the king was not prepared to surrender real political power. Nor did his officials expect him to. They supposed that absolutism could be saved on condition that the *Helstat* was run more efficiently. The estates were given the right to petition the crown and advise the government on legislation affecting the finances and general administration in their respective halves of the state, because the officials believed this would serve the useful purpose of revealing the needs of the people, drawing attention to abuses in the administrative system and keep the government informed of the trend of opinion in the *Helstat*. The franchise was a very restricted one with a high property qualification conferring a vote on only three to four per cent of the population, for governments would listen only to the opinions of the educated few. Members were elected directly; this was an uncommon practice in the early nineteenth century, avoided by most governments because of its Jacobin connotations; it was adopted in the *Helstat* in order to stimulate interest in the estates on the part of the politically reliable middle class. But where fear of the *Ritterschaft* did not enter into the calculations of the officials, the limits to their liberalism were quickly apparent. The sessions of the estates were not open to the public. Debates could be reported only in the *Ständezeitung*, a journal edited by the members and censored by the government. There were no guarantees of the citizen's fundamental rights, a commonplace of continental constitutions. Nor did members enjoy legal immunity. In fact, judged by the standard of the Norwegian constitution of 1814 and the Belgian constitution of 1830, the constitution of 1834 amounted to very little; it merely afforded the king's subjects an opportunity of expressing their views on matters of local importance while denying them any share in real power.

The constitution was accompanied by important administrative changes in the duchies. There was growing awareness in official circles that Lornsen's criticism of the stagnant administrative system had been abundantly justified. Already in the 1820's the government had agreed that the separation of administrative and judicial functions was a desirable and beneficial reform; Lornsen's intervention ensured that there would be no further delay. Some of the king's advisers, like the heir to the throne, Prince Christian, would have preferred separate authorities for Schleswig and Holstein, but O. Moltke and P. C. Höpp, while opposed to the union of the duchies' estates, were prepared to recognize the administrative unity of the duchies;[1] this seemed a harmless concession once separate estates had been agreed upon, and it might even placate those who still pressed for a united estates. So in 1834 the dual powers of the *Obergerichte* came to an end, their judicial functions were taken over by a court of appeal for both duchies in Kiel and their administrative functions by the Schleswig-Holstein government at Gottorp castle; this new authority, supervised by the *Statthalter*, was intended to form an intermediate authority between the *Schleswig-holsteinische Kanzlei* and the *Amtmänner*.

The king's officials congratulated themselves on the discovery of a formula for the preservation of absolutism. Their confidence was misplaced. It proved impossible to contain the political aspirations of the people within the strait-jacket of a consultative assembly supplemented by the efforts of paternalistic officials. The inevitable result of the constitution, here as elsewhere in Europe, was the growth of political consciousness, so that within twenty years absolutism had been destroyed for ever in the *Helstat*.

[1] Jansen, *Zur Lornsenschen Bewegung*, Z 24 p. 208, O. Moltke to Höpp, 13 Nov. 1830.

Europe was awakening in the 1830's from her long winter sleep. Economic and social change was at last beginning to dissolve the traditional pattern of society inherited from the eighteenth century. The duchies benefited from the growing demand for food in those countries embarking on industrialization. Their cattle exports increased in value from four million *Reichsbanktaler* in 1833 to six million *Reichsbanktaler* in 1838. Prices of wheat and cattle rose and remained at a high level throughout this and the next decade. The population of the duchies was increasing and the towns were growing in size. These changes gradually eroded the old order of things and accentuated the need for modernization of the archaic commercial, administrative and judicial structure of the *Helstat.* Inevitably the estates became a focal point around which a public opinion eager for reform could crystallize. An essential catalyst in this process was the creation of a political press; this began in the duchies in the summer of 1830 with the publication of the *Kieler Korrespondenz Blatt* by the young liberal Theodore Olshausen. This paper remained the leading journal in Schleswig-Holstein for the next twenty years. It was soon followed by many other local papers, all of them showing an interest in those political issues so carefully avoided by the middle class at the beginning of the century. True, the spell of loyalty to the crown remained unbroken but undoubtedly the mood of the people was beginning to change at last. If one man could claim credit for this development, it was Lornsen; the constitutional and administrative changes of 1834 represented a complete vindication of his criticism of the state; they were also a living testimony to the important political truth that the ideas rejected by the Establishment today are often accepted by it tomorrow. Once the people had advanced a step further to the realization that opposition to the crown could produce beneficial results for the whole community, then the days of absolutism were assuredly numbered.

Naturally it took time to effect this mental metamorphosis. The lives of the mass of the people were at first little affected by the changes of 1834. Only the educated minority, actively interested in public affairs, received the constitution with positive expressions of approval. The older liberals were perfectly satisfied with it, because constitutions in their eyes were primarily a device for removing stagnation in the administrative and legal systems and not a lever for altering the balance of political power in favour of the middle class. Falck, their spokesman, combined regret at the failure to unite the estates with a conviction that the Prussian estates, shorn of their landed element, represented the ideal constitution.[1] The young liberals were naturally critical of the government's failure to endow the estates with considerable financial powers, but they agreed with their leader, Peter Lorenzen, that the estates were better than nothing.[2] Even Lornsen in distant Rio de Janeiro felt that representation of the various classes and the direct election procedure left nothing to be desired.[3] Only the members of the *Ritterschaft* registered a solemn protest in July 1831, declaring the estates to be a mere administrative device which could not supersede the old constitution of which the *Ritterschaft*, as a corporate body, was the last surviving remnant. But internal dissension, lack of strong leadership and suspicion of their former allies, the middle-class intellectuals, had combined to reduce the political influence of the landowners very considerably.

Political life in the 1830's was still dominated by the conservative academicians of Kiel university. The moderate views of Falck, Hegewisch and Adam Moltke, an enlightened member of the *Ritterschaft*, commended themselves, not only to the officials and great landowners as one might expect, but to the middle class as a whole. This was largely because the small farmers, basking in the unaccustomed glow of material prosperity and rooted in the immediate locality, were slow to recognize their own political importance and were inclined to endorse the conservative views of the older liberals. The young liberals, who desired a modern constitution conferring real financial and legislative power on the middle class, including the small farmers, lacked popular support and constituted only a tiny minority of

[1] C. Petersen, *Nikolaus Falck und die Entstehung des Schleswig-Holsteinischen Gedankens*, pp. 280–1.

[2] Jansen, *op. cit.*, p. 378.

[3] Jansen, *op. cit.*, p. 408, to Balemann, 2 Dec. 1834.

those who were politically active. A few lawyers in the towns, some journalists, especially Theodore Olshausen of Kiel and H. Hansen, editor of the *Eckernförder Wochenblatt*, a lonely representative of the *Ritterschaft* in Count Magnus Moltke, and the liberal leader, a radical-minded Haderslev shopkeeper, Peter Lorenzen; that was the total strength of those liberals who regarded themselves as the heirs of Uwe Jens Lornsen.

It was significant that all those interested in politics in the duchies accepted the fundamentals of the *Landesrechte* as defined by Falck in the 1820's. That was to be expected of the *Ritterschaft* and the older liberals. But even the young liberals treated the *Landesrechte* with respect and made little reference to the Rights of Man or to the Belgian, French and Norwegian constitutions. To some extent this was because they realized, like Uwe Lornsen, that arguments emphasizing the historical continuity between the medieval estates and a modern constitution impressed the tradition-conscious people of Schleswig-Holstein, whereas abstract theories repelled them. But in a more profound sense it was a tribute to Kiel university, where most of them were educated in the 1820's, that these young men accepted as an integral part of their political heritage the idea of the inseparability and independence of the duchies within the *Helstat*.

At first sight defence of the *Landesrechte* might seem the ideal political platform, capable of uniting all shades of political opinion in the German estates. To some extent it did so; Falck's motion for the union of the two German estates, shelved at the first meeting of the Schleswig estates in 1836, was accepted by an overwhelming majority at the second meeting in 1838. This represented the first victory for the *Landespartei*, as it was now customary to call those who were loosely associated in defence of the *Landesrechte*. Outside the estates the *Schleswig-Holsteinische Blätter*, edited by C. Heiberg, supplied the *Landespartei* with an organ for arousing wider interest in the *Landesrechte* between meetings of the estates.

But the *Landesrechte* could only remain a common denominator in political life as long as no one attempted to define the precise nature of the common constitution to which all paid lip service in

1838. Serious political discussion soon revealed the absence of common ground between *Ritterschaft* members, clinging tenaciously to privileges, still dreaming of a resuscitated medieval estates, and liberal members for whom the *Landesrechte* were only a signpost on the road to a Norwegian-type constitution. This fundamental cleavage was thrown into sharp relief by the fate of Berwald's motion. This motion, in which the liberal member, F. Berwald, sought financial powers for a united estates, was decisively defeated by twenty-seven votes to thirteen in the Schleswig estates in 1838. The implication was obvious; the *Landespartei* had agreed, out of respect for the *Landesrechte*, that it was desirable to unite the estates; but the thought of using them as a means of gaining political power for the middle class clearly horrified most members.

Other pressures were at work widening this gulf and disrupting still further the superficial unity of the *Landespartei*. In the 1830's the growing need for the modernization of the state raised innumerable practical issues of administrative and financial reform, including questions of tax reform, control of the budget, reorganization of urban and rural administration and revision of the customs system. This development inevitably accelerated the emergence of party attitudes, compelling the members to declare their basic political philosophy. The result was that the conflict between conservative and liberal deepened, and the small band of German liberals looked with increasing favour on Danish liberals as their natural allies against reactionary conservatism.

Not only did this ideological conflict attenuate the political efficacy of the *Landesrechte*, but the existence of separate estates constituted an additional danger. For if the government proceeded energetically with the modernization of the *Helstat*, people might in time cease to believe in the inseparability of the duchies and accept separate estates as the price of an efficiently-run state. This was a real danger as long as the small farmers failed to use their political power. There were many, like the Frisian farmers on the west coast, who were traditionally attached to the crown, hostile to the *Ritterschaft*, preoccupied with material problems, and inclined to the view that the existing estates were preferable to a united body dominated completely by the *Ritterschaft* and upper middle class.

The growth of political consciousness in Schleswig-Holstein was modest compared with Denmark. At first the events of 1830 aroused much less interest in the kingdom of Denmark than in the duchies. The position was quickly reversed. The first elections to the Danish estates were followed by a growth of political consciousness undeniably more virile than in Schleswig-Holstein. The academicians and officials, who formed the backbone of the liberal movement in Copenhagen, were much more radical in outlook than their German colleagues; this was because the latter were inhibited by the conservative influence of aristocratic landowners and lacked the stimulus of a great capital city like Copenhagen. In Denmark the political conflict between liberalism and absolutism was more clearly delineated and sharper in tone, because Danish liberals were not inhibited by past history or aristocratic connections in their campaign for the union of their estates and the ordering of their public finances. Their demand for an efficiently-run state was motivated not by an interest in the medieval past of Denmark but by rational considerations and admiration for Norwegian practices. Their main support came from a middle class traditionally opposed to the pretensions of aristocracy and well organized through the Press Society, an association which played a major role in the growth of Danish liberalism. The society was founded in 1835 in protest against censorship regulations which the government, anxious to curb the embryonic political press, had introduced after the new radical paper, *Faedrelandet*, had attacked absolutism. By 1838 the Press Society had established branches all over Denmark, spreading liberalism from Copenhagen to middle-class circles in the small towns and creating a formidable, well-organized and articulate opposition to absolutism.

One of the most interesting features of the liberal movement in the *Helstat* in the 1830's was the intimate relationship between German and Dane referred to above. There were many instances of this; when *Faedrelandet* was launched as a daily paper in 1834, Olshausen's *Kieler Korrespondenz Blatt* sent friendly greetings to fellow liberals and when Lornsen committed suicide in 1838 his memory was honoured in Copenhagen as well as in Kiel. The liberal leaders corresponded regularly with each other, Lehmann with Lorenzen, Olshausen with J. Hage and C. N. David. When in Kiel or in Copenhagen they stayed in each other's homes and discussed the common problem facing them as political allies in the struggle against absolutism and conservatism. They were seeking the same administrative, financial and military reforms and the abolition of all feudal jurisdictions. They were equally concerned to secure freedom of the press and publicity of proceedings in their respective estates and they favoured the same type of constitution conferring political power on the middle class. It could not, of course, be denied that the Danes regarded the *Landesrechte* of their German friends as outworn aristocratic privileges of no significance in the modern world. Moreover, on the rare occasions when national questions were discussed, a fundamental divergence of opinion about the legal status of Schleswig was revealed. Danish lawyers and historians considered that Schleswig had been incorporated in the Danish kingdom in 1721, a point of view irreconcilable with the German belief in the independence of the duchies as guaranteed by the *Landesrechte*. But these considerations did not impair the friendship between German and Danish liberals, because questions of practical reform absorbed their interest for most of the 1830's. They understood that their hopes of a better future would recede still further, as a radical liberal, H. R. Claussen of Kiel, remarked to O. Lehmann, if the small band who were of like mind about fundamentals were to quarrel about minor matters, such as the frontier between the German and Danish languages and the exact definition of the legal status of Schleswig.[1] Only isolated and perceptive individuals, in particular Uwe Lornsen, felt intuitively that this friendship would only be of temporary duration and would ultimately be wrecked on the rocks of the Schleswig question.

In the second half of the 1830's a cloud no bigger than a man's

[1] P. Bagge and P. Engelstoft, *Danske politiske Breve*, etc., I, no. 188, p. 259, 20 April 1838.

hand appeared on the horizon, casting the first shadow over the relations between German and Dane. The cloud was the so-called Danish awakening in Schleswig, a development fraught with momentous consequences for the future of the *Helstat.*

In the past the fact that a Danish dialect was very widely spoken in Schleswig, especially in the north, had assumed neither political nor national significance. The North Schleswig farmers, living in isolated communities in this sparsely populated area, did not share to any appreciable extent in the cultural life of Denmark or Germany. Little was known about them in Copenhagen or in Holstein. Educated Germans in Schleswig regarded this dialect—'a corrupt form of Danish' in Dahlmann's words[1]—as a relic from the past doomed to inevitable extinction. They certainly did not suppose that Schleswig was any less German in character because some Danish was spoken there. True, attention had been drawn to some of the administrative and political implications of this by Pastor Aagaard in 1815 and by C. Paulsen in 1832, but interest in these matters was strictly limited to middle-class circles and quickly waned. The small farmers were quite unmoved by these literary controversies. They felt no kinship on account of their dialect with Danes north of the Kongeaa, and when questioned on the subject were perfectly content to describe themselves as 'Holsteiner' or in some cases as 'Danish Holsteiner'.[2]

The Danish movement in Schleswig owed everything in its initial stages to the work of a handful of dedicated men led by Christian Paulsen and Christian Flor. Paulsen, 'the first Sønderjyde',[3] was born in Flensburg of German parents and educated at Göttingen university and later in Copenhagen. Though he came from a German-speaking home, he picked up Danish in the streets of Flensburg, a town proud of its Danish associations. During a long stay in Copenhagen in 1820 he fell in love with the capital, was impressed by its cultural wealth and attracted by the liberal sentiments of its upper middle class. It was a turning-point

[1] Varrentrapp, *op. cit.*, p. 13.

[2] N. F. S. Grundtvig, *Politiske Betragninger med Blik paa Danmark og Holsteen,* Kiøbenhavn, 1831, p. 62.

[3] Fabricius, *op. cit.*, p. 121. Sønderjylland is the old Danish name for Schleswig.

in his life. Henceforth he considered himself Danish by blood as well as by inclination; he began to write his diary in Danish instead of German. In 1824 he secured an appointment as lecturer in legal history at Kiel university. He now regarded it as his mission in life to assist the peoples of the *Helstat* to know each other better and in particular to strengthen the cultural ties between Schleswig and Denmark. He was by no means unsympathetic in principle to Lornsen's attempt to secure a constitution, for he too had been a *Burschenschaftler* while in Germany. But he was repelled by the young Frisian's brash manner and incautious remarks and appeared as a witness for the prosecution at Lornsen's trial. In 1832, at the tail end of the controversy over Lornsen's pamphlet, Paulsen wrote a pamphlet highly critical of the German demand for a united estates for the duchies—separate estates he willingly accepted.[1] He drew attention to the special legal position of Schleswig and emphasized the fact that Schleswig had been completely Danish for over a thousand years and that over half the people spoke a Danish dialect. Language was a holy thing for Paulsen. He insisted that it must be preserved because it was the essential medium for the expression of the cultural values and idiosyncrasies of a people. To arrest the decline in the use of Danish and preserve Danish cultural values, Paulsen suggested that Danish be used as the administrative language in North Schleswig and that some Danish be taught in German schools in North Schleswig towns. He also commended these measures to his readers as a means of preserving the *Helstat*. Schleswig, half-Danish and half-German, was the essential link between Denmark and German Holstein. By preserving the Danish spoken in Schleswig, the ties with Denmark would be strengthened without prejudice to the association with Holstein and the unity of the *Helstat* would be preserved. The pamphlet did not arouse much interest in the duchies; but later in 1832, on Flor's advice, Paulsen visited Copenhagen where he received a friendly welcome from the king and found several prominent officials in the *Schleswig-holsteinische Kanzlei*, as well as the influential Otto Moltke, sympathetic to his point of view.

[1] P. D. C. Paulsen, *Für Dänemark und für Holstein.*

Paulsen's interest in Danish-speaking Schleswig was encouraged by his friend Christian Flor, a colleague at Kiel university, who had lectured on Danish language and literature since 1826. Flor was an energetic and determined propagandist for the Danish way of life; a native of Copenhagen, he was under the spell of Grundtvig's romanticism and filled with a burning love for his mother tongue. Flor regarded himself as a missionary in Kiel disseminating Danish cultural values among the German upper class. In the 1830's he proved himself an organizer of great ability, playing the major role behind the scenes in the Danish awakening. Like Paulsen he sought to preserve the Danish tongue in Schleswig. But Paulsen, being a native of Schleswig, was reluctant to see the existing political relationship between Schleswig and Denmark disturbed and showed no enmity towards the German language as such; he even advocated the teaching of German in the Danish schools of North Schleswig to meet local needs. Flor, on the other hand, was, both by temperament and origin, more aggressive in outlook, eager to reconquer ground lost to the Germans and was probably thinking already of that intimate political association between Schleswig and Denmark, which was the essence of the Eiderdane position in the 1840's.

Although many high officials in Copenhagen sympathized with Paulsen, it soon became obvious that they were not prepared to arouse controversy by introducing the measures he advocated. So Paulsen went to the people, touring North Schleswig in 1834 and 1835, seeking to interest prominent citizens in the preservation of Danish but meeting with only limited success. In 1836 he aroused considerable interest with a new pamphlet in which he stated in unmistakable terms his conviction that the Danish nationality of North Schleswig rendered illusory the German dream of an independent Schleswig-Holstein in personal union with Denmark.[1] Moreover, on the basis of documents shown him by Otto Moltke, Paulsen maintained that the Danish succession law had been introduced into Schleswig in 1721, a factor which would loosen the association between the duchies in the fullness of time.

[1] P. D. C. Paulsen, *Über Volkstümlichkeit und Staatsrecht des Herzogtums Schleswig; nebst Blicken auf den ganzen dänischen Staat.*

Early in 1835 Paulsen decided to try and persuade the Schleswig estates to petition the crown for the introduction of Danish in the courts and the administration in areas where Danish was used in church and school. Acting on the advice of Otto Moltke, he approached Nis Lorenzen, a well-known farmer and Danish-speaking member for Haderslev district. Lorenzen soon collected over 600 signatures to a petition requesting these changes. Flor probably wrote the speech which Nis Lorenzen delivered in the estates in June 1836 in support of his motion.[1] The stamp of Flor's personality was evident in the sharp attack on German officials who refused to learn Danish and in his assertion that only officials would oppose this motion. But it should be remembered, added Nis Lorenzen, that the officials were there for the sake of the people and not vice versa. Officials who could not be bothered to learn Danish were not welcome in these areas, for they lacked sympathy for the people and had no interest in their affairs. Despite the belligerent tone of the speech the atmosphere in the estates remained friendly and Nis Lorenzen's motion was sent to committee from which, owing to lack of time, it did not emerge.

At this time Paulsen managed to interest the Danish press in the Schleswig problem. He persuaded C. F. Wegener, a Sorø teacher, to write an article on language conditions in Schleswig for *Københavnsposten*. In this article Wegener praised Nis Lorenzen but launched a bitter attack on Andreas Petersen, a member of the Schleswig estates, who had just moved a motion in favour of some German instruction in North Schleswig schools. 'Petersen', wrote Wegener, 'wants 150,000 men to learn the language spoken by the officials, whilst Nis Lorenzen wants the officials to learn the language of thousands of farmers.' [2] In October, again at Paulsen's instigation, a similar article by J. Hage was featured in the liberal paper *Faedrelandet*. As a result of the work of Paulsen and Flor and of the effects of the debate on the Nis Lorenzen motion, the Press Society's attention was drawn to North Schleswig. Orla Lehmann, a rising young liberal, became interested in the problem and was instrumental in persuading the society, at its annual general meeting in November 1836, to support cultural work on

[1] *St. Z.*, Schleswig, 1836, pp. 529–30.
[2] *Kjøbenhavnsposten*, 1 July 1836.

behalf of the Danish language in Schleswig. The speech of this gifted orator aroused great interest in Denmark and was followed by a very considerable increase in the membership of the society during the winter of 1836.

The decision of the Press Society to interest itself in Schleswig represents a turning-point in the history of the duchy. But it does not mean that the Danish liberals had become nationalists overnight; Orla Lehmann, a prominent figure since the November speech, was not yet an Eiderdane but primarily a liberal who felt impelled to defend the inalienable right of a people to keep its native tongue. '... my interest in Danish in Schleswig,' he told his friend, C. Sørensen of Haderslev, 'springs from my love of the people and of the down-trodden and ill-treated common man. My anger at the German yoke in the Danish-speaking part of Schleswig is no different from that which I would feel if, for example, the Russians were to impose their language on the Poles.' [1]

It is true that even in the 1830's there were some traces of Eiderdanism in Lehmann's belief, shared by many Danes, that Schleswig had never been part of Germany—*Eidora Romani imperii terminus* as the Latin tag ran[2]—and that the Danish succession law had been introduced into Schleswig in 1721, further strengthening the ties between Schleswig and Denmark. But Lehmann did not deny that close ties existed between the duchies. Indeed, should the connection between Holstein and Denmark be terminated in the near future, he expected Schleswig to follow Holstein into the Confederation. Much as he resented the germanization of Schleswig by the Holstein aristocracy, he had no desire to reverse the process by compelling Germans to become Danes. Reason and respect for the Rights of Man excluded that possibility. He only insisted that the so-called 'terrorization' of Danish-speaking people by German officials should cease and that the Press Society be given complete freedom to reawaken the Danish spirit by distributing literature and founding newspapers. Eventually Schleswig would have to choose between Denmark and Holstein—he excluded the possibility of an independent Schleswig. When the

[1] Bagge and Engelstoft, *op. cit.*, I, no. 207, p. 288, 1 Nov. 1838.

[2] The Roman Empire ends at the Eider river.

moment arrived for this final choice, all he insisted on was that the decision be made, not by the Holstein aristocracy or by the Danes, but by the people of Schleswig. True, he felt that once the unnatural germanization of Schleswig had ceased, the free choice of the people would reveal a natural preference for Denmark; but whatever their decision, Lehmann was prepared to abide by it at this time.

The attempt of the Press Society to make Schleswig conscious of its Danish character started a controversy between German and Dane which has lasted into our own day. German historians in the nineteenth century—and later for that matter—regarded the Danish awakening as a completely artificial agitation, largely inspired and supported by Danes from Copenhagen and very limited in its influence even in North Schleswig. In the eyes of Danish historians, on the other hand, the awakening is a memorable episode in the Danish national story, a glorious crusade to render articulate sentiments for so long obscured by the German superstructure of Schleswig. For the Danes Schleswig, in Paulsen's apt phrase, was 'a Danish body in a German dress'.[1] But the Germans never wavered in their belief that the duchy was essentially German in history and superstructure and to a large extent in language also.

On the face of it there seemed to be reasonable prospects for the success of the Danish movement in Schleswig in the late 1830's. Danish was still spoken well to the south of the present frontier and, as indicated already, the legal status of Schleswig was shrouded in obscurity, with a large body of Danish opinion firmly convinced that the duchy was an integral part of the Danish kingdom. The Danish movement might well have attracted considerable support among the small farmers and townsfolk of Schleswig. It was royalist to the core and was imbued with a democratic, anti-aristocratic spirit, attractive to the 'small man' and the lower social groups who were naturally hostile to the German official class. This antipathy was religious as well as social in origin; the rationalist views of the officials and academicians had aroused deep resentment among the orthodox Lutheran farmers ever since the turn of

[1] Paulsen, *Für Dänemark und für Holstein*, p. 30.

the century, when an abortive attempt had been made by German pastors to introduce a new liturgy into the churches of North Schleswig. Against this favourable background it was possible for the organizers of the Danish movement to hope for considerable success, especially north of Flensburg fiord. Active workers were few and far between, but made up for this by their devotion to the cause. They included N. C. Nissen, a bookbinder's apprentice in Haderslev, merchants like P. C. Koch and C. Sørensen and the crippled watchmaker and amateur astronomer, F. Fischer of Åbenraa, an indefatigible propagandist of whom it was said that, if the last trumpet did not sound in Danish on the Day of Judgement, he would not leave his grave. The story of this small band of dedicated men is a moving episode in the history of Schleswig, for they faced not only the formidable opposition of German officialdom, but soon found many people in North Schleswig reluctant to give them unconditional support in their efforts.

It was not long before the activities of the Press Society evoked an unfavourable response on the German side. Lehmann's speech to the Press Society evoked immediate protests in the duchies; Falck, most moderate of men, denounced it as interference in their internal affairs and when approached shortly afterwards by the Press Society to write a history of Schleswig, he refused on the grounds that he knew only the united state of Schleswig-Holstein.[1] Fears that the activities of the Press Society were the thin edge of the wedge, leading ultimately to the incorporation of Schleswig in Denmark, did not subside throughout 1837, and were substantially increased by certain developments in the summer of 1838.

Just after the new session of the Schleswig estates began, late in May, Peter Lorenzen, the radical leader, caused a minor sensation when he produced a copy of Olsen's map of Schleswig, recently published by the Press Society; he protested vigorously against the name Sønderjylland used on that map to describe the duchy instead of the customary name Schleswig.[2] Lehmann admitted later that the society had erred in failing to insert the German name as

[1] *Proben Schleswig-Holsteinischer Pressfreiheit*, etc., pp. 132–6.
[2] *St. Z.*, Schleswig, 1838, p. 38, p. 55.

well, although he minimized the importance of the incident, declaring that no one intended to incorporate Schleswig.[1] But the damage had been done. The incident aroused great bitterness in the estates and reference was made to it during the debate on Nis Lorenzen's motion. As Count C. D. Reventlow shrewdly commented, it would take hundreds of years to efface the effects of the Press Society's thoughtless blunder.[2]

That was not all. On 15 June the first edition of the Danish newspaper *Dannevirke* appeared. The very name increased the apprehensions of many Germans for it referred to the ancient fortifications, running westwards from the town of Schleswig, which had originally marked the northernmost expansion of the Germans in the ninth century. With the enthusiastic Danish nationalist P. C. Koch as editor, *Dannevirke*, the first non-German paper to appear in Schleswig, became a most important medium for the propagation of Danish culture in the duchy.

In the same month Schleswig was referred to during the debate in the Viborg estates on J. P. With's motion for the union of the Danish estates. With admitted that Holstein was part of Germany, but declared that Schleswig was part of Denmark and even suggested partition as a solution of the Schleswig problem. A. S. Ørsted, the royal commissioner, promptly rejected the suggestion but later on another member of the estates spoke of the possibility of union between the Danish and Schleswig estates. It is true that these were isolated comments of which there was no trace in the final petition requesting the union of the two Danish estates. But the remarks did not pass unnoticed in Schleswig.

The cumulative effect of these developments on the German attitude was revealed during the debate in July and August on the Petersen and Nis Lorenzen motions. Andreas Petersen, member for Kristiansfeld district, had reintroduced his motion proposing that in rural schools in Danish-speaking districts—that is in the area where Danish was spoken in church and school—three hours' instruction a week be given in German during school hours

[1] Bagge and Engelstoft, *op. cit.*, I, no. 229, p. 330, O. Lehmann to P. Lorenzen, July 1839.

[2] *Ibid.*, no. 220, p. 312, P. Lorenzen to O. Lehmann, 22 Feb. 1839.

to those children whose parents requested it. An additional cause of irritation to German members was the appearance at this time of an inflammatory attack on Petersen's motion in *Københavnsposten*.[1] It was no more necessary for Danes to learn German than for Germans in Schleswig to learn Danish, maintained the writer of the article. In his opinion the motion was a plain violation of the Rights of Man and part of an attempt to extirpate Danish in the duchy. This article was interpreted by the German members as proof positive of the existence of a party inimical to German cultural values and opposed to the spread of the German language.[2]

Petersen and Nis Lorenzen—who had also reintroduced his motion for the second time—were quite prepared to support each other's motions, for they were conscious of no incompatibility between the use of Danish in the courts and the provision of some instruction in German for those who desired it. They readily agreed that their motions be examined by the same committee; this decision was taken by the estates after Falck, the president, had pointed out that, as a certain party wished to sow the seeds of disunity among them, the best way to indicate to Danish-speaking people that they did not need foreign aid to guarantee them their rights, was to refer both motions to the same committee.

During the debate on the committee report no voice was raised against Petersen's motion. There was undoubtedly a genuine desire, especially in the northern *Harden* of Haderslev *Amt*, for some instruction in German.[3] No one disagreed with Petersen's contention that people in North Schleswig came into closer contact with the Germans in Schleswig and Holstein than with Danes and that a knowledge of German was essential for apprentices who frequently learnt their trades in Germany, for women in domestic service, for recruits stationed in German barracks and for farmers selling their cattle in the towns of Schleswig and Hamburg. Provided that the instruction remained optional, nothing but

[1] 15 June, 15 July 1838. [2] *St. Z.*, Schleswig, 1838, pp. 590–1.

[3] In the first year following the implementation of the 1840 rescript, 183 teachers gave some tuition in German for payment. P. Lauridsen, *Da Sønderjylland vaagnede*, III, p. 43. Even before 1840 village schools in the southern half of North Schleswig had taught some German. O. Scheel, *Eine Fehldeutung und Legende*, etc., pp. 104, 107.

good could come of the measure proposed. The motion was subsequently carried by thirty-eight votes to one at the end of the debate.

The almost unanimous adoption of Petersen's motion probably facilitated the passage of Nis Lorenzen's motion, which proved much more controversial and was finally carried by twenty-one votes to eighteen with four abstentions. Once the Petersen motion had been carried, some German members probably found it easier to vote for Nis Lorenzen's motion in the belief that German would spread as easily in North Schleswig as it had in Angeln and would ultimately remove the need for the use of Danish in the courts. This argument was advanced in an interesting report on the Petersen and Lorenzen motions sent by the Gottorp government to Copenhagen in March 1837.[1] This report, prepared by German officials, pointed out that the Danish-speaking population in North Schleswig did not consider itself to be either Danish or German. But as both languages were spoken in the towns, the officials hoped that German would spread from there to the rural areas as had been the case in East Prussia. This desirable state of affairs would be facilitated by the introduction of some German instruction in the schools. They were much more cautious about the Nis Lorenzen motion. It was felt that however just the demand might be, only slight concessions were advisable. Most revealing of all was the comment that a complete replacement of German by Danish in the courts could be envisaged only if it was accompanied by an effective school reform introducing German into North Schleswig and breaking down the isolation in which the people lived.

Those members who spoke in support of Nis Lorenzen's motion during the debated were moved largely by ethical considerations. They condemned the use of German by officials and lawyers in Danish-speaking North Schleswig simply because it was unnatural and contrary to the dictates of reason and justice that public affairs be conducted in a tongue alien to the district.[2] Opponents of the motion made much of the difficulties which individual officials might experience in using Danish. But the North

[1] Lauridsen, *op. cit.*, I, p. 22. [2] *St. Z.*, Schleswig, 1838, p. 587.

Schleswig members, A. Jaspersen and P. Alexandersen, quickly retorted that the wishes of the people, expressed in eighteen petitions to the estates, were surely more important than the inconvenience suffered by a few officials.[1] Democratic arguments of this kind were not, however, to the liking of most supporters of the motion. They preferred to avoid this issue, maintaining that it was in any case an academic point, as most of the officials involved had at least some understanding of Danish and would surely find no difficulty in perfecting their knowledge. There was general agreement that the higher courts and the Gottorp government should not be required to use Danish; it was felt that difficulties were confined to the lower courts where they could be quite simply overcome by introducing the language spoken by the people. It was finally agreed that officials working in North Schleswig and able to use Danish should do so immediately. Lawyers and notaries were exempted from this provision by a narrow majority on the grounds that they must be free to use whichever language their clients preferred. When vacancies for official posts occurred in North Schleswig, steps should be taken to ensure that successful candidates had that spoken and written knowledge of Danish which the rescripts of 1811 and 1812 obliged them to possess. It was further agreed that Danish translations of royal and college proclamations be signed and given equal authority with the German original. A proposal that there be Danish translations of proclamations from the Gottorp government and of pronouncements from the high court of appeal was rejected.

The opponents of the motion denied the existence of any genuine need to justify these changes. They were swift to cast doubt on the authenticity of the petitions, suggesting that Danish propaganda adequately explained the disproportion between the number of petitions requesting these changes and those requesting German in the schools.[2] The supporters of the motion were undoubtedly embarrassed at this juncture by the fact that all the petitions had not been as moderately worded as those from Haderslev *Amt* and the east coast; the estates had also received a 'monster' petition bearing 1,200 signatures, requesting not only the intro-

[1] *St. Z.*, Schleswig, 1838, pp. 597, 599, 613. [2] *Ibid.*, p. 592.

duction of Danish in the administration and courts but in church and school wherever Danish was spoken. This was no careless phrase. The theme that Central Schleswig was Danish had been developed by N. Nissen in the *Itzehoer Wochenblatt* in July 1837 and he and Koch were responsible for this petition.[1] It aroused the misgivings of many members partly because they disliked the radical format, and partly because the Germans were never at any time prepared to agree to any drastic modification of the superstructure of Schleswig. However much Danish might be spoken in Central Schleswig, the Germans considered that the use of their language in church and school for generations made any change quite unthinkable.

Nis Lorenzen owed much to Falck for his prompt intervention in the debate at this critical point. Falck sympathized with the motion but realized that the unfortunate 'ultra petition', as he called it, might ruin the motion's chance of success. So he deliberately minimized the importance of all petitions on the subject, observing that the general maxim of those who organized petitions was 'first come, first served'. More to the point was his own long and intimate experience of Tønder *Amt*, which convinced him that the introduction of Danish was both just and necessary.[2]

The opponents of the motion argued that the existing system worked well enough and rendered the motion superfluous. As wills and contracts were already executed in Danish, the people of North Schleswig had really no grounds for complaint. More serious was the allegation made by supporters of the motion to the effect that the use of German in court resulted in inaccuracy; it was pointed out that oral examination of witnesses was conducted in Danish but statements were taken down in German and read back in translation, so that in effect a Danish witness was testifying to the accuracy of a German document. The Duke of Augustenburg, a leading opponent of the motion, argued that these fears were groundless.[3] Errors in translation would almost certainly be

[1] A. Scharff points out in *Aus den Anfängen der Kämpfe um Sprache und Volkstum in Nordschleswig*, p. 51, that some signatories of the 'monster' petition were in fact opposed to interference in Central Schleswig.

[2] *St. Z.*, Schleswig, 1838, p. 594. [3] *Ibid.*, pp. 598–9, 599–600.

noticed by other members of the court and be corrected at once when statements were read back. But, on the other hand, if documents were written in Danish in the lower courts, difficulties would most certainly arise when the documents were referred to the higher courts where a knowledge of Danish could not be presumed, and where errors in translation would certainly pass unnoticed.

That was not all, the duke continued. The language spoken in North Schleswig was not High Danish but a dialect. So great was the difference between the two that the duke maintained that if he spoke to North Schleswig members in their own dialect, in the presence of a Danish teacher, the latter would barely understand the conversation. It followed from this that if High Danish was used in court, serious difficulties were bound to arise. What was the point of compelling German officials to try and translate the untranslatable idiom of North Schleswig into a language which the people of North Schleswig did not understand? In fact, the duke's argument was of doubtful validity for, as another member pointed out, High Danish was easily understood in Nørrejylland, where a Low Danish dialect was spoken as in North Schleswig.[1] German officials might have found it difficult to master High Danish to perfection, but it was surely reasonable to suppose that the people of North Schleswig would find it easier to understand High Danish than High German.

The duke was never impressed by democratic arguments. Established practice appealed more to him. In particular he drew attention to the similarity between the situation in North Schleswig and that in Flanders and Alsace.[2] In 1837 one of the conspirators involved in the Louis Napoleon plot had been tried at Strassburg. As he understood no French the proceedings were translated for him. But it never occurred to anyone to introduce German into the courts of Alsace on this account because everyone recognized that French was the language of educated people in Alsace just as German was the language of educated people in North Schleswig.

Some opponents of the motion went further, maintaining that

[1] *St. Z.*, Schleswig, 1838, p. 612. [2] *Ibid.*, p. 617.

even in North Schleswig the vast majority of the people knew German as well as Danish and did not, therefore, need Danish in their courts. There was every reason for avoiding change, in the opinion of these members, because trade with the south and schooling in German would gradually reduce the very small number of those who knew no German at all. Significantly enough, P. Hamckens argued that it was unethical to agree to changes which would encourage Danish-speaking people to preserve their language and even to think of spreading it in Schleswig, however remote their chances of success. The fact of the matter was that Hamckens, like many Germans, confidently assumed that North Schleswig would be germanized as rapidly as Angeln had been at the turn of the century.[1] Falck tried to disillusion him, insisting that there was no prospect of German becoming a universal language in the near future, and pointing out that even where the use of German had increased, as in the southeast of the duchy, it had only done so because forcible methods had been used to supplant Danish.[2] But the words fell on stony ground. The Germans remained firmly convinced of the cultural superiority of their language. Hensen, the member for Schleswig town and a bitter critic of the Press Society, bluntly affirmed that German was more important than any other language for the people of North Schleswig, for was it not a generally accepted principle that one derived greatest educational benefit from a knowledge of German?[3]

This does not mean that the opposition wished to impose an absolute veto on the use of Danish in the courts. On the contrary; thirty-one members supported Drohse's proposal that only officials with a knowledge of Danish should be appointed in North Schleswig in the future. In this way difficulties could be resolved without having recourse to drastic modifications of the existing system. This was the crucial point for opponents of the motion; at all costs they were determined to preserve the German superstructure of Schleswig for this, not the language spoken by the people, determined the national character of the duchy. 'The duchy of Schleswig is German,' said Drohse. 'The system of

[1] *Ibid.*, pp. 607–8. [2] *Ibid.*, p. 609. [3] *Ibid.*, p. 592.

government and the laws have been German from time immemorial. Legal proceedings are conducted in German, the upper courts, the high court of appeal and the Schleswig-Holstein government all use German and the officials are educated in German at the university.' [1] But the Nis Lorenzen motion, by modifying the superstructure of the duchy, would weaken the bonds between the duchies and assist the Danes to annex Schleswig; for, as the Duke of Augustenburg pointed out, the introduction of Danish logically implied the introduction of Danish law or of Danish officials ignorant of German law, and this, he warned members, might lead ultimately to the separation of the German- and Danish-speaking parts of Schleswig.[2] This fear was uppermost in Drohse's mind when he bluntly declared, in his final speech, that the administrative and legal system of Schleswig could not be changed just to please one small district.[3]

The fact that Nis Lorenzen's motion was carried, albeit by a narrow majority, indicated that the Schleswig estates wished to treat the language question as a purely administrative matter and not as a pawn in a national conflict between German and Dane. Rational considerations and humanitarian sentiment guided most members towards this favourable conclusion. Most of them were imbued with the spirit of the eighteenth century, and simply wanted to improve the administrative system by removing what seemed to them a glaring injustice and an irrational practice. They steadfastly refused to allow their judgement to be clouded by national prejudice which appeared to inspire the activity of a lunatic fringe of Danes eager to stir up trouble between the two peoples. Nor could the members agree that they had endangered the independence of the duchies by their decision, as the minority would have them believe. There seemed no reason to doubt the continued goodwill of the overwhelming mass of their Danish neighbours at this time. Supporters of Lorenzen's motion were correct in thinking that most Danish liberals regarded the work of the Press Society in Schleswig as exclusively cultural in nature, and secondary to the task of obtaining financial powers for a

[1] *St. Z.*, Schleswig, 1838, p. 597.
[2] *Ibid.*, p. 615.
[3] *Ibid.*, p. 612.

united Danish estates. They were also correct in supposing that very few Danes were thinking of the annexation of Schleswig in terms of practical politics. With few exceptions, the Danes, like the Germans, had no desire to exacerbate relations between the two halves of the *Helstat* either by raising the contentious question of the legal status of Schleswig or by allowing the language question to become the plaything of party politics.

The majority were confirmed in their belief that the fears of the minority were grossly exaggerated by the attitude of the members for North Schleswig.[1] On this occasion Nis Lorenzen had avoided the provocative language of 1836 when Flor had written his speech. Nis Lorenzen spoke for all the North Schleswig members, when he declared that they considered themselves an inseparable part of Schleswig and had no desire to be separated from Schleswig-Holstein.[2] Attention was also drawn in the committee report to the fact that, with one notorious exception, all the petitions from North Schleswig had been strongly critical of those individuals who were trying to make party capital out of the legitimate grievances of the people, and who seemed bent on sowing the seeds of hatred between German and Dane.[3]

The cautious attitude of the people of North Schleswig helps to explain the surprisingly slow progress made by the Danish movement in the late 1830's. *Dannevirke* had commenced its career in a blaze of publicity, but the number of readers remained around 350 until the beginning of 1841, most of them being teachers and pastors in Haderslev *Amt*. The truth was that those who took an active interest in politics in North Schleswig were, with few exceptions, extremely wary of support from Copenhagen. They were not ungrateful for Danish assistance to help preserve their cultural heritage and to secure the right to use Danish in the courts. But they were quick to resent interference in their internal

[1] A. H. Posselt (replaced by Thomsen in 1838), Petersen, Nis Lorenzen, Steenholdt, Alexandersen, Ebbersen (replaced by Bonefeldt in 1838) and P. Todsen represented the seven electoral districts of North Schleswig (lesser landowners). H. C. Jensen and P. Nielsen represented Flensburg town, Peter Lorenzen, Haderslev town and Klestrup, Arroeskiøping.

[2] *St. Z.*, Schleswig, 1838, p. 76.

[3] *Ibid.*, p. 591.

affairs. Nis Lorenzen, for example, did not hesitate to resign at once from the Press Society in protest against the political undertones of the Olsen map. Even N. Hanssen and C. Sørensen, men deeply involved in the Danish awakening, were always inclined to suspect the existence of political designs behind the activities of the Press Society. To some extent this was the instinctive reaction of isolated provincials suspicious of sophisticated intellectuals like O. Lehmann. But it was also indicative of a very real and deep attachment to their native soil. They were natives of Schleswig, proud of their Danish cultural heritage but as strongly opposed to the idea of incorporation in Denmark and subjection to the *Kongelov* which that implied, as they were to germanization. They were conscious that their higher material standards separated them from their Danish-speaking brothers in Nørrejylland, and they accepted the association with Holstein as part of their political heritage. Their representatives in the Schleswig estates voted without hesitation for the union of the two estates. In politics North Schleswig tended to be liberal, its nine members forming the backbone of the small liberal group led by Peter Lorenzen and Count Magnus Moltke; most petitions requesting financial powers for a united estates came not from South Schleswig but from Haderslev *Amt*, and six of the nine North Schleswig members had supported Berwald's motion in 1838.

The growth of the Danish movement in Schleswig was retarded still further by the gradual revelation of the depth of the differences which separated the North Schleswig liberals from their Danish associates. These differences, which assumed crucial importance in the following decade, are illustrated by the correspondence between the young Danish liberal, Orla Lehmann, and the North Schleswig radical, Peter Lorenzen, in 1839.[1]

Peter Lorenzen declared at the beginning of the correspondence that their common aim as liberals was the overthrow of absolutism as quickly as possible in both halves of the *Helstat*, so that their generation could enjoy the Rights of Man. To this end they must subordinate differences of opinion arising out of past history. It was all a matter of reflexes; if they changed places they would

[1] Bagge and Engelstoft, *op. cit.*, I, nos. 218, 219, 220, 223, 224, 229.

inherit different historical traditions. What was certain was that nothing would alter the determination of Schleswig to resist incorporation in Denmark. Lorenzen was bitterly critical of *Dannevirke* which, in his opinion, had betrayed the cause of freedom and cast itself into the arms of absolutism by attacking the *Landesrechte*. It was essential that the Danes realize that, as well as a common belief in the Rights of Man, the North Schleswig liberals had the good fortune to possess an invaluable antidote to absolutism in the *Landesrechte*. The extension of the absolutist *Kongelov* to Schleswig would not only be a denial of natural right. It would also be a violation of the independent status of the duchies inside the *Helstat* as guaranteed by the *Landesrechte*. 'We are merely using our historical rights', observed Lorenzen, 'to wage a battle which the people in the Danish kingdom cannot wage.'[1] If the Danes regarded loyalty to the *Landesrechte* as evidence of separatist designs, it grieved him to hear it. Surely Lehmann could understand that detestation of absolutism did not imply any ill will towards the Danish people? No one could deny that *Dannevirke* had repudiated the *Landesrechte* and upheld Carl von Wimpfen's thesis, that Schleswig had been incorporated in Denmark in 1721 and was now subject to the *Kongelov*.[2] No wonder North Schleswig believed that *Dannevirke*, under the guise of defending the nationality of Schleswig, was trying to create bad blood between Dane and German, in order to prepare the way for the seizure of the duchy. As long as *Dannevirke* persisted in this policy co-operation with Danish liberals would be difficult, because Copenhagen was generally recognized as the driving force behind Koch and Flor. This agitation conducted by *Dannevirke* repelled the duchies, and might in time even turn people's thoughts towards separation from the kingdom. As responsible liberals they ought to avoid the dissipation of their best forces in this miserable internecine warfare which only played into the hands of their worst enemy, absolutism.

O. Lehmann was quick to reply that his interest in Schleswig

[1] *Ibid.*, no. 220, p. 312, 22 Feb. 1839.

[2] C. von Wimpfen, *Geschichte und Zustände des Herzogtums Schleswig oder Südjutland von den ältesten Zeiten bis auf die Gegenwart*, Flensburg, 1839, p. 323.

was not inspired by national prejudice, but solely by democratic feelings and by his hatred of German tyranny in Schleswig. 'In the name of nature and justice, which is mightier than the force and guile of men, I protest against the most shameful tyranny on earth, namely, to rob a people of its nationality and language. This takes precedence over all constitutional questions.' [1] Anyone who disagreed with this was, in his opinion, lying when they spoke of their love of freedom. P. Lorenzen could not disagree with these democratic sentiments, but, like many others in Schleswig, he remained uneasy about Danish intentions. He imagined, erroneously, that Lehmann was an Eiderdane before the latter had arrived at that position; hence P. Lorenzen supposed that Lehmann's interest in the national unity of the Scandinavian peoples was the key to his Schleswig policy and that he was really seeking to strengthen Scandinavia by leading Schleswig into a renewed Calmar Union. When the hour of freedom struck in Europe and the Germans, Italians and Poles obtained their independence, P. Lorenzen saw no reason why the duchies should not join a Scandinavian Union and so secure political freedom—always provided that it was the free choice of the people and not the work of *Dannevirke* agitators. If, on the other hand, Holstein was drawn into the 'German vortex', Schleswig would probably follow voluntarily or by force or perhaps North Schleswig might adhere to Denmark and South Schleswig to Germany. But, he concluded, all this was pure speculation about which they could do very little. Basically P. Lorenzen was uninterested in national questions which seemed to him a mere distraction from the primary liberal task of overthrowing absolutism.

P. Lorenzen was justly critical of Lehmann's exaggerated picture of conditions in Schleswig. Whether the Holstein dukes had used force to separate Schleswig from Denmark five hundred years ago or not, P. Lorenzen neither knew nor cared. But he was quite certain that North Schleswig was not at present groaning under a German tyranny as Lehmann alleged. The real source of oppression was the absolutist Danish government, not the German officials. Nor was it anything but a travesty of the facts to suppose,

[1] Bagge and Engelstoft, *op. cit.*, I, no. 219, p. 306, Feb. 1839.

as Lehmann did, that Central Schleswig was only prevented from declaring its Danish sympathies by the terrorization of officials. With the exception of Angeln, where there was admittedly cause for complaint, there was no question of tyranny south of the Flensburg-Tønder line. Even in Angeln what had been done could not be undone. It was now a fact that German-speaking people in that area did not wish to speak Danish. The unpleasant truth was that the Danish nationality could no longer be awakened in Central Schleswig, whatever Lehmann or Nissen might think. Nor had P. Lorenzen heard of any attempts to germanize the people in North Schleswig, where, in his experience, the two peoples were on the friendliest footing. He warned against attempts to replace German by Danish in church and school in the North Schleswig towns. This would arouse the hostility of German and Dane alike because German had been used there, as in Central Schleswig, for hundreds of years. P. Lorenzen was generally satisfied with existing conditions, though he regretted that prohibitive costs made it impossible to provide Danish as well as German schools in the towns. He wanted Danish to be used in court, but not because he thought there was any question of tyranny or violation of the Danish nationality—Danish was, he believed, in general use in the administration already and ordinary people usually left legal intricacies to the judge and lawyers in court. He had supported Nis Lorenzen's motion simply because reforms, such as the introduction of a jury system, were impossible as long as German was used in court. In short, P. Lorenzen's attitude to the language question was typical of many educated people in North Schleswig, who were invariably bilingual, as he was, and had lived in peace with their German neighbours for generations. To them language was purely a matter of convenience and not a symbol of national affinity. They were deeply suspicious of people who attached exaggerated importance to either language at the expense of the other, for they realized instinctively that amicable relations and civilized conduct between peoples in a frontier district were dependent on the absence of national antagonisms. As for the official use of Danish in North Schleswig, there seemed no reason for Danish-speaking people to suppose, after the Schleswig estates accepted Nis

Lorenzen's motion, that their German friends were lacking in an understanding of local needs.

Nor could P. Lorenzen agree with Lehmann that the Schleswig-Holstein liberals were really the enemies of Denmark, seeking to break away from the kingdom and establish an independent state. P. Lorenzen firmly repudiated the charges of separatism which were already being levelled at the *Landespartei* in certain Danish newspapers. 'An independent Schleswig-Holstein is in my eyes a chimera,' he declared bluntly. 'But a constitutional Schleswig-Holstein in honourable union with a constitutional Denmark is a possibility and the only solution of the problem.' [1] He insisted throughout the correspondence that his intimate knowledge of Schleswig-Holstein liberals and of their political ideas convinced him that they were the heirs of Lornsen accepting the *Helstat* as he had done, and working within this framework for constitutional advances. They wanted neither incorporation in Denmark nor separation from Denmark, but simply the continuation of the traditional relationship between the duchies and the Danish kingdom.

P. Lorenzen's views both on the language question in Schleswig and on the aims of the Schleswig-Holstein liberals were much more realistic and far less clouded by national prejudice than those of Lehmann. The Schleswig problem was far more complex than Lehmann supposed and could not be satisfactorily explained in terms of terrorization by German officials and separatist designs by German liberals in league with the reactionary Duke of Augustenburg.

All the same, Lehmann showed much greater perception than Peter Lorenzen in forecasting the course of future development. The latter insisted, somewhat naïvely, that he did not know a single Schleswig-Holstein liberal who would refuse to respect the real wishes of the people in the language question. It was nonsense to say that a united Schleswig-Holstein estates would have the power to—or would want to—oppress the Danish nationality. 'My fellow countrymen,' P. Lorenzen remarked, 'are not so foolish as to believe that they need support absolutism because their

[1] Bagge and Engelstoft, *op. cit.*, I, no. 220, p. 312, 22 Feb. 1839.

language is oppressed, when any educated person is aware that malpractices which occur in a few places can and will be eradicated to the satisfaction of everyone concerned.'[2] In other words P. Lorenzen had complete faith in the good intentions of his German colleagues.

But Orla Lehmann sensed that some of the Schleswig-Holstein liberals were already anti-Danish. If this was not so, then why had so many of them opposed the Nis Lorenzen motion in 1838 and why did liberals like C. F. Heiberg refer to the Danish language in disparaging terms? Lehmann, like Uwe Lornsen, had an intuitive appreciation of the tremendous power of national sentiment. He had a shrewd suspicion that when the hour of freedom struck in Europe a national crisis would flare up in Schleswig, revealing the falsity of the idyllic picture of German-Danish relations drawn by P. Lorenzen, and relegating constitutional questions to the background of the political arena. Lehmann, like Uwe Lornsen, felt that national sentiment would prove a more powerful impulse to action than liberal conviction.

For the discerning there had already been some significant indications of the power of national sentiment at the second meeting of the Holstein estates in the autumn of 1838. The tone of the meeting had certainly been more subdued than that in Schleswig and little interest was shown in the *Landesrechte*. A motion for the union of the estates had not even emerged from committee; during the debate there was little comment when one speaker warned the estates against close relations with Schleswig, 'a province more or less incorporated in Denmark'.[2] But there was unanimous approval for H. Löck's motion demanding the discontinuance of the practices of using Danish at the installation of officials, of publishing official proclamations and laws in both languages and of requiring officials to possess a knowledge of Danish. They were gratified, declared Löck, that their duke was also king 'in a neighbouring foreign country', and they respected the language and literature of that foreign country. But the official use of Danish in Holstein implied a position of inferiority which they would not

[1] *Ibid.*, no. 224, p. 319, 19 April 1839.
[2] *St. Z.*, Holstein, 1838, p. 876.

tolerate. The Danes would rightly complain if German was used when their officials were installed in office, if their laws were published in German and if their officials were required to possess a knowledge of German. The Germans felt the same way about the use of Danish. Nor did Löck hesitate to suggest that, whereas a knowledge of Danish enabled one to communicate with a million people, those who learned German could communicate with thirty million people.[1] It was indeed a significant pointer to future developments that liberals and conservatives, who were so deeply divided over motions seeking financial powers for a united estates, closed their ranks in defence of the national independence of German Holstein.

[1] *St. Z.*, Holstein, 1838, pp. 904–8.

VII

The fateful years, 1839, 1840

THROUGHOUT the 1830's political life in the duchies was dominated by the spirit of the eighteenth century. It was the era of Falck when public affairs were the concern of a privileged few, the officials and academicians, who were guided in their deliberations by reason and humanitarian sentiment, and who remained staunch in their loyalty to the crown and indifferent to national idiosyncrasies. The years 1839 and 1840 were undoubtedly the most critical and fateful in the history of the *Helstat*. They constitute a climacteric separating the peaceful years of the 1830's from the turbulence and strife of the 1840's and 1850's. In these decades the texture of political life was radically altered. New forces were stirring in Europe, old loyalties were losing their spell as the era of Metternich drew to a close, the masses of the people were at last being drawn into politics and—most fateful change of all for the *Helstat*—nationalism superseded humanitarianism as the dominant impulse to political action. Three events in this period suggested that national animosities would dominate the 1840's and disrupt the old harmony between German and Dane on which the *Helstat* rested; firstly, there was the emergence of the New Holstein movement; secondly, developments in Denmark following the death of the old king at the close of 1839 and, finally, the rejection of the language rescript by the Schleswig estates in 1840.

New Holsteinism originated in the articles written by Theodore Olshausen, radical-minded editor of *Kieler Korrespondenz Blatt*, in the summer of 1839.[1] These articles appeared at a critical juncture in the affairs of the *Landespartei*. Relations between the liberal and

[1] 8, 11, 18, 25 May. 19, 26, 29 June. 6, 24 July.

conservative wings of the party had been severely strained since the decisive defeat of liberal motions seeking financial powers for a united estates. These motions had been moved by Peter Lorenzen in the Schleswig estates and by Lorentzen of Kiel in the Holstein estates in 1838. The determined opposition of *Ritterschaft* members on these occasions made it quite evident that there was little hope of a modern constitution based on the *Landesrechte*. If the conservatives had their way absolutism would be superseded by an equally obnoxious *Junkerherrschaft*. It almost looked as if real political advance would be possible only when the Germans adopted the more radical policies favoured by their Danish colleagues.

An additional cause of dissatisfaction was the situation in North Schleswig, where the Danish movement was at last making perceptible progress. A second Danish newspaper, *Åbenraa Ugeblad*, appeared in 1839 and despite great difficulties the editor, F. Fischer, built up a circulation of about 200 readers in and around Åbenraa within a few years. This was followed in 1840 by a third newspaper, *Flensburger Zeitung*, which, though written in German, supported the Danish movement. In the summer of 1839 Nis Hanssen, a Copenhagen theological student and brother-in-law of P. Koch, founded *Selskabet for dansk Laesnings Udbredelse i Slesvig* to organize the distribution of Danish literature in Schleswig.[1] This was an important event for the Danish lending libraries, which soon began to circulate in North Schleswig, were used by many who did not read newspapers. N. F. Grundtvig now began to interest himself in the Schleswig problem; there was talk of a *Folkehøjskole*;[2] Danish actors performed in Haderslev and von Wimpffen published the first history of Schleswig to be written from a non-German standpoint. In Copenhagen public meetings addressed by N. Hanssen and Lehmann drew attention to North Schleswig, while in the background the Scandinavian movement began to take shape. The cumulative effect of these developments, following the acceptance of the Nis Lorenzen motion by the Schleswig estates, was to arouse serious misgivings among many

[1] The society for the distribution of Danish publications in Schleswig.
[2] People's college.

Germans who now feared that the action of the estates had only encouraged the growing ambition of the Danes. To some Germans this seemed to suggest that the *Landesrechte* were not only useless as a foundation for a modern constitution, but were equally incapable of preserving the independence of the duchies—for was not the official use of German an integral part of the German superstructure, which preserved the unity and independence of Schleswig-Holstein against Danish aggression?

In the first of his controversial articles, published in May 1839, Olshausen expressed profound dissatisfaction with the behaviour of the *Landespartei* in recent months. He boldly challenged the basic assumption that Schleswig and Holstein formed a single state with a right to a common constitution. It was evident that Holstein had a much better chance of obtaining a constitution than Schleswig, for clause thirteen of the federal constitution applied in the former but not in the latter duchy. Schleswig was really the stumbling block. In the past Holstein had failed to obtain a constitution simply because it had preferred to maintain the old association with Schleswig, and had even weakened its case by trying to revive the antiquated common constitution of medieval times. The German Confederation had declared that constitution null and void as long ago as 1823, and the recent defeat of the motion moved by Lorentzen of Kiel surely proved how slim the chances were of obtaining a modern constitution along these lines. By continuing to insist on a common constitution the *Landespartei* was really playing into the hands of absolutism, making it easier for the Danes to refuse the legitimate requests of Holstein. Nor was it by any means certain that Schleswig-Holstein formed a single state as Dahlmann alleged. Some people believed that Schleswig and Holstein were only provinces in the *Helstat*, others thought that Holstein was a German state and Schleswig a Danish province or even an independent state. Amidst such confusion there was only one logical and rational course open to Holstein—let it abandon attempts to secure a common constitution, forget the *Landesrechte*, sever its connection with Schleswig and seek a constitution as a member of the German Confederation.

But Olshausen had not broken with the *Landespartei* because he believed constitutional advance to be the only object of political action; on the contrary. The decisive consideration for Olshausen was the indisputably German character of Holstein. 'Germany for ever and before everything—then Schleswig-Holstein,' he announced in a memorable phrase.[1] Holstein had to look southwards for a constitution because it was obliged to seek 'the closest spiritual association with everything German'.[2] The Confederation had been a great disappointment in 1814. But it had now become the star of hope for all Germans, as day by day it drew the German states closer through the *Zollverein*, the railway network and the growing industrialization of the country. Holstein must not be excluded from this development even if a democratic constitution were offered it elsewhere (i.e. by the Danes); 'for a people must not sacrifice their nationality for the sake of a constitution with non-nationals'.[3] Nationality, 'the strong and Divine bond of the natural law', was infinitely more powerful than any constitutional arrangement. It would be far better for Holstein to wait until the great German nation obtained political freedom than to share a constitution with foreigners.

Holstein could not wait for Schleswig, because Schleswig was not indisputably German or at least—and this was probably the real cause of Olshausen's hesitation in 1839—the Germans had not established the German character of the duchy beyond dispute. Schleswig was nationally immature, in his opinion, because the people wished to remain 'Schleswiger', a concept which, like 'Schleswig-Holsteiner', lacked national significance. Olshausen was mystified and irritated beyond measure by the miserable provincialism of these people. At a time when German national feeling was again stirring south of the Elbe, why could the people of Schleswig not see that neither Schleswig nor Schleswig-Holstein, but only Germany was a satisfactory fatherland for Germans? Schleswig had enjoyed the best of both worlds in the past by virtue of its anomalous position. But now it must decide as soon as possible whether it was German or Danish and give political expression to its decision by joining Denmark or entering the German Confederation. He insisted, like his Danish friend Lehmann

[1] *K.K.B.*, 11 May. [2] *K.K.B.*, 18 May. [3] *K.K.B.*, 6 July.

at this time, that the decision must be a democratic one, taken by the people of this neutral territory in accordance with their own wishes and without pressure from outside. Like Lehmann, he toyed with the possibility of partition, but on the whole seems to have considered this unlikely, probably because the advances made by the Danish movement were still fairly limited in the summer of 1839.

Olshausen's views on the language question are highly interesting. True to his radical convictions, he considered that the Danish-speaking inhabitants of North Schleswig should use their own language in court and in the administration as they did in church and school. But the high courts must remain German, because the duchies formed an administrative entity and a Danish minority must give way here to a German majority. Nor had he any criticism to make of conditions in Central Schleswig apart from a cautious comment to the effect that possibly Danish was given too little recognition in this part of the duchy. He believed that officials should possess a knowledge of Danish, but German must be retained in higher education because German was a superior cultural medium. It was not disrespectful to the Danes to point out that they had produced no original philosophy, and that German science had attained a higher level than Danish. The Danish-speaking people of Schleswig could not, therefore, regard it as a hardship to learn German for their cultural advancement. In short, Schleswig should remain culturally German.

Olshausen seems to have hoped at this time that Schleswig would opt for Germany rather than Denmark. He thought that the succession question might soon result in the separation of Schleswig from Denmark, thus facilitating the entry of the duchy into the Confederation. On several occasions he emphasized that he was as reluctant as anyone to separate the Germans in Holstein from the Germans in Schleswig even temporarily. Separation was justifiable only because national sentiment necessitated it; 'Our fate depends on Germany,' he wrote to Peter Lorenzen, 'why then should we not associate ourselves, as soon as possible and as closely as possible, with Germany? The fact that Holstein can do this sooner because it is able to do so will not prevent Schleswig doing it later, if it can do so and desires to do so.'[1] When Schleswig had made its decision and entered the Confederation—thus placing its German character beyond dispute—a common constitution with Holstein would be eminently desirable.

By 1841 Olshausen had abandoned the hope that the whole of Schleswig would choose to enter the German Confederation; as the tide of German nationalism began to rise again south of the Elbe, the growing strength of the Danish movement in Schleswig was thrown into sharper relief. Reluctantly Olshausen had to admit that Schleswig was divided in its national allegiance and that partition was the only practical solution. The refusal of the *Landespartei* to accept the logic of this argument brought forth devastating criticism from his pen, especially after the rejection of the language rescript.[2] It was patently illiberal, he argued, to deny the Danish-speaking people in North Schleswig their natural right to use Danish as their official language. The Germans could either recognize this right or else, if they denied this right as the Schleswig estates had done without even waiting to see the rescript in operation, they must accept the logical alternative—partition. If parity of esteem could not be established between the two languages, then separation was the obvious course and would be mutually beneficial as in the case of Holland and Belgium. There was a prophetic ring about his final observation that if the Germans continued to deny this natural right in North Schleswig and still opposed partition, then they would have to resort to force to preserve the unity of Schleswig. He was equally critical of those Germans who claimed that Schleswig was completely German in character and that even the Danish-speaking population, with few exceptions, wanted to become German. If this was so—which Olshausen denied—then it was a sad proof of the extent to which the Germans had succeeded in suppressing the true feelings of these people. If Schleswig was as German as these gentlemen alleged, then why had it not set the seal on its national character by requesting admission to the Confederation? The fact of the matter

[1] A. E. Møldrup, *Breve fra Th. Olshausen til P. Hjort Lorenzen 1831–9*, p. 389, 22 June 1839.

[2] *K.K.B.*, 1841, 26, 29 May. 2, 23 June. 3 July. 14 Aug. 18, 29 Sept. 6 Nov.

was that Schleswig had no desire to do this and even his opponents had to admit that the reluctance of Schleswig to take this step seriously weakened the case of the *Landespartei*.

The New Holsteiner, as their enemies called them, or the German Party, to use their own less well-known name, had only a limited appeal in Holstein. The editors of the Preetz, Oldesloe and Wandsbek *Wochenblätter* sympathized with Olshausen, and in the west of Holstein, especially in Ditmarschen, the ideas of the New Holsteiner found favour. But the two Ditmarschen members, together with H. R. Claussen, the Kiel radical, represented the total political strength of the New Holsteiner in the Holstein estates in 1842. The iconoclastic and heretical ideas of the New Holsteiner naturally aroused great resentment in the ranks of the *Landespartei*. Many members were completely unnerved and thrown into confusion by these devastating attacks on their political beliefs, and they bitterly resented strictures on their provincial outlook. No doubt the *Landespartei* was quite right in thinking the New Holsteiner over-optimistic about the chance of Holstein obtaining a modern constitution in the German Confederation at this time; no doubt the *Landespartei* was also right in supposing that the *Landesrechte* were becoming part of the political heritage of ordinary people to a much greater extent than the New Holsteiner realized. But only time could prove the *Landespartei* right on these points. Meanwhile the cogency of Olshausen's arguments and the defection of so eminent a liberal shook the *Landespartei* out of its complacency and exposed the inconsistencies in its attitude. Many Germans tried to avoid the issue by branding as traitors all those who disagreed with them. But there were others who reluctantly admitted the need for an agonizing reappraisal of inherited political attitudes, to meet the situation created by the new stirrings of national feeling in Germany and the progress of the Danish movement in Schleswig.

The repercussions of Olshausen's political heresy were not restricted to Holstein. In July 1840 the *Landespartei* suffered another severe blow when the leading Schleswig radical, Peter Lorenzen, resigned from the *Landespartei*. Throughout the 1830's Lorenzen had worked loyally for a common constitution for the duchies in honourable union with a constitutional Denmark. But doubts about the *Landespartei* had begun to cross his mind ever since the conservative wing of the party defeated his liberal motion in the Schleswig estates in 1838. Olshausen's articles increased these doubts. By his breach with the *Landespartei* Olshausen had retarded the cause of freedom, seriously weakening the radical camp and playing into the hands of reactionary elements. Furthermore, Olshausen had made the inclusion of Schleswig in the Confederation a *sine qua non* for a common constitution. This condition was quite unacceptable to P. Lorenzen for, like most people in Schleswig, he wished to preserve the anomalous status of the duchy. Moreover he was firmly convinced that Schleswig's chances of obtaining a democratic constitution would be seriously impaired, if it was drawn into the Confederation to please the aristocratic clique who now dominated the *Landespartei*. Indeed the rising tide of Danish liberalism convinced him that there was now much more likelihood of constitutional advance in Denmark than in the Confederation. Yet how could Schleswig share in the fruits of the imminent destruction of Danish absolutism if Olshausen expressly excluded all constitutional partnership with the Danes? Retirement from active politics seemed the most sensible course until the *Landespartei* had clarified its attitude and regrouped its forces.[1]

The bitter German opposition to the language rescript in the early summer of 1840 was the last straw. P. Lorenzen had never been interested in national questions, which merely diverted attention, in his opinion, from the main task of destroying absolutism. But his democratic soul was shocked by the clear violation of liberal principle implied in the German refusal to concede equality of status to the Danish language. Moreover, his great political opponent, the conservative duke of Augustenburg, was exploiting the language question in order to establish himself in a preeminent position in the councils of the *Landespartei*. Already in the spring and summer of 1840 the duke had launched bitter attacks

[1] Bagge and Engelstoft, *op. cit.*, I, no. 230, pp. 334–5, P. Lorenzen to O. Lehmann, 26 July 1839.

on P. Lorenzen in the *Itzehoer Wochenblatt,* accusing him of treason in supporting Nis Lorenzen's motion in 1838. It became increasingly clear that there was no place for a democrat in this anti-Danish and ultra-conservative party. A thorough reappraisal of his political position could no longer be delayed. In June, after discussions with his radical friends, I. W. Joachimsen of Flensburg and H. de Wolff of Haderslev, P. Lorenzen decided to leave the *Landespartei.*[1] In August, shortly before the estates met, he resigned his seat, declaring himself unable to work any longer for a Schleswig-Holstein constitution.

So at last P. Lorenzen had to admit that Orla Lehmann had been right after all. P. Lorenzen now denounced the illiberal, anti-Danish propensities of the *Landespartei* as fervently as Lehmann had done and found a basis for co-operation with the latter in July 1839.[2] P. Lorenzen ceased to bother about Holstein, concentrating exclusively on the task of obtaining a constitution for Schleswig. He agreed with Lehmann that Schleswig must remain in a state of suspended animation, poised between Denmark and Holstein until the people decided their own political future. For neither he nor Lehmann were Eiderdanes at this time; they both insisted on the democratic right of the people of Schleswig to make up their own minds. P. Lorenzen was aware that there was considerable political apathy in Schleswig, attributable in his opinion to the absence of a free press and the intimidation of the people by the officials. He intended, so he informed his electors, to devote himself to the task of enlightening the people about the relative merits of the constitutions they might expect from Denmark and Holstein.[3] He realized that this might well be a slow and arduous task, for German resistance to the Danish movement—with which he was now associated—stiffened after the publication of the rescript. But if Denmark succeeded in overthrowing absolutism in the near future, then the situation would be completely transformed. The people of Schleswig would no longer fear the Danes, but would 'shake off their chains and go over to their

[1] *Ibid.*, no. 290, p. 434, P. Lorenzen to O. Lehmann, 24 June 1840.
[2] *Ibid.*, no. 229, pp. 330–4, O. Lehmann to P. Lorenzen.
[3] Skau, *op. cit.*, p. 122.

Danish brothers'.[1] Somewhat naïvely he supposed that the Germans in the towns of North Schleswig and perhaps even in South Schleswig would realize—if it was properly explained to them—that Schleswig had no expectations of freedom in a Confederation indirectly 'under the knout of Russia', and would opt for Denmark. Equally naïve was his belief that it would be easy to reassure the Germans that a democratic constitution would guarantee them the use of their language more effectively than the old arbitrary absolutist system had done. P. Lorenzen simply could not conceive that national sentiment might prove a much more potent impulse to action than reason and a belief in democracy.

The second event which made 1839 a decisive year for the *Helstat* was the death on 3 December of King Frederik VI. The passing of the *Herzensherzog*,[2] ruler of the *Helstat* for fifty-five years, first as regent and then as king, moved the people as profoundly as the death of Queen Victoria moved the British nation in 1901. Frederik had been a homely figure, a man of no great intelligence or gifts, but a conscientious and diligent ruler with a deep sense of obligation towards his subjects. He had endeared himself to his people more than most kings by his long association with them in good times and bad, from the days of the liberation of the serfs to the establishment of provincial estates, and he had built up a very real fund of devotion to his person which helped to sustain the *Helstat* during the crisis years 1813 and 1814. With his death an era came to an end.

His successor, King Christian VIII, had many of the qualities of kingship. He was a man of great personal charm, considerable intelligence and ability, a fluent conversationalist and patron of the arts with wide cultural and humanitarian interests. In the popular mind he had always been associated with the Norwegian constitution of 1814; as a young prince he had been sent to Norway in 1813 by King Frederik VI to restore confidence in the four hundred year old connection with Denmark. His efforts were in vain, for a few months later Denmark had been compelled to

[1] Bagge and Engelstoft, *op. cit.*, I, no. 290, p. 434, P. Lorenzen to O. Lehmann, 24 June 1840.

[2] 'Most dearly beloved duke.'

sue for peace and surrendered Norway to Sweden. But the Norwegians did not relish the prospect of Swedish rule and declared their independence, electing Prince Christian their ruler after he had reluctantly accepted the new liberal constitution drawn up by the Eidsvold constituent assembly. Unfortunately the Great Powers were not prepared to allow peoples to decide their own destiny and within a few months they had forced Christian out of Norway. Norway kept her constitution but remained united with Sweden by dynastic ties until 1905. The legend of Christian's liberality was not dimmed with the passage of the years. Ever since the serious illness of the king in 1837, Christian had been the hope of the Danish liberals. When he finally ascended the throne at the end of 1839, there was very considerable excitement in Copenhagen where liberals confidently expected a constitution in the near future. They were soon disillusioned. Christian confirmed the late king's ministers in office and politely but firmly rejected numerous addresses, which poured in from all parts of the *Helstat* requesting a constitutional monarchy of the Norwegian pattern. The liberal experiences of his youth lay twenty-five years behind this middle-aged ruler. Since then he had become a respectable member of the Establishment. As a member of the *Statsraad* he had been closely associated with the government for several years, and his visit to the Tsar and to Metternich in 1838 had only confirmed him in his determination to avoid precipitate action in these matters. He was intelligent enough to see the need for further modernization of the state, but he was not prepared to destroy the basis of his power to please Copenhagen students.

The impressive political agitation of the winter of 1839 failed in its immediate objective. Nevertheless, it constitutes a turning-point in the history of Danish liberalism. The death of the old king had removed those psychological inhibitions which had impeded constitutional advance for so long. At last Danish liberals felt free to make demands which would never have been made in King Frederik's lifetime. The Danish liberal movement was at last changing in character; young men, like Orla Lehmann, D. G. Monrad and C. Ploug, played a leading role in the organization of addresses to the crown. The liberalism favoured by the older generation of officials was basically eighteenth century in conception; Algreen Ussing, the liberal leader of the 1830's, stood for the rationalization of the financial and administrative machinery of government, within the limits permitted by the existing political framework of the estates. The loyalty of the older liberals to the crown was unquestioned. They fought for freedom of the press and for publicity of proceedings in the estates simply because these were essential safeguards of administrative efficiency. But the younger generation of liberals, the students, the journalists and junior officials, represented a more fundamental challenge to the power of the crown. They wanted to alter the existing balance of political power, by diminishing the power of the crown and conferring extensive financial and legislative power on the middle class. The agitation in the first few weeks of King Christian's reign was a clear indication that advanced liberalism of this kind would dominate the political life of the 1840's, as the reformism of Ussing had dominated the preceding decade.

One feature of the new liberalism soon to assume tremendous significance for the course of Danish history in the next three decades, was the intimate association between liberal and national ideas. When *Faedrelandet*, the Danish liberal weekly, became a daily on 1 January 1840, Orla Lehmann told P. Ç. Koch that the paper was intended not only to promote the cause of constitutional advance and secure essential rights for the citizen, but to defend the Danish nation and the Danish language against all insults and oppression, especially where it was hardest pressed in North Schleswig.[1] It would also disseminate information about the Nordic character of the Danes and deepen the belief of the people in their Scandinavian past. For Denmark, declared *Faedrelandet*, was not only a member of the West European cultural community. She belonged to Scandinavia as well by reason of her geography, past history, racial ties and common culture.

The new king was also aware of the significance of nationalism. Christian had been interested for many years in the position of the Danish language in Schleswig. He had conversed with Paulsen and accepted a copy of his pamphlet in 1832. In the following

[1] Bagge and Engelstoft, *op. cit.*, I, no. 235, pp. 340–2, 26 Nov. 1839.

year he had spoken in the *Statsraad* in support of Danish during the deliberations on the constitutional law of 1834.[1] He deprecated the germanisation of Schleswig and considered that Danish-speaking people had every right to the official use of their language. He proposed that Danish be used in court wherever Danish was used in church and school (i.e. in North Schleswig) and that proclamations from the Schleswig-Holstein government be issued in both languages in Schleswig. The proposals were shelved, for the old king and most of the high officials feared that any alteration of the *status quo* would arouse unwelcome controversy. Christian commented gloomily that the decision of the *Statsraad* meant the abandonment of Schleswig to germanization for a long time if not for ever.[2] The Danish awakening raised his hopes once more; he interceded with the king on behalf of P. C. Koch to secure permission for the publication of *Dannevirke* and he gave financial support to lending libraries in 1838. These actions did not pass unnoticed in the duchies. Falck, writing to Dahlmann in April 1840, openly expressed the fear that there was substance in the rumours that the king was 'Danish-minded' and hostile to the idea of a united Schleswig-Holstein.[3]

The rumours did less than justice to King Christian. He was certainly much more sympathetic to the Danish movement than King Frederik had ever been. But he never allowed his national preferences to dominate his political thinking. The North Schleswig problem was for him primarily a political and not a national problem. Christian perceived that the affinity between the Danish spoken in North Schleswig and in Denmark was a factor of the utmost political significance because it would strengthen the ties between Schleswig and Denmark—there was no stronger bond between peoples than a common tongue as the king appreciated. But this would not loosen the ties between Denmark and Holstein because the long association between the duchies was also a factor of political importance; it meant that if Schleswig stayed with Denmark, then so would Holstein. In short the preservation of the *Helstat* was his primary objective, the Danish spoken in Schleswig

[1] A. D. Jørgensen, *Kristian VIII og Nordslesvig*, pp. 59, 62.
[2] *Ibid.*, p. 64.
[3] Liepmann, *op. cit.*, p. 161.

was only a means to this end. King Christian was concerned only to preserve the Danish language, not to extend it because this would only endanger the delicate political balance between Schleswig and Denmark. The king expressly warned P. C. Koch that he must not increase tension between the two nationalities by using his new paper to attack the Germans; Koch's task was only to preserve that which was Danish, not to regain what was clearly German.[1]

King Christian was naturally pleased with the Schleswig estates' petition on the language question which he inherited on his accession to the throne. It gave him an opportunity which he was swift to seize. His officials were ordered to draft a directive immediately, giving effect to the changes requested by the estates. His eagerness to act in this matter and the method chosen may well have been influenced by a feeling that the mood of the Germans was already changing;[2] instead of submitting a draft law to the estates and enabling them to reconsider their request, King Christian decided in favour of a royal pronouncement, the language rescript of 14 May 1840. The rescript ordered the Schleswig-Holstein government to ensure that Danish was used in place of German for legal and administrative purposes in those areas where Danish was used in church and school, i.e. in North Schleswig. Those officials able to comply with this instruction should do so with effect from 1 January 1841. The Danish translations of royal ordinances and college patents would in future be accorded parity of esteem with the German texts. In the schools of North Schleswig teachers able to give tuition in German would be allowed to give three hours a week private tuition for payment to children whose parents requested it, but outside school hours. In future all teachers would be required to satisfy the local church officials, before appointment, that they possessed an adequate written and spoken knowledge of German. Tuition would then be given free of charge to those who desired it.

The rescript, more than any other event in those fateful years,

[1] Lauridsen, *op. cit.*, I, p. 208, P. C. Koch to C. Flor, 24 Nov. 1838, cf. p. 105, C. Flor to P. C. Koch, 3 Oct. 1837; p. 114, 7 Nov. 1837.

[2] A. S. Ørsted, *For den danske stats opretholdelse i dens helhed*, p. 265.

ensured that national animosity between German and Dane would thrust constitutional questions into the background of the political arena throughout the 1840's. In itself it was a modest document, for King Christian desired only to remedy the grievances of the North Schleswig Danes. Very wisely he had finally decided not to tackle the delicate problem of Central Schleswig, as the monster petition of 1838 had urged. Yet despite its moderation, the rescript caused considerable excitement in the towns of Schleswig, comparable, in the opinion of Storm, the member for Husum, to that caused by the rescript of 1813.[1] Falck was undoubtedly correct in maintaining that there was fairly general satisfaction if little enthusiasm for the rescript in the countryside of North Schleswig.[2] It was the small but vociferous German minority in the towns whose indignation knew no bounds in the summer of 1840. Falck and Olshausen welcomed the rescript as an overdue reform, but they were in a very small minority. More typical was C. Heiberg's denunciation of it in the *Kieler Korrespondenz Blatt* as a blatant attack on the nationality of Schleswig and a violation of the duchies' rights.[3] Even a more restrained observer, Heinrich Reventlow-Criminil, royal commissioner at the estates, said in his report to the king that the officials, far from creating intense public feeling in this matter, merely reflected a sentiment shared by all classes[4]—a comment which was probably true of the Germans in the towns and some of the farmers in South Schleswig.

The Germans regarded the rescript with grave suspicion because it appeared at a time when their fears of Danish ambitions were already growing. The Danish movement had been gaining ground in North Schleswig since 1839, certain Danish newspapers were adopting a hostile attitude towards the Germans in matters concerning the duchies, and some rather ominous developments were taking place in the Danish estates in 1840. When the Roskilde estates met in July, addresses were received from Lolland, Falster and Langelund requesting full financial powers for the

[1] *St. Z.*, Schleswig, 1840, I, p. 567.
[2] Liepmann, *op. cit.*, pp. 165–6, Falck to Adler, 11 Nov. 1840.
[3] 11 and 15 July 1840.
[4] Fabricius, *op. cit.*, p. 262.

united estates of Denmark and Schleswig. The royal commissioner, Ørsted, was sharply critical of the petitions, but could not prevent the acceptance by forty-four votes to twenty-three of a motion suggesting that financial matters might be discussed jointly by the three estates, although the majority denied that this would lead to the incorporation of Schleswig in Denmark. When the Viborg estates met in October they, too, were of the opinion that financial ties between the estates were desirable, as long as the independence of Schleswig was respected. Some members were prepared to go much further. A leading radical, J. P. With, told a correspondent that he and his friends were ready to petition for a common constitution for the three estates and had already approached some Schleswig members, winning over a number of them to this idea.[1] Seen against this general background the rescript assumed sinister proportions; it was interpreted by the Germans as proof positive that the new king was 'Danish-minded' and eager to play his part in transforming Schleswig into a Danish province.

The alarm of the Germans soon found expression when the Holstein estates met in the summer of 1840. The Holstein members were at last aroused out of their lethargic indifference towards Schleswig. In 1838 D'Aubert's motion for the union of the estates had been buried in committee. In 1840 it was accepted with alacrity by thirty-three votes to eight. During the debate Balemann, president of the estates, a moderate conservative and friend of Falck, declared that the time had come for Holstein to make its position clear, for there were those in Denmark who demanded the incorporation of Schleswig.[2] Neither he nor D'Aubert supposed that the government had designs on Schleswig. But it was undeniable that Danish liberals were stretching their arms out towards the duchy and had welcomed the rescript as a step towards the separation of Schleswig from Holstein.[3] It must be made clear to them that the river Kongeaa was not only a physical barrier between Denmark and the duchies, but a political and legal

[1] Bagge and Engelstoft, *op. cit.*, I, no. 294, pp. 440-1, J. P. With to J. F. Schouw, 7 July 1840.

[2] *St. Z.*, Holstein, 1840, pp. 102-3.

[3] *Ibid.*, pp. 87-8.

barrier as well. The veteran radical, Löck, warned the people of Schleswig that a union of the estates would be inconceivable if their estates favoured the introduction of a foreign language into the duchy, because members from Holstein could not be expected to speak Danish in a united estates.[1] Perhaps this threat had some influence on the proceedings in Schleswig later in the year although most members in Itzehoe did not take it too seriously. There seemed no need to worry about what they regarded, significantly, as a 'Danish dialect still spoken in part of Schleswig'. No one had used it in the Schleswig estates in the past or seemed likely to do so in the future.

When the Schleswig estates met in the autumn vigorous opposition to the rescript could be anticipated. The estates lived up to expectations. By an overwhelming majority they reversed their previous decision and petitioned for the suspension of the rescript. This was a momentous event, a real turning-point in the history of Schleswig and of the *Helstat*, the effects of which were felt for many decades.

There were sound reasons for discussing the rescript as members felt that clarification was required on a number of points. It was not clear whether lawyers were affected by the order or not, although expressly excluded in the 1838 petition. The rescript ordered the immediate use of Danish by all officials, whereas the petitioners had expected it to be used immediately only by those able to do so, future vacancies being filled by officials having a knowledge of the language. The position of those few officials unable to speak Danish remained obscure. Nor was it clear whether litigants would be permitted a choice of languages. Finally, it might be argued that the king should have submitted a draft law to the estates, instead of announcing the changes in a royal proclamation.

It was quickly apparent that T. Steenholdt, who formally moved the suspension of the rescript, was concerned much less with textual ambiguities and with the alleged impracticability of the measure, than with the political implications he feared lay behind the Danish movement.[2] A North Schleswig member,

[1] *Ibid.*, p. 560.

[2] *St. Z.*, Schleswig, 1840, I, p. 38.

Steenholdt had supported Nis Lorenzen's motion in 1838, but since then had come round to the view that the petitions requesting these changes were entirely the work of Danish agitators working for *Dannevirke*.[1] There was, he said, neither need nor desire for change in North Schleswig. The rescript would adversely affect the status of German, a knowledge of which was indispensable for commercial transactions with the south. It was also regarded as a first step towards incorporation in Denmark, an eventuality which he and his electors regarded as a grave misfortune to be avoided at all costs. These fears were shared by other members. Storm observed that people feared that Danish propaganda was favourably received in most exalted circles. The hasty publication of the rescript was not calculated to allay such fears.[2] It was significant that those members mainly responsible for the committee report, Storm, J. G. Gülich and the duke of Augustenburg, prefaced their findings with a long historical preamble, emphasizing the connection between recent developments and the attempts made after 1807 and in 1816 to encourage the use of Danish in the duchies;[3] the Danish movement, springing into prominence after Lehmann's speech to the Press Society, was merely a new form of the age-old Danish ambition to annex Schleswig and, like earlier attempts, was completely dependent on support from Denmark.

It was a great misfortune that fear of the Danish movement loomed so large in members' minds in 1840, because it made them underestimate the need for change which many had recognized in a calmer frame of mind two years previously. It was certain, as Falck insisted on the basis of his personal experience, that the demand for change was genuine, not the fabrication of Danish agents.[4] Even Gottfriedsen, member for Sønderborg in place of Peter Lorenzen and an opponent of the rescript, admitted that, in his work as notary in his native Haderslev *Amt*, he used only Danish when drafting wills and inventories.[5] Small wonder that

[1] He had been alarmed by Nis Hanssen's letter inviting him to organize petitions for the union of the three estates. Max Rasch, *Thies Hansen Steenholdt 1784–1850*, pp. 183–4.

[2] *St. Z.*, Schleswig, 1840, p. 567.

[3] *Ibid.*, II, *Beilagenheft*, pp. 292–300.

[4] *Ibid.*, I, p. 521.

[5] *Ibid.*, I, p. 526.

the royal commissioner, Count Heinrich Reventlow-Criminil, a supporter of the rescript, inferred from Gottfriedsen's remarks that the people would use Danish exclusively in jurisprudence, given the opportunity.[1]

With considerable justification the minority, who supported the rescript, maintained that their opponents had failed to consult the masses of the people who welcomed the changes. 'Only the shepherds, the officials, were asked their opinion, not the flock, the people,' commented P. Nielsen bitterly.[2] One of their leading opponents, Gülich, even admitted that he knew little of conditions in North Schleswig and could not say whether the people wanted Danish or not.[3] He opposed the rescript on the basis of inquiries amongst educated people in his constituency, Åbenraa. Naturally he had not bothered to interview uneducated people, he added, for their opinions did not matter. As for the eleven petitions from North Schleswig denying the need for any change, Nis Lorenzen soon revealed their unrepresentative character.[4] He estimated that these petitions, all written in meticulous official German, were signed by no more than two hundred farmers in all and some of these could be discounted, especially from Tønder, Åbenraa and Løgumkloster, where German was used in church and school.

The main argument used by opponents of the rescript was significant. They felt that the majority of 1838 had failed to examine the legal aspect of the question thoroughly, but had allowed themselves to be guided by an indeterminate instinct for natural justice. Since then many members had realized their error and the general public had expressed, in no uncertain manner, its fear that the ancient legal framework of Schleswig would be endangered by the rescript. Humanitarian and utilitarian considerations alike must be subordinated to the infinitely more important consideration that the duchy had a duty to safeguard its independence by preserving the unity of the legal system. Drohse declared bluntly that, far from the legal system being adjusted to serve the needs of the subjects, the latter must conform to the language and laws of their country.[5] In effect the majority was insisting on the need

[1] *Ibid.*, I, p. 528. [2] *Ibid.*, I, p. 39. [3] *Ibid.*, I, p. 529.
[4] *Ibid.*, I, p. 566. [5] *Ibid.*, I, p. 573.

for preserving intact the German superstructure of the duchies, because it was regarded as an essential guarantee of their independence. The natural right of the individual to use his mother tongue must be subordinated to this need in the interests of national survival. The well-being of the duchies, as Gülich put it, was at least as important as the wishes of the people.[1] In short, some of the illiberal implications of the national idea were at last beginning to emerge on the German side.

The duke of Augustenburg, one of the leading opponents of the rescript, argued that people in one geographical area have need of a common tongue. In the case of the duchies, over and above the local dialects, educated people possessed a common tongue in German. This language was a vehicle for German culture, to which all aspired, and it must therefore be used exclusively in legal matters as it was in the university and other institutions.[2] Gottfriedsen and H. C. Jensen also insisted that German be retained in the courts because the laws were German. If Danish was introduced it would lead to the introduction of Danish officials and the exclusion of German lawyers from South Schleswig. This would endanger the nationality of Schleswig, for in time Danish law would replace German law as the Danish language could not adequately express German legal concepts. The duchy would then be as good as incorporated in Denmark.[3]

In reply to these points the minority argued with considerable force that the use of a second language in litigation would not have the disastrous effects feared by their opponents.[4] After all, German was not the only official language in Schleswig; was not Danish used in many churches and schools and in many legal matters? In any case, the laws of Schleswig were not German laws but the Danish *Jydske Lov* translated into German. The minority admitted that their opponents were not seeking to forbid absolutely the use of Danish in court, but that was not enough. It was intolerable for a people to be dependent on the goodwill of officials for the use of their native tongue; in any civilized community this was generally recognized as a natural right. The

[1] *St. Z.*, Schleswig, 1840, I, p. 529.
[2] *Ibid.*, I, p. 539.
[3] *Ibid.*, I, pp. 526–8, 570.
[4] *Ibid.*, II, *Beilagenheft*, pp. 727–36.

minority was quite prepared to defend the right of Frisians and Low Germans to use their own languages in court, and they expected similar treatment for the Danish language. They indignantly rejected their opponents' undemocratic argument that, as only a very few litigants had no knowledge of German, changes in the existing system were hardly justifiable.

The opponents of the rescript repeated the argument used in 1838, namely, that the language spoken in North Schleswig was not High Danish but a dialect composed of Low German and Low Danish.[1] In these circumstances the use of High Danish in court would be a pointless complication; it would be equally unintelligible to the North Schleswig litigants and to the German lawyers. To which the minority replied that there was nothing unusual in the use of a Danish dialect in North Schleswig—there were always discrepancies between written and spoken languages. But it was arguable that the people of North Schleswig would understand High Danish at least as well, if not better, than High German. For, as the royal commissioner observed, people who understand High Danish in church and school will surely understand it in court?[2] If they understood it in Jylland, where according to some members the dialect deviated more from High Danish than that spoken south of the Kongeaa, there would be no difficulty in North Schleswig. The minority felt that their opponents were far too preoccupied with the difficulties which German officials might experience and not sufficiently interested in the wishes of the people. If German officials found it difficult to learn Danish—a task surely not beyond the ability of a cultured man—then the people of North Schleswig would not be averse to seeing official posts occupied by natives, who did not experience these difficulties. But if the Germans refused to recognize their language, 'the chief mark of nationality', North Schleswig would lose confidence in the judges and courts. Worse still, Danish might be driven out of their churches and schools—for there were deep-rooted fears on the Danish as well as the German side in 1840. The minority openly stated their belief that many Germans in the duchy (if not in the estates) considered the complete extirpation

[1] *Ibid.*, II, pp. 306–7.

[2] *Ibid.*, I, p. 525.

of Danish a desirable objective. The rescript had been welcomed in North Schleswig as a first step towards the reversal of the germanization process, for only if Danish was used for legal and administrative purposes could a proper balance be preserved between German and Dane.

Not that the minority had much sympathy for Danish activity in Schleswig. It was indeed a striking testimony to the strength of local patriotism in Schleswig that the minority—the *Siebengestirn*[1] as the Germans called the five North Schleswig members, supported by the two Flensburg members—were as opposed to Professor Flor as they were to the duke of Augustenburg. 'The minority', these members declared, 'have stated more than once and repeat again, that the Danish-speaking people of Schleswig desire only their language and nothing else and that, although they are Danish by nationality, nevertheless they belong politically to Schleswig; they desire no other connection with the kingdom than the existing one, they do not want Danish law or the Danish legal system, but they do desire alterations and improvements in the present legal system.' [2]

The debate ended in a victory for the opponents of the rescript. By thirty-three votes to nine they accepted Steenholdt's motion for its suspension.[3] It was decided by twenty-two votes—with the consent of the North Schleswig members be it noted—to retain that part of the rescript providing for schooling in German, although disappointment was expressed that it was to be given outside school hours. A strong minority of twenty wished to suspend even this part of the rescript, arguing that private tuition would make German an unpopular subject with children, whose natural desire after school hours would be for relaxation. These members suggested that the king order those schools in North Schleswig which were not already giving some German instruction, to do so where possible.

The decision of the Schleswig estates was a crucial one because,

[1] Seven star constellation or *Syvstjerne* (Danish).

[2] *St. Z.*, Schleswig, II, *Beilagenheft*, 1840, p. 736.

[3] The *Siebengestirn* was supported on this occasion by two Germans, Boysen and Jaspersen—'*ni trofaste*', as the Danes called them.

although there was little chance of the king bowing to their wishes, it implied that the Germans were unwilling to concede parity of esteem to a language spoken or understood in dialect form by a large part of the duchy. Allowance must be made for the considerable apprehension of the Germans—for which incautious Danish newspapers and agitators were to blame—and for the fact that the duke of Augustenburg exploited this issue in his own dynastic interests. But it was undoubtedly a severe blow to peaceful coexistence between German and Dane upon which the *Helstat* rested. The lack of tactical sense displayed by the Germans could not fail to confirm the growing feeling in North Schleswig that there were people anxious to extirpate the Danish language. The partition of 1920 lay implicit in the refusal of the Germans to concede parity of esteem. Had the Germans been willing to make sacrifices in North Schleswig, they could almost certainly have retarded the progress of the Danish movement—for the oppositional attitude of many North Schleswig members in the estates was motivated primarily by dislike of officialdom, not by any hatred of Germans. At a time when national sentiment was stirring north and south of the Kongeaa, the tactless decision of the Schleswig estates threatened to transform local friction between German officials and Danish farmers into a national conflict between German and Dane.

That does not mean that the Germans were worse than other peoples in this respect. A few years later the Danes behaved in exactly the same fashion when facing an analogous situation in the Faroe islands, for the illiberal implications of the national idea were universal in their application. The Danish refusal to allow the Faroese people to use their own language in church and school was as much a violation of natural right as the German refusal to concede parity of esteem to Danish. Originally ruled from Norway, the Faroe islands had been subjected to Danish influences at the time of the Reformation. The Danish language had replaced Icelandic in church and in the courts and the island was now administered almost exclusively by Danish officials. In 1844 the Roskilde estates decided to substitute Danish for Faroese as the medium of instruction in the schools—a much more radical step than that proposed by Petersen for North Schleswig. During the debate at Roskilde familiar arguments appeared to justify this action; Faroese was only a mixture of Icelandic and Danish, it was not worth preserving and as there was no written Faroese language it could not be a medium of instruction in schools or a subject of tuition. No one could deny that the superstructure of the Faroe islands was Danish, Danish was the language of church and school and of educated people, nearly everyone had some knowledge of Danish and all regarded it as a superior cultural medium. These were all old friends in a new setting. It was finally agreed to permit the use of Faroese in schools alongside Danish, but only as an interim measure until parents were able to teach their children Danish. Was this very different, asked Svend Grundvig, from the attitude of the Germans towards the teaching of Danish in Schleswig?[1]

Before the estates dispersed there was further evidence of growing animosity between German and Dane during the debate on Storm's motion for the abolition of the Danish translation of the *Ständezeitung*.

The Germans were easily able to show that low sales figures made continued publication of this paper uneconomical. Only six copies had been sold in 1838 and fourteen in 1840, compared with several hundreds of the German paper. This discrepancy was not really surprising, remarked Gülich, because the educated classes interested in politics were either German or German-speaking.[2] The duke of Augustenburg added that seven of the fourteen Danish copies sold in 1840 had been bought by subscribers with a knowledge of German. On this basis one might as well publish a French version, provided half a dozen Frenchmen were resident in the duchy.[3] On the other hand, there is no doubt that even the German paper ran at a loss despite its circulation; the North Schleswig members suggested, quite rightly, that the real reason for the small circulation of the Danish paper was the thrift of local farmers who preferred to club together to buy one copy, which

[1] *Dansken paa Faroerne Sidestykke til Tysken i Slesvig*, Kjøbenhavn, 1845.
[2] *St. Z.*, Schleswig, 1840, I, p. 47.
[3] *Ibid.*, I, p. 710.

then circulated in the village, rather than procure copies individually as wealthy German townsfolk did.

But the Germans did not confine themselves to arguments based on sales statistics. They saw an opportunity to defend the German superstructure of Schleswig, by denying that there was any specific obligation under the 1834 law to publish the proceedings of the estates in two languages simply because the North Schleswig population knew no German. 'The Schleswig estates', stated the committee report, 'are German in organization, the debates are conducted in German and all the work of the estates is effected in German. Therefore, only the German paper can be the official paper and only that paper can be regarded as essential to the functioning of provincial estates.' [1] However desirable it was that the Danish-speaking people of Schleswig should understand the debates, the Germans would not admit that they had any rights in this matter. Storm argued that, as the proceedings were conducted in German, a knowledge of that language was essential for those wishing to follow the debates. This applied, he added significantly, to members as well as to electors.[2] The duke of Augustenburg admitted that there could be no question of compelling electors to elect members possessing a knowledge of German; but it was clearly in their interests to do so, because members were not there to represent parochial interests but to take part in debates on matters of general significance, which required a knowledge of the common language, German.[3] The Germans felt that people who read the Danish paper could read the German one as well, and even those who had no German need not be deprived of information, for had not *Dannevirke* recently announced its intention of publishing the most important debates?

The *Siebengestirn*, led since Peter Lorenzen's resignation by Nis Lorenzen, counter-attacked vigorously.[4] They insisted that half the duchy spoke nothing but Danish and had a right to know what went on in the estates. The royal commissioner upheld them in their contention that to comply with the intentions of the 1834 law publication in both languages was necessary. As long as two

[1] *Ibid.*, II, *Beilagenheft*, p. 402.
[2] *Ibid.*, I, pp. 707–8.
[3] *Ibid.*, I, p. 711.
[4] *Ibid.*, II, *Beilagenheft*, pp. 404–8.

versions were published Danish speakers could obtain the information they required. But if only the German version was published, difficulties would arise. Electors in Danish-speaking areas would naturally request their members to speak Danish in the estates so that their speeches would appear in that language in the paper. Members had a right to have their speeches published in the original language, but had never insisted on this as long as proceedings were published in both languages. But they would be obliged to insist on their rights if only one version appeared. However good their German might be, their electors would insist on Danish speeches. If Storm's motion was carried and 'the stamp of contempt set on our language', the Germans could be quite sure that the North Schleswig members, many of whom had always found German a strain, would use only their native Danish in the estates. That this was no idle boast was made clear by Nis Lorenzen's use of Danish earlier in the debate, after a visit from D. G. Monrad.[1] Despite the warning the Germans decided by thirty-two votes to seven to publish the Danish version of the *Ständezeitung* only if fifty subscribers requested copies. On this ominous note a most eventful session of the Schleswig estates came to an end.

[1] H. Jensen, *De danske Staenderforsamlingers Historie*, II, p. 288.

VIII

The beginning of the national conflict, 1842

THE *Landespartei* had been thrown into a state of complete confusion by the forward march of events since 1838. The inevitable differences in political outlook between conservative and liberal revealed in 1838, had deepened with the passage of the years. As it became increasingly clear that the *Landesrechte* were incapable of sustaining liberal demands for a modern constitution, dissatisfied radicals followed Olshausen and Peter Lorenzen out of the party. The left wing was weakened and thrown into a state of dispondency by these defections. Even those who remained in the party were hard pressed by the relentless logic of the New Holsteiner and compelled, like W. H. Beseler, to reinterpret the *Landesrechte* in a fashion displeasing to the conservative wing of the party. It seemed fair to assume, in the first half of 1840, that the *Landespartei* was on the eve of dissolution.

But the process of disintegration was arrested by a diagonally-opposed tendency operating to preserve the unity of the party. The strength of the party lay basically in an instinctive and deeply-rooted loyalty to Schleswig-Holstein, and a determination to preserve the autonomous position of the duchies inside the *Helstat*. A challenge to their fundamental loyalties was the one eventuality capable of alerting all shades of opinion in the *Landespartei*. The Danish movement in Schleswig, the rescript and the relentless attacks of the New Holsteiner seemed to represent just such a challenge to the unity and German character of the duchies. The result was that growing apprehension about Danish intentions began to overshadow differences between conservative and liberal especially in Schleswig. Significant changes in the texture of the party reflected this new preoccupation with national questions. By

1840 the Duke of Augustenburg had emerged as the dominant figure in Schleswig, Falck's influence was rapidly waning and last, but by no means least, a new national liberal group appeared in the Schleswig estates.

Wilhelm Hartwig Beseler exemplified the new national liberal attitude soon to become the dominant political posture south of the Elbe. A native of Schleswig, Beseler studied law at Heidelberg and Kiel universities in the 1820's. In 1828 he settled in Schleswig Town, where he soon built up a flourishing legal practice. An ex-*Burschenschaftler*, he was an enthusiastic supporter of U. J. Lornsen, whom he met during the latter's abortive tour of Schleswig in November 1830 and in whose defence he wrote his first political pamphlet.[1] This was a turning point in his life, for ever after he remained a devoted admirer of Lornsen, Beseler's 'court of final appeal' in political questions. He played no active part in the politics of the 1830's, but by 1840 was writing regularly for the *Itzehoer Wochenblatt*. This paper, founded in 1817, had replaced the *Kieler Korrespondenz Blatt* as the semi-official organ of the *Landespartei* and was rapidly becoming the most important political journal in the duchies. It was in the columns of this paper that Beseler launched bitter attacks on the New Holsteiner in 1840 and 1841. By now he had become a political figure of some importance and secured election as member for Tønder in 1841.

Beseler, like Olshausen, appreciated the tremendous power behind the national sentiment stirring in the Germany of 1840. Like Olshausen he was bitterly critical of the local patriots who saw no further than the confines of the duchies, remaining blissfully ignorant of the onset of a new age. But there their agreement ended. For Olshausen was a democrat who believed that the national future of Schleswig-Holstein must be determined solely in accordance with the wishes of the people. Holstein presented no problem in this respect, but the growth of the Danish movement in Schleswig proved that this duchy was nationally divided. To speak of the 'unity' of 'Schleswig-Holstein', as the *Landespartei* did,

[1] *Beleuchtung der Broschüre betitelt: Einige Worte über die Schrift des Herrn Canzleiraths Lornsen über das Verfassungswerk in Schleswig-Holstein*, Leipzig, 1830.

was pretentious nonsense. In these circumstances the only democratic solution for Schleswig was partition.

The national liberal answer to Olshausen was of crucial importance for Schleswig-Holsteinism for decades to come. At first sight, it certainly seemed as if the principle of nationality was incompatible with the thesis of a united Schleswig-Holstein; in the north the Eiderdanes claimed that the only national solution was the abandonment of Holstein and the incorporation of Schleswig in Denmark, while in the south the New Holsteiner maintained that it was necessary to abandon Schleswig in order to secure the immediate entry of Holstein into the Confederation. The national liberals produced a new variant, or rather they boldly reasserted the old belief that not only Holstein, but the whole of Schleswig as well was 'nationally' German by virtue of its German superstructure. They rescued the *Landespartei* from indecision and restored its badly shaken faith in the *Landesrechte* by breathing a new national spirit into the traditional local patriotism on which the party was based. They were the most bitter opponents of the Danish movement and of the rescript, adamantly resisting all attempts to give Danish equality of status with German inside or outside of the estates; as the storm clouds gathered in the north and the hour of national decision drew nigh, the national liberals insisted that any alteration of the German superstructure would automatically weaken the defence mechanism of the duchies and endanger its independence. It is true that Beseler, driven into a corner by Olshausen in 1840, admitted that if North Schleswig wished to become part of Denmark, partition was the only practical solution.[1] But this admission, as well as his formal proposal in 1842 that Haderslev *Amt* be ceded to Denmark, was only a tactical manœuvre; it was designed to obviate the necessity for the application of the principle of self-determination, by compelling North Schleswig to make up its mind and enter the Confederation at once. The national liberals were utterly opposed to the loss of any part of Schleswig-Holstein; '*Das ganze Schleswig-Holstein soll es sein*' might well have been their watchword.[2] Partition

[1] *Itzehoer Wochenblatt*, nos. 41 and 47, 1840.

[2] 'Nothing less than the whole of Schleswig-Holstein.'

appealed as little to them as to the Eiderdanes, because the claims of Eiderdane and German national liberal alike rested primarily on historical traditions and territorial ambition, not on the will of the people. History, not the democratic right of self-determination, had the last word in Schleswig. The national political attitudes north and south of the Kongeaa illustrate once again the important political truth that liberal and national ideas become incompatible beyond a certain point, and that when this point is reached liberal principle is frequently sacrificed in the interests of national survival, as U. J. Lornsen had prophesied a decade before. National sentiment did not dissolve the old association between the duchies as Olshausen expected; reinterpreted by German national liberals, it infused a new and potent ideological content into old historical claims.

It was significant that national liberals played a leading role in resisting the enforcement of the rescript. As reports from the *Schleswig-holsteinische Kanzlei* revealed that very few of the forty officials concerned knew no Danish, the king decided that the rescript must come into force on 1 January 1841. Some lawyers determined to prevent this by refusing to use Danish in court. The strike was successful. In February 1841 lawyers in North Schleswig were permitted to continue using German in court if they wished. In March the *Obergericht* lawyers, organized by Beseler, declined to handle Danish documents in cases referred to them from the lower courts. Another royal concession followed, permitting the optional use of German in contracts and other legal documents. This resistance not only reduced the effectiveness of the rescript,[1] but it also reflected the more realistic note of politics in the 1840's. Unlike Falck and his colleagues twenty years before, the liberals of the 1840's were not satisfied with words or inhibited by a sense of loyalty to the crown. They were perfectly prepared to resort to direct action to sabotage policies of which they disapproved.

[1] It was enforced most thoroughly in Haderslev *Amt*, in most of Åbenraa and Sønderborg *Amter*, but was ignored in Tønder *Amt*. F. Gribsvad, *Hvad fortaeller retsprotokollerne om retsproget i Nordslesvig?* in *Afhandlinger tilegnede arkivmandar og historikeren Rigsarkivar Dr. A. Linvald*, København, 1956, p. 128.

The 1841 elections confirmed the growing importance of national liberalism. There was as yet little sign of it in Holstein but in Schleswig the election of Beseler, Tiedemann and Gülich heralded the entry of a sharper, more aggressive national tone into the political life of the duchy. In North Schleswig the Danish position was also strengthened by the election of Peter Lorenzen for Sønderborg. He soon proved himself an intrepid and able leader of the *Siebengestirn*, which now consisted of Posselt, Petersen, Nis Lorenzen and Jepsen supported by the two Flensburg members, Jensen and Nielsen; Steenholdt had gravitated into the German camp and Steffens, the Duke of Augustenburg's *protégé*, had replaced Bonefeld for Sundeved and Als. This does not mean that the *Siebengestirn* had become a Danish national party. The members of the *Siebengestirn* were Danish only in the sense that they shared in the Danish cultural heritage and fought for parity of esteem for their language. They were not Eiderdanes but natives of Schleswig, anxious to defend their native soil against both Eiderdanes and German nationalists. True, they had opposed Henningsen's motion for the union of the estates in 1840 but largely as a protest against the suspension of the rescript. It is clear from the debate that the people of North Schleswig did not desire to end the association with Holstein, but only to avoid changes in the *status quo*—such as the inclusion of Schleswig in the Confederation—for which they saw no need.[1] They were equally opposed to forcible incorporation in Denmark, although they agreed with Peter Lorenzen that when Denmark obtained a constitution the Schleswig people would voluntarily associate with the Danes to share in this freedom.

In Denmark, as well as in Germany, national questions began to preoccupy the people at the beginning of the 1840's. In May 1842 Orla Lehmann's historic Eiderdane speech heralded the emergence of Danish national liberalism as a considerable political force.

Previously Lehmann, like Olshausen, had believed that the national future of Schleswig was a matter for the people of Schleswig to settle. Naturally he expected a decision favourable to Denmark. Once the Holstein aristocracy, Lehmann's *bête noire*, had

[1] *St. Z.*, Schleswig, 1840, pp. 251–3, 255–6.

ceased to interfere in Schleswig and the Danes were able to explain their case without hindrance, the scales would fall from the people's eyes and they would see that their best interests would be served by association with Denmark, from whom a democratic constitution could confidently be expected.

By 1840 Lehmann's attitude was changing. He now assumed that Schleswig was completely Danish in character; not only was Danish spoken in half the duchy—which was probably true—but even South Schleswig was not entirely German or lost irrevocably to Denmark in his opinion. No longer was Lehmann thinking exclusively in terms of a people's natural right to use their native tongue and determine their own political future. He began to speak of the will of the Danish people to hold on to Schleswig and of the need for Denmark to possess the Eider frontier. He could still have the best of both worlds in December 1840, for he believed that a democratic decision by the Schleswig people would secure this frontier for Denmark, and as long as the will of the Schleswig people remained in the centre of his political thinking, he had not arrived at the Eiderdane position.

In May 1842 he delivered his first 'Eiderdane' speech at a meeting in Copenhagen held to celebrate the establishment of the estates eight years before.[1] What is the Danish fatherland? he asked. Did it extend to the Eider, to the Schlei or only to the Kongeaa? He left his audience in no doubt as to the answer. The Danish frontier was the Eider river. He flatly rejected the idea of a partition of Schleswig, a possibility which he, like Olshausen and Peter Lorenzen, had toyed with in the past. Schleswig must choose between Denmark and Germany. No one denied that Holstein was part of Germany. As for the old association between Schleswig and Holstein, that was purely aristocratic in nature and had no political significance. The Eider was obviously the frontier between Germany and Denmark and, as an independent Schleswig was an anomaly which did not exist in international law, Schleswig must be part of Denmark. Lehmann still believed that the Schleswig people would be repelled by 'aristocratic' Holstein and would welcome association with 'democratic' Scandinavia; but the im-

[1] A. Thørsoe, *Den danske Stats Historie*, etc., pp. 488–91.

portant point was that the national frontier of Schleswig was no longer dependent on the democratic right of the people to decide their own future. The Eider frontier was an indispensable requirement for the Danish state, justified by history, by international law, by an identity of material interest between Schleswig and Denmark, by a common succession and last, but by no means least, by the military needs of the Danish state. The *Helstat* could still continue in being, for Lehmann did not exclude the possibility of association between Holstein and the Danish state. But he drew a sharp distinction between dynastic unity of this kind and national unity which made Schleswig an integral part of Denmark.

The Eiderdanes, like the German national liberals, were exploiting national sentiment to reinforce traditional claims to Schleswig. They could hardly deny that two distinct national groups lived in the duchy although they disagreed about the numerical strength of these groups. But neither thought that the existence of these groups invalidated their claims to the whole duchy. They both maintained either that the minority shared their point of view, or else that it was in the best interests of the minority to form part of another state. The implication was obvious enough; Eiderdanes and German nationalists were denying the democratic right of self-determination to these minorities because they wished to retain intact an area historically associated with their own national group. Danes and Germans were equally guilty of sacrificing liberal principle in the interests of what they considered to be national survival.

Lehmann gained considerable notoriety in the duchies after his speech in Copenhagen because of the strong terms in which he referred to the *Landespartei* and to the *Admiralstaat* project. In the 1840's there was talk in Germany of using Holland or Denmark as a base for a future German navy. In the *Augsburger Allgemeine Zeitung* a writer suggested that Denmark join the German Confederation as an *Admiralstaat*, so that when Germany was united her merchant navy might be protected by the Danish fleet. The writer believed that Denmark stood to gain under this arrangement, because her pseudo-independence could only survive so long as it suited the Great Powers to respect it. Also, naval costs were heavy burdens for small powers and in the *Zollverein* markets could be found for Danish agrarian produce. If the Danes were still unconvinced, then they should realize that Germany was growing in strength and that it was clearly in Danish interests to join in a common navy. Lehmann vigorously rejected the project. He had the authors of the *Admiralstaat* as well as the *Landespartei* in mind, when he remarked that Denmark to the Eider was the Danish demand and that the Danes 'were ready to defend our old Dannevirke against both the treasonable cries of the Nordelbinger and all sea-sick German bird catchers, lusting for conquest. If it is necessary we will inscribe on their backs with our swords the bloody proof that Denmark will not have it so.' [1]

Lehmann's speech in May 1842 contained the essence of Danish national liberalism. A year previously, in the spring of 1841, the essentials of the German case had been restated when U. J. Lornsen's last will and political testament was published by Georg Beseler, W. Beseler's brother.[2] In *Die Unionsverfassung Dänemarks und Schleswig-Holsteins* the prophet of Schleswig-Holsteinism reasserted, in classic form, the demand that the duchies be given a common constitution and be accorded the status of an independent state, the grand duchy of Nordalbingien, bound only by dynastic ties to Denmark. This voice from the grave came at the psychologically correct moment for national liberalism. It provided the Germans with a clear, concise and up-to-date exposition of their case, decked out in the language of the *Landesrechte* to which Lornsen had paid special attention after 1830, feeling that the people of Schleswig-Holstein would accept his case more readily if he found historical justification for it.[3]

Both Eiderdanes and German national liberals were prepared to preserve the external framework of the *Helstat*—for the time being at any rate—always provided that the balance of power was altered in their favour internally. Yet the seeds of an inevitable

[1] A. Thørsoe, *Den danske Stats Historie*, etc., p. 491.

[2] *Die Unionsverfassung Dänemarks und Schleswig-Holsteins; eine geschichtliche staatsrechtliche und politische Erörterung von Uwe Lornsen.*

[3] Pauls, *op. cit.*, pp. 101–3, U. Lornsen to F. Hegewisch, May 1832.

conflict were already present in the Danish demand for '*Danmark til Ejderen*'[1] and the German demand for an independent Schleswig-Holstein. For even if Schleswig was allowed a good deal of local autonomy when united with Denmark, this would still be incompatible with the German concept of the duchy as an integral part of the Schleswig-Holstein state. Contemporaries, as usual, did not feel that a conflict was inevitable. There was some justification for this complacency, for the excitement aroused by the rescript had died down by the end of 1841, and on the eve of the fateful meeting of the Schleswig estates in 1842 a much quieter political atmosphere prevailed.

One important factor contributing to the relaxation of tension was the policy of the new king. Christian was as concerned as his late cousin had been to preserve the *Helstat*. But, unlike his predecessor, King Christian was a gifted and intelligent humanitarian, an enlightened conservative aware of new social forces stirring in Europe and perceptive enough to see the need for flexibility in meeting the liberal challenge of the age. Change was essential for the survival of the state. But what kind of change? King Christian was quite unprepared to make political changes of the kind demanded by the younger generation of Danish and German liberal. But he was a hard-working autocrat, with a real zest for the prosaic business of state, eager to deal with the arrears of work left by King Frederik and sweep away the accumulated lumber of centuries. With an able minister, A. S. Ørsted, behind him, Christian determined to win the respect and loyalty of his subjects by transforming the antiquated and cumbersome *Helstat* into a unitary centralized state. His autocracy would at least be efficient, well-run and attuned to the needs of a new age. These aspirations had some bearing on the improved political atmosphere in 1842, because the majority of King Christian's subjects were uninterested in politics. In Denmark Lehmann had relatively few supporters outside the towns, while in the duchies ordinary people were much less perturbed by the rescript than proceedings in the estates might lead one to suppose. Loyalty to the crown was still a powerful soporific and it was a reasonable assumption that most of

[1] 'Denmark down to the Eider.'

King Christian's subjects would accept with gratitude the material benefits which this able administrator intended to confer on them. If he succeeded in his objective, radicalism would be isolated and neutralized, starved of that mass support without which it could not become a serious political danger to the crown.

He set about his task of modernizing and centralizing the administrative structure of the *Helstat* with zest. Attempts were made to break down the old-fashioned prejudice of the officials against the modern departmental system of government as opposed to the collegial system. Encouragement was given to the modernization of agriculture, state expenditure was reduced and revenue collection improved. To draw closer the component parts of the state, communications were improved, a common road policy was devised, and the building of railways was encouraged with the construction of lines between Flensburg and Husum and Kiel and Altona. Reform of the penal code was taken in hand and in 1842 a long overdue re-organization of the army and navy commenced. As a result of this reform historic regiments in the duchies were dissolved and Schleswig-Holstein battalions were sent to Denmark on garrison duty. In this way the old demarcation line between the duchies and Denmark in military matters was eliminated. This was an important reform, because improved organization and the amalgamation of military units strengthened the most important physical weapon at the disposal of autocracies in the early nineteenth century.

It was perhaps rather surprising that these radical military changes aroused little adverse comment in the duchies. That the changes were accomplished with ease was a first fruit of the appointments to high office made at the beginning of 1842; King Christian desired to conciliate opinion in the duchies and turned to his natural allies, the conservatives, who were as opposed to radicalism and as concerned about the preservation of the *Helstat* as he was. That was the reason for the Prince of Noer's appointment to the *Statthalterschaft* and to the post of general officer commanding in Schleswig-Holstein, and of the Holstein brothers, Josef and Heinrich Reventlow-Criminil, to the posts of president of the *Schleswig-holsteinische Kanzlei* and foreign minister respectively. It is true that the prince was suspicious and only accepted his appointment when reassured by King Christian that the relationship between the duchies and Denmark would not be altered. The appointments were welcomed in the duchies, doing much to reassure the Germans that the king's intentions were above suspicion, and that the rescript was not, as they had feared, the first of a series of measures designed to incorporate Schleswig in Denmark. The appointments were tangible proof that the king was a respectable conservative quite out of sympathy with tiresome demagogues like Lehmann.

King Christian had no reason to fear any repetition of the unpleasantness of 1840. Had he not recently made considerable concessions to German lawyers in North Schleswig? He could surely rely on his conservative friends, with their vested interest in social order, to understand that national animosities would only set German against Dane, shake the foundations of the *Helstat* and—worse still—play into the hands of radicals. For his part, King Christian was always careful to observe strict impartiality towards his German and Danish subjects. He was not a 'national' king despite his interest in North Schleswig. As explained earlier, his Danish sympathies were always subordinated to the political task of preserving the *Helstat* by strengthening the ties between Schleswig and Denmark, and thus, via Schleswig, between Holstein and Denmark. It was a source of encouragement to him and a justification of his policy that interest in the troublesome language question was generally declining in the summer of 1841.

King Christian might have been one of the most honoured kings in the history of Denmark. As the creator of a modernized autocracy, run efficiently and impartially in the interests of Dane and German alike, he might well have won the gratitude and loyalty of the overwhelming mass of his subjects and delayed the disruption of the *Helstat* for generations. Unfortunately for King Christian the 1840's were not as uneventful as the previous decade had been. If only King Frederik had possessed the vigour and insight of his successor he could have done much to preserve the *Helstat* in the 1820's and 1830's, as he had done (if only nominally) in the late eighteenth century under the able direction of A. P.

Bernstorff. King Christian's reforms came too late because it was not in his power to guarantee the peaceful political conditions essential for the success of his experiment. What was the alternative? Had he accepted the logic of nationalism he might perhaps have transformed the *Helstat* into two nationally homogeneous states, united only in the person of the ruler. Such a policy was much too daring for a middle-aged sovereign who had witnessed the loss of Norway in his youth and felt that the preservation of the state was a sacred obligation. Enlightened absolutism seemed the safest policy. That it failed was not his fault, but rather his misfortune.

When the Holstein estates met in the summer of 1842 their attitude to certain government proposals suggested that King Christian's policy was already doomed to failure. The most important of these proposals envisaged the creation of committees functioning between meetings of the four estates. This would supply an element of continuity hitherto lacking and enable the king to benefit by the advice of his estates at all times. This was no subtle scheme for the enslavement of the Germans but merely part of the plan for modernizing the *Helstat.* Yet conservative and liberal alike expressed their disapproval of the proposal and voted almost unanimously against it, fearing that it might diminish the authority of the German estates.

A similar fate overtook the proposal for the amalgamation of the church and school organization of Schleswig-Holstein with that of Denmark. These proposals were considered incompatible with the independence enjoyed by the duchies, for 'different nationalities could never understand each other completely'.[1] The estates were not prepared to sacrifice their independence for the sake of the *Helstat* however grateful they were for the recent appointments, which they described, significantly, as 'a pledge of security for our national interests'.[2]

The estates had expressed themselves politely if firmly about these proposals, for a spirit of restraint and moderation characterized the proceedings in Itzehoe. This was partly because members

[1] *St. Z.*, Holstein, 1842, II, *Beilagenheft*, II, p. 216.
[2] *Ibid.*, I, pp. 62-3.

were flattered by the appointment of prominent Holstein noblemen to high office, and partly because they were coming under the spell of a new member, a well-known nobleman, Count Friedrich von Reventlow of Preetz, a man of moderate conservative views who was rapidly proving himself a powerful political personality in Holstein.

Such moderation was hardly to be expected when the Schleswig estates assembled in October. P. Lorenzen was now spokesman for the North Schleswig group and certain to cross swords with his bitter opponent, the Duke of Augustenburg, and with the newly elected national liberal members. There were rumbles of thunder during the debate on the address of thanks. P. Lorenzen objected to the words 'German duchies' on the grounds that Schleswig never had been, was not and never would be German, either nationally or politically.[1] Beseler intervened at once to reaffirm the German character of Schleswig.[2] It was no insult to Denmark to say that the duchies differed from the kingdom and were not subject to the *Kongelov*. It would of course be foolish to deny the existence of a Danish-speaking population in North Schleswig with whom the Germans desired to be on good terms. But, Beseler concluded, that did not alter the German character of Schleswig, any more than the presence of an Italian minority in the Tyrol prevented that frontier district being part of Germany.

A few weeks later a number of private motions moved by national liberals led to further skirmishing. H. Tiedemann moved the separation of the duchies' finances from those of Denmark; G. Claussen protested against the proposal to establish a branch of the *Dansk Nationalbank* in Flensburg, and the fiery Gülich, in most provocative fashion, demanded the removal of the words *Dansk Eiendom* from ships registered in Schleswig-Holstein and the introduction of a Schleswig-Holstein flag for these ships. It is true that these clashes between the *Siebengestirn* and the national liberals involved only a handful of members. Perhaps the Prince of Noer was correct in supposing that most members attached little importance to these altercations and that those involved acted out of

[1] *St. Z.*, Schleswig, 1842, I, p. 68.
[2] *Ibid.*, I, pp. 73, 79–80, 103.

sheer caprice.[1] Nevertheless, Gülich's motion led to a particularly sharp altercation between P. Lorenzen and his opponent and was the ostensible cause of the former's decision to use Danish.

Gülich based his motion on a petition in which certain Åbenraa shipowners declared that the words *Dansk Eiendom*[2] and the absence of their own flag robbed them of their national pride, making them dependent on Denmark as subjects were dependent on rulers. Speaking to the motion Tiedemann declared roundly that these words were offensive to the German national pride of the duchies.[3] If these words were branded on his property he would erase them and take the consequences, because his property was German property and he was subject to the king of Denmark only in his capacity as duke of Schleswig. The estates refused to accept the motion in its original provocative formulation. But they accepted its substance shortly afterwards in an amendment to customs regulations. Speaking on this occasion Gülich ended his peroration with the cry 'Away with the brand of slavery!'[4] Neither the royal commissioner, Josef Reventlow-Criminil, nor the president, Falck, rebuked him for his improper remark. When Count Magnus Moltke drew attention to it, the commissioner declared lamely that he would have rebuked Gülich had he heard the remark. P. Lorenzen boldly defended the words *Dansk Eiendom*.[5] Bitterly he recalled an age when it had not been thought dishonourable to be a Danish citizen or a degradation to sail under the *Danebrog*. Whereupon Beseler intervened to support his friends and to add that there was much else besides these words to justify their dissatisfaction, in particular, the removal of their old emblems from the Schleswig-Holstein regiments.

It was after the debate on Gülich's motion that P. Lorenzen decided to speak nothing but Danish in the estates. In the past he had been reluctant to agree to Flor's suggestion that the North Schleswig members should speak Danish in the estates. Now, after a final consultation with Flor, P. Lorenzen made up his mind. The

[1] C. F. Wegener, *Über das wahre Verhältnis des Herzogs von Augustenburg*, etc., p. 44.

[2] Danish property.

[3] *St. Z.*, Schleswig, 1842, I, pp. 652, 671.

[4] *Ibid.*, I, p. 662.

[5] *Ibid.*, I, pp. 662–3.

acidulous comments of the national liberals were only one reason for his decision. Still a democrat rather than a nationalist, P. Lorenzen had been bitterly disappointed by the appointment of Holstein noblemen to high office. The king, it seemed, preferred to rely on the advice of his German conservative friends rather than on the goodwill of the Danish people. If constitutional progress was ever to be made was it not essential, by a solemn public protest, to remind the king of the democratic rights of Danish-speaking people?

So on Friday, 11 November, immediately after the Gülich amendment had been carried by twenty-eight votes to six, P. Lorenzen began to address the estates in Danish instead of his customary German which he spoke to perfection.[1] The law of 1834 did not forbid the use of Danish in the estates. Otto Moltke had informed C. Paulsen that it was certainly the *Statsraad's* intention that Danish be allowed,[2] and Höpp, royal commissioner to the estates, informed North Schleswig members, at the first meeting of the estates, that they could speak Danish if they wished. J. Klestrup, member for Aerø, availed himself of this opportunity in 1836 and Nis Lorenzen was allowed to speak Danish in 1840. On that occasion only fleeting protests came from Pastor L. Lorenzen and the royal commissioner had acted as interpreter.

When P. Lorenzen started to speak Danish, the royal commissioner declared that he could not understand him. Falck at once admitted P. Lorenzen's right to use Danish but declined to act as interpreter. No one seriously challenged P. Lorenzen's right to speak Danish. The difficulties centred round the minutes; Storm, the secretary to the estates, declared his inability to understand P. Lorenzen and to keep minutes of the speech. He added that unless German was used in the estates, members might as well stay at home. Beseler maintained that German must be used in the minutes for it was the official language of the estates, although he had to admit that the 1834 law offered no positive guidance on this point. P. Lorenzen was on the point of replying to his opponents

[1] Proceedings of 11 Nov. in *St. Z.*, I, pp. 718–20.

[2] Fabricius and J. Lomholt-Thomsen, *Flensborgeren Professor Christian Paulsens Dagbøger*, p. 187, 4 May 1832.

when Falck cut him short, adjourning the meeting before most members fully comprehended the issue raised by a competent German speaker's sudden preference for Danish.

Over the weekend the members grasped the point. Consequently the meeting on Monday, 14 November, was never far removed from uproar most of the time.[1] P. Lorenzen tried in vain to submit a motion to the president in which he demanded that officials appointed by the estates should have a knowledge of Danish. Falck refused to accept it because it was written in Danish. In the petition, printed later in *Faedrelandet*,[2] P. Lorenzen defended his decision to speak Danish on the grounds that half the duchy spoke it and, although a knowledge of both languages was desirable, there was no valid reason why Danish-speaking members should be compelled to speak German when German-speaking members were not obliged to learn Danish. He had no personal preference for either, using both in everyday life. But his patience was exhausted. He regretted his former use of German in the estates, and now resolved to speak nothing but Danish in the estates as a protest against the contempt in which the Germans held his mother tongue.

The national liberals, quick to see the significance of P. Lorenzen's action, were determined to have his head. Storm, Tiedemann, Gülich and Beseler urged that he be forbidden to speak Danish because of his knowledge of German. In cases of necessity they were prepared to allow the use of Danish by members ignorant of German. But not by P. Lorenzen. Falck tried desperately to lower the temperature of the debate, pointing out, in reply to Beseler, that he could not forbid any member to speak Danish but at the same time Falck insisted that the minutes be written in German. The duke of Augustenburg, 'white as a sheet'[3] and quivering with fury, intervened to suggest that the power of deciding whether P. Lorenzen spoke Danish or not, lay not with the president but with the members as a whole. Falck could not bring himself to accept the duke's novel argument. The

[1] Proceedings of 14 Nov. in *St. Z.*, I, pp. 722–5.

[2] In J. Ottosen, *Peter Hjort Lorenzens historisk Gerning*, pp. 108–10.

[3] *Ibid.*, p. 111, P. Lorenzen to C. Flor, 14 Dec. 1842.

tense scenes culminated in P. Lorenzen's declaration that he would continue to speak Danish until forbidden to do so by the king or until physical force was used against him. Nor did he consider that the president could claim jurisdiction in a matter upon which the 1834 law was inconclusive. Perplexed and thoroughly embarrassed by the turn of events, Falck adjourned the meeting before it got completely out of hand.

On Monday, 14 November, some thirty members of the estates met at the duke's house and agreed that the members of the estates and not the president, must decide the issue. They warned Falck that unless he took steps against P. Lorenzen they would leave the estates.[1] Falck's nerve broke at last and reluctantly he sided with P. Lorenzen's enemies. When the crucial meeting of the estates opened on Wednesday Falck made a last desperate attempt to keep the peace and save his reputation.[2] P. Lorenzen had fully demonstrated his loyalty to his principles but there the matter must end, said Falck; Lorenzen must now speak German again. There was no objection to a North Schleswig member speaking Danish if he could not speak German, and, turning to the assembled members, Falck asked for and obtained confirmation of this ruling. P. Lorenzen retorted that he would only cease speaking Danish when ordered to do so by the king.

Tumult broke out in the hall. Falck asked the members whether they would allow P. Lorenzen to speak Danish. They replied in the negative, only Jepsen and Nielsen, one of the Flensburg members, supporting P. Lorenzen at this point.[3] P. Lorenzen challenged the legality of Falck's action in consulting the assembly. Falck thereupon forbade him to speak. P. Lorenzen persisted. Was he being ordered to remain silent because he was speaking in Danish? Falck replied that this was so. P. Lorenzen appealed to the royal commissioner for a ruling on the legality of the proceedings, but Reventlow-Criminil remained silent. Meanwhile there were

[1] Bagge and Engelstoft, *op. cit.*, II, N. Falck to A. Ørsted, 19 Nov. 1842.

[2] Proceedings of 16 Nov. in *St. Z.*, I, pp. 769–71.

[3] Nis Lorenzen and Posselt were absent but Petersen and Jensen of Flensburg remained silent. According to Lauridsen, *op. cit.*, III, p. 122, Jensen disapproved of Peter Lorenzen's conduct.

loud cries of order on all sides and, as P. Lorenzen had technically disobeyed the president, Falck ordered him to leave the hall. Defiantly P. Lorenzen retorted that he yielded only to force. Amid shouts that he be expelled forthwith, Falck adjourned the meeting, adding that he would see that P. Lorenzen did not have access to the next meeting.

Physical force proved unnecessary for the same afternoon P. Lorenzen sought out Falck and Reventlow-Criminil and came to terms with them. He would return to his place at the next meeting but would refrain from speaking Danish until his petition to the king had been answered. In this petition[1] he defended his use of Danish as a protest against the persecution of that language by an assembly which had dared to discuss motions disruptive of the unity of the state.

The dramatic scenes in Schleswig aroused unprecedented interest throughout the length and breadth of the *Helstat*. It was a decisive moment in the history of these years for at last the animosity which had been growing between German and Dane in recent years erupted in public, confirming and deepening national prejudices on both sides of the Kongeaa and placing national questions in the forefront of the political arena much to the dismay of all true friends of the *Helstat*.

There was great indignation in Schleswig where P. Lorenzen's action was generally interpreted by Germans as a deliberate declaration of war on their nationality. The *Itzehoer Wochenblatt* had been right after all in supposing that Nis Lorenzen's use of Danish in 1840 was the prelude to the decisive battle for the national future of Schleswig. Addresses began to arrive at the estates, some supporting P. Lorenzen, others denouncing him. The latter were by no means restricted to the Germans for Beseler's recent motion for the cession of Haderslev *Amt* had confused the issue. Many who approved of P. Lorenzen's stand now disowned him, fearing that the Germans in retaliation might surrender North Schleswig to Denmark. As for P. Lorenzen, he now slept with pistols near his bed for hooligans had demonstrated outside his house in Schleswig, bombarding the windows and doors with stones.

[1] In L. Skau, *Peter Hjort Lorenzen*, pp. 202–4.

Political development in Denmark was profoundly affected by the events in Schleswig. Suspicion of German intentions had been growing in Danish political circles since the petition for the suspension of the rescript in 1840. The ascendancy of the duke of Augustenburg and the appointment of his brother to high office added to these suspicions. The treatment of P. Lorenzen was the last straw. It caused widespread indignation in Denmark and shifted the centre of gravity decisively from constitutional questions to the national problem in Schleswig. All shades of political opinion were aroused by this new evidence of German determination to treat Danish as an inferior language and to separate the duchy from Denmark—for so the Danes interpreted references to the German Confederation made in Schleswig in December. Much as conservative circles regretted it, the radical Eiderdanes grew rapidly in importance.

The Viborg estates were in session at this time. The radical leader, J. P. With, had been fully informed of events in Schleswig by P. Lorenzen. 'All Denmark admires your stand', he wrote to his friend[1] and he threw himself with zest into his self-imposed task of opening 'the Jutish campaign against the Nordelbinger'.[2] He moved that the estates petition the king, firstly, to protect the rights of the Danish nationality in Schleswig and secondly, to defend the state against separatists. Ørsted, the royal commissioner, regarded the outbreak of a national conflict as little short of disastrous and vigorously opposed With. An old friend of Falck, Ørsted defended the latter's conduct in the Schleswig estates and sharply criticized Lorenzen's behaviour as unnecessarily provocative. But he could not prevent a modified version of With's motion being carried by forty-six votes to three. Ørsted's decline in popularity dated from this meeting, especially since he forbade all mention of the debate in the *Ständezeitung*. Even his conservative friends disapproved of his conduct for, as one of them remarked, 'on the subject of the Schleswig-Holsteiner I share my fellow-countrymen's views whatever political colour they may

[1] Bagge and Engelstoft, *op. cit.*, II, no. 471a, p. 226, J. P. With to P. Lorenzen, 18 Nov. 1842.

[2] *Ibid.*, no. 483a, p. 252, J. P. With to P. Lorenzen, 3 Dec. 1842.

be'.[1] The simple fact was that men like Falck and Ørsted belonged to a different era. They could not and did not wish to accommodate themselves to the harsh and alien spirit of the 1840's, and suffered inevitable political eclipse in consequence. In their petition the Viborg estates expressed the grave anxiety which the activity of the German party had caused in Denmark since 1840, and their fear that the Germans intended to separate Schleswig from Denmark. The Germans could rest assured that no one wished to alter the status of Schleswig, which remained part of the Danish state but with its own administrative and legal machinery. Nor did anyone seek to harm the German nationality, 'as far as it really extends'—for they were critical of the use of German in church and school in those parts of Schleswig where Danish was spoken. But above all the Viborg estates insisted that Danish enjoy parity of esteem with German, and they solemnly declared their intention of supporting the crown in all steps deemed necessary to defend the Danish language and the ties binding Schleswig to Denmark.

In Copenhagen some prominent Eiderdanes organized an address to the king expressing similar sentiments. A big public demonstration was held and hundreds of signatures collected, for as J. Schouw remarked, 'there was very bitter feeling here regardless of class or political conviction'.[2] The intensity of feeling in the city was reflected in the warmth of the reception accorded P. Lorenzen during his visit in December. The crown prince openly expressed sympathy with him. During his audience with the king, Lorenzen had the satisfaction of hearing Christian express his displeasure with the Schleswig estates and assure his visitor that as he was a Danish king he would never let Schleswig go.[3] But in private King Christian was equally displeased with the Viborg estates and inclined to look upon P. Lorenzen as a demagogue.

Back in Schleswig there had been renewed discussion about the use of Danish. The question rose again when Nis Lorenzen, the

[1] Bagge and Engelstoft, *op. cit.*, II, no. 475, p. 276, Caspar Paludan-Müller to Prof. N. Høyer, 23 Dec. 1842.

[2] *Ibid.*, no. 477, p. 236, J. F. Schouw to P. Bruun, 29 Nov. 1842.

[3] J. Ottosen, *P. Hjort Lorenzens besøg i København ved nyaarstid 1843*, S. A. Flensburg, 1895, p. 23, P. Lorenzen to C. Flor, 15 Jan. 1843.

only Eiderdane in the assembly, suddenly commenced to speak Danish during the debate on 23 November. His North Schleswig colleagues were divided in their attitude. Petersen was prepared to speak German despite his electors' desire that he speak Danish, because he felt that one language must be used in the estates.[1] But Posselt thought that he must speak Danish in future in protest against the veto imposed on its use by the Germans.[2] On this occasion there was no tumult in the estates, merely lengthy discussion about the adequacy of Nis Lorenzen's German. Beseler and Gülich considered it adequate but most members disagreed. Finally, Nis Lorenzen was allowed by twenty-six votes to nine to speak Danish, although the estates refused to accept his contention that he had an absolute right to speak Danish whenever he wished to do so.

In December the estates debated the government proposal for the creation of estates committees, already rejected in Itzehoe. It was significant that Beseler and Gülich prepared the committee report on this proposal.[3] They not only recommended the rejection of the proposal as expected, but boldly suggested that Schleswig enter the German Confederation. They were naturally concerned to remove an obvious inconsistency in their case, upon which Olshausen had played so skilfully in the past. If Schleswig was in the Confederation it would then be able to claim that common constitution with Holstein demanded by Dahlmann in 1816. It would also serve as an impressive demonstration to Denmark that attempts to annex Schleswig—such as the Viborg Estates' proposal to unite the three estates in 1840—were doomed to certain failure. There was another immensely important advantage. If Schleswig joined the Confederation it could participate fully in the upward surge of national development which would lead Germany to the pinnacle of power and fame in the not too distant future. The committee report admitted that similar estates committees had been favourably received in Prussia, but only because that was a homogeneous state. The Danish state, on the other hand, consisted of two halves no more closely associated than

[1] *St. Z.*, Schleswig, 1842, I, p. 983.
[2] *Ibid.*, p. 984.
[3] *Ibid.*, II, *Beilagenheft*, pp. 123–48.

Austria and Hungary. In each half different political conditions prevailed, symbolized for Denmark by the *Kongelov* and for the German duchies by the magic date 1460. Amalgamation of the two halves was, in these circumstances, a moral impossibility.

During the debate Beseler and Gülich gave expression in classic form to the burning national sentiment and faith in Germany which activated national liberals in the 1840's. Beseler emphasized the danger from Denmark, against which the duchies could be secured once Schleswig was in the Confederation. But there was much more to it than that. An emotional note, usually absent from his cogent and legalistic speeches, suddenly intruded. 'Anyone,' he remarked, 'who has watched the development of German national life cannot doubt the growing might of Germany. If I believe this and am mistaken, then I prefer to be mistaken along with enlightened statesmen, kings and emperors' sons, with my worthy citizens and fellow-countrymen and with the spirit of the German nation. This spirit is growing vigorously and is the certain pledge that the future of Germany will be a great and splendid one. Political forms will have to accommodate themselves to this spiritual development for the things of the mind always triumph in the end. Anyone who can see no further than Schleswig or Schleswig-Holstein is guilty of small-town provincialism. I love Schleswig-Holstein, my fatherland, as dearly as anyone in this room. But my mental horizon is not bounded by the Königsau, Eider or Elbe or by the sanddunes of Sylt or by the shores of Aerø. I live in the great German fatherland. That is the source of my happiness and pride. Anyone who is content to think of Schleswig-Holstein as his only fatherland, will not be able to find a satisfactory answer to those vital questions which are being asked at the present time.' [1]

No less fervent a confession of faith in Germany's future came from Gülich. Whether or not Denmark's future lay with Scandinavia, Schleswig's future would be completely German, he maintained. He reminded members of the legend of Barbarossa, sleeping in the Kyffhäuser, awakening and hanging his sword on a dry branch, which immediately blossoms forth and casts its

[1] *St. Z.*, Schleswig, 1842, II, *Beilagenheft*, pp. 1073–4.

shadow over the entire earth. Barbarossa was awake when Germany's youth drove out the Corsican but then Barbarossa had fallen asleep again. The time of reawakening was not far distant, for the men of the north were convinced that the Eider was not the frontier of Germany. 'So it behoves us all,' he concluded, 'to see to it, as far as in us lies, that those who live to see this great day, shall not be fainthearted men.' [1]

Moving as these speeches were, it is most significant that, although a large majority rejected the proposal for estates committees, twenty-six of the thirty-nine members also voted for the deletion of all reference to the inclusion of Schleswig in the Confederation. The conclusion was inescapable. Traditional provincial patriotism still provided the primary impulse to action for most members of the *Landespartei*. They were instinctively hostile to any attempt to alter the status of Schleswig, whether from the Danish or German side. Enthusiastic references to Germany were received politely but coolly. The royal commissioner, a good friend of the duchies, declared that the relations between the component parts of the *Helstat* were no concern of the estates, an opinion endorsed by most members. He dryly remarked, after Gülich's emotional peroration, that the member's prophetic gift could not alter the plain fact that the German frontier lay at present on the Eider.[2]

The royal declaration read out to members during the debate by the royal commissioner was most reassuring in this respect. The king declared that he had no intention either of incorporating Schleswig in Denmark or of allowing it to enter the Confederation. He would maintain 'the legal basis on which the independence of Schleswig and the connection with Holstein depended'. Reventlow-Criminil had, after consultation with the Prince of Noer, taken it upon himself to omit the words 'under the Danish crown' at the end of the sentence in order to make the declaration even more acceptable to the estates. Many members agreed with Storm that their doubts were allayed by the declaration. References to Schleswig were now unnecessary, for the demand that the duchy enter the Confederation had been inspired solely by a

[1] *Ibid.*, p. 1696. [2] *Ibid.*, p. 1697.

desire to protect it against Danish aggression.[1] C. Rönnenkamp added the reflection that in any case it would not be much fun to be in the Confederation, because it was a union of princes not of peoples; he even doubted whether it was in the material interest of Schleswig to join. The *Zollverein* would probably fail for it was hardly conceivable that what Napoleon had failed to do by force in the Continental System, could be achieved by German writers.[2] In any case Schleswig could share in the great German intellectual heritage without being in the Confederation. Boysen added, shrewdly, that the idea of Schleswig's entry into the Confederation lacked popular roots and was favoured by very few indeed.[3]

In vain did Beseler plead with them not to reject association with the Confederation merely because Schleswig's independence seemed at present secure. 'What is at stake here,' he said, 'is that the spirit of the German nation has begun recently to soar upwards so rapidly that one does not need to possess prophetic insight to see whither it is going.'[4] The members remained unimpressed. They were prepared only to defend the *status quo* in 1842, because their patriotism was still restricted to the land between the Kongeaa and the Eider.

Finally, the estates debated the rescript of 2 December which contained King Christian's reply to P. Lorenzen's petition. It was obvious that the king was anxious to settle this delicate matter as quickly and equitably as possible. He did not hesitate to reprimand P. Lorenzen for disobeying the president's call to order on 16 November. But he could not accept the German members' contention that they alone should decide who spoke Danish. The king insisted on the natural right of Danish-speaking members to use their native tongue, and requested his estates to devise a procedure to facilitate this. Danish speeches would still be translated into German by the secretaries, for the king agreed that the minutes must be kept in German as before. The commissioner considered that the new rescript allowed P. Lorenzen to speak Danish (which he did), but did not allow him to have his speeches recorded in Danish. As the secretaries declared their inability to understand

[1] *St. Z.*, Schleswig, 1842, II, *Beilagenheft*, p. 1705.
[2] *Ibid.*, p. 1703.
[3] *Ibid.*, pp. 1721–2.
[4] *Ibid.*, pp. 1743–4.

him, the entry 'He continued to speak Danish' was made in the minutes whenever he spoke.

The majority report on the rescript, drafted by Storm, Rumohr and Pastor L. Lorenzen, made it abundantly clear that the estates would still not concede parity of esteem to Danish.[1] They recognized that language not only allowed man to express his deepest emotions but imprinted a national character on him. Therefore no one ever thought of forbidding the use of local dialects, Frisian, Low German or Low Danish, by people in their daily lives. But who could doubt that High German was far superior to these dialects as a cultural medium and was spoken by the educated and official classes? These arguments buttressed up their main contention, which was, as always, that the German superstructure of the duchies must not be altered. High German was the official language, used in all matters appertaining to the unity of Schleswig-Holstein. It would almost certainly be a violation of natural right to forbid the use of dialects in everyday life. But natural right must be subordinated to the rights of existing institutions in the interests of good government. Thus in the estates only German must be spoken, because the exclusive use of one language was essential to facilitate the free exchange of ideas and discussion of the duchies' welfare which the estates were established to promote. Unless one agreed with Talleyrand's quip that language was devised to conceal thought, rational necessity alone surely dictated the use of German, not of Danish which many did not understand.

In fact the committee even felt that a knowledge of German was a *sine qua non* for a member if he wished to make proper use of the estates. A man without this knowledge should in conscience decline election. Even North Schleswig invariably returned German-speaking members because they appreciated the wisdom of this. How could it possibly be an insult to Danish if German was used as a business language, when it was the tongue of educated people with the authority of centuries behind it? Finally, they considered new legislation to regulate the use of Danish in the estates unnecessary. The present practice, whereby members

[1] *Ibid.*, II, *Beilagenheft*, II, pp. 561–74.

decided on the merits of individual cases, was quite adequate. Indeed, in the opinion of the committee the practice would never have been questioned had not a certain party, intent on causing mischief, made an issue of it.

These arguments were violently assailed by P. Lorenzen, Nielsen, Jepsen, Posselt and Nis Lorenzen.[1] They insisted that a language spoken by half the duchy must be accorded parity of esteem with German. Reference to the traditions of centuries did not impress them. It was their task not to preserve but to destroy the German superstructure of the duchies imposed on Danish-speaking people by tyrannical officials. The fact that most members of the estates spoke German merely indicated how unnatural the present position was, and how essential it was to insist on recognition of the right of Danish-speaking members to speak Danish and have their speeches recorded in Danish. Petersen, still hoping to prevent language questions from becoming the plaything of contending nationalisms, devised a compromise formula. He proposed that those unable to speak German be allowed to use Danish on condition that a procedure was devised to guarantee the recording of their speeches in German. But he could muster only two votes for his compromise.

All the same, it was evident from the debate that there were limits to the influence exerted by the national liberals. Beseler, Tiedemann, Hamckens, Berwald and Steffens all spoke in support of a motion, moved by B. Lüders and Fries, that the use of Danish be completely forbidden when the new estates assembled after the 1847 elections. As German-speaking candidates were usually available, no difficulty need arise, but if Danish-speaking members were returned, their electors must take the consequences. Beseler would even have forbidden the use of Danish in the next estates so convinced was he that its continued use could only lead to more trouble.[2] He attacked Falck bitterly, blaming the present rescript on the latter's failure to put P. Lorenzen in his place long ago—comments which were not well received for most members still had an affectionate regard for the well-meaning if ineffectual

[1] *St. Z.*, Schleswig, 1842, II, *Beilagenheft*, II, pp. 1003–5.
[2] *Ibid.*, I, pp. 1960–5.

president. With relentless logic Beseler accused the members of illogicality. They had just demonstrated the impossibility of allowing Danish to be spoken and yet wanted to allow certain members to continue the practice. Nor was he moved by appeals from Storm that on humanitarian grounds those unable to speak German must be treated as special cases.[1] Beseler retorted that the government had made the language question a matter of principle and the estates must deal with it as such and not on humanitarian grounds.[2] Tiedemann added that if Danish were allowed in the estates, far better let North Schleswig become part of Denmark where members could speak as much Danish as they wanted.[3] Gülich warned members that this was not just a simple language question for the proceedings in Viborg showed that the Danes wanted to annex Schleswig. He reminded members of the lawyers' strike two years ago, hinting strongly that if the government insisted on new legislation in this matter there might soon be as few members sitting in the estates as there had been German lawyers accepting Danish briefs.[4]

Most members considered the national liberal viewpoint far too extreme and their prophecies of further conflict in the estates, if Danish was permitted, too pessimistic. Pastor L. Lorenzen expressed the feelings of the majority—including the duke of Augustenburg—when he remarked that there would be no trouble in future if the old procedure was adhered to. There had been no trouble when Klestrup spoke Danish in 1836 nor when Nis Lorenzen had spoken Danish at the present meeting for, unlike Peter Lorenzen, neither spoke for the sake of it. To accept the national liberal argument would be to abandon the path of moderation trodden in the past, and to ignore the fact that Schleswig was a frontier area where two languages were normal. 'One would have to be filled with passion and prejudice not to take account of these conditions,' he concluded.[5] He understood that lawyers delighted in logical and precise argumentation, but in the rough and tumble of life justice must temper legal abstractions. By thirty-four votes to six it was decided that members lacking

[1] *Ibid.*, I, pp. 1971–2. [2] *Ibid.*, I, pp. 1972–3. [3] *Ibid.*, I, pp. 2070–2.
[4] *Ibid.*, I, pp. 2060–1. [5] *Ibid.*, I, p. 1976.

sufficient German be allowed to speak Danish until the next estates, when it was to be expected that Danish districts would elect German speakers. No legal definition of the use of Danish was considered desirable as this would imply the recognition of a right to speak that language in the estates.[1] Shortly afterwards this memorable meeting ended and the members dispersed, still in excited mood, to their homes in time for the Christmas celebrations.

[1] 'One could hardly imagine anything more impertinent' observed the king on receiving news of this decision. A. D. Jørgensen, *op. cit.*, p. 116, 22 Dec. 1842.

IX

The age of mass politics

At the beginning of the 1840's affairs of state were still the traditional preserve of the upper classes, the landowners and officials, with a sprinkling of lawyers and journalists living on the periphery of high society. Interest was sometimes displayed by wider circles of the population when the estates happened to be in session and were discussing questions of particular interest to ordinary people, such as the burden of taxation. But between meetings there was very little sustained interest in politics outside the circle of urban intellectuals, for the material problems of everyday existence completely absorbed the attentions of the phlegmatic people of Schleswig-Holstein. Even the rescript of 1840 had aroused only fleeting interest in the Schleswig towns and although interest lingered on for some time after the estates dispersed, it had certainly died down by the end of 1841.

But by the middle of the 1840's much wider circles of the population were beginning to take a sustained interest in politics whether the estates were meeting or not. The protests which arrived at the Holstein estates in 1844 revealed a degree of popular interest which was generally maintained up to 1848. This was part of a general European phenomenon. Everywhere in Western Europe the dominant upper classes sensed that the age of elegance was passing, and that they were on the threshold of a new era when the numerical strength of the multitudes would give them a decisive voice in the affairs of state. Unless the upper classes directed this new force into politically acceptable channels, the days of their dominance were clearly numbered. The gentlemen of the *Landespartei* had other reasons for seeking a popular following. They were anxious not to share the fate of Lornsen, 'a commander without an army', in the difficult days that lay ahead, for after the Eiderdane speech and the Peter Lorenzen incident many feared that the decisive battle for Schleswig might not be long delayed.[1]

The national liberal wing of the *Landespartei* now came into its own for the popularization of political ideas was a task much more congenial to men like Beseler, Gülich, Tiedemann and Hansen than to aristocratic landowners or even to older liberals like Falck. National liberals had been the first to see in the events of 1842 a declaration of war by the Eiderdanes on the German nationality. They agreed with Karl Lorentzen that 'when the struggle for freedom commences again in Europe, the decisive factor will be how far popular consciousness has been given a political orientation and schooled to take part in the affairs of the fatherland'.[2] In their propaganda they did not hesitate to appeal to the national sentiment latent in the German population and to emphasize the connection between the preservation of the duchies' independence and the future of Germany, a connection which their conservative colleagues were still most reluctant to admit if it implied major alterations in the *status quo*.

In the field of propaganda the Danes had six years' lead over the Germans. The Press Society had been engaged in cultural propaganda since 1836, founding and circulating Danish newspapers and lending libraries. True, progress was slow and the society had not much support outside Haderslev *Amt* and part of Åbenraa *Amt*. But by 1843 the Danish movement acquired additional impetus with the commencement of the Skamlingsbank festivals and the establishment of the *Slesvigske Forening*.[3]

The popular festivals held annually at the Skamlingbank were unique. They did not fail to impress North Schleswig. In a beautiful natural setting 6,000 people, many from Denmark, gathered together in May 1843 to see J. G. Drewsen, a leading Danish nationalist, present P. Lorenzen with a silver drinking horn bearing the inscription *Han vedblev at tale dansk*,[4] and to listen to

[1] *Itzehoer Wochenblatt*, no. 46, 1840.

[2] *N.K.B.*, Oct. 1844, pp. 670–1.

[3] The Schleswig Society.

[4] 'He continued to speak Danish.' These words were entered in the minutes of the Schleswig estates in 1842 whenever P. Lorenzen spoke Danish.

Laurids Skau, talented young organizer and new leader of the Danish movement. The North Schleswig festivals reached a peak with the memorable 1844 gathering, when 9,000 spectators listened to speeches by Orla Lehmann, by Grundtvig and by the young Scandinavian C. Ploug.

The *Slesvigske Forening*, founded in June by farmers from Haderslev *Amt* and directed by Laurids Skau, has the distinction of being the first successful popular society founded in Schleswig. There was much support for its cultural and political activity along the east coast of Haderslev *Amt*. By the end of 1843 it had a membership of 70 increasing to 400 in 1844. The society received considerable financial support from Danish societies and played a major role in the foundation of the *Folkehøjskole* at Rødding, a project dear to the hearts of all Danish leaders. This school, built by popular subscription, was opened in November with the historian, C. F. Wegener, as the first principal. It formed a focal point for Danish efforts in Schleswig and helped to inculcate a love of Danish culture in its pupils.

Once the Germans decided to build up a popular following, they soon made up for lost time. In the important field of popular journalism they scored a major victory. This was not only due to the work of the duke of Augustenburg; many local news-sheets in Schleswig-Holstein were blossoming into political journals at the beginning of the 1840's as new production techniques made them an increasingly effective medium for influencing an ever-widening circle of readers. It was of vital importance for the *Landespartei* that these journals, almost without exception, accepted the *Landesrechte* as immutable political verities. One of them, the *Itzehoer Wochenblatt*, edited by P. S. Schönfeld, rapidly attained a pre-eminent position as the organ of the *Landespartei*, with W. Beseler and the duke of Augustenburg as regular contributors. Another important journal was the fortnightly *Neuen Kieler Blätter*, inspired by the circle of young and enthusiastic students associated with J. G. Droysen. In its columns was reflected the preoccupation of this decade with the unification of Germany, as well as a growing realization of the commercial and geographical importance of the duchies to a united Germany.

'The unification of Germany is a task which every good patriot must help to complete,' remarked H. Carstens in the first number. 'This task will be in the mind of the *Neuen Kieler Blätter* at all times. The readers will see this in every line of the journal even if it is not blazoned forth in every article.' [1]

The uniform political orientation of all these journals did not fail to create a public opinion sympathetic to the *Landespartei*. Beseler remarked shrewdly that the *Itzehoer Wochenblatt*, with between 6,000 and 8,000 subscribers and possibly 300,000 readers, was worth more than an army to the party.[2] It was no less important that the Danish monopoly of reporting the affairs of Schleswig-Holstein in the German press was at last being broken by young writers like L. Stein, K. Samwer and K. Lorentzen. The *Landespartei* had always been able to rely on support from the Hamburg press, simply because the economic interest of that city in the neighbouring duchies made their political fate a matter of the greatest interest. From now on sympathetic reports began to appear in the influential and respectable *Augsburger Allgemeine Zeitung*. Only in North Schleswig did the Germans fail to obtain a favourable hearing. Neither the Haderslev *Lyna* nor the *Sonderburger Wochenblatt*, appearing in Danish editions, attracted any considerable body of readers away from *Dannevirke* or the *Åbenraa Ugeblad*.

The Germans had ensured that educated opinion was solidly on their side in most of Schleswig-Holstein. But this was only the beginning of wisdom. How could an intimate and durable relationship be established with the masses of the people, most of whom were not regular readers of the *Itzehoer Wochenblatt* and the *Neuen Kieler Blätter*?

Attempts to interest the people in the traditional type of political association were almost universally unsuccessful. The German liberals failed in the 1830's to create any organization comparable to the Press Society. Even after 1842, when conservative as well as liberal approved of this activity, no progress was made. Falck's

[1] *N.K.B.*, I, 1843, p. 5.

[2] P. von Hedemann Heespern, *Die Herzogtümer Schleswig-Holstein und die Neuzeit*, p. 640.

suggestion that a society be formed to promote the teaching of German in schools, to establish a Danish paper in North Schleswig and a German paper in Copenhagen to explain their viewpoint, evoked a lukewarm response. The younger generation disliked the last proposal, feeling that the old harmony between German and Dane could not be restored as easily as the older politicians seemed to think. National liberal proposals for a Patriotic Society to promote liberal principles and the German way of life, to further popular education and to organize gymnastic displays were no more successful—perhaps because well-known agitators like Gülich and Heiberg were associated with the project.[1] Only in the vicinity of Haderslev was a society founded in March 1844 by local landowners to counteract the *Slesvigske Forening's* propaganda. The society, with a membership of 150, became the *Schleswig-Holsteinischer Patriotischer Verein*[2] in 1845. But up to 1846 it had no anti-Danish bias; its German-speaking members were content to be natives of Schleswig, and spent their time improving the yield and quality of their crops. The truth was that the inhabitants of Schleswig-Holstein were easy-going, friendly people who were perfectly content to leave politics to the members of the estates whom they knew and trusted. What need had they of newfangled political clubs, membership of which would at the very least entail financial outlay?

The Germans could not compete successfully with the Danes in this type of political association. But they discovered in the popular festival a much more efficacious and impressive vehicle for political propaganda. The importance of these festivals lay in the fact that people who could not be induced to join political societies, and who probably did not—or could not—read papers regularly, were brought together in their thousands for several hours on end at some of the most important gatherings. On such occasions unique opportunities existed for moulding the political outlook of these mass audiences.

At the beginning of the 1840's popular festivals, both *Volksfeste* and *Sängerfeste*, were in an embryonic state. The *Volksfeste*

[1] P.A., III, C 60, Pastor L. Lorenzen to the duke, 15 Nov. 1843.
[2] The Schleswig-Holstein Patriotic Society.

probably originated in electoral meetings in the towns and developed freely after the prohibition imposed on public meetings in 1838 had been removed at the insistence of the estates in 1840. The first *Volksfest* was held in Kiel that year although not until 1843–4 did *Volksfeste* assume considerable dimensions. The *Sängerfeste* grew out of the *Liedertafeln* or glee clubs, established in nearly all towns between 1839 and 1842 and enjoying considerable popular support. The *Sängerfeste* were meetings at which various *Liedertafeln* assembled to render popular music. In time they became indistinguishable from *Volksfeste*, except that the former were held only in towns, the latter in rural areas as well. The heyday of the popular festivals commenced with the Süderbrarup (Angeln) meeting in 1843 and culminated in the Eckernförde *Sängerfest* of 1845, with outstanding successes in June 1844 at the North Frisian *Volksfest* and in July at the Schleswig *Sängerfest*.

The festivals followed a general pattern with local variations. A suitable geographical promontory was selected on which to erect tents for meals and side shows, triumphal arches and platforms for choirs and speakers. Invariably one or more *Liedertafeln* were invited to grace the proceedings and a formal dinner was arranged to which as many of the significant political personalities as cared to attend were invited. For the crowds who flocked to the festival, amusements were organized with dancing and fireworks in the evening, all liberally interspersed with addresses of a political nature delivered by W. Beseler, Tiedemann, Gülich, Heiberg and Hansen and enlivened by patriotic songs rendered by the choirs. The dinner for the guests, usually commencing in the late afternoon, was a quite considerable affair, distinguished by an inordinate number of toasts for which the people of Schleswig-Holstein were notorious and by further political discourses. As night fell on the festive scene, rockets were fired from the surrounding hills, bonfires blazed on others and a torchlight procession to the market square of the nearby town in the early hours of the morning rounded off the proceedings.

The atmosphere engendered by the oratory, the songs, the liquid refreshment and the abundance of political emblems, banners and flags was calculated to make a profound impression on the participants in these festivals. Naturally many were attracted only by the spectacle and the amusements.[1] Some were offended by the anti-Danish tone of the speeches and bored by their length.[2] But there is little doubt that the festivals did much to familiarize the people with the leading personalities and political ideas of the *Landespartei*. At these intimate gatherings, so often punctuated by emotional displays of national sentiment, the national liberal speakers succeeded in establishing close bonds with their audience where newspapers and political clubs would have failed.

It was here that the popular song proved an asset of inestimable value which the Danes could never equal. From their earliest days the *Liedertafeln* were politically inclined and nationally conscious. At the first popular gathering, the Kiel *Volksfest* of 1840, the loyal toast was quickly followed by a toast to the 'great German fatherland'. The popular song soon proved a most efficacious medium for awakening the national feeling of the people. National liberals were alive to the significance of this. Through the medium of popular songs, observed Hansen, politics could be brought closer to the people, gripping and enkindling their hearts, 'where words could not and should not do so'.[3] Heiberg, another prominent orator, believed that the great mission of the *Liedertafeln* was to unite all branches and classes of the German people through the power of harmony for the popular song was the harbinger of German freedom.[4] It was no accident that patriotic songs already well-known in Germany—including *Was ist des deutschen Vaterland?* and *Freiheit die ich meine*—were firm favourites with the *Liedertafeln*.

These popular songs helped to awaken a feeling of national consciousness in German-speaking audiences and to weaken that

[1] J. Jensen, *Nordfriesland in den politischen und nationalen Entwicklungen des 19ten Jahrhunderts 1797–1864*, pp. 101–6, is most careful not to overestimate the effect of festivals in Nordfriesland.

[2] P. K. Iverson, *Kniplingskraemer Jens Wulffs dagbøg*, p. 124.

[3] H. Hansen, *Deutsche Volks und Sängerfeste in Schleswig-Holstein besonders das am 1, 2 und 3 Juni gefeierte Deutsche Volks und Sängerfest in Eckernförde*, Altona, 1846, p. 34.

[4] *Ibid.*, pp. 111–12.

deeply-rooted spirit of local patriotism which dismayed and repelled J. G. Droysen in 1843.[1] People hitherto indifferent to the great world outside the duchies were suddenly transported, on the wings of song, from the *engere Heimat*, Schleswig-Holstein, to the great German fatherland to which they owed allegiance and from which they could derive spiritual sustenance. The efficacy of the popular song reached a peak in July 1844 when *Schleswig-Holstein meerumschlungen*[2] was rendered for the first time at the Schleswig *Sängerfest*. It was an immediate and overwhelming success and was popularized throughout the duchies in the columns of the *Itzehoer Wochenblatt*. By 1845 it had become a popular patriotic song in Germany after the Würzburg festival. It is perhaps no exaggeration to claim that this song did more than anything else to activate the national sentiment latent in the German-speaking population. The song paid tribute to the people's natural affection for Schleswig-Holstein, emphasized the German character of the duchies, '*Deutsche Sitte hohe Wacht*',[3] and established an implicit connection between the defence of the duchies' independence and the national future of the German fatherland.

When Beseler introduced the new song at the Schleswig *Sängerfest* he made the connection explicit in memorable prose. 'Today we are celebrating a beautiful festival on German soil, a German *Sängerfest*. When dawn is breaking in the early hours of the morning and the glittering stars are wrestling with the nocturnal darkness and the morning mists, the lark soars up into the pure air singing his song full of joy and hope. So may the German song become a lark of promise for the German people struggling for light and freedom and may it announce with joy the approach of day. May the lark soon be followed by the German eagle, winging his way upwards into the rays of the rising sun and protecting us all beneath his mighty wings. German men and women, I ask you to join with me in a hurrah so loud and heartfelt that it will resound far over the countryside from this lovely place and find

[1] R. Hübner, *Johann Gustav Droysen Brief Wechsel I, 1829–1851*, p. 235. J. G. Droysen to F. Perthes, 26 Feb. 1843.

[2] Schleswig-Holstein surrounded by the sea.

[3] 'The guardian of the German way of life.'

a thousandfold echo in the distant mountains of the German plateau. Long live the song of the German people.' [1]

It was not only on the German side that a new ideological content was infused into the contest between Eiderdane and Schleswig-Holsteiner. In Denmark the Scandinavian movement began to assume importance after the Upsala meeting and the foundation of the *Scandinavsk Selskabet*[2] in 1843. The literary Scandinavianism of the 1830's had emphasized the cultural unity and common heritage of the three northern kingdoms. It was replaced after 1843 by a movement with wider appeal, supported especially by student circles in Denmark, and working for the political and military union of the three kingdoms. The romantic and emotional appeal of the Scandinavian mystique was apparent in C. Ploug's speech at the Skamlingsbank in 1843, and in O. Lehmann's peroration to enthusiastic students at the Reithaus in 1845. For Scandinavians the three kingdoms represented the only fatherland and the Scandinavian mission was to uphold the cause of freedom in Europe:

> '*da skal det frie*
> *magtige Norden*
> *føre til Seieren*
> *Folkenes Sag.*' [3]

The Schleswig problem assumed a new urgency in a Scandinavian setting. The defence of the rights of Danish-speaking people in Schleswig concerned all Scandinavians, for was not Schleswig an outpost of the Scandinavian way of life? It was a *Morgengabe*[4] which Denmark would lead into a new Calmar union founded, not on outmoded dynastic ties, but on the will of the people and the democratic constitution of 1814. Thus the Scandinavian movement reinforced Eiderdane claims to Schleswig, much as the movement for German unification reinforced the claims of the Schleswig-Holsteiner. C. Ploug and O. Lehmann on the one hand, and K. Lorentzen on the other, had discovered in the heady

[1] O. Beseler, *Wilhelm Hartwig Beseler*, etc., p. 19.
[2] The Scandinavian Society.
[3] 'The free and mighty north will lead the people's cause to final victory.'
[4] Dowry.

wine of the new ideologies powerful reinforcement for their respective historical claims to Schleswig.

The *Landespartei* was deeply indebted to another successful song for the popularization of the Schleswig-Holstein slogan *op ewig ungedelt*. This slogan soon became famous throughout the duchies and Germany. It was based on a phrase in the 1460 charter to which Dahlmann had first drawn attention in 1816. The phrase was not in popular circulation in his time. During the 1830's Hegewisch made several attempts to popularize it, changing the word order and publishing his versions beneath pictures of Christian of Oldenburg and U. Lornsen. One of these versions enjoyed wide popularity in the duchies at the beginning of the 1840's. It was Becker's *Rheinlied* which inspired A. W. Neuber, leader of the Åbenraa Germans, to write his poem, *Sie sollen es nicht haben, das heilige Land der Schlei.*[1] The poem ended with the words:

se scholln tosammen blieben
op ewig ungedelt.[2]

The press popularized Neuber's poem in 1844 and in the following year at Eckernförde *Sängerfest*, when the poem was set to music for the first time, banners bearing the slogan already decorated the festive scene. In the last line of the poem the *Landespartei* had at last discovered a concise and popular formulation of its fundamental thesis that the inseparability of the duchies guaranteed their German character and independence. The new catchphrase, together with the red, white and blue Schleswig-Holstein flag and coat of arms, which appeared shortly afterwards, were of inestimable value to the *Landespartei*. The constant display of these tangible and vivid but unofficial symbols of the independent status claimed for the duchies, familiarized the general public with the abstract concept of a Schleswig-Holstein state united only by dynastic ties with Denmark.

The Germans were careful to adjust their propaganda to suit particular localities.[3] Reference could be made to the *Landes-*

[1] They will not get the sacred land of the Schlei.

[2] They will remain together, always undivided.

[3] Even the proud particularism of the Frisians was put to good use by the Schleswig-Holsteiner. The old motto, *Lever duad as slaav*, was pressed into ser-

rechte at all popular festivals. In Holstein references to the German fatherland were frequent. In Schleswig stress was laid mainly on the ties with Holstein, Orla Lehmann and the Eiderdanes were frequently attacked, but care was taken not to antagonize North Schleswig by raising the contentious language question. There were, however, a few contemporary problems which could be raised without constraint. One such issue, which aroused widespread interest in both duchies, was that of finance.

The allegation that there had been unfair discrimination against the duchies in fiscal matters over a number of years proved a most effective propaganda weapon. It attracted the interest of all classes, particularly the small farmers who were generally unimpressed by emotional rhetoric about the German fatherland but were always interested in lightening the burden of taxation. Nor was it difficult for the Germans to prove—to their own satisfaction at least—that the existing fiscal arrangements represented a violation of the *Landesrechte*, the sheet anchor of the duchies.

It was significant that one of the national liberals, Tiedemann, a powerful and persuasive orator, made this question his speciality. He started with the tax reassessment of 1802 to substantiate his general thesis that the burden of taxation had always been inequitably shared between the duchies and Denmark. In 1813 Denmark, faced with national bankruptcy, had established a *Riksbank* for the *Helstat*, imposing a liability of 14,000,000 *Riksbanktaler* on the duchies and 18,900,000 *Riksbanktaler* on Denmark. But later in 1813 the finance college reduced the total liability of the Danish landowners by 12,500,000 *Riksbanktaler*, reapportioning this sum so that the duchies bore 5,000,000 *Riksbanktaler* and Denmark 7,000,000 *Riksbanktaler*. Tiedemann alleged that the duchies had paid 6 per cent interest not only on the original liability of 14,000,000 *Riksbanktaler*, but on an additional 5,000,000 *Riksbanktaler* as well. This made the total liability 19,000,000 *Riksbanktaler* as opposed to a Danish liability of only 6,500,000 *Riksbanktaler*. In fact the *Riksbank* project had not materialized. In its place a private *National Bank* was established in 1818 from which the German

vice as a rallying cry for the defence of 'German freedom' against 'Danish aggression'. Cf. J. Jensen, *Nordfriesland*, p. 101.

landowners contracted out. Tiedemann concluded that the duchies had, over a period of thirty years, paid in capital and interest a total of 38,000,000 *Riksbanktaler*. At Haddeby festival, held in his honour in 1843, Tiedemann insisted that the duchies had been cheated out of this money, as little of it had been spent on improving the amenities of Schleswig-Holstein. Legal proceedings were taken against him for this remark, but he was acquitted after a most able defence by Beseler during a trial which aroused widespread interest in the duchies.

Tiedemann reached the pinnacle of his fame as an orator in connection with the government proposal to establish a branch office of the Danish *National Bank* in Flensburg. In the Schleswig estates in 1842 G. Claussen registered a protest against this proposal, and Tiedemann moved that the duchies' finances be separated from Denmark and regulated by a separate *Landesbank*. During the debate Beseler voiced the fears of the national liberals that the branch office would endanger the independence of the duchies. No doubt it would confer substantial commercial benefit on them. But would not the people of Schleswig-Holstein react as unfavourably as the Belgians would if a London bank tried to establish a branch in their country?[1] The government paid scant attention to these protests but Tiedemann, encouraged by growing opposition to the proposed branch office, pressed ahead with his *Landesbank*. He popularized the project during the winter of 1843, speaking at over sixty meetings and exhorting the general public to subscribe the necessary capital. The money was raised, all classes subscribing to the fund, and the *Landesbank* opened its doors in Rendsburg in the spring of 1844, a month or so before the branch office of the *Nationalbank* was opened in Flensburg. When the latter commenced operations, Tiedemann's appeals to the people to refrain from patronizing the new branch met with considerable success. Societies were even formed in some towns to prevent the circulation of Danish notes, so considerable was public interest in this question. All shades of opinion from Reventlow-Preetz and Falck to Beseler and Storm were united on this issue, for the *Landesbank* was depicted as an essential guarantee of the financial

[1] *St. Z.*, Schleswig, 1842, p. 1165.

independence of the duchies, which was threatened by the establishment of the Danish branch office. Tiedemann, remarked Reventlow-Preetz, had taken the bull by the horns and by his pioneering work had ensured their ultimate victory.[1] It had been a most successful exercise in the art of mass politics, immensely gratifying and encouraging to the *Landespartei*. The Germans were able to employ the same arguments with equal success to obstruct the attempts which the government made in the late 1840's to unify the coinage of the *Helstat*, by withdrawing the old Hamburg, Lübeck and Schleswig-Holstein silver coinage and replacing it with a uniform paper and copper coinage. It was unfortunate but inevitable that these well-intentioned and sensible efforts to modernize the *Helstat* should have foundered on the rocks of intransigent German nationalism.

Finally, in the academic world, the Germans had the advantage of the Danes. They had only Rødding *Højskole* to sustain their efforts. But the Germans had Kiel university behind them and derived from it intellectual sustenance in the 1840's. German universities were again playing an active role in politics as they had done a quarter of a century previously. Johann Gustav Droysen, the new professor of history at Kiel university, was the prototype of the political professor of this decade and the spiritual heir of Dahlmann. A vigorous and forthright personality and ardent national liberal, Droysen believed that the problem of the duchies attained true perspective only in the context of German development. Arriving in Kiel in 1840, Droysen had been appalled by the tenacity with which the people of Schleswig-Holstein clung to their local traditions and shocked by their indifferent attitude towards Germany. Droysen resolved to wage all-out war on this pernicious provincialism and kept his promise. In his well-attended lectures on modern history and in his celebrated speech at the *Verdunfeier* of 1843,[2] he elaborated with fierce eloquence on his major thesis that the connection between the duchies and the

[1] F. Hähnsen, *Tiedemann-Johannisberg. Ein Schleswig-Holsteinischer Führer*, p. 46.

[2] Celebrations held in honour of the partition of Charlemagne's empire at Verdun in 843 and the emergence of separate 'German' and 'French' kingdoms.

German fatherland was of crucial importance to both. His iconoclastic spirit and the more realistic trend of political thinking in the 1840's was reflected in his contempt for the *Helstat*.[1] Old-fashioned balance of power theories might justify the existence of this historical and national anachronism, but that was no durable basis for a modern state. The Belgians had done well to ignore such nonsense in 1830. The whole concept of balance of power was fraudulent, in his opinion, and tenable only as long as peoples were politically immature and inarticulate, or, like the English, obtained their mastery at the expense of the oppressed Irish. The only tolerable and permanent basis for relations between states was autonomous national development and the pursuit of national interest. If this affected the *Helstat* adversely Droysen saw no cause for regret. Like Beseler, Droysen pinned his hopes on Germany, never doubting for a moment that a great future lay ahead of her people.

Droysen was always acutely aware of the vital role which a liberal Prussia would play in the unification of Germany.[2] But Prussia must recognize the importance of the duchies both for herself and for the new Germany. Without Schleswig-Holstein there could not be a powerful Germany and without the will to create Germany there could be no independent Schleswig-Holstein. Prussian interests were bound up closely with the duchies, for it was here that she would find the indispensable basis for the future sea-power of Germany and obtain compensation for the loss of Ems. Strategically the duchies formed a neck for the German body, rendering Germany especially vulnerable to attack and directly endangering the security of the Prussian state. Droysen believed that Russia, the great enemy of Germany, was trying to obtain control of the Sound, the Bosphorus of the north; with this end in view Russia was intriguing in Copenhagen and supporting the anti-German policy of the government. Counter measures from Prussia were clearly imperative both in her own interests and in those of the duchies and of Germany. Otherwise

[1] Liepmann, *op. cit.*, p. 214. J. G. Droysen to W. Arendt, 5 March 1845.

[2] E.g. Hübner, *op. cit.*, pp. 298–300, to W. Arendt, 18 Nov. 1844, pp. 351–5, to W. Arendt, 22 April 1847, pp. 381–4, to J. v. Gruner, 30 Jan. 1848.

the new Germany would not be strong enough to fulfil her mission of defending Central Europe against 'the ice floes from the east and the volcano from the west'.[1] Droysen strove continually to explain the commercial and strategic importance of the duchies to his friends in the Prussian foreign office, but with little success.

In the duchies Droysen's influence was considerable. His classes were attended by several men of ability, including Karl Samwer, Lorenz Stein, founder of the student society *Albertina*, Karl Lorentzen, editor of the *Neuen Kieler Blätter*, Friedrich Harms, Wilhelm Nitzsch and Theodore Mommsen. Droysen was asked to chair the serious political discussions which these young men started in 1842. Out of this circle of students, doctors and lawyers emerged the project for the *Nord Deutsche Blätter*, a paper which would, it was hoped, demand the separation of Schleswig-Holstein from Denmark under its own prince, work for German unification by arousing national sentiment in the duchies, and support the struggle of the Germans in Schleswig.[2] Droysen was bitterly disappointed when the name of the paper was altered to *Neuen Kieler Blätter*.[3] This was yet another testimony to the potency of conservative influences in the *Landespartei*. Men like Reventlow-Preetz and Falck still thought of Germany primarily as a *Kulturnation*. They admired and shared in the German cultural heritage so substantially enriched in the last half century. But even when they admitted the need—as in 1846—for some closer political tie with Germany, they were concerned only to guarantee the independent status of Schleswig-Holstein in the *Helstat*, not to give expression to feelings of national sentiment. The *Helstatsførelse* retained its magical power over the minds of the older generation right down to the revolution. Even Droysen seems to have envisaged the continuance of personal union with Denmark as late as 1848.[4] But there can be little doubt that many of the younger generation had scant respect for dynastic ties and would have welcomed complete independence.

[1] G. Droysen, *Johann Gustav Droysen*, I, p. 259.
[2] L.A.S. 399, Lorentzen 18, draft project 1842 undated.
[3] Liepmann, *op. cit.*, pp. 195–6, J. G. Droysen to T. Olshausen, 26 July 1843.
[4] Hübner, *op. cit.*, p. 382, J. G. Droysen to J. v. Gruner, 30 Jan. 1848.

If we compare the results of the organizational activity of the *Landespartei* with those of the Danish movement, the success of the Germans is both obvious and impressive. The whole of Holstein, South Schleswig and a considerable area in Central Schleswig had been won over to the Schleswig-Holstein cause by the middle of the 1840's. It was a tribute to the effective nature of their work that in the spring of 1848 no resistance was offered to the provisional government in the area south of the Flensburg–Tønder line. In the towns of North Schleswig, particularly in Tønder and Åbenraa, the socially and politically influential German minority co-operated wholeheartedly with the government. Only in Haderslev did the government fail to secure recognition.

It was hardly surprising that Holstein and South Schleswig supported the Germans once the national sentiment of the people had been awakened, because the area was almost entirely German-speaking. But north of the Schlei-Dannevirke line there was probably as much Danish as German spoken even in the late 1840's. Yet it is undeniable that the Danish movement failed to obtain much support outside Haderslev *Amt*, the northern half of Åbenraa *Amt*—where commercial ties between Åbenraa and Copenhagen and the work of Fischer strengthened the Danish connection—Sundeved and the island of Als, where most of the teachers and pastors were influenced by the ancient connection with the bishopric of Odense. *Dannevirke's* circulation was restricted to the same area. Two hundred of their 705 subscribers were resident in Denmark, one hundred were resident in Haderslev *Amt* and the remainder were scattered over the countryside between Haderslev and Tønder. Similarly, over half of the sixty or seventy lending libraries circulating in Schleswig were in Haderslev *Amt*, although a very few extended as far south as Kappeln on the Schlei.

There were several reasons why the Danish movement was confined to a small area of Schleswig. The deeply ingrained provincialism of the duchy was a factor of major importance. The conservative-minded and phlegmatic people of Schleswig-Holstein were as repelled by the prospect of incorporation in Germany as they were by the thought of becoming part of Denmark. On balance they were probably far more suspicious of Danish than of German propaganda because the Schleswig-Holstein movement did at least seek to preserve the *status quo*—before 1846 the *Landespartei* opposed the inclusion of Schleswig in the Confederation; on the other hand the *Slesvigske Forening* insisted on the severance of the connection with Holstein, promising Schleswig local autonomy but only inside the Danish state.

In Central Schleswig there were other factors at work restraining the Danish movement; although much Danish was still spoken in this area, the attachment of the people to the German spoken in church and school proved a most serious obstacle to the spread of Danish cultural values. In addition the small farmers were aware that their prosperity depended on southern cattle markets, which made close ties with Germany a necessity. There were also some faint memories of the Gottorp connection still lingering on in certain parts of Central Schleswig.

In general the power of the Establishment was arrayed on the side of the Germans throughout Schleswig-Holstein. Most German pastors, lawyers and senior officials were naturally sympathetic to the *Landespartei*. This was especially true of the younger generation for those who had been educated at Kiel university in the 1820's were now attaining positions of importance, as Lornsen had prophesied. The social importance of the official classes in an agrarian society as well as their monopoly of political power, both locally and at Gottorp castle, made it easy for the *Landespartei* to conduct its organizational activities under the most favourable circumstances. But the party paid a price for the favours of officials and landowners. It remained sensitive to the interests of the upper classes and lacked the genuinely popular character of the Danish movement in which small farmers, rural teachers, minor officials and some artisans played an active part.[1]

Finally, a most important reason for the German success was the fact that their organizational activity coincided with a period when the use of Low German was on the increase in Central Schleswig. It is difficult to overestimate the social and political

[1] Cf. Bagge and Engelstoft, *op. cit.*, II, no. 526, p. 326, P. C. Koch to A. Tang, 23 July 1843.

importance of the ethnographical changes which had been taking place in this area since the beginning of the century. In Angeln and along the west coast of Schleswig the forward movement of the German language was of inestimable benefit to the *Landespartei*. It was no coincidence that the centre of gravity of the popular festivals lay in South and Central Schleswig where the cause of the *Landespartei* was favoured by the growing popularity of the German tongue. It is a common experience that the most aggressive nationalism is usually found in frontier regions where two nationalities are in close contact. Central Schleswig was no exception. The festivals in their turn accelerated the process of germanization—particularly in Angeln—and gave it a political orientation favourable to the *Landespartei*. In Holstein, on the other hand, the Germans were much less active because on the estates of the *Ritterschaft*, which lay in the east of the duchy and in southeast Schleswig, the preoccupation of the tenants with their material needs and the dislike of the landowners for the popular festivals rendered these areas less accessible to sustained organizational activity. Nor was any significant progress made in the marshlands of western Holstein where local patriotism was still a powerful and all-pervading force.

X

The Duke of Augustenburg

LOOKING back over the history of the century separating us from the 1840's, a century moulded by the force of nationalism, it is tempting to assume that contemporaries must have seen in the national conflict between German and Dane the most significant historical force at work in their times. Some did appreciate the power of nationalism; but most did not; this was especially true of the older generation for whom loyalty to a personal ruler was a deeply-rooted and potent sentiment, a conditioned political reflex. But loyalty to a national group seemed a rather unsavoury concept redolent with revolutionary connotations; only the ignorant would attach much importance to national differences. Views such as these were still quite common among educated people in the 1840's, because memories of the cosmopolitan humanitarianism of the eighteenth century died hard. It is not, therefore, surprising that many people regarded the succession question as a matter of greater moment for the *Helstat* than national differences.

Difficulties about the succession arose when it first became clear that the male line of the house of Oldenburg, which had ruled the *Helstat* since 1459, was approaching extinction.[1] King Christian, on his accession to the throne in 1839, was faced with a serious long-term problem. His son, Frederik, had no male heirs; King Christian's brother, Frederik Ferdinand, had no children and the late monarch, Frederik VI, had only female heirs. When these three princes, Christian, Frederik and Frederik Ferdinand, were dead there would be no more male heirs by agnates remaining in the Glückstadt or royal branch of the house of Holstein-Sonderburg.

Provision had been made to meet this contingency in 1665

[1] See appendices B and C.

under the *Kongelov* which allowed cognates to inherit the crown of Denmark. The usual interpretation of the law, in the circumstances of the nineteenth century, was that after King Christian's sister, Juliane, died without issue, the crown would pass to his younger sister, Charlotte, wife of Wilhelm, *Landgraf* of Hesse Cassel, and from her to her son, Friedrich Wilhelm and his heirs.

There was another less common interpretation which brought King Frederik VI's children into the picture. This was based on a literal interpretation of certain clauses in the *Kongelov* which gave prior right to the children of agnates, whether male or female, over the children of cognates, whether male or female.[1] As Frederik Ferdinand, Charlotte and Juliane were respectively sixteen, nineteen and twenty years older than Christian's son, Frederik, and Wilhelmine, one of King Frederik's daughters, it seemed likely that Charlotte would die before the last male heir, King Frederik VII.[2] In this case the female heirs of the agnate, King Frederik VI, must be preferred to the male heirs of the cognate Charlotte. That meant that the crown would pass to Caroline (Wilhelmine's senior by fifteen years) and then to Wilhelmine. If she died without heirs, the crown would be claimed by her cousin, the duke of Augustenburg, who would be the nearest male to this cognate, or more probably by his son, Friedrich August.

On the whole the former interpretation of the *Kongelov* was more tenable from a legal point of view, for even if Charlotte did die before King Frederik VII it seemed sensible to suppose that the crown should pass via the aunts of the dead king to his cousin, rather than via female cousins to his half cousins.

But legal considerations were not the only or even the most important ones; had they been, then the succession question could have been safely left to the professors of jurisprudence. The real difficulty was that dynastic changes might easily result in the breakup of the state because the succession was not uniform in all parts of the *Helstat*. No one disputed that the female succession applied in Denmark. But Holstein, it was generally agreed, would

[1] *Lex Regia*, clauses 27, 28, 32, 36.

[2] In fact she outlived King Frederik VII by a few months but in 1863, under the treaty of London, Christian of Glücksburg succeeded.

revert to the Schleswig-Holstein-Sonderburg-Augustenburg or cadet branch of the house of Holstein-Sonderburg, since the charter of 1460 explicitly stipulated that only the male heirs of Christian I could succeed to the duchies. The position in Schleswig, on the other hand, was much more complex. The general consensus of opinion, especially in Denmark, favoured the view that the female succession had applied there since 1721. Even Dahlmann, while dissenting from the view that the absolutism of the *Kongelov* applied to Schleswig, never disputed that the succession was the same as that in Denmark.[1] This view was not shared by Falck nor by the head of the house of Schleswig-Holstein-Sonderburg-Augustenburg, Christian Karl Friedrich August, better known in history as the duke of Augustenburg.

The situation facing King Christian was not unique. During the reign of King Christian VII in the previous century, there had seemed a possibility of the male line dying out. The reigning monarch's son, Frederik (later to become King Frederik VI), had only female heirs and Christian's brother, Ferdinand, had no issue at that time. A. P. Bernstorff saved the situation by arranging a marriage in 1786 between the king's daughter, Louise Augusta (whose father was almost certainly Struensee), and the head of the cadet branch, Friedrich Christian. If the male heirs by agnates had died out, the crown of Denmark would have passed to the nearest cognate, Louise Augusta, and from her to the heirs of her marriage. If she had a male heir he would succeed in the duchies as well as in Denmark, being head of the cadet branch. The eventuality did not arise because in September 1786 a male heir, Christian VIII to be, was born to Frederik, the king's brother, and six years later another heir, Frederik Ferdinand. The first male child of Louise Augusta's marriage was Christian August, born in 1798.

His father, Friedrich Christian, was one of the leading rationalists of his day and a bitter enemy of the political Romanticism of Emkendorf. He kept a vigilant eye on the succession and as a member of the *Statsraad* had protested vigorously against the proposed

[1] Dahlmann, *Wort über Verfassung in Kieler Blätter*, I, p. 294; but Falck, *Handbuch des Schleswig-Holsteinischen Privatrechtes*, II, Altona, 1831, p. 43.

incorporation of Holstein in Denmark in 1806, fearing that this would exclude his house from the succession by introducing the female succession into the duchies. He was further incensed by the treatment his brother received at the hands of King Frederik VI in connection with the candidature to the Swedish throne, and he resigned in protest from the *Statsraad* in 1810. The estrangement of the duke from the king was of considerable historical significance, for the duke spent the last years of his life (he died in 1814) researching in the family archives. He claimed, on the basis of these researches, that the rights of his family had been ignored in 1806 and in 1810 and he maintained that only males could succeed to the duchies. Clearly he had visions of his house succeeding to the entire *Helstat*, for he was quick to point out that the state would collapse and the duchies would be lost to Denmark unless the succession laws were altered in the near future. These findings were not published because various Danish correspondents strongly advised Friedrich Christian against it. But the findings were accepted with filial piety by his son and formed the basis of Christian August's dynastic claims advanced many years later.

The marriage expedient of 1786 was resorted to on more than one occasion. In 1815 Prince Christian's second marriage to Caroline Amelia, sister of the duke of Augustenburg, may well have been designed to reinforce the family ties between the royal and cadet branches. It certainly seems probable that King Frederik VI's attempt to forbid the marriage of the young Duke Christian August to the lady of his choice, a certain Countess Danneskjold-Samsø, was inspired by a wish to unite him in matrimony with Caroline, one of the king's daughters, in order to strengthen the connection between the duchies and the kingdom. Eventually Frederik relented and allowed the duke to marry his fairy princess. But it is significant that Schimmelmann remarked, on the occasion of the birth of the duke's son in 1821, that the child might be destined one day to rule over their descendants.[1]

The succession question became a matter of public interest with the appearance of Christian Paulsen's pamphlet in 1836.[2] In it

[1] J. Gebauer, *Christian August. Herzog von Schleswig-Holstein*, etc., p. 51.
[2] *Für Dänemark und für Holstein.*

Paulsen defended his thesis that the *Kongelov* applied not only to the whole of Schleswig but even to some parts of Holstein, leaving only part of the duchy to the cadet branch. Paulsen alleged that, when the Gottorp portions of Schleswig were reunited with the royal portions in 1721, the duke of Augustenburg had formally renounced all claim to Schleswig and to parts of Holstein. The present position was clearly unsatisfactory and likely to lead to renewed partitions of the duchy reminiscent of medieval times. To avoid this melancholy eventuality, Paulsen favoured the extension of the *Kongelov* to all parts of Holstein.

Christian August had shown a passing interest in the succession question over the years, in the intervals between his frequent visits to Schleswig, Hamburg and Odense race-courses where he was a well-known and ardent follower of the turf and an expert breeder of race-horses. In 1824 he took time off to write an essay for a German newspaper, in which he challenged the view advanced by a Danish writer that the *Kongelov* applied to Schleswig. In the early 1830's he corresponded with Dahlmann, seeking further information about his dynastic claims. But Dahlmann pleaded lack of time to undertake the necessary research. No doubt it also occurred to the father of Schleswig-Holsteinism that little constitutional progress could be expected if the illiberal Augustenburg brothers succeeded to the *Helstat*.[1]

Faced with a new and serious challenge from the pen of the well-known Kiel professor, the duke was obliged to devote some time to a detailed refutation of Paulsen's thesis. It was perhaps a not uncongenial task, for Christian August had been irritated already by the king's failure to appoint him *Statthalter*—a post he had always coveted—when that office fell vacant in 1836. The result of the duke's labours was the *Hallische Schrift*,[2] published anonymously in 1837 and favourably reviewed in the *Kieler Korrespondenz Blatt*.[3] The duke flatly rejected Paulsen's allegation that the act of homage made by his ancestor in 1721 had in any

[1] Gebauer, *op. cit.*, p. 78.

[2] *Die Erbfolge in Schleswig-Holstein. Eine historische Beleuchtung der Behauptungen des Herrn Professor Paulsen in der Schrift derselben*, Halle, 1837.

[3] 16, 19, 23 Aug. 1837.

way affected the rights of the cadet branch. Like his father he stoutly affirmed that only the male line could succeed in both duchies.

These pamphlets aroused a certain interest in the succession question which was kept alive by publications such as von Wimpfen's history of Schleswig in 1839, a work which refuted the duke's claims, and by C. F. Heiberg's refutations of von Wimpfen in the *Schleswig-Holsteinische Blätter*, but of course the prospect of the question acquiring more than academic interest was still fairly remote.

The duke was neither well-known nor popular in the duchies at this time. Little was known of the Augustenburgs, save only that they 'spoke Danish, loved horses and were never to be seen'.[1] Nor was the duke a particularly attractive personality. A natural autocrat, proud, overbearing, obstinate and opinionated, he had few friends and many prejudices although he was certainly not lacking in intelligence and ability. At his home, Gravenstein, he lived the life of a country gentleman devoted to the chase, a pastime which often clouded relations with his tenants, for the duke clung tenaciously to his feudal privileges.

It was his political activity in the Schleswig estates which made him a well-known figure in the duchies. He possessed a *Virilstimme*[2] in the estates and by virtue of his pre-eminent social position was the natural leader of the Schleswig conservatives. At the first meeting of the estates he quickly demonstrated his real political ability and fitness to be their spokesman.

On occasion his conservatism was mildly progressive, *vide* his motion for the abolition of all customs dues and the introduction of free trade—this was one of the rare occasions when the duke's arguments were supported by P. Lorenzen. The duke's enlightenment did not, however, extend to the concept of constitutional government. True, his visits to England bred in him a certain admiration for the English parliamentary system, but largely be-

[1] Lotte Hegewisch, *Erinnerungen früherer Stunden für letzte Stunden*, Kiel, 1902, p. 99.

[2] As holder of the Augustenburg *Fideikommissgüter* in Schleswig, he was entitled to a seat in the estates.

cause it allowed the aristocracy to play an important part in the management of public affairs. It was characteristic of him that he warmly applauded the Dutch king's resistance to the Belgian rebels in 1830.[1] He was opposed to a united estates for the duchies and throughout the early 1830's his letters were full of gloomy jeremiads repeating the traditional lamentation of conservatives, that the new provincial estates would cost money and confer little real benefit on the duchies. He was particularly critical of the generous representation given the small farmers, remarking that they were the least enlightened class in the population and morally degenerate into the bargain.[2]

As one might expect the duke was a vigorous and bitter opponent of radical liberalism as represented by U. Lornsen and P. Lorenzen. In the duke's eyes these men were dangerous demagogues bent on the destruction of the established social order, an opinion in which he was confirmed when Peter Lorenzen had the audacity to seek some mitigation of the stringent game laws in the interest of the tenants. Naturally the duke was regarded with aversion by most radicals. G. Claussen refused to trust 'the Tory archduke', fearing that he would use everyone for his own ends. Impressed by warnings from G. Claussen and Hansen, Peter Lorenzen finally rejected the continual exhortations of Hegewisch that he work closely with the duke.

The basic illiberalism of the Augustenburg brothers was clearly revealed when the estates met in 1838. Bitter clashes between the duke and Peter Lorenzen electrified the atmosphere and polarized, around these antithetical personalities, the growing divergence between conservative and liberal. The duke voted for the union of the estates, the only matter on which conservative and liberal could agree, but he opposed Berwald's motion for financial powers for the estates and fought tenaciously against P. Lorenzen's attempts to abolish the jurisdictional powers of landowners. P. Lorenzen's suspicions were confirmed. One could expect little

[1] Bagge and Engelstoft, *op. cit.*, I, no. 10, p. 13, Christian August to Grev Danneskjold-Samsøe, 11 Jan. 1831.

[2] A. Heils, *Augustenborgske Breve til I. G. Adler og P. Hjort*, pp. 92–3, duke to J. G. Adler, 3 Dec. 1842; pp. 94–5, 17 July 1833; pp. 95–6, 8 Aug. 1833.

from the Augustenburg brothers. They had 'at last dropped the mask' and made public the tacit alliance between the Establishment and the government.

By this time there were fresh developments in the succession question. King Frederik VI had raised the question with the Great Powers, Austria, Prussia and Russia. The attitude of Tsar Nicholas was especially important. Not only was he the most powerful ruler in Europe but, as head of the house of Holstein-Gottorp, he might raise claims to certain parts of Holstein. The powers were sounded as to their reaction should the succession laws be altered so that the *Kongelov* applied to all parts of the *Helstat.* Prince Christian personally informed the Tsar and Metternich of his cousin's wishes, meeting with a not unfavourable response. Evidently King Frederik was prepared to offer Lauenburg to the duke of Augustenburg and obtain for him a seat in the Federal Diet if he would renounce his claims to the duchies. The duke got wind of these secret negotiations and promptly wrote to the Tsar in December 1838 in defence of his claims, only to receive a noncommittal reply in the following spring.[1] F. C. Dankwart, the king's secretary, was awaiting the royal signature to new instructions, which would have sent him to Gravenstein to commence negotiations for a renunciation of the Augustenburg claims, when the old king died in December 1839.

Not only in the diplomatic field did the duke feel obliged to defend his dynastic claims. These seemed equally endangered by parties seeking to alter the status of the duchies. He was firmly opposed to the New Holsteiner and even more disturbed by the activity of the Press Society in Schleswig. He shared with many Germans the belief that the Press Society was working for the ultimate incorporation of Schleswig in Denmark. Consequently concern for the claims of the cadet branch was uppermost in his mind when he and his brother opposed the Nis Lorenzen motion in 1838.

The duke's denial during the debate that he was anti-Danish was spontaneous enough, for Danish and German conservatives alike attached little significance to national sentiment. Education,

[1] P.A. III D2, Tsar to duke, 4 March 1839.

the duke observed to a friend, should enable one to overcome personal and national prejudices.[1] He disagreed most emphatically with people who attached an exaggerated importance to their mother tongue. An educated man should speak several tongues and by so doing would shed provincial or national attitudes and shun these juvenile prejudices. His own children spoke as much Danish as German, English or French. It was immaterial to him whether they were educated in a Danish or German environment. The family, as the Prince of Noer remarked, was as much Danish as German and they were born in and partly educated in Denmark. Danish as well as German was spoken at home and they had many educated Germans and Danes among their friends.[2]

The duke's prominent role in the opposition to the Nis Lorenzen motion had, therefore, nothing to do with national antipathies. Rather he was concerned to preserve the monopoly enjoyed by the German language in administrative and legal matters, because this symbolized the unity of Schleswig-Holstein and safeguarded his dynastic claims. Behind the technicalities of his speech lay a real fear that the introduction of Danish would lead to the separation of the German and Danish-speaking parts of the duchy, an eventuality which it was in his interests to avoid at all costs.[3]

His opposition was coloured by intense dislike of the radicalism of Peter Lorenzen and of other North Schleswig members associated with the Nis Lorenzen motion. The motion annoyed him because it represented a popular protest against the might of German officialdom. The duke refused to entertain the revolutionary notion that officials might exist to serve the people. On the contrary, he attacked the changes proposed by his opponents on the ground that they would seriously interfere with the careers of those who were aspiring to official positions. In practice it would restrict official posts in North Schleswig to natives of the area and furthermore, as the university was a German institution, it would surely be unfair to make a knowledge of Danish a prerequisite for advancement.[4]

[1] Heils, *op. cit.*, pp. 133–4, Duke to P. Hjort, 6 Oct. 1844.
[2] Heils, *op. cit.*, p. 211, Prince of Noer to P. Hjort, 20 Feb. 1846.
[3] *St. Z.*, Schleswig, 1838, p. 615. [4] *Ibid.*, p. 598.

His speeches inevitably attracted attention in Denmark where many people began to suspect that he was hostile to their way of life. Unflattering references to the duke began to appear in the leading papers, *Faedrelandet*, *Københavnsposten* and *Folkebladet*. These suspicions seemed justified by the attitude of the Augustenburg brothers during the debate on the *Ständezeitung* shortly before the end of the Schleswig estates.

The Viborg estates had decided to send free copies of their journal to those members of the Holstein and Schleswig estates placing an order for it. The Schleswig estates reciprocated this offer by proposing to send free copies of their journal, in German and Danish, to those members of the Danish estates who requested them. The duke seemed determined to make an issue of it, demanding that the Danish edition be distributed only in North Schleswig. Those members of the Danish estates who requested copies of the Schleswig journal should be supplied only with the German edition—for did not the Danish estates supply only one edition, namely the Danish, to those German-speaking people in the duchies who were interested in their proceedings? What must be avoided at all costs, remarked the duke in an unfortunate passage, was a situation where anyone who thought he would like to read the proceedings of the Schleswig estates in Danish, instead of German, the official language, could be supplied with an official translation.[1] His brother, the Prince of Noer, maintained that a Danish translation was not necessary, and added bluntly that sentiments of generosity must not be permitted to prejudice the issue.[2] The committee elected to consider the petition actually proposed that only a German edition be published, as only fifty-three Danish copies of the Schleswig journal had been sold and only six of them inside the duchy. Reasonable counsels prevailed later, when a considerable majority decided to continue the publication of both editions, but in separate numbers. It was most significant that after this debate Danish conservatives like Bishop Fogtmann, commenting on 'the puerile and unintelligible behaviour' of the brothers, referred to a general conviction in

[1] *St. Z.*, Schleswig, 1838, p. 78.
[2] *Ibid.*, pp. 459–60.

Denmark that the Augustenburgs were trying to separate the duchies from the kingdom.[1]

The accession of King Christian VIII posed a new problem for Christian August, as relations between the duke and the new sovereign, his brother-in-law, had never been particularly cordial. They did not improve after the visit of the duke and duchess to Copenhagen in May 1840 for the silver wedding celebrations and coronation ceremony. The duke, a stickler for etiquette, was deeply offended when precedence was given to the Hessians at formal functions. He was also disappointed at the king's failure to discuss the succession question; with only three men standing between the male line and extinction, an accommodation was surely an urgent necessity. King Christian was well aware of this but was in fact seeking to solve the problem at the expense of the Augustenburgs, by arranging a suitable marriage for his son, Frederik.

1840 was an important year in the duke's political career, in the course of which he made a determined and successful bid to obtain control of the *Landespartei*. His great enemies, the radicals, were in retreat, dispirited after the defection of Olshausen. The moment seemed opportune for establishing the ascendancy of conservative forces in the party and driving out his *bête noire*, Peter Lorenzen, whose democratic influence among the farmers of North Schleswig irritated the duke beyond measure. Nor did the duke fail to perceive that by enhancing his own reputation as leader of the *Landespartei*, he could strengthen his dynastic claims. The language question and in particular the rescript in May 1840 supplied him with the means of realizing these ambitions. The growing perturbation with which conservatives and liberals regarded developments in North Schleswig drew the party together in defence of the duchies, obscuring the ideological differences which had damaged the duke's reputation in the past. Radicals like Peter Lorenzen who favoured the official use of Danish in North Schleswig were isolated, driven out into the political wilderness and upbraided for betraying the German way of life

[1] Bagge and Engelstoft, *op. cit.*, I, no. 197, pp. 268–9, to P. Hjort, 20 July 1838, p. 237, 21 Aug. 1838.

in Schleswig-Holstein. At the same time the reputation of those members who had fought Nis Lorenzen's motion tooth and nail under the leadership of the duke was considerably enhanced.

The duke now dominated the estates, sitting on all important committees, directing the attack on the rescript and ensuring by his vigorous intervention that the estates reversed their decision of 1838. It was also a victory for conservatism, as the royal commissioner, Reventlow-Criminil, shrewdly observed; for it was the duke's influence which was decisive in securing the rejection of all liberal measures, especially Gülich's motion demanding a constitution for a united estates.[1] By the end of 1840 Christian August had clearly superseded Falck as titular head of the *Landespartei*. The duke's championship of the German resistance to the rescript made him a popular figure in the duchies although his reputation suffered in Denmark. He was now the object of frequent attacks in the Danish press, where he was depicted as the very incarnation of all anti-Danish separatism. Even the reluctance of the new sovereign to follow a liberal policy was ascribed to the sinister influence of his aristocratic brother-in-law during King Christian's visit to Gravenstein in 1838.

The duke's ability as a polemical writer helped him to consolidate his position in the *Landespartei*. Early in 1838 he saw the need for a press campaign to counteract the propaganda of *Dannevirke* and the democratic influence exerted by Peter Lorenzen on the farmers of Als. He commenced his career as a writer in the spring and summer of 1840, with a series of articles bitterly attacking Peter Lorenzen for his support of Nis Lorenzen. In the early 1840's the duke's articles appeared regularly in the *Itzehoer Wochenblatt* and on occasion in the Husum, Rendsburg and Sønderborg *Wochenblätter*. He met deficits on the Haderslev *Lyna* out of his own pocket, subsidized a Danish edition of the *Sonderburger Wochenblatt* (*Sønderborger Ugeblad*), and paid for special issues of articles and committee reports too long for publication in the press.

He played an active and prominent role in organizing resistance to the rescript outside the estates. Besides lodging a formal protest

[1] Fabricius, *op. cit.*, p. 262.

on the grounds that the rescript infringed his powers of jurisdiction in Als and at Gravenstein,[1] he informed the agents and officials on his estates that he expected them to declare their inability to implement the rescript. In December 1840 Krogh, *Amtmann* of Tønder, suggested that a strike of lawyers would be a most efficacious means of preventing implementation of the rescript. For as another correspondent, B. Schow, *Bürgermeister* of Haderslev, remarked, 'without lawyers the functioning of the law is as much impaired as if there were no courts. Consequently the rescript is for all practical purposes suspended.'[2] The duke listened to this advice and seems to have been implicated in the strike which followed in 1841 and resulted in substantial modifications of the rescript.

The publication of U. J. Lornsen's book by Georg Beseler in the spring of 1841 could not have occurred at a more opportune moment for Christian August.[3] Between meetings of the estates people tended to lose interest in the language question which had temporarily united the party around the duke. Thoughts turned once more to the ideological conflict between conservative and liberal, still smouldering on to remind members of the *Landespartei* that the duke remained the enemy of their constitutional aspirations. At this critical moment the duke might well have lost ground in the party had it not been for Lornsen's book, *Die Unionsverfassung*, in which the liberal prophet of Schleswig-Holsteinism supported the dynastic claims of the Augustenburgs. One of Lornsen's objectives in writing his popular history had been to clear up the very considerable confusion existing in the public mind about the succession.[4] Neither Dahlmann nor Falck had accepted the Augustenburg claims, much less had they attached any political significance to them. Dahlmann believed that the female succession applied in Schleswig, while Falck, though accepting the Augustenburg contention that only the male line could succeed there, was of the opinion that certain parts of Holstein were subject to the female succession and might be separated

[1] P.A. III 3d.
[2] P.A. III D 3b, to duke, undated.
[3] See p. 160.
[4] Pauls, *op. cit.*, pp. 250–3, U. Lornsen to F. Hegewisch, 4 July 1835.

from Schleswig if the succession changed. Lornsen cut through the confusion with characteristic boldness, reducing the *Landesrechte* to three essentials: firstly, the duchies of Schleswig and Holstein formed the state Schleswig-Holstein; secondly, the same succession applied to all parts of this state and thirdly, Denmark and Schleswig-Holstein would remain united by dynastic bonds only as long as there were male heirs by agnates in the royal line.[1] This was an historic moment in the history of Schleswig-Holsteinism. The dynastic claims of the cadet branch had been recognized as essential to the defence of Schleswig-Holstein, becoming an integral part of the *Landesrechte* with the blessing of Lornsen, idol of the young liberals.

It was popularly but erroneously assumed by many Danes that the Augustenburg brothers were seeking to disrupt the *Helstat*, and make Christian August ruler of an independent Schleswig-Holstein. Naturally the duke was as anxious to uphold the claims of the cadet branch as his father had been. But, like his father, he believed that the disruption of the *Helstat* could be prevented if the *Kongelov* was altered so that the cadet branch could succeed to the Danish throne. Radicals like Olshausen and Lehmann, anxious to refashion the state along national lines, could look forward with eager anticipation to the disruption of the *Helstat*. But not the conservative Augustenburgs. They had as much to lose as their royal brother-in-law. They had a common enemy in radicalism—the most likely beneficiary if the *Helstat* broke up—and a strong vested interest in the perpetuation of the existing social order. This was ample justification for the rapprochement of 1842 which made the prince of Noer *Statthalter*. Peter Lorenzen never understood this. He supposed that the king had simply been outmanœuvred by the Machiavellian tactics of the brothers. Commenting on the prince's appointment, Lorenzen exclaimed melodramatically: 'the king has given the stamp of legality to the

[1] Lornsen never completely overcame his suspicion of the Augustenburgs. Writing to his father in July 1835, he commented that one could never rely on princes. Once the succession in Denmark was altered in their favour, that would probably be the end of their Schleswig-Holstein patriotism. W. Jessen, *op. cit.*, p. 175.

uprising by supplying it with a leader. Now the outbreak is only a matter of time.'[1] This was very wide of the mark; the political activity of the Augustenburgs was inspired by a desire to preserve the *Helstat* not to disrupt it.

The duke made this very clear when writing to the prince in April 1842.[2] The prince, extremely critical of the Danish royal house in the past, had second thoughts after his new appointment.[3] He now urged the duke to go to Copenhagen, try to come to terms with the king and neutralize the anti-Augustenburg feeling prevalent in Denmark. This spadework was essential if the Augustenburgs were ever to succeed to the Danish throne. In his reply the duke emphasized the need for extreme caution. Any attempt to conciliate the Danish people in the near future would fail and excite speculation in Denmark about his aims. If he put his dynastic claims first and showed a willingness to flatter the Danes for his own ends, he might well turn public opinion in the duchies against him. A great many people in Schleswig-Holstein desired separation from the kingdom, in the duke's opinion, and favoured the Augustenburg claims as a means to this end. These people would become enemies the moment he attempted to perpetuate in his own person the connection with Denmark. But if he waited on events the outcome would be very different. The king would turn to the cadet branch in the end, because his own plans would be rendered impracticable by the refusal of the Augustenburgs to renounce their irrefutable claims. Sensible people in Denmark would surely understand that the connection with the duchies could not be maintained by force but only by negotiation and that unless something was done to prevent it, the connection with Holstein would most certainly be severed when the Danish male line died out. The conclusion was inescapable; if the *Helstat* was to be preserved the Augustenburgs must succeed in Denmark.

Shortly afterwards the duke visited Copenhagen to refute allegations appearing in *Faedrelandet*, to the effect that his own marriage had not received the sanction of the late king. King and

[1] Skau, *op. cit.*, p. 149. [2] P.A. III D 2a, 11 April 1842.
[3] P.A. III D 2a, 27 and 29 March 1842.

duke met at Schloss Sorgenfrei one summer's afternoon and discussed the question uppermost in their minds.[1] The king opened the discussion with the allegation that the duke was primarily to blame for the bad blood between them. In the first place the duke was considered by many people to be the leader of a party seeking to separate the duchies from Denmark. Secondly, had he not published the *Hallische Schrift* there would have been no talk of a different succession in the duchies. The duke replied, somewhat evasively, that his constant opposition to democratic currents in the estates was surely sufficient proof that he was not attempting to found a party. As for the *Hallische Schrift*, it had been his duty to refute Paulsen and defend the well-established rights of the cadet branch. It was not his fault that differences in the succession laws had existed since the seventeenth century. In reply the king conceded that parts of Holstein might be subject to different succession laws from Denmark, but he insisted, come what may, that Schleswig remain part of Denmark. It was his duty as king to preserve the *Helstat* and to this end he was prepared to offer compensation for a renunciation of the Augustenburg claims. The duke flatly rejected this offer, maintaining that he was in honour bound to his late father to uphold the claims of his house.

Moreover the duke argued that the Augustenburg claims were the duchies' best line of defence against incorporation in Denmark; for there was no doubt that the Germans would regard the introduction of the Danish succession law as proof positive of Denmark's desire to annex the duchies. It was significant that the duke tried to associate his claims as intimately as possible with the defence of the duchies. This was not because he wished to become ruler of an independent Schleswig-Holstein, but simply because he calculated that he could use the duchies as a lever to move the king. With the German duchies behind them, the Augustenburgs would be in an unassailable position. It would dawn on Christian, not only that the Augustenburgs could not be bought off, but that if he resisted their claims indefinitely he would lose the duchies as

[1] The duke's version in J. G. Droysen and K. Samwer, *Die Herzogtümer Schleswig-Holstein und das Königreich Dänemark*, etc., pp. 164–8. The king's version in A. D. Jørgensen, *op. cit.*, S.A. 1895, pp. 109–11.

well. Should the Danes desire to avoid this melancholy outcome, renunciations were certainly necessary. This was no concern of his, the duke added piously, for he would never seek a crown not his by right. But it seemed obvious to him that the cognates must make the sacrifice, because Denmark was more anxious to maintain her connection with the duchies than the duchies were to maintain their ties with Denmark. This was certainly an exaggeration designed to give added point to the duke's argument, for he was well aware that *Helstatsførelse* was still a potent psychological force in Schleswig-Holstein. Nor was Christian August as disinterested as he pretended to be in the possibility of an accommodation favourable to the cadet branch.

Astute politician though he was, it is clear that the duke grossly underestimated the difficulties he was creating for himself as a result of his successful career in the Schleswig estates. He possessed sufficient tactical sense to realize that the Danish liberals could not be won over to his point of view in 1842. But he did not comprehend that his chances of obtaining the Danish crown were steadily declining with the passage of the years, simply because he had associated himself too closely with the Germans, permanently alienating Danish opinion from the cadet branch. The duke did not realize this simply because he had an aristocratic contempt for public opinion. Writing to his brother-in-law, the duke referred to the hostile attitude of Danish liberals who were trying to turn public opinion against him by alleging that he was anti-Danish. He remarked that he was indifferent to what these people said or thought about him. He refused to do anything calculated to win 'so-called popularity of which I am contemptuous in the highest degree'.[1] His views would not change whatever the mob might say about him. The duke was shrewder than many conservatives in recognizing the usefulness of the press as a propaganda weapon, and extremely dexterous in his manipulation of persons and situations to forward his dynastic claims. But, like most conservatives, he failed completely to appreciate that the entry of the masses into politics was the most significant development in the

[1] Bagge and Engelstoft, *op. cit.*, I, no. 251, pp. 370–1, to Grev Danneskjold-Samsøe, 28 Dec. 1839.

nineteenth century. Consequently he underestimated the growing importance of popular anti-Augustenburg feeling in Denmark as a factor likely to influence government policy in the future. He confidently assumed that needs of state, the king's desire to preserve the *Helstat* and the well-established claims of the cadet branch were the only important considerations, which must prevail ultimately over all else including the popular prejudices of Germans and Danes.

The discussions between the king and the duke at Schloss Sorgenfrei ended in complete deadlock. Neither side was prepared to give way. King Christian faced the future full of confidence for it seemed possible that his son, remarried in 1841, might have a male heir. Failing this, the king saw no need for a renunciation by the cognates in favour of a brother-in-law who had resisted all appeals to abandon his claims in the interests of the state, had indulged in party politics and had made anti-Danish utterances.

The duke was equally certain that the cadet branch must eventually secure the throne of the *Helstat*. But in the months that followed, the political situation deteriorated sharply with the onset of the national conflict. When the duke launched his attacks on Peter Lorenzen in the Schleswig estates, he was probably embittered by the realization that national animosities would destroy that peaceful coexistence between German and Dane so indispensable for the preservation of the *Helstat*, and would seriously prejudice his dynastic ambitions. He continued to exert a moderating influence on the *Landespartei* after 1842, opposing with success the national liberal demand for the entry of Schleswig into the Confederation. He was reluctant to associate himself too closely with the national liberals who were undermining his conservative influence in the party and, always averse to popular acclamation, he did not appear at *Volksfeste* or *Sängerfeste*. Nor did he approve of the widespread discussion of the succession question in the early 1840's, preferring to wait until the question assumed practical significance.[1]

The duke's innate conservatism was illustrated by his reaction to suggestions made in certain Danish circles regarding the

[1] P.A. III D 2a, Falck to duke, summer 1842.

Augustenburg claims. A regular correspondent, Professor P. Hjort, suggested in 1843 and again in 1844 that, in the event of the extinction of the male line, a Danish prince of the Oldenburg house would be preferable to a Hessian soldier's son.[1] For his part the duke must sever his connections with the Schleswig-Holsteiner, allow his sons to be educated as Danish princes and cultivate the friendship of Danish politicians.

It was characteristic of the duke that in his reply he concentrated upon the legal aspect of the problem.[2] He and his sons could not claim, strictly speaking, to be 'Danish princes'. They were not princes of the blood as were all the male and female heirs of King Frederik III. Nor were the Hessians able to claim this, as he was quick to point out. But as long as the *Kongelov* remained in force, the female succession applied to Denmark and the Hessians would presumably be the lawful heirs. Only if this law was repealed or if the Hessians renounced the throne, could he and his sons become heirs to the throne. There was, of course, no doubt about his succession in the duchies; when the male line died out the cadet branch would automatically secure a ducal crown.

Christian August was not prepared to become king of Denmark by will of the people, should the Danes take matters into their own hands when the male line died out. That would be a gross violation of established rights in which he could not possibly acquiesce. Revolutionary action of any kind was abhorrent to the duke; he felt that people who resorted to violence only did so because their arguments were unconvincing. He repeated his assertion made at Schloss Sorgenfrei that he would never stretch out his hand towards a crown which was not his by right.

This did not mean that he thought the Hessians should be allowed to secure the throne. Far from it. If they succeeded he prophesied disunity and confusion in Denmark. Even supposing the Danes accepted a foreign prince as their king—and much

[1] L.A.S. 399 Samwer 40, P. Hjort to duke, 26 Dec. 1844.

[2] Heils, *op. cit.*, pp. 135–6, duke to P. Hjort, 2 April 1845. Later, when the Danes accused the duke of instigating the *Erhebung*, this letter was published in *A.A.Z.*, 4 and 5 March 1849, with a commentary emphasizing the correctness of the duke's attitude in 1845.

opposition could be anticipated—the duchies would not accept him. Behind the duchies stood the German princes who would not permit a German princely house to be deprived of its rights, much less allow the Danes to make a Hessian prince duke of Holstein. The blunt truth was that Germany stood to gain politically and commercially if Holstein entered the Confederation as an independent state. It was equally certain that Schleswig would not relish the rule of the Hessians. Finally, if the Hessians succeeded to the throne it was quite likely that absolutism would collapse in Denmark and with it the female succession. This would weaken still more their tenuous hold on the throne and destroy completely the basis of their claims.

He concluded that if the Danes wished to preserve the *Helstat*—a laudable aim of which he approved—then they must rectify the error of 1660. The *Helstat* could be preserved but only if the cadet branch of a house which had ruled the duchies and Denmark for four centuries came to the throne. The Great Powers, with their vested interest in the *status quo*, were more likely to approve of this arrangement than of the accession of a foreign dynasty opposed in the duchies and disliked in Denmark. It was characteristic of the duke that he tacitly assumed that the growing desire of the duchies for separation—caused he believed by the prospect of the Hessian succession—would automatically disappear once the Augustenburgs ascended the throne.

The duke was equally cautious when the Eiderdane, L. Skau, outlined his fantastic plan to Pastor H. W. Meyer in January 1846.[1] Skau suggested to Meyer, a friend of the duke's, that Christian August must surely have realized by now that he could not defeat the Hessians. They had the Danish people and Russia behind them. But if the duke came to an understanding with the Danish radicals a great career would be open to his family. If he wished to seize this opportunity, he must jettison his anti-Danish prejudices, improve his personal relations with the king and crown prince, evince an interest in constitutional government and

[1] P.A. III D8, 7 Jan. 1846. Cf. Bagge and Engelstoft, *op. cit.*, III, no. 728, pp. 160–1, L. Skau to A. Tscherning, 4 July 1846; no. 729, pp. 162–4, A. Tscherning to L. Skau, undated.

marry his younger son, Christian, into the Swedish royal family, thus paving the way for a Scandinavian union. If Russia objected to changes in the *Kongelov*, the Danes could rely on English and French support. As for Holstein and Lauenburg, they would be given to the eldest son, Friedrich. Skau was confident that his plan, which would place the duke or his son on the Danish throne, would prove attractive to the Augustenburgs and would be supported by C. Flor and A. Tscherning.

Nothing came of these suggestions or of the remarks made by the Danish radical, Captain Tscherning, during a dinner party at Gravenstein in June 1844.[1] Tscherning observed that dynastic squabbles were a matter of indifference to Eiderdanes. They were concerned only to ensure that the Danish state extended to the Eider. The fate of Holstein was not their business. But it so happened that the Hessians were intimately associated with Russia, the *bête noire* of all democrats. In these circumstances Tscherning welcomed the possibility of a change of succession in favour of the Augustenburgs. The duke was uninterested in suggestions of this sort because they made the Augustenburg succession dependent on the will of the Danish people. In any case he shrewdly suspected that little would come of them. Duty and expediency happily coincided in Christian August's case, convincing him that he must remain on the firm ground afforded by his claim to Schleswig-Holstein and avoid the pitfalls implicit in the Danish suggestions. As always he comforted himself with the thought that the Hessians would find it too difficult to succeed to the throne and ultimately the cadet branch would come into its rightful heritage.

The succession question entered a new phase in 1844 when King Christian tried to strengthen the claims of the Hessians by marrying Frederik of Hesse into the Russian royal family. The Russian minister, Count Nesselrode, made the suggestion to Christian in the autumn of 1842, when it became evident that the second marriage of King Christian's son, Frederik, would not be blessed

[1] J. Clausen, *Af Orla Lehmanns Papirer. Bidrag til Danmarks Tidshistorie i det 19 Aarhundert*, København, 1903, pp. 80–5, A. Tscherning to O. Lehmann, 19 June 1844.

with children. In July 1843 Frederik's engagement to Princess Alexandra was announced and the marriage followed in January 1844. King Christian attached great importance to the marriage alliance, feeling confident that Frederik would succeed without difficulty to the Danish throne now that he had the most powerful autocrat in Europe as a father-in-law.

But with Danish and German liberals the marriage alliance was most unpopular. In Denmark there was despondency for it seemed clear that the Russian connection would strengthen Frederik's natural disinclination to bestow constitutional liberties on his subjects. In the duchies there was much alarm. It was rumoured that the Russians might renew their claims to the Gottorp parts of Holstein, for the arrangement negotiated with Tsar Paul in 1773 had applied only to the male descendants of the Danish royal line. There was talk of Kiel passing into Russian hands as the result of secret arrangements which it was supposed had been the price of the marriage alliance. Partly because of these fears, public interest in affairs of state did not decline as usual after the dispersal of the Schleswig estates. The national liberals in particular were quick to see that these fears could be put to good use when popularizing the programme of the *Landespartei*; a new note of urgency was added to the exhortation that Schleswig-Holstein must seek closer association with Germany.

The duke was especially concerned by reports in *Dannevirke* and elsewhere in 1843 that Russia and Prussia had secretly agreed to guarantee the association between the duchies and Denmark. Fearing that this agreement might have been made at the expense of his claims, he decided to visit Germany with his family and enlist the support of the German princes. In Cologne he met the two most powerful princes in North Germany, Friedrich Wilhelm IV, the new ruler of Prussia, and Ernst August of Hannover. In Wiesbaden he discussed his claims with Leopold, king of the Belgians, and later with Ludwig of Bavaria, Friedrich August of Saxony and last, but certainly not least, with Metternich. He did not meet with any notable success during the visit and, characteristically, decided not to repeat his trip the following year because of the hostile reception it received in Denmark.

In the second half of the 1840's the duke gradually lost his freedom of manœuvre and was taken prisoner by the forces he had tried to exploit in his own interests. Between 1840 and 1842, when politics were the concern of an educated minority, it was still possible to use the Schleswig-Holstein movement as a weapon in his campaign to persuade King Christian of the need for altering the succession in his or his son's favour. With the onset of the national conflict in 1842, national antagonisms deepened, making acceptance of his claim to the *Helstat* a remoter possibility. In Denmark he became a symbol of popular anti-German feeling; for once the German national liberals had espoused his claims to Schleswig-Holstein he was committed almost irretrievably to their side—as he seems occasionally to have suspected. Even within the *Landespartei* his dominant influence declined although, as subsequent chapters will show, he always remained an important figure rendering valuable political services to the Germans for whom he symbolized the independence of Schleswig-Holstein.

XI

1844

THE year 1842 ended on a melancholy note for all who had the interests of the *Helstat* at heart. It was a bitter moment for the king. In the first two years of his reign King Christian had been confident that he could retain the loyalty of his subjects by a vigorous policy of modernization and conciliation. The general approval which greeted the new appointments made in January 1842 encouraged him to believe that he had turned the corner, and was winning the approval of all conservatives by his policy. But now it lay in ruins, for with the sudden outbreak of the national conflict the internal peace so essential for the success of the policy was shattered and its beneficent effects on the *Helstat* were obscured. Naturally the king was filled with anxiety and foreboding as he looked into the New Year of 1843; 'I ask God to give me wisdom and strength,' he wrote in January, 'to resolve these contentious issues exaggerated by both sides. The Schleswig-Holsteiner are trying to germanize Schleswig, the Danish radicals are trying to separate Schleswig from Holstein. Kings should stand above parties and try to maintain things as they are, allowing Schleswig to remain an independent duchy under the Danish crown and respecting whatever language is used by their subjects.'[1] Brave words but a forlorn hope, for once German and Dane ceased to look upon each other as equal partners, the fate of the *Helstat* was sealed. Only an accident of history and the intervention of the Great Powers allowed it to remain intact for another twenty-five years.

One should not attach undue importance to inflammatory newspaper articles and speeches by young politicians who often find in the magic of the spoken word compensation for their exclusion from the seat of power. Much more alarming were ominous

[1] A. D. Jørgensen, *op. cit.*, *S.A.*, 1895, p. 116, 1 Jan. 1843.

signs that national animosities were penetrating the apparatus of government at the highest levels. Friction between Danish and German officials had developed to such an extent that the prince of Noer feared an imminent crisis; 'No one would believe how rapidly we are approaching a complete breakdown,' he wrote in the summer of 1843.[1] His reports as *Statthalter* now made little impression on a monarch who had begun to regard the prince as an agent of his enemies, the Schleswig-Holsteiner. Senior German officials, presided over by Count Reventlow-Criminil, remained at their posts only with the greatest reluctance, while the younger officials, contemporaries and admirers of Lornsen, found their duties increasingly irksome in what was for them a foreign city. Similarly in the armed forces, restless since the 1842 reform had dispersed the Schleswig-Holstein regiments, the German rank and file were increasingly resentful of Danish words of command and on bad terms with their Danish officers. The prince of Noer informed his brother, at the end of 1843, that the military could no longer be relied upon, and that in the key fortress of Rendsburg Danish and German officers were on such bad terms with each other that all social intercourse had ceased.[2]

It is a commonplace in history that rulers, like other men, are rarely free to accept the logic of events. Even if King Christian had believed the collapse of the *Helstat* to be inevitable, his instinctive reaction and his sense of duty would have obliged him, like Metternich, to play his part in propping up a mouldering edifice. In fact, once the king had recovered from his momentary fit of depression, the situation assumed a more roseate hue. After all, should an heir be born to his son, Frederik, the succession would be secured. His subjects, German and Danish alike, would surely rejoice to see the *Helstat* preserved in this way and, with the Russian connection behind him, the future could be faced with equanimity. Until the happy event occurred, a judicious mixture of blandishments and threats would serve to overawe the Eiderdanes and the 'professors and lawyers' in the Schleswig-Holstein movement. On the one hand King Christian continued to combat

[1] P.A. III C 5, prince of Noer to duke of Augustenburg, 27 Aug. 1843.
[2] P.A. III C 5, 5 Dec. 1843, 20 Dec. 1843.

the claims of the duke, seeking to discredit him in the eyes of the Great Powers, while on the other hand he showed a conciliatory spirit in his dealings with the German estates. In this mood he issued a patent letter on 29 March in a last attempt to solve the problem which had ostensibly sparked off the national conflict in 1842.

The Schleswig estates had failed to devise a procedure which would allow Danish-speaking members to take an active part in the deliberations as envisaged in the rescript of December 1842; the king, therefore, ordered the *Schleswig-holsteinische Kanzlei* to work out a provisional solution and submitted its findings to the estates for discussion. It was proposed in the patent letter that members unable to speak German should inform the president of the estates of this fact at the beginning of the session. They would then be allowed to speak Danish. Statements made by members regarding their inability to speak German must not be questioned by the estates. But speeches made by these members would be entered in the minutes in a German translation. This meant that the secretaries would require a knowledge of both languages in order to take the minutes and to translate into German any private members' bills handed to the president in Danish.

It seemed a reasonable enough compromise which, while accepting the German argument for one official language, insisted that the right of non-German speakers to participate fully in debate be safeguarded by a proper procedure, and be no longer dependent on the will of the majority. But, as the unfavourable Danish reaction was soon to demonstrate, the time had passed when questions affecting relations between German and Dane could be settled rationally and impartially by royal fiat.

The *Slesvigske Forening* was the first to announce its displeasure. At the annual general meeting in May a resolution was passed roundly condemning the patent as a betrayal of Danish interests. P. Lorenzen now expressed regret at his own forbearance in the past and declared bitterly to Ploug that 'the Danes in Schleswig will not be taken in by this crowned comedian any longer'.[1] In P. Lorenzen's eyes the patent was nothing more nor less than a

[1] Skau, *op. cit.*, p. 270, 23 May 1844.

betrayal of the natural right to speak Danish, because all the North Schleswig members, except Nis Lorenzen, could speak German well and would now be obliged to recommence using that language. Rather than endure this humiliation Peter Lorenzen preferred the honourable course of resignation from the estates, to be quickly followed by Posselt, Jepsen and Nielsen. The *Slesvigske Forening* endorsed their action and prompted by P. Lorenzen, who wished to force the hand of his Copenhagen friends, passed a motion sharply critical of the 'German' king who had betrayed the nation and made Denmark a laughing stock abroad. The same bitter spirit overflowed in Skau's open letter to the king and coloured the speeches of P. Lorenzen, Lehmann and Grundtvig at the Skamlingsbank meeting in July which was attended by over 9,000 people and presided over by Skau.

In Denmark the public reaction was equally unfavourable. The Copenhagen radicals had no difficulty in organizing a monster petition which was presented to the king by prominent citizens in May. 20,000 people signed this petition expressing support for the king's attempt to maintain the *Helstat* and protect the Danish nationality in Schleswig. This was the first fruit of a genuinely popular national movement which spread from the capital to the provincial towns. By now the Schleswig cause had become a popular one and all classes in town and country alike were contributing to collections for the establishment of Rødding *Højskole* opened in the same year.

When the Viborg estates met in July it was quickly apparent that the members were fired by this national spirit and convinced that the 'Schleswig-Holstein party' desired to break away from Denmark. There were frequent protests about German advisers misleading the king and demands that only men loyal to the state be put at the head of affairs in Schleswig-Holstein. It was significant that in a motion moved by a prominent liberal, Schytte, the maintenance of the state now took precedence over demands for a free constitution. When Schytte had moved a motion calling for financial powers for a united Danish estates, he had suffered defeat because ideological differences between conservative and liberal were as strong as ever. But on questions affecting the national honour the ranks were closed north of the Kongeaa—J. E. Larsen's motion demanding action to preserve the unity of the state was accepted by forty-five votes to three despite Ørsted's ineffectual protests. In their petition the Viborg estates maintained that the kingdom and the duchies formed one state with a common ruler, common colleges and a common *Statsraad*, and they called for a joint committee of all four estates to decide the questions at present affecting the unity of the state. Their sympathy for the Eiderdanes was evident in their concern for the Danish nationality in Schleswig, and in their demand for an assurance that the king's remarks to the Schleswig estates in December 1842 had not been intended to prejudice the rights of the crown over that duchy.

Had the Schleswig estates, meeting in July, reacted in like fashion the national conflict would have flared up again. But the meeting passed off quietly for several reasons. In the first place, the Germans were naturally satisfied with a patent which recognized the primacy of their language. Secondly, although the proceedings at Viborg aroused both indignation and suspicion in Schleswig, this was offset to some extent by welcome signs that the king would no longer tolerate the strident voice of the Danish radicals. The apparatus of autocracy had lumbered into action. Skau was prosecuted for his open letter, Copenhagen newspapers publishing the letter were confiscated, proceedings were instituted against the *Slesvigske Forening* and its meetings were forbidden. Whatever the Danish estates might say, the king could be relied upon to keep the mob at bay. Thirdly, the absence of Peter Lorenzen and his colleagues contributed materially to this peaceful atmosphere, for the remaining North Schleswig members, Petersen, Nis Lorenzen and Jensen, were all men of moderate views unlikely to offer serious opposition to the Germans. As for the members who replaced the absentees, one was a friend of the duke and two were eager to speak German. So moderate opinion prevailed, Falck, not Beseler, was elected president and the members seem to have made a conscious and deliberate effort to avoid offensive remarks and hasty utterances.[1]

[1] Bagge and Engelstoft, *op. cit.*, II, no. 596, p. 477, J. Reventlow-Criminil to Ørsted, 27 July 1844.

This did not signify any alteration in their opinions. Falck, prompted by the duke and eager to retain the confidence of the meeting, vigorously defended those actions of the last estates to which the king took exception in the royal address. That hardy annual, the motion for the union of the estates, was opposed only by Jensen, the member for Flensburg. Lüders' motion for the separation of Schleswig-Holstein's military forces from those of Denmark and for the establishment of a separate officers' training school was carried by a large majority. So was Tiedemann's motion for the separation of the finances of the duchies from those of the kingdom. When the *Sängerfest* was held in Schleswig there was general agreement that the meeting adjourn to allow members to participate in the celebrations.

It was only when the patent was discussed that any substantial difference of opinion manifested itself. This originated not with the North Schleswig members but with the national liberals, whose intransigent attitude towards the use of Danish in the estates aroused opposition from the moderate-minded majority.

Beseler, the recognized leader of the national liberals, led the attack on the patent. A skilful and formidable debater, he made much of legal technicalities, arguing that the patent amounted to a provisional law which ought to have been submitted to the estates before publication. For in as much as the patent conferred a legal right on Danish-speaking members to use their language, it amounted to an amendment of the basic laws of 1831 and 1834 which could not be altered without the estates' consent.

Behind this clever dialectical display there lay more fundamental reasons for Beseler's opposition. As always, the essential point was that the German language be preserved intact as a symbol of the unity of the German duchies. 'The state,' he declared, 'must be governed by one idea expressed in the assembly in the form of one language.' [1] This was not peculiar to Schleswig, he continued. Other consultative assemblies had appreciated the necessity of according absolute primacy to one language. That was why the Hungarian estates decided in 1843 to use Magyar instead of Latin in their deliberations. It was important to notice

[1] *St. Z.*, Schleswig, 1844, p. 2356.

that the language selected was that of the people who had conferred a distinct national character on the crown lands of St. Stephen. Even the greatest conservative of them all, Metternich, had realized that the use of more than one language in an estates would endanger the stability of the state. 'In affairs of state,' said Beseler, 'one should always keep the state in mind and not allow free rein to a sense of justice which could cause the dissolution of the state.' [1] As for the language dispute in Schleswig, he had always believed this to be purely political in its origins, engineered by foreigners to assist them in the attainment of political objectives inimical to Schleswig-Holstein. Because of this he feared that the patent would merely encourage the political machinations of these people and lead ultimately to the break-up of the Schleswig estates. For this reason he was utterly opposed to the patent and, as a native of Schleswig-Holstein, he could only advise the estates to reject the document. But Beseler never lost sight of the wider implications of the dispute between German and Dane; 'As a German I stand here on the frontiers of my fatherland and will do nothing which could result in the alienation of the smallest piece of German territory.' [2]

The majority were not convinced by his eloquence. Nor was the committee appointed to study the patent united in its findings. Rumohr and Nis Lorenzen agreed with Beseler and Gülich that there had been no need to devise a special procedure to deal with language difficulties in the estates. But, unlike Beseler and Gülich, they were prepared to accept the patent because it recognized the essential point, namely, that German remain the official, but not the only, language of the estates and it attempted to minimize the difficulties consequent upon the use of two languages. Steenholdt, a national liberal, had to admit that the government could hardly be censured for devising measures to assuage the passions aroused in recent years.[3] He, for one, would accept the patent as the lesser of two evils. Count Reventlow-Jersbek, a member of the *Ritterschaft*, agreed with him. In the first place these measures had been quite unnecessary but now it seemed wiser to accept a law which

[1] *St. Z.*, Schleswig, 1844, p. 2026.
[2] *Ibid.*, p. 2356.
[3] *Ibid.*, p. 2035.

clarified the position and ensured that members could not sabotage the work of the estates in future.[1] No doubt this was a thoroughly illogical position, as the duke of Augustenburg pointed out;[2] but twenty-one members were satisfied with it and prepared to accept a provisional law based on the patent. This was a victory for common sense although a large minority, fifteen in all, approved of the doctrinaire intransigence of Beseler and Gülich.

Moderate conservative influences dominated this meeting of the estates. There was no reference to the German Confederation. Gülich's motion for a constitution conferring financial and legislative power on a united estates was not carried, although Gülich went out of his way to mollify the conservatives, by basing his constitution on the *Landesrechte* and agreeing that the *Ritterschaft* be represented in the new body. It was disagreement about the details of this representation which rendered the task of the committee a difficult one. In the debate which followed there was no unanimity of opinion and no final decisions were taken. This was a common phenomenon in the history of the *Landespartei*. When there was no external threat—real or supposed—to the independence of the duchies, the *raison d'être* of the party disappeared, and the internecine strife between conservative and radical broke out again. This was clearly reflected in the press. The *Kieler Korrespondenzblatt* rejoiced to see the *Landespartei* in imminent danger of breaking up into the more logical party formations of democrats and aristocrats.[3] Karl Lorentzen, the national liberal editor of the *Neuen Kieler Blätter*, boldly declared that adherence to the *Landesrechte* could lead only to contradictions and illogicalities. These beliefs should be abandoned and common sense applied to the solution of contemporary problems.[4] It was significant that the *Rendsburger Wochenblatt* resurrected Olshausen's radical views on national questions, demanding the partition of Schleswig and the inclusion of the German areas in the Confederation.

King Christian seemed to have good reason for facing the future with confidence after the dispersal of the Schleswig estates. The

[1] *Ibid.*, pp. 2036–7, 2360–61.
[2] *Ibid.*, p. 2385.
[3] *K.K.B.*, 1844, nos. 63, 71, 78.
[4] *N.K.B.*, 1844, pp. 662–71.

Danish radicals were subdued, the *Landespartei* was less united than before and the edge had been taken off the language dispute. The king was favourably impressed with the good reception accorded him by his subjects during his visit to North Schleswig in the summer of 1844 and reassured by the peaceful atmosphere he found there. The effectiveness of his measures against the *Slesvigske Forening* was proved by the submissive behaviour of Skau and Nissen when interviewed by the king at Føhr. Moved by their pleas, King Christian allowed the *Forening* to resume its activities in 1845.

Then one day in early August the situation was suddenly and dramatically transformed. Princess Alexandra gave birth to a son, the long-awaited heir. But there was little time for rejoicing; mother and child died the same day. This was a tragedy of the first magnitude for the *Helstat.* Not only was the succession question as far from solution as ever but King Christian's hopes of an intimate association with the Romanov dynasty had perished overnight. This was not all. A few weeks later the claims of the duke of Augustenburg were strengthened by the appearance of Karl Samwer's book.[1] A young lawyer and pupil of J. G. Droysen, Samwer had been researching into the succession question for some time, eventually arriving at conclusions favourable to the duke's claims. Hegewisch sent the proofs of Samwer's book to the duke. Instantly aware of its political value, the duke undertook responsibility for its publication and instructed his agents to see that it was brought to the notice of various European courts.[2] Samwer was flattered by the attentions of the duke and readily agreed to significant alterations in the text of his introduction, drawing attention to the possibility of the Augustenburgs succeeding to the throne of the *Helstat* if certain cognates were removed from the line of succession.[3] At no time did Christian August lose sight of this, the most desirable solution for his family.

The work of this obscure provincial lawyer made a consider-

[1] *Die Staatserbfolge der Herzogtümer Schleswig-Holstein und zugehöriger Lande*, Hamburg, 1844.

[2] L.A.S. 399 Samwer 40, to his mother, 22 March 1844.

[3] P.A.D. 13, K. Samwer to duke, 4 Oct. 1844, L. A. S. Samwer 40, duke to K. Samwer, 20 Oct. 1844.

able impression both in the duchies and in Germany, too, thanks to the duke. The fact that a young man of national liberal persuasions could write a defence of the Augustenburg claims seemed to indicate that the duke's bitterest opponents were at last overcoming their hostility to him. Samwer's book was generally welcomed by the *Landespartei* for his demonstration of the justice of the Augustenburg claims supplied it with a new and timely refutation of Danish claims to Schleswig, and reinforced the German case for an independent Schleswig-Holstein.

King Christian was not alone in supposing that these new developments would seriously prejudice his chances of preserving the *Helstat*. When the Jylland estates met in Roskilde in October, a few days after Samwer's book appeared, they took an early opportunity of expressing their concern at the growing strength of the Schleswig-Holsteiner. 'They are the enemies of the Danes,' declared J. C. Drewsen. Another liberal, Larsen, proposed that measures be taken immediately to defend the Danish nationality in Schleswig and to separate the administration of Schleswig from that of Holstein. Lehmann supported the motion wholeheartedly, for this was a matter 'affecting the honour and salvation of the Danish nation and the Danish language'.[1] It was agreed unanimously that the king be petitioned to take the necessary steps in this matter.

But the motion which made this a memorable meeting was moved at the end of October by Algreen Ussing, Mayor of Copenhagen. Ussing, leader of the moderate liberals in the 1830's, was concerned above all else to preserve the *Helstat* and felt, in common with many of his fellow countrymen, that the time had come to invoke the power of the crown against the Schleswig-Holsteiner to frustrate their separatist designs. Ussing proposed, therefore, that the king issue a solemn declaration to the effect that the *Helstat* constituted a single indivisible dominion and that the succession to it was governed by the *Kongelov*. Ussing also called upon the king to take whatever steps were necessary against those who expressed opinions to the contrary in this matter. Although the Eiderdane members were more interested in the union of

[1] H. Jensen, *op. cit.*, II, p. 384.

Schleswig and Denmark than in the preservation of the dynastic *Helstat*, nevertheless, for tactical reasons, they supported a modified version of Ussing's motion.

This motion, moved by so distinguished a public figure, carried overwhelmingly by fifty-nine votes to two and supported wholeheartedly by Danish public opinion, would in any case have caused grave concern in Itzehoe where the Holstein estates had just assembled. It was, however, the behaviour of Ørsted, the royal commissioner, which aroused the gravest misgivings. In the past Ørsted had been a popular figure in the duchies for he could usually be relied upon to oppose motions obnoxious to the German estates. But not in October 1844; during the debate on Ussing's motion he remarked that the controversy about the succession question might well induce the government to consider adopting the energetic measures advocated by Ussing in order to put an end to further argument. He agreed with Ussing's interpretation of the events of 1721 and 1806, and he admitted that a royal declaration affirming the unity of the *Helstat* would be ineffective, unless accompanied by a prohibition on public discussion of the succession question. As royal commissioner he would raise no objection if the estates adopted Ussing's motion, and made known their wishes to the king who would undoubtedly be glad to receive their petition.

These sympathetic comments by a hitherto impartial figure caused a sensation in the duchies. It was believed that Ørsted must at least have ascertained in advance that the king was favourably disposed towards the Ussing motion, and might well have been authorized by the king to make the comments in question.[1] Some Germans believed that the Russians were the villains of the piece; J. G. Droysen was 'quite certain' that Ørsted had acted with the king's consent, given after secret consultations with Count Nesselrode, the Russian foreign minister and a recent visitor to Copenhagen; were not the Russians seeking to dominate the Baltic Sea and would not their interests be better served if the coastline was controlled by a subservient Denmark rather than by a united

[1] Bagge and Engelstoft, *op. cit.*, II, no. 638, pp. 532–3, J. Reventlow-Criminil to Ørsted, 7 Nov. 1844.

Germany?[1] In fact King Christian was very far from pleased with the behaviour of the Roskilde Estates; 'The embers have been scattered with this motion of Ussing's and they have been re-kindled in the duchies,' he lamented to Ørsted.[2]

The apprehensions of the king were soon justified. At first the Holstein estates could scarcely believe their ears and continued their deliberations as usual, hoping that the king would dissociate himself from Ørsted's remarks. But as the days slipped by and the king did not do this, the indignation of the Germans knew no bounds. They readily placed the worst possible interpretation on the incident. The king, on whom they had relied to keep the Danes at bay, had turned traitor. He had shown his true colours at last, siding with the Danes against the Germans. Seen in this light the Ussing motion assumed a sinister significance. Was it not the first step towards the incorporation of the duchies in Denmark, a revival of Guldberg's policy after 1806 and a most serious threat to the independence assured them by the *Landesrechte*? The Germans were particularly incensed by the suggestion that this question could be solved by royal fiat, and that physical force should be used to compel them to accept an interpretation of the succession diametrically opposed to their beliefs. Whatever the intentions of the Danes, one thing is certain; their tactics betrayed a serious lack of psychological insight into the mentality of the people of Schleswig-Holstein. One of the few things certain to offend these phlegmatic people was an attack, whether intentional or not, on their ancient traditions and proud sense of independence. The reaction to the Ussing motion was most impressive; throughout November many addresses and petitions arrived in Itzehoe, thirty-eight from towns and rural areas in Holstein and thirty-seven from Schleswig. No one could have wished for a more energetic and widespread response, as J. G. Droysen remarked with satisfaction.[3] This was proof indeed that the *Landespartei* had succeeded in creating a public opinion favourable to its point of view.

Some parts of Schleswig-Holstein responded more readily than

[1] Hübner, *op. cit.*, p. 301, J. G. Droysen to J. von Grüner, 18 Nov. 1844.
[2] H. Jensen, *op. cit.*, II, p. 395, 28 Nov. 1844.
[3] Hübner, *op. cit.*, p. 299, J. G. Droysen to W. Arendt, 18 Nov. 1844.

others. The towns were naturally well-represented, for petitions could be easily organized in urban centres. Rural areas varied a good deal. Many addresses came from the west coast of Schleswig, from Angeln and generally from Central and South Schleswig, i.e. from areas where *Volksfeste* had been held most frequently. For this reason Schleswig was affected much more than Holstein. Only the north and southeastern corners of Schleswig did not participate in this agitation. But in Holstein much of the countryside remained apathetic, especially where great landowners had their estates, although in February 1845, after a dignified pause, the *Ritterschaft* did send a solemn protest to the king which met with general approval in the duchies.

The address drafted by J. G. Droysen and signed by all the prominent political figures in Kiel, was typical of the sentiments expressed in many petitions. In fact copies of the Kiel address were circulated in many parts of the duchies and formed the basis of other petitions. Droysen followed current practice in distinguishing carefully between 'their gracious monarch' and his 'treacherous advisers' who were counselling the use of force against his German subjects. The petitioners expressed their confidence that the king would reject this nefarious advice and protect the duchies. It might or might not be in the interests of the Danish kingdom to incorporate the duchies in Denmark. What was quite certain was that such attempts were a violation of the *Landesrechte* which afforded protection to the duchies 'in everything affecting their national feeling and aspirations'.

By this time Ussing's motion had been substantially amended. The references to the indivisibility of the *Helstat* and the use of force were omitted. In its final form the petition merely requested the king to declare that the *Kongelov* applied to all parts of the *Helstat*. Ørsted had expressed regret at the misunderstandings caused by his remarks. But these signs of repentance did not satisfy the Holstein estates. On 23 November Reventlow-Preetz registered a formal protest against Ørsted's contention that Schleswig had been incorporated in Denmark in 1721, and against his approval of the suggestion that discussion of the succession question be prohibited. The time had come for Holstein to speak out.

Reventlow-Preetz moved that an address be sent to the crown explaining the legal status of the duchies, drawing attention to the indignation of the people and protesting against any infringement of their independence.[1] The members were not deterred by the commissioner's observation that Ørsted had spoken without consulting the king, and that Ussing's motion was only designed to preserve the unity of the state. There was unanimous agreement that the motion be sent to committee to which Reventlow-Preetz, Löck, the veteran liberal, and Balemann, the friend of Falck, were elected.

The debate on the committee report was dignified and restrained in tone. The ranks were closed, conservative and liberal being united in sharp condemnation of Ussing's motion. Not only was it a violation of their well-established rights but the threatened use of force was an indignity which aroused them to anger. Such threats seemed, in the eyes of the law-abiding people of Schleswig-Holstein, conclusive proof of the basic weakness of the Danish position. But there was a genuine desire for reconciliation with the Danes. Expressions of respect for the Danish people, as distinct from the Roskilde radicals, were not infrequent during the debate. Everyone shared the hope of H. R. Claussen, the New Holsteiner, that the king would soon appreciate the justice of their arguments. But they were quite determined not to compromise on a fundamental issue. The stubborn and instinctive tenacity with which they clung to their medieval traditions was reinforced by awareness of the power of German national feeling. No conservative quarrelled with H. Koch's reference to the Danes as 'a foreign nation with foreign customs, sentiments and language'.[2] Löck wished to live in peace with the Danes, but felt this was impossible as long as they thought of themselves as the dominant race and of the duchies as conquered provinces.[3] Tiedemann warned the Danes that it was not only a difference in succession laws which precluded the incorporation of the duchies in Denmark. Equally important was the connection with the Confederation and the nationality of Schleswig-Holstein; 'nationality,' said

[1] *St. Z.*, Holstein, 1844, pp. 788, 814–18.
[2] *Ibid.*, p. 1813. [3] *Ibid.*, p. 1836.

Tiedemann, 'is one of the most powerful, if not the most powerful, of all spiritual forces. It is more potent than the power of money and any attempt to destroy or suppress it would be a quite vain and highly dangerous enterprise.' [1]

The petition, carried unanimously on 19 December, reiterated the profound conviction of the Holstein estates that the events in Roskilde threatened their independence. In order to refute Ørsted's contention that Schleswig had been part of Denmark since 1721 and Holstein since 1806, the petitioners restated the three essential points contained in the *Landesrechte*. Firstly, the duchies were independent states. Secondly, only the male line could succeed in the duchies and, thirdly, the relationship between the duchies was close and intimate. These were the points emphasized by Lornsen in *Die Unionsverfassung*, and endorsed by Samwer whom Reventlow-Preetz and Balemann had consulted before drafting the petition.

The legal arguments advanced by Ørsted were quickly disposed of. The 1806 patent had simply meant that Holstein was no longer a member of the Holy Roman Empire but an independent state. In this connection attention was drawn to the protests of the then duke of Augustenburg against the patent. Nor had the reincorporation of the Gottorp and royal parts of Schleswig in 1721 affected the independence of that duchy. This had been established in 1658, a fact acknowledged by the king in 1842. There could be no doubt, said the petitioners, that only the male line was entitled to succeed in the duchies. But if the Roskilde estates had their way the duchies would become part of Denmark; they would be reduced to the status of provinces and Holstein would cease to be on an equal footing with the other members of the Confederation. Even absolute rulers could not alter well-established rights unilaterally. 'Past history,' they observed darkly, 'teaches us that on innumerable occasions perjury and civil war have been the unavoidable consequence of such attempts.' [2] Finally, the petitioners protested against the threatened use of physical force by the Danes to impose their will on the duchies. Legal rights could

[1] *St. Z.*, Holstein, 1844, p. 1833.
[2] *Ibid.*, *Beilagenheft*, II, p. 392.

be suppressed by these methods but never altered, much less destroyed.

Most significant of all was the reaction south of the Elbe. In December a motion was carried in the Brunswick estates, expressing the hope that the government would consider measures to safeguard the independence not only of Holstein but also of Schleswig on account of the close union between the duchies. The Brunswick government was not unsympathetic and the Prussian *chargé d'affaires* in Brunswick signified his approval of the motion. Early in 1845 the second chamber in Baden expressed similar sentiments, conservative and liberal alike condemning the reticence of the Federal Diet in this matter. 'Schleswig-Holstein,' declared F. Hecker, the South German radical, 'is a bulwark of the German Empire, it is a German border land fighting for its ancient rights, for its fatherland and its language. Anyone whose heart burns for the German fatherland, anyone who takes a brotherly interest in the fate of the most distant corner of German soil and has not been engulfed by narrow-minded particularism, must do what he can by word and deed and, if need be, by the sword to make certain that not an inch of German soil is alienated from Germany.' [1]

These signs of German national feeling took the duchies somewhat by surprise. But, though unexpected, this sympathy was no less welcome to the younger generation of national liberals, the pupils of J. G. Droysen. They responded with alacrity. In December a new poem, *Deutschlands Einheit*, appeared in the *Neuen Kieler Blätter*, warning the princes that if they were not mindful of their duty to the Confederation the people would rise up as in 1813 and take the swords from the hands of the princes. Then 'the trumpets will sound, the smoke of battle will rise high in the air and with the help of God we will win the new battle for freedom'.[2]

The success of the Würzburg *Sängerfest* in the summer of 1845 revealed a significant degree of general interest in and popular sympathy for the duchies in Germany. Twenty-five prominent Schleswig-Holsteiner were invited to the *Sängerfest*. They were

[1] *N.K.B.*, 1845, Jan. 1, p. 11. [2] *N.K.B.*, 1844, Dec. 1, pp. 732–3.

greeted like conquering heroes on their journey through Germany to Würzburg, where 20,000 choral singers from all parts of Germany had assembled. Bauditz of Eckernförde spoke at the festive dinner of the spirit of unity and love of the great German fatherland which animated all those living on the northern frontiers of Germany. Their only desire was to enter into an even closer union with their brothers in the south. The meeting reached its climax with the singing of the new Schleswig-Holstein song. This made a tremendous emotional impact on the *Sängerfest*. It was greeted with thunderous applause. D. von Liliencron, a young national liberal in the audience, remarked that it was the Schleswig-Holsteiner who had at last broken down the frontiers between the thirty-six German states, and created overnight a united people who embraced each other like brothers, with tears in their eyes.[1] The song, the coat of arms and the new flag, exhibited at Würzburg for the first time, soon became well known in Germany, symbols of the new association established in the popular mind between the duchies and the German fatherland.

This was a development of the utmost importance for the duchies in which the German press played a vitally important role. J. Abrahamson, a prominent Eiderdane, complained that nine out of every ten Germans he met accepted the arguments of the Schleswig-Holsteiner without question, simply because this was the only side of the case presented in the German press. That was why the Germans believed that Schleswig was a German-speaking province, that Danish was a kind of German, that the Danes were aggressors seeking to danize Schleswig, rob the people of their rights and incorporate them in Denmark. They were told that a similar fate awaited Holstein and Lauenburg and that the Danes looked upon the duchies as milk cows to be exploited in the interests of Denmark.[2]

[1] D. von Liliencron, *Up ewig ungedeelt. Die Erhebung Schleswig-Holsteins im Jahre 1848*, Hamburg, 1848, p. 12.

[2] Bagge and Engelstoft, *op. cit.*, III, no. 668, pp. 9–11, J. Abrahamson to Professor Flor, 28 March 1844; appended address by J. Abrahamson to *Slesvigske Hjaelpeforening*, pp. 11–25.

Abrahamson was instrumental in persuading the Eiderdane publicists to do battle for the minds of the German public. A committee was set up in Copenhagen, articles explaining the Danish case were sent to the influential *Augsburger Allgemeine Zeitung* and an interesting exchange of ideas between German and Danish writers followed in 1845 and 1846.[1] The Eiderdanes failed to break the monopoly of reporting enjoyed by the Schleswig-Holsteiner but the exchanges helped to clarify the issues at stake.

The Eiderdanes presented their case skilfully. In the first article they maintained boldly that there was no real justification for the quarrel between German and Dane since their peoples had a common mission to protect Europe against the great power slowly stirring in the east. Admittedly the Scandinavians expected Schleswig to become part of the new northern kingdom and, in as much as the Germans resisted this, a conflict between Dane and German was always a possibility. But seen in a wider setting, might not a united Scandinavia co-operate with a united Germany and act as mediator between east and west, preserving the balance of power in Europe? It was an attractive theme which appealed to many Germans and Danes in the mid 1840's. Karl Lorentzen, for example, writing in the *Neuen Kieler Blätter*, regretted the refusal of the Danes to recognize the autonomy of the duchies, because he believed it to be in the common interest of both peoples to remain united against 'the aggressive designs of the east' and 'the commercial despotism of the west'.[2] Dahlmann wrote from Frankfurt in the same vein; Scandinavia allied with Germany would be a haven of German culture in northern Europe. She would place her fleet at Germany's disposal and when the storm did at last break, hundreds of thousands of German warriors would come to her assistance.[3] Lars Hierta of Sweden spoke of Germany as the ally of the Swedes and Danes against the danger from the east, and as late as 1849 Jakob Grimm agreed with P. A. Munch of Norway, that Scandinavia and Germany were destined to become

[1] *A.A.Z.*, 1845, nos. 282, 297, 359, 360. 1846, nos. 12, 43, 59, 66, 95, 96, 121.

[2] *N.K.B.*, 1844, Oct. 1, p. 633.

[3] Springer, *op. cit.*, II, p. 141.

more closely associated so that they might count for something in Europe.[1]

For tactical reasons the Eiderdanes were compelled to minimize the implications of their claim to the Eider frontier. They presented the Schleswig problem as exclusively cultural and ethnographical in nature and capable of easy solution. The Germans had only to abandon their attempts to extirpate Danish, concede equality to the Danish language and allow Schleswig to join Denmark of its own free will; in short the arguments used by Lehmann before he became an Eiderdane in 1842.

The German writers were not prepared to abandon Schleswig and accept the Eider as the northern frontier of a united Germany. In their articles they repeated the old arguments. German was the official language and cultural medium of Schleswig. The people of Schleswig did not regard themselves as Danes and, judging by the relatively slow progress made by the Danish movement, did not wish to become part of the Danish state. But, in contrast to the Eiderdanes, the German writers grasped the nettle firmly. The Schleswig problem was not primarily a cultural or ethnographical problem. Essentially it was a matter of power politics and historical frontiers as Lehmann was well aware. It was Danish interference in the internal affairs of the duchy in recent years, and the Danish refusal to recognize the independence of Schleswig as a historical reality which lay at the bottom of the estrangement. Only when the Danes abandoned their attempts to incorporate Schleswig in Denmark, could their two peoples co-operate in the manner envisaged by the Eiderdanes.

The events of 1844 left their mark on the *Landespartei*. 'The archdanes,' Hegewisch observed shrewdly, 'were the real saviours of the duchies.'[2] Once again a threat to the independence of Schleswig-Holstein, real or supposed, had closed the ranks of the party. It did more than that. It closed the ranks of the Germans with the suspension of the activities of the New Holstein party. Olshausen signed the Kiel address and in Itzehoe H. R. Claussen

[1] M. Gerhardt and W. Hubatsch, *Deutschland und Skandinavien im Wandel der Jahrhunderte*, Bonn, 1950, pp. 335–6.

[2] L.A.S. 399 Samwer 41, undated letter.

supported with enthusiasm the petition to the crown. The pressure of events had compelled the New Holsteiner to abandon the idea of a neutral Schleswig deciding its national allegiance in the fullness of time. It seemed that they had either to defend the independence and integrity of Schleswig-Holstein against Danish aggression, or else acquiesce in the abandonment of the whole of Schleswig to the Danes. Nor could Holstein go it alone, for the Algreen Ussing motion seemed to threaten Holstein as much as Schleswig. In the interests of national survival the New Holsteiner turned to the *Landespartei*. They found it a more congenial party than in 1839, for since then the centre of gravity had moved to the left. National liberals, like Droysen and Beseler, agreed with the New Holsteiner that Schleswig must one day enter the Confederation and they shared the enthusiasm of the New Holsteiner for Germany. It was with the greatest satisfaction that the national liberals observed the recent display of interest south of the Elbe in the affairs of the duchies. 'We recognize', wrote Karl Lorentzen, 'that the question does not only concern Holstein or Schleswig-Holstein but the whole of Germany, and under the German banner we stand united.' [1]

The duke of Augustenburg had also profited by the events of 1844. The Holstein estates, by solemnly upholding the rights of the male line, had conferred national significance on his claims. With characteristic caution he resisted the pleas of Reventlow-Preetz and Samwer that he make his own public protest against Ussing's motion. Perhaps he thought the Holstein estates' protest adequate, or more probably he was as reluctant as ever to become a popular figure. But he did not miss this opportunity of arresting the decline in his influence inside the *Landespartei*. He was aware that exclusive dependence on conservative support had its limitations. Conservative landowners could be relied upon to defend their *Heimat* Schleswig-Holstein, but they had little wish to become the subjects of a petty sovereign from Gravenstein. It was the national liberals who welcomed his dynastic claims, seeing in them a means of loosening the ties with Denmark in the natural course of events. On the other hand, there was still much suspicion

[1] *N.K.B.*, 1844, Oct. 11, p. 676.

of the haughty aristocrat; some of the younger liberals, the 'ultras' as Christian August dubbed them, believed that he would rule his dominions like an old-time despot and shrewdly suspected that he was really seeking the crown of the *Helstat*.[1] Their support was conditional on his renunciation of all claim to the Danish throne. The duke was not likely to give way on that point. But it is significant that in the early spring of 1845 the duke decided to meet the national liberals halfway by abandoning his stubborn opposition to a Schleswig-Holstein constitution. Writing to a Danish friend, he observed that one day the *Kongelov* would be overthrown and conservatism with it, unless conservatives took an interest in constitutions. If they placed themselves at the head of the constitutional movement they could lead it. That did not mean, he added in a revealing passage, an alliance with liberalism or support for liberal proposals. No, conservatives ought to decide the content of party programmes and inform the liberals of their terms.[2]

There was an equally important rapprochement between the liberal middle class and the conservative *Ritterschaft* at this time. Count Reventlow-Preetz, the leading nobleman in the duchies, supported by a small but active minority of the *Ritterschaft*, was prepared to pay heed to the spirit of the times. This was partly because he recognized the need for national solidarity and partly because he and his colleagues feared political isolation in an age of mass politics. A shrewd and able politician, Reventlow-Preetz believed that the *Ritterschaft* should not oppose the people as a matter of principle but rather lead them along the paths of righteousness and support measures in keeping with the needs of a new age. This was conservatism at its best. Refusal to follow this advice would ruin them, as Reventlow-Preetz understood perfectly well. '. . . a *Ritterschaft* isolated from the people, regarding it as a duty to oppose every progressive step and natural development of the people, lacks virility, will have no influence with the people

[1] L.A.S. Samwer 41, duke to Samwer, 26 Feb. 1845. P.A. III D, Samwer to duke, 3 March 1845.

[2] Bagge and Engelstoft, *op. cit.*, III, no. 745, pp. 182–3, duke to Grev G. Holck Winterfeldt, 17 Aug. 1846.

and will be regarded with contempt even by the government.'[1] Men of moderate liberal persuasions were equally aware that in time of crisis they could not dispense with the *Ritterschaft*. These powerful landowners, backbone of the Establishment, still exerted great economic and social power in the countryside, especially in Holstein. It was obvious that unless the landowners were broadly in sympathy with liberal aspirations, the rural population could not be mobilized in its entirety. To facilitate a rapprochement the liberals were prepared to abstain from attacking the *Ritterschaft*, feeling that German unity was a safer political slogan than German freedom in such troubled times.

These structural changes in the *Landespartei* did not make it any easier to reach agreement in the immediate future on the substance of a modern constitution as demanded by the liberals. But there was at least more general acceptance in conservative circles of the need for a constitution and, therefore, less likelihood of a recurrence of the ideological strife which had torn the party asunder in 1839. Above all, there was unanimous agreement that the *Landesrechte* afforded an indispensable basis for the defence of Schleswig-Holstein in the testing time which lay ahead. It was this that rallied the Germans around the *Landespartei*, making it stronger and more united at the beginning of 1845 than ever before.

[1] T. Regensburg, *Brevvexling fra 1846–1847 mellem Graf Reventlow (Preetz) og Grev C. Moltke*, p. 219, Reventlow-Preetz to C. Moltke, 26 Dec. 1846.

XII

The open letter

BY the early spring of 1845 conditions had slowly returned to normal. In the duchies there was a general feeling that the events of the previous autumn had cleared the air and impressed the Danes. The king had accepted the petition of the Holstein estates without comment and no attempt had been made to remove the prince of Noer from the *Statthalterschaft*. Did this not imply that the king was at last realizing the impossibility of annexing the duchies? The duke of Augustenburg was quite convinced that only the timely action of the estates had saved the day and prevented a declaration in support of Ussing.[1] This widespread somewhat naïve optimism, coupled with the fact that the estates were not due to meet until 1846, caused a general diminution of interest in politics in 1845. There was little the Germans could do to revive it; the *Volksfeste* had outlived their usefulness but the age of the mass meeting had not yet arrived. In any case the Germans were on the defensive, because at long last the king had decided to take steps to bring the *Landespartei* to heel; the powers of the press censor were suddenly increased, the first casualty being the *Neuen Kieler Blätter* which ceased publication in May. This was followed by the banning of the so-called Schleswig-Holstein flag in July. The Danish movement did not fare much better in 1845: in March it suffered a most grievous blow with the death of Peter Lorenzen.

The initiated were of course well aware that this was not peace but merely an extended armistice. 'The exasperated feelings between the duchies and Denmark proper at no time previous has been so violent as at present,' wrote Sir William Wynn, the British ambassador to Denmark, in August.[2] Several high officials

[1] L.A.S. 399 Samwer 41, Samwer's note.

[2] F.O. 22 149, Wynn to earl of Aberdeen no. 15, 28 Aug. 1845.

expressed grave anxiety about the future as the bad feeling between German and Dane in official circles deepened with the passage of time.[1] King Christian could no longer work with the *Schleswig-holsteinische Kanzlei*, relying more and more on Danish officials for advice. The sad truth was that the old confidence between the peoples of the *Helstat* had gone for ever; it had been destroyed by national prejudice which clouded and distorted the relationship between German and Dane at all levels in society. The popular press played a not inconsiderable part in this melancholy development; the average German was persuaded by the papers he read that the aggressive designs of the Danes were the cause of all the trouble; on the other hand the average apolitical Dane was convinced by his press that present difficulties were due entirely to the separatist aspirations of the Schleswig-Holstein party. In the eyes of the Germans the king-duke was pandering to the Danes and wanted to incorporate the duchies in Denmark; in the eyes of his Danish subjects King Christian was inspired solely by an honourable desire to preserve the unity of the *Helstat*. These mutual misunderstandings and suspicions completely destroyed the pattern of loyalty and obedience on which the *Helstat* had rested for generations. Only physical force could hold together peoples whose viewpoints had become so antithetical.

The king was now deeply concerned about the future. He had never approved of Ussing's motion—'*une proposition inconvenante*' as he called it—which had been completely misunderstood by the Holstein estates. Ussing's intention had been to prevent the dismemberment of the *Helstat*, not to annex the duchies as the estates pretended. Certainly the king had accepted their petition without comment, but he observed in his diary that he would have to consider carefully how to reject the shameless allegations of the Holstein estates. This would have to be done promptly and with determination, for 'one could scarcely expect any reconciliation between the contending viewpoints. The government must not hesitate on that account to express its opinion about the rights and wrongs of the matter and take firm action against all disturbers of the peace and against anyone seeking to disrupt the Danish

[1] L.A.S. 399 B. H. Rathgen 4a, to his wife, 19 Aug. 1845.

monarchy.[1] This was the heart of the matter. It would, he wrote later, have been unpardonable weakness in a monarch and would only have encouraged separatism, had he not dealt firmly with the audacious assertion of the Holstein estates that the ties with Denmark would be dissolved immediately, once the male line had died out.[2] Christian had been driven at last to the conclusion that decisive action could no longer be delayed. He did not consider that the estates, whose powers were purely consultative in nature, had any business to meddle in these matters. But since two of them had done so, he felt compelled to resolve the contentious succession issue within the next eighteen months before the estates reassembled. Further equivocation seemed likely to accelerate the drift to civil war or revolution. He must choose finally between Roskilde and Holstein. Because he was so firmly opposed to the Augustenburg succession, there remained only one possible course of action—a declaration of his intention to maintain the unity of the *Helstat* by supporting the cognate succession at all costs.

As the months passed King Christian persuaded himself that his dearest wish, the preservation of the *Helstat*, coincided with the aspirations of all patriotically-minded men—not excluding members of the Holstein estates—who would assuredly welcome a declaration to this effect. The only people likely to object were those perennial trouble-makers in the Schleswig-Holstein party, who wanted a new state '*à la Lornsen*' and who were only awaiting a favourable opportunity to break completely with Denmark and enter the German Confederation. These separatists, the Schleswig-Holsteiner, were the cause of all his trouble. Now the time had come to put them in their place. Persuasion and conciliation had failed; it was the turn of physical force, the last weapon of absolute monarchy. Thus when disturbances occurred in North Schleswig in the summer of 1845, King Christian immediately banned the offending Schleswig-Holstein flag. But this only sparked off further unrest in the duchies, illustrating the real dilemma facing the king. The Schleswig-Holstein movement enjoyed widespread

[1] A. D. Jørgensen, *op. cit.*, *S.A.*, 1895, p. 159, beginning of 1845.

[2] R. Hansen, *Zur Geschichte der dänischen Politik 1840–48*, Z 42, p. 330, Christian to Graf Blome, 31 March 1847.

popular support, so that measures directed primarily against 'lawyers' and 'officials' automatically stimulated popular discontent. Six years before it would have been very different. But by 1846 the distinction, commonly drawn by King Christian and his advisers between the small group of 'disloyal agitators' and the 'faithful mass' of his people, lacked political validity. In this age of national conflict, nurtured and sustained by a popular press, politics were ceasing to be the preserve of the educated minority. The masses were at last becoming politically articulate, a momentous development which conservatives like King Christian failed to evaluate correctly.

In January 1845 King Christian began consultations with his ministers seeking their advice on the next step. Ørsted and Heinrich Reventlow-Criminil counselled caution, advising the appointment of a royal commission to examine the relevant documents in the succession question at its leisure. Other advisers, including A. W. Moltke and Steman, believed that the time for action had arrived. They advised the king to issue a declaration upholding the commonly held Danish opinion that the *Kongelov* applied to Schleswig and parts of Holstein. King Christian sided with the conservatives and in February appointed a commission composed of the foreign minister, Heinrich Reventlow-Criminil, the director of the foreign office, Dankwart, the Danish ambassador to the Confederation, von Pechlin, the secretary of the *Statsraad*, J. G. Adler, and the president of the *Dänische Kanzlei*, Steman. In the summer of 1846 the findings of the commission were submitted to the *Statsraad* and discussed for three critical days. Should a public declaration be made at once or should the findings be submitted first to the estates? The Reventlow-Criminils and, ironically enough, Ørsted opposed precipitate action. This time their advice was ignored. The *Statsraad*, with the approval of King Christian, voted in favour of a declaration which a senior official, P. G. Bang, was instructed to draft. This declaration, published on 11 July and known as the open letter, precipitated a crisis rocking the *Helstat* to its foundations.

In the open letter King Christian declared that the circulation of erroneous opinions about the future of the *Helstat* in the event of the extinction of the male line, had compelled him to submit the succession question to a royal commission. The commission had decided that the female succession applied in Lauenburg and in Schleswig. Christian solemnly announced his intention of upholding this finding. He admitted that it was still not clear whether the female succession also applied to certain parts of Holstein. However, he assured the people of Holstein that it would be his constant endeavour to clarify the position in order to maintain the *Helstat*. There was, he hastened to assure the people of Schleswig, no intention of encroaching upon their cherished autonomy or of altering the existing association between the duchies in any way. Schleswig would remain, what it had always been, an autonomous duchy inseparably united with the Danish monarchy. The declaration was signed by the king and by all the members of the *Statsraad*.

It is deceptively easy to say with hindsight that King Christian would have been better advised to have instituted negotiations with the Great Powers and with the claimants to the throne in an attempt to solve the question by mutual agreement. That was how the powers solved it, temporarily, in 1852. But in the circumstances King Christian felt it his bounden duty to invoke the authority of the crown as soon as possible against views which seemed prejudicial to the maintenance of the *Helstat*. The Holstein estates would undoubtedly offer some resistance and no doubt there would be echoes in Germany. But, on the other hand, the moral power of the crown was still considerable enough for King Christian to assume that his subjects would ultimately abide by his decision. His friend O. Blome, a former ambassador to Russia and a friend of Nesselrode, encouraged the king in this belief.[1] Blome believed that there was no general desire in the duchies for separation from Denmark—which was undoubtedly true—nor was there likely to be any desire for separation provided that the association between the duchies was not disturbed—and King Christian certainly intended to respect the *status quo*. Were not the scales weighed very heavily in favour of

[1] R. Hansen, *Zur Geschichte der dänischen Politik 1840–48*, Z 42, p. 297, Graf Blome to Christian, 13 Dec. 1844.

the Danish connection by the mutual benefits of continued association, consolidated by centuries of common history and underpinned by the power of habitual allegiance to the crown? The Great Powers would surely approve of his action for, like King Christian, they believed that the *Helstat* in its present form was an indispensable guarantee of the balance of power in northern Europe. For that reason the claims of the Augustenburgs had received scant attention at most European courts.

All the king's advisers did not share his optimism. Josef and Heinrich Reventlow-Criminil had both opposed the declaration, remaining in office only because they feared their resignation might precipitate revolution in the duchies. 'Today the king has lost the duchies,' commented Dankwart unhappily as the king appended his signature to the open letter.[1] Dankwart was right. The historian K. Jansen, then a student in Kiel, put his finger on the heart of the problem, observing shrewdly that the king, quite naturally, saw nothing unjust in his desire to preserve the *Helstat*, nor did he intend to violate established rights which he had always respected. What he and others like him failed to appreciate was that the succession question had ceased to be a purely dynastic issue affecting only court circles. It had become part of a wider national conflict between German and Dane and could no longer be settled by royal fiat alone.[2]

In Denmark reaction to the open letter was encouraging. Moderate opinion, represented by A. Ussing and P. G. Bang, wholeheartedly endorsed the sentiments behind it. The Eiderdanes were less enthusiastic, having little interest in the *Helstat*. *Faedrelandet* regretted the king's references to the connection with Holstein, feeling that he ought to have incorporated Schleswig instead of talking about its independent status inside the *Helstat*. But they were encouraged to hope for more in the near future by King Christian's references to the duchy as an inseparable part of the Danish monarchy.

[1] L.A.S. 399 Samwer 41, Samwer's note. Cf. P. Bagge and P. Engelstoft, *op. cit.*, III, no. 800, pp. 276–7, Dankwart to C. Bille, 9 Jan. 1847.

[2] G. E. Hoffmann, *Die Lebenserinnerungen von Karl Jansen*, Z 78 Neumünster, 1954, p. 249.

If King Christian had really expected the duchies to accept his open letter in a spirit of dutiful obedience, he was quickly disillusioned. The Holstein estates assembled in Itzehoe on 15 July. At the first meeting the commissioner read out the royal address which curtly rejected the 1844 petition; the king went on to warn members that the commissioner would refuse to accept any petition dealing with matters outside the purview of the estates; such petitions must not be mentioned in the minutes or in the *Ständezeitung*. This was the authentic voice of absolutism hardly calculated to reassure members stunned by the open letter. At first many members wanted to leave Itzehoe at once, but it was finally agreed that the members stay and give the government a last chance. A committee was elected to draft a reply to the address and the estates subsequently accepted almost unanimously a draft prepared by Reventlow-Preetz and couched in uncompromising terms.

It would be treason to the duchies, declared the estates, if they obeyed the king and refrained from using their right of petition at a time when the established rights of the duchies were being attacked. It was their bounden duty not to rest until they obtained satisfaction in this matter. They refused to accept any of the theses contained in the open letter and reiterated the three points made in their petition of 1844—the duchies were inseparably united, they formed the state of Schleswig-Holstein, and they could be ruled only by the male line. In matters affecting the succession, it was not within the power of rulers to create new rights or to annul existing ones. They admitted frankly that the fate of the *Helstat* was not the first concern of the people of Holstein: 'they feel they are Germans and they desire above all else to secure the integrity of their duchy as part of the German fatherland.' [1] Holstein was no Danish province but a sovereign state and equal partner with Denmark. 'We know of no lost battles or treaties which could deprive the duchy of its independence . . . patiently and silently we have borne the burdens laid upon us by our ruler in dark days. We cannot believe that our obedience and submis-

[1] *Schleswig-Holsteins Gegenwart*, Hamburg and Leipzig, 1846, p. 14. The address is not in the *St. Z.*

siveness have cost us our rights and that the confidence placed by your loyal servants in Your Majesty and his predecessors has been misplaced.' [1] This address was handed on 24 July to the royal commissioner who returned it to the estates with the comment that he could not accept addresses of this nature, but assuring them that there was no intention of interfering with the association between the duchies.

Rebuffed by the crown, the estates turned to the German Confederation. The widespread interest Germany had shown in the affairs of Schleswig-Holstein made it certain that the estates would have a more favourable reception than the *Ritterschaft* had when it petitioned the Federal Diet in 1823. 'The Schleswig-Holsteiner,' remarked H. R. Claussen the ex-New Holsteiner, 'are greeted rapturously as the guardians of the German way of life, defending Germany's frontiers against the menace from the north.' Nor had the duchies been slow to reciprocate these sentiments. For, in his opinion, the people did not really care whether their future ruler was a cognate or an agnate. The driving force behind them was the resurgence of national feeling, the desire to attain national independence. It was, therefore, an historic moment for the Holstein estates; '. . . not only the inhabitants of the duchies but a considerable section of German opinion is looking towards us in a mood of tense expectancy . . . this is not just a question of our freedom, it is a question of nationality and of German interests.' [2]

H. R. Claussen wanted the estates to lodge a formal protest in Frankfurt against interference with their established right of petition. Most members, in what was still a very conservative assembly, felt this too extreme a step, likely to frighten the Diet away. They settled for the more moderate proposal of Balemann that the Diet simply be informed of what had happened. Throughout these proceedings all protests from the royal commissioner were studiously ignored. Finally, the estates dispatched the relevant documents, the 1844 petition and the open letter to the Diet, together with a letter drawing attention to the violation of their right of petition, to the king's declared intention of annexing

[1] *Ibid.*, p. 21.
[2] *St. Z.*, Holstein, 1846, p. 39.

Holstein, and to the termination of the association between Schleswig and Holstein which was implied in the open letter.

The work of the estates was completed. On 4 August Reventlow-Preetz announced that he could not remain a member of the estates as long as he was unlawfully constrained in the exercise of his duties. His resignation was the signal for similar declarations from thirty-four members who followed him out of the hall, despite the commissioner's entreaties to avoid precipitate action. Only five members stayed to the bitter end to hear the commissioner formally adjourn the session a few days later. This was the first step on the road to revolution, wrote the commissioner to his friend Jensen.[1] Some Germans, like Beseler, condemned it as a tactical blunder, depriving the movement of its top leadership at a critical moment. But the general public approved of 'the Holstein secession' as the only honourable course open to the estates.

Whilst the estates were still in session, there had been an impressive demonstration of the temper of popular feeling at the Neumünster mass meeting on 20 July. Arranged months before, the meeting was completely transformed in character by news of the open letter. Beseler presided over the meeting which approved enthusiastically an address drafted by Karl Lorentzen, Tiedemann and Olshausen. This address to the estates, signed by 1,500 people, restated the three principles enunciated in 1844, and roundly condemned the open letter, not only because it disregarded these principles, but because it conflicted with their national loyalties. 'For we have no wish to maintain the connection between the duchies and the Danish kingdom any longer than is necessary in the natural course of events and under the existing order of succession. If, by the will of Providence, the male heirs of the senior royal line should die off, we would then wish to sever all connection with a foreign state and, under our own duke, play our full part in the development of our great German fatherland now striving to attain national unity.' If the king would not listen to his estates, then they must warn the German Confederation that the affairs of Schleswig-Holstein concerned Germany. 'Let all the

[1] L.A.S. 399 Jensen 63, 28 Aug. 1846.

German people know that they must not stand idly by should the tragic fate of Alsace and Lorraine occur here.' [1] The British ambassador to Denmark was deeply impressed by this bold language, 'which would almost amount to treason in a more constitutional country'.[2] It did not fail to impress contemporaries because here, for the first time, was a clear public statement of the duchies' wish to terminate the Danish connection at the earliest possible moment.

Excitement ran high in the towns throughout the late summer. There were protest meetings in Kiel, followed by disturbances in the streets when Olshausen was arrested. A curfew was imposed on Kiel but it did not prevent fresh disturbances when a Danish officer, Colonel Hoeg, arrived in September to assume the regimental command laid down by the Duke of Glücksburg. For the first time the king was received in silence by his subjects during his annual visit to the duchies. There were catcalls outside the royal residence in Schleswig, and L. von Scheel, the unpopular new head of the Gottorp government, had his windows smashed by the mob. To some ardent nationalists like J. G. Droysen these signs of animosity between the people and the authorities were most welcome. There was now no need to fear—as there had been two years before—that the duchies might agree to patch up their differences with the Danish crown. 'The breach between king and people is complete and fully understood right down to the lowest levels of the population,' he observed with satisfaction.[3]

The climax came with the Nortorf mass meeting, held outside Neumünster on 14 September. Some young admirers of Olshausen decided to stage a demonstration, much against the advice of Beseler, Samwer and K. Lorentzen. Thousands turned up at the appointed hour and approved an address modelled on that of Neumünster. The sudden appearance of a troop of cavalry with orders to disperse the meeting might have led to serious disturbances, had not Tiedemann urged moderation on the crowds and encouraged the organizers to close the meeting. The timely

[1] *Hamburger Nachrichten*, no. 174, 24 July 1846.
[2] F.O. 153, Wynn to Palmerston, no. 27, 26 July 1846.
[3] Hübner, *op. cit.*, p. 337, Droysen to W. Arendt, 6 Sept. 1846.

appearance of a locomotive between demonstrators and cavalry gave the former time to beat a hasty retreat. The crisis passed off, but the Schleswig-Holsteiner heeded the warning and avoided further mass meetings. They realized that an open conflict with the authorities would result in the imposition of further restrictions and would most certainly seriously weaken their influence over the law-abiding masses of the population.

High society followed the lead given by Itzehoe and Neumünster. After characteristic hesitation, the duke of Augustenburg sent a formal protest to the king on 30 July defending the rights of the agnates. Similar protests were received from Karl of Glücksburg and from the grand duke of Oldenburg. The prince of Noer, after remaining at his post as long as possible at his brother's instigation, finally tendered his resignation on 13 August, when asked to give a written undertaking to respect the open letter. Public opinion was particularly impressed by the resignation of the well-respected Holstein nobleman, Count J. Reventlow-Criminil, from the *Schleswig-holsteinische Kanzlei*. Shortly afterwards the ambassador to Russia, Count Rantzau, and the ambassador to Prussia, Count Reventlow-Altenhof, both Holstein noblemen, tendered their resignations.

Matters were not improved by the king's determination not to tolerate any opposition to the open letter. He had refused to accept any petition from the Holstein estates and ordered the dissolution of that body when it appealed to the Confederation. After the Neumünster meeting the *Amtmann* was dismissed for incompetence, Beseler and Karl Lorentzen were charged with *lèse-majesté* and sedition, and local authorities were sternly admonished to forbid all mass meetings in future. Olshausen was arrested for his part at a meeting in Kiel, but was released later from Rendsburg prison and returned to Kiel in triumph. The judiciary was encouraged to impose heavy sentences for breaches of the peace, the press censorship became more severe, and the correspondence of the duke of Augustenburg was regularly examined at Flensburg post-office. The appointment of Karl Moltke as president of the *Schleswig-holsteinische Kanzlei* aroused indignation in the duchies, for this arch-conservative, a son of Adam Moltke, was a willing servant of absolutism and bitter opponent of all that the *Landespartei* stood for. The majority of the advisers of the Gottorp government were summarily dismissed and the powers of the new head of government, L. von Scheel, were increased. The *Statthalterschaft*, symbol of the unity of the duchies, remained vacant and military command in the duchies was given to a Danish officer, Major General von Lützow.

The blunt instrument of autocracy made a deeper impression on the duchies than the second open letter issued on 18 September from Plön where the king was celebrating his birthday. In this new letter King Christian, while still upholding the cognate succession, made a belated attempt to placate his German subjects. He asserted that the open letter had been grossly misinterpreted by his enemies, and he assured his 'dear and faithful subjects' that there was no intention of interfering with the association between the duchies or with the ties between Holstein and the Confederation. But it was too late for conciliatory speeches. The usual deputation from Kiel university and town did not call on him in Plön. The local aristocracy stayed at home and when Reventlow-Preetz did seek an interview, his request was rejected by the angry monarch. This merely widened the breach between the crown and the conservative *Ritterschaft*, for Reventlow-Preetz commented bitterly that he had no alternative but to throw himself into the arms of the Augustenburgs.[1] He accepted an invitation to the birthday celebrations of the duchess of Augustenburg at Gravenstein. In previous years these celebrations had attracted only the duke's racing associates. This year many members of the Holstein estates and other influential political figures attended, and drank toasts to the union of the German estates proposed by the duke.

Memorable as these events were in the history of Schleswig-Holstein, they were overshadowed by the great upsurge of national feeling in Germany. 1846 ranks with 1813, 1848 and 1870 as a vintage year for German nationalism. 'Legitimists, liberals, radicals, Catholics, Protestants, dogmatists, rationalists, pantheists, Austrians, Prussians, Saxons, Franks, Swabians, Bavarians all rose as one man' in defence of the duchies, commented General

[1] Lotte Hegewisch, *op. cit.*, p. 133.

von Radowitz.[1] Only a few extreme conservatives, including an obscure young Prussian O. von Bismarck-Schönhausen, remained unmoved by the general enthusiasm. Innumerable declarations in support of the duchies poured in from *Landtage* and universities, from mass meetings and societies of every kind throughout the length and breadth of Germany. Typical of the sentiments expressed in these declarations was the motion adopted by the Hanoverian *Landtag*, calling on the Federal Diet to speak out boldly in defence of the independence and German nationality of Lauenburg, Holstein and Schleswig. Foreign powers, said Lang, the mover of the motion, had been quick to take advantage of Germany over the Luxemburg question when she was weak. Now the tremendous enthusiasm for the fatherland and the determination of the people to resist further encroachments on German soil, made it certain that Germany would stand behind the duchies in resisting Danish attempts to annex them.[2] All the great figures of the academic world, Dahlmann, Grimm and Gervinius, declared their support for the duchies, individually and collectively, at the Frankfurt *Germanistentag*. At a popular level resurgent nationalism found expression in the verses of the Lübeck pamphleteer, Geibel:

'*Wir wollen keine Dänen sein, wir wollen Deutsche bleiben.*' [3]

'All Germany,' remarked a contemporary, 'is looking with confidence to the people of the duchies who have proved how dearly they value their German honour and German ancestry . . . the question of the German duchies is a vital one for Germany . . . for if Denmark should succeed in making even one village Danish, the die would be cast for Germany and our people could then be numbered among the dead nations in Europe.' [4]

The wave of popular enthusiasm reached the thrones of the German princes, compelling them to swim with the tide and express at least token sympathy for the duchies. A few, like King

[1] J. von Radowitz, *Wer erbt in Schleswig? Eine Rechtsfrage*, Karlsruhe, 1846, p. 1.

[2] *Hamburger Nachrichten*, 29 July 1846.

[3] 'We don't want to be Danes, we want to remain German.'

[4] T. Klein, *Der Vorkampf deutscher Einheit und Freiheit*, Berlin, 1914, pp. 84–5.

Ludwig of Bavaria, were only too pleased to do so. Others, like the rulers of Hanover and Saxony, expressed polite sympathy for the agnates, while King Friedrich Wilhelm IV voiced his disapproval of the open letter and talked vaguely of supporting the duchies. In Vienna even the arch-conservative Metternich expressed disapproval of the Danish measures. Much as he disliked the growth of German radicalism and believed the integrity of the *Helstat* to be an indispensable element in the balance of power in northern Europe, he had to admit, as champion of the principle of legitimacy, that princes could not arbitrarily disregard well-established rights. 'The people are not there for the sake of kings, but kings for the sake of the people. They are the repository of the rights of their people and should protect and defend them. That is why the person of a king is sacred and monarchy an eternal institution.' [1]

The interest displayed by ruling circles in the claims of the agnates was most gratifying to the duke of Augustenburg. Yet it is significant that Christian August was still not greatly interested in becoming ruler of an independent Schleswig-Holstein. In a revealing letter to King Friedrich Wilhelm IV, Christian August argued that the open letter had not been published in order to preserve the *Helstat*. That objective could be attained much more easily and certainly by altering the succession in favour of the agnates. Had this course been adopted, he added, neither the duchies nor Germany would have had an excuse to interfere in the dynastic question. It would have concerned only the Danes.[2]

Further proof of the duke's desire for the crown of the *Helstat* is afforded by his correspondence with Professor Hjort of Copenhagen university. The duke recognized frankly that the succession question had become a mere pawn in a power political struggle between German and Dane, with the duchies as the prize. In this setting the significance of the succession question was that it enabled the Germans and Danes to justify their respective claims

[1] R. v. Fischer Benzon, *Zur Geschichte der Jahre 1839–47*, Z. 35, p. 224, Baron Löwenstein to H. Reventlow-Criminil, 2 Oct. 1846.

[2] C. Boysen, *Der offene Brief in seiner Auswirkung auf die Berliner Politik*, Z. 67, pp. 366–7, 26 Sept. 1846.

to the duchies. But what chance had one million Danes of winning a struggle against forty million Germans? 'The time is past', the duke wrote, 'when this question can be decided east of the Belt and north of the Kongeaa. Should this question ever be resolved in present circumstances, it will be resolved on the other side of the Elbe.' [1] Certainly the Great Powers wished to preserve the *Helstat*. But that could be done without imposing the Danish succession on the duchies. All that the Danes need do to preserve the monarchy was to alter the succession in favour of the agnates. Once they did this they would automatically remove German pressure from their throats, because they would destroy all legal justification for interference by the Confederation in the internal affairs of the *Helstat*. In fact the duke was trying to exploit the force of German nationalism, using it as a lever to compel the Danes to recognize that they could not keep the *Helstat* intact by force. But he still cherished the naïve, aristocratic illusion that popular animosity between German and Dane would become a factor of no importance the moment the Danes recognized the error of their ways, and called the Augustenburgs to the throne.

On 16 September the Federal Diet published its reply to the petition of the Holstein estates. Reassured by the pacific declarations of the Danish representative, the Diet had decided that there were no grounds for complaint at present. It was confident that the Danish king would give due consideration to the rights of the agnates, the Holstein estates and the Confederation in the succession question. The Diet asserted its right to express an opinion in this matter and it ruled that the refusal to accept petitions from the Holstein estates was a violation of the constitution of 1831. The Diet timidly acknowledged the patriotic sentiments of the people, but hastened to add that governments must take steps to restrain popular demonstrations. With this danger in mind, it advised the immediate introduction into Holstein of the Federal law of 1834 forbidding mass meetings. Widely criticized in Germany for its complacency and excessive timidity, the declaration of the Diet was approved in the duchies perhaps because little had been expected from Frankfurt. In fairness to the Diet, it must be remembered

[1] Heils, *op. cit.*, p. 169, 27 Dec. 1846.

that, as its writ did not run north of the Eider, it was extremely difficult for that body to defend the unity of Schleswig-Holstein. Under popular pressure the Diet had at least moved very far beyond the completely negative attitude it adopted in 1823.

By now it was October and the members were beginning to assemble in Schleswig for the sixth meeting of the estates. With von Scheel as royal commissioner and Beseler and the duke leading the assembly, stormy scenes could be predicted. It was an ominous sign that only seventeen members attended the customary dinner given by the commissioner on the eve of the formal opening. The remainder, with Beseler and the duke well to the fore, dined at a local inn. The next day Beseler was elected president of the estates, with the approval of the duke and by an overwhelming majority. This choice was a testimony to the popularity of Beseler, now at the height of his political career, and a clear sign that Falck's day as oracle of the party was over. The temper of the members had hardened since 1844 and in consequence the national liberals were able to exert great influence over the meeting, moving most of the important motions; Tiedemann demanded the withdrawal of the open letter, Gülich an alteration of the existing system of government to bring it into line with 'the demands of public morality and justice', H. K. Esmarch the separation of the finances of the duchies from those of Denmark, and Hansen the entry of Schleswig into the Confederation.

One of the sensations of the meeting was the motion for a constitution moved by the duke of Augustenburg, whose opposition to such motions in the past had done much to secure their rejection. Now he considered the people mature enough for a constitution which would enable them to defend their threatened rights. He proposed, therefore, that a draft constitution conferring financial and legislative powers on the Schleswig-Holstein estates be submitted to the joint estates. The motion was referred to committee by thirty-nine votes to two, despite von Scheel's protests that the estates were not competent to discuss matters affecting Holstein. By his decisive step Christian August had finally removed one of the major causes of friction between conservative and liberal, thus helping to preserve the solidarity of the party in face of the common enemy; he had been obliged at last to recognize the need for prompt action to forestall radical motions liable to prejudice the cause of the duchies in the eyes of the ruling classes. By sponsoring the motion the duke did not improve his standing in Denmark. But he was most careful to give the most influential German princes prior warning of his intentions, for fear they assumed he had thrown in his lot with radicalism and withdrew their support from him.

The national liberals could not always rely on the support of the other members. When Gülich demanded the dismissal of Karl Moltke, all the oratory of Beseler—who vacated the president's chair to support his colleague and delivered an impassioned attack on the 'political immorality' of the government—could not persuade the majority, the duke included, to accept so radical a step. Most members still conceived of their function as essentially defensive in character. In that spirit they accepted Esmarch's motion for the separation of the finances of the duchies from Denmark and Hansen's motion that Schleswig join the Confederation. It was a great triumph for the national liberals and a testimony to the changed temper of the estates, that Hansen's motion was carried by thirty-nine votes to three. Beseler had been right when he prophesied in 1842 that the idea of Schleswig entering the Confederation would gain ground year by year, and would eventually win universal approval as the idea of a united estates had done.[1]

Hansen restated the essentials of the German case. Schleswig was German because the superstructure of the duchy—the administrative and legal language, the language used in the schools and by educated people—was German. The fact that some Danish was spoken in North Schleswig should not deter the king from entering the Confederation as duke of Schleswig. There were Polish minorities in Silesia and Italian minorities in the Tyrol but were not these territories in the Confederation? He was prepared to forgive King Frederik VI's lack of foresight in not taking this step. But times had changed and King Christian must realize that the people of Schleswig-Holstein felt they were part of the German nation. 'It is no longer sufficient in the year 1846 to feel that

[1] *St. Z.*, Schleswig, 1842, pp. 1743–4.

you are German and can retain your German character wherever you happen to live. Complete peace of mind can come only with the knowledge that you belong politically to Germany. Speaking personally, I say that this German point of view is more than enough to convince me . . . that the greatest benefit, which it lies within the power of His Majesty to bestow on us, would result from acceptance of our petition in this matter.' [1]

Hansen had no time for the idea of an independent Schleswig. He saw only the long centuries of German influence in the duchy. 'Who is there whose vision is so narrow, whose heart is so devoid of affection that he wants to be separated politically from Germany at this moment in the renaissance of the German nation, just because Schleswig is his fatherland? . . . whatever course the development of our great fatherland may take in the near or distant future, it is our duty and our privilege, as true sons of the fatherland, to share in the joys and sorrows of Germany, as far as in us lies, and to work with might and main to give her a future rich with blessings.' [2]

Not everyone who supported the motion was as carried away by national sentiment as Hansen, Beseler, Gülich and Tiedemann. Many, like Count Reventlow-Jersbek, had in the past opposed an *Anschluss* with Germany on political grounds. They changed their minds simply because conditions had changed. It now appeared that closer relations with the Confederation were essential for the defence of Schleswig against the Danes. Hansen argued speciously that the Confederation had jurisdiction over Schleswig, because article two of the federal constitution committed the Confederation to defend the independence and inviolability of German states, while article eleven committed all members to defend not only the Confederation but every German state against attack. Was not Schleswig a German state and did not violation of the association between Schleswig and Holstein constitute an attack on an established right?[3] All the same, national liberal speakers were careful to reassure conservatives that the king would suffer no diminution of his authority by entering the Confederation.

[1] *St. Z.*, Schleswig, 1846, p. 99. [2] *Ibid.*, p. 103. [3] *Ibid.*, pp. 100–1.

The only opposition came from the North Schleswig members, Petersen, Nis Lorenzen, Jepsen, Nielsen and Jensen. The strongest argument against an *Anschluss* was, in their opinion, the simple fact that no one wanted it. It was a good point. Many German speakers were compelled to concede that most people in Schleswig did not desire an *Anschluss*. G. Claussen admitted, quite frankly, that if his electors were consulted most of them would oppose it although they would very likely be unable to rationalize their attitude. 'But is it not the same with all questions of high politics? These are simply outside the range of their judgement.'[1] But whatever his constituents said he would continue to support Hansen's motion. For this was a matter where the estates must be allowed to make up their own mind, unembarrassed by such trivial details as the opinions of those who had elected them. Klestrup and Steenholdt hastened to endorse these undemocratic sentiments. Most of their electors would also oppose an *Anschluss*. Most farmers would not even know what the Confederation was, observed Klestrup.[2] But as these people would certainly want to preserve the old association with Holstein, the estates should accept Hansen's motion; for it was quite clear to Klestrup and Steenholdt, if not to their more obtuse electors, that this association could only be preserved within the framework of the Confederation.

Hansen urged the estates, quite rightly, not to pay too much attention to the petitions they had received on this subject. But he was clearly guilty of exaggeration when he maintained that 70 of the 108 petitions favoured an *Anschluss*.[3] Most of them only attacked the open letter. In fact there was little support for an *Anschluss* even in the towns of North Schleswig although naturally rather more support in Central and South Schleswig. Positive opposition to an *Anschluss* was expressed in twenty petitions bearing thousands of signatures from Haderslev *Amt*. The signatories declared their desire to remain independent both of Germany and Denmark. This was the authentic voice of provincial Schleswig,

[1] *St. Z.*, Schleswig, 1846, p. 378.
[2] *Ibid.*, p. 411.
[3] Fabricius, *op. cit.*, pp. 330–1.

morbidly suspicious of all innovations and anxious that 'things should remain as they have always been'.[1]

There were many tense scenes at this meeting of the estates, due largely to the high degree of personal animosity between the new and unpopular commissioner, von Scheel, and the new president of the estates, Beseler. This dislike was mutual and of long standing. They first crossed swords when von Scheel announced that he could decide on his own initiative whether or not to forward the formal address of the estates to the king. As Scheel disliked references in this address to the three principles of 1844 and its denunciation of the open letter, he decided not to accept it. If his intention was to provoke the estates into voluntary dissolution he failed. All that happened was that the estates registered their solemn protest and continued their deliberations; at a private meeting, the members had decided not to force a dissolution but rather to 'throw the odium of such a measure on the government who are equally anxious to avoid it'.[2]

Von Scheel's second attempt was more successful. He suddenly announced that all government legislation must be expedited before private petitions were debated. This novel interpretation of clause 50 of the law of 1834 did not commend itself to the members. It was generally believed that von Scheel intended by this stratagem to secure the assent of the estates to all government legislation, and then order dissolution before the more controversial private motions had been reached. Beseler clashed sharply with von Scheel, flatly refusing to give priority on the agenda to the twenty-two government bills. If Scheel's interpretation of clause fifty was accepted, then the estates would lose all independence and be completely at the mercy of the government. Von Scheel persisted, returning a few days later with a royal letter confirming his interpretation. The estates agreed almost to a man that they could not accept what amounted to an infringement of their essential right of petition. They continued to debate private motions in the absence of the commissioner. On 24 November they accepted by overwhelming majorities the motions of the duke and Hansen. On

[1] A. D. Jørgensen, *op. cit.*, *S.A.*, 1895, p. 170.

[2] F.O. 22 153, Wynn to Palmerston, no. 51, 12 Nov. 1846.

30 November Beseler forwarded these petitions, with two government bills for good measure, to von Scheel.

The moment of decision had arrived. On 3 December von Scheel replied that he had forwarded the government bills to the king, but had returned the other petitions. After Beseler read out this reply on 4 December, the duke rose to declare that he found it impossible to remain there any longer as the estates were obviously impeded in the exercise of their duties.[1] He walked out of the hall followed by the majority of the members. Only the five members from North Schleswig remained to hear Beseler adjourn the meeting. Ten days later a sharply worded royal proclamation dissolved the estates, the last to meet in Schleswig-Holstein before the revolution, and with that a most memorable year in the history of the *Helstat* came to a close.

[1] *St. Z.*, Schleswig, 1846, pp. 563–5.

XIII

The revolution

THE last year before the revolution passed almost without incident. It was a deceptive calm, the lull before the storm, as contemporaries understood full well. Sir William Wynn, writing to Palmerston, observed that 'the tranquillity proceeds . . . more from want of opportunity of publicly expressing their opinion than from any spirit of conciliation on either side'.[1] The king was still powerful enough to repress all overt signs of disaffection, but this only made the fire 'glow more fiercely under the ashes'.[2] The prince of Noer was certainly not alone in his belief that a great political crisis would occur when the estates met in 1848.

As the *Vormärz* moved to a close the *Landespartei* was redoubling its efforts to establish firm connections with Germany. Before the Schleswig estates dispersed, the German members met privately to discuss future policy. A very few, like the impetuous Tiedemann, were thinking of an armed uprising. 'A new era is on the way. No more words. The issue will have to be decided by the sword,' he exclaimed dramatically to his wife.[3] The majority of the estates had not got as far as this. Their immediate concern was to ensure that the duchies had powerful allies standing by their side in the hour of trial, which their instincts told them might lie in the immediate future. Naturally they turned to Germany, commissioning Tiedemann to approach the governments of South Germany on their behalf, while the duke agreed to sound the courts of Hanover, Brunswick and Mecklenburg.

In February came the announcement that the king of Prussia had consented to call a meeting in Berlin of representatives from

[1] F.O.22 157, Wynn to Palmerston, 8 April 1847.
[2] J. G. Droysen and K. Samwer, *op. cit.*, p. 264, Prince of Noer to king, 5 Jan. 1848.
[3] Tiedemann, *op. cit.*, p. 85.

the various provincial estates. This momentous event aroused great excitement in liberal circles. Great changes would surely not be long delayed when the most powerful autocrat in North Germany deemed the time appropriate to redeem promises made by his predecessor regarding a constitution. In fact, the king was a good deal more anxious to secure money for building a railway to East Prussia, than to bestow a modern constitution on his subjects. However, it was the appearance that mattered most in the spring of 1847, and many prominent Schleswig-Holsteiner flocked to Berlin, among them Beseler, Olshausen, Tiedemann and G. Claussen, all of them anxious to witness the opening of the *Vereinigter Landtag* and to try and interest the members in the affairs of the duchies. J. G. Droysen, a frequent visitor to Berlin in the past, was particularly well placed to work behind the scenes on behalf of the duchies. He was instrumental in getting a motion in support of the duchies put before the *Landtag* in June, and he persuaded influential members to ask their colleagues to express their sympathy for Schleswig-Holstein at the end of the meeting. However modest the success of the *Vereinigter Landtag* might appear by material standards—and the members were certainly disillusioned by the king's behaviour—nevertheless, Droysen expressed the confidence of contemporaries that from these small beginnings epoch-making changes in internal and external policy would soon follow. These changes, he wrote to a friend, W. Arendt, would not be restricted to Prussia, because the whole European system associated with the Holy Alliance had really rested on the essential basis of Prussian illiberalism. It was reasonable to suppose that once the pivot was removed, the system would fly apart. The duchies would certainly benefit from all this because at last they could be sure of that support so essential if they were to remain German. He was especially elated at the success of his conversations with his foreign office friends. His persistent efforts in this direction were at last bearing fruit. His friends were beginning to appreciate how fortunate it was for Prussia that the affairs of the duchies had captured the attention of Germany. 'I hope, in short, that Prussian diplomacy in Copenhagen will now play a role worthy of her. They are beginning to see that it is precisely there that the great battle against Russia is to commence, a conflict which we need not fear as long as we have courage and popular support . . . the scales are falling from their eyes in Berlin . . . the night is ending and day is breaking,' he concluded.[1]

Conservatives, too, were conscious of the imminent climacteric in the affairs of Schleswig-Holstein. In January 1847 a petition, drafted by Reventlow-Preetz on behalf of the *Ritterschaft*, was presented to the crown. This document, observed Sir William Wynn, 'was no less remarkable for the language such as the absolute monarchs of this country have not, for the last two centuries, been accustomed to hear—as for the early opportunity taken of transmitting it and the determination it shows of keeping alive the spirit at present existing in the duchies'.[2] The *Ritterschaft* stood foursquare behind the national liberals, bluntly informing the crown that the moment of decision was not far distant in the long-standing quarrel between duchies and crown. There were two alternatives. Either the king continued to violate the duchies' rights, forcing the *Kongelov* on them at the point of the bayonet, or he respected their rights and granted them a constitution. Indeed it was essential, the petition continued, that he take the latter step for his repressive measures had already lost him the affection of his German subjects. To regain it something more than the existing estates was needed in 1847.

The king rejected this and another more moderately worded address sent to him in May. Yet on the face of things reconciliation between crown and *Ritterschaft* seemed highly probable. After all, the king must surely realize that the optimism of 1846 had been misplaced. For how long could he continue to employ force against his German subjects without tearing the *Helstat* asunder? Nor were the conservative landowners at all happy to find themselves in permanent opposition to their king-duke.

[1] Hübner, *op. cit.*, pp. 351–5, J. G. Droysen to W. Arendt, 22 April 1847. Others were less optimistic. Samwer thought most of the visitors from Schleswig-Holstein were dissatisfied with the Prussian attitude. L. A. S. Samwer 40, Samwer to Woldemar, 27 April 1847.

[2] F.O.22 157, Wynn to Palmerston, 5 Feb. 1847.

Sooner or later a political explosion might occur, bringing with it rebellion and social upheaval. National liberals might face this prospect with equanimity, but never conservatives. With these thoughts uppermost in his mind, Count Reventlow-Preetz turned to K. Moltke in the autumn of 1846. But the correspondence which followed revealed differences of outlook so fundamental that a rapprochement finally proved impossible.

Karl Moltke's autocratic views left little room for compromise. Reventlow-Preetz had, in his opinion, become the unwitting dupe of a small group of malevolent individuals bent on destroying the existing order of things, and employing all manner of illegality to this end. These people were extremely dangerous, for by pretending to have justice on their side, they had persuaded honourable men like Reventlow-Preetz to join them, giving the latter the illusion that their opinions were valued. Whatever they said, these people were separatists guilty of high treason, for they were seeking to transform the duchies into an independent state (whether under the same ruler as Denmark or not was immaterial), and to include Schleswig in Germany. The Danes, on the other hand, had no wish to disturb the *status quo* by incorporating the duchies in Denmark. So there could be no question of compromise with the treasonable Schleswig-Holsteiner. Subjects must remember their Christian duty to obey the ruler. His power was unlimited and his rulings on dynastic and constitutional matters must not be questioned. If subjects forgot these elementary truths, force would be used to bring them to their senses. As for the members of the *Ritterschaft*, if they did their duty they would be seeking to preserve the *status quo*, as they had done in 1831 when they denounced Lornsen. Finally, if Reventlow-Preetz wished to serve the state, as he alleged, his best course of action would simply be to withdraw from all political activity.

Reventlow-Preetz disagreed profoundly with this absolutist view of politics. He denied that he was seeking to serve the interests of any party. He cherished his independence of mind and considered morality much more important than politics. The defence of the duchies he regarded as a moral obligation incumbent upon the members of the *Ritterschaft*. By doing their duty they would, incidentally, protect the people against leaders with dubious motives. There was surely justification for their present alarm because, whatever the government said, the Danes clearly wished to incorporate the duchies in Denmark. This would undoubtedly intensify the national conflict between the Germans and Danes, for as part of Denmark the former would not enjoy equality of treatment with the latter in the administration of the state. Unless the Danes abandoned their designs on the duchies, more and more people would conclude that separation from Denmark was the only way of securing their rights. In the past he had been most reluctant to envisage this painful possibility, for he 'feared few things as much as becoming a citizen of a little duodecimo state with a duodecimo prince peeping into every pot and through every cellar window' and treating the duchies like a country estate.[1] There was no need for separation; personal union could easily be preserved, provided that the duchies were treated as equals and given a constitution as a tangible sign of their independence—for he insisted that Schleswig-Holstein formed an independent state. As for the *Lex Regia*, would it not be easy to buy off the Hessians who had expectations of a throne in Germany? The *Lex Regia* had been introduced with popular approval. It could be annulled in the same way. He would continue as always to speak his mind freely for duty and conscience were the mainsprings of his political activities. He flatly rejected Moltke's contention that absolute rulers could interfere arbitrarily with established rights. If absolute submission to the will of the crown was the only basis on which Moltke thought a reconciliation possible, then Reventlow-Preetz was not interested. He broke off the correspondence in May 1847, closing the last letter with the words, 'we have nothing but our conviction that our rights are firmly established. We make use of no other weapon than the spoken word. God will not refuse His aid to those who, trusting in Him, enter upon this desperate struggle joyfully and resigned to His Will.'[2]

[1] Regensburg, *op. cit.*, p. 223, Reventlow-Preetz to C. Moltke, 22 March 1847.

[2] *Ibid.*, p. 254, Reventlow-Preetz to C. Moltke, 4 May 1847.

It was a decisive moment. All hopes of reconciliation had ended, and shortly afterwards Reventlow-Preetz turned to the national liberals. In the early autumn he met Beseler in Schleswig, discussing with him certain measures, including the establishment of a provisional government and the occupation of Rendsburg fortress, which a sudden emergency might necessitate. They met at Beseler's request, for the latter was now fully convinced that a conflict with Denmark was imminent,[1] and was anxious to co-ordinate policy with the leader of the *Ritterschaft*.

The stresses and strains inside the *Helstat* were accentuated throughout 1847, as Moltke tried to prove that strong government was not only good government (as every absolutist knew) but would even become popular in the duchies, once the trouble-makers had been silenced. For he clung pathetically to the pretence that the Schleswig-Holsteiner were a small minority of malcontents lacking all general support in the population. That day was long past. Consequently his 'firm measures' merely drove the opposition underground and strained the loyalty of the duchies to the utmost. The press censorship was applied more rigorously than ever before. The *Itzehoer Wochenblatt* was forbidden to print political articles, the *Hamburger Neue Zeitung* was banned and the *Kieler Korrespondenz Blatt* came close to suspension. The sale of all political literature was forbidden and new regulations made the holding of mass meetings virtually impossible. Had it not been for the personal intervention of the king, von Scheel would even have dissolved all political societies including the *Schleswig-Holsteinischer Patriotischer Verein* and the *Slesvigske Forening*. As mentioned already, legal proceedings were taken against prominent political figures, including Karl Lorentzen and Beseler, for their part in the Neumünster meeting. Beseler was acquitted but Lorentzen was sentenced to a term of imprisonment.

National animosities were burning as fiercely as ever in North Schleswig as the elections to the new estates revealed. The towns returned men of national liberal persuasions, prominent opponents of the Danes in the previous estates like Beseler, Gülich and

[1] '*Wenn Michel jetzt nicht seine Schlafmütze ablegt, nehme ich die Tonsur*', L.A.S. 399 Lorentzen 3, W. Beseler to K. Lorentzen, 22 March 1847.

Esmarch, all of them securing increased majorities. Danish representation was increased from four to six seats, clearly implying that there was little support for an *Anschluss* in North Schleswig. Nis Lorenzen and Jepsen were re-elected but, significantly enough, Posselt and Petersen were replaced by men of pronounced nationalist views, Hans Kryger and P. L. Wiimh. H. C. Bladt defeated Steffens for Sundeved and Als, and Klestrup, now a supporter of the *Landespartei*, was replaced in Aerø by C. H. Brandt. Jensen and Schmidt, who replaced Nielsen, were returned for Flensburg. The signs were that had the estates met as planned in 1848, clashes between German and Dane would have been both frequent and acrimonious.

The prospects seemed brighter for the Danish movement in 1847. At last the Danes obtained a monopoly of reporting in North Schleswig after *Lyna* fell foul of the censor. In May the king ordered all lessons at Haderslev school to be given in Danish. In June a Danish teachers' training college was established in Vonsbaek. There was talk of a Danish school in Åbenraa and of new regulations which would compel students from Schleswig to attend Copenhagen university instead of Kiel. This challenge to German cultural domination of the north increased the tension between German and Dane, especially in the towns where brawls between rival factions became a frequent occurrence.

King Christian did not relax his efforts throughout 1847 to secure the support of the Great Powers for the preservation of the *Helstat*. In May, on the advice of Nesselrode, the king instructed Baron Löwenstein, Danish ambassador in Vienna, to inquire whether Austria and Prussia would be willing to issue an immediate declaration upholding the integrity of the state. King Christian calculated that this would help the authorities to restore popular confidence in the monarchy. The response was far from encouraging. The powers certainly appreciated the strategic importance of the *Helstat* as a factor in the balance of power, but felt that a solemn guarantee could be given only if the Danes negotiated a satisfactory settlement with the agnates. Opinion was now moving strongly in favour of recognition of the agnates' claims. The Tsar was favourably disposed towards them. Louis Philippe in the winter of 1847 informed Karl of Glücksburg that an alteration of the *Lex Regia* was the only possible solution.[1] Prince Albert spoke against the female succession in the queen's presence,[2] and Metternich had felt for some time that the principle of legitimacy necessitated a renunciation by the Hessians.

After this rebuff, Christian began to have serious doubts about his policy. The position was undoubtedly grave. The Great Powers would not support him against the Augustenburgs, all hope of reconciliation with the *Ritterschaft* had to be abandoned by the summer, and Moltke's firm measures had clearly not restored the confidence of the duchies in the crown as anticipated. There remained the possibility of winning popular support by constitutional change, very much in the public mind since the *Vereinigter Landtag* meeting. King Christian had shown great interest in this, sending a minor official to Berlin to act as his observer. Some of his ministers now recommended similar changes for the *Helstat*. By August King Christian had overcome his natural repugnance for 'this last extreme'; writing to a friend, he observed that he was prepared to come to terms with the idea of constitutional government, but he would do so 'with skill and dignity for a king ought not to descend to the level of his people in constitutional matters but rather raise them to his own level'.[3] In short, an agonizing reappraisal could no longer be delayed. A constitution would, he hoped, give a new lease of life to the *Helstat*, overcome the resistance of the duchies, win them back to their old loyalties and strengthen the crown at the crucial stage in any future negotiations with the agnates. If the estates were consulted during these negotiations—as Reventlow-Criminil suggested they might be—it seemed not unreasonable to hope that gratitude for a new constitution would make them reconsider their support of the Augustenburgs. The king's decision represented a major change of policy, a last expedient certainly—but what transpired in 1848

[1] P.A. III D. 8, K. Samwer to duke of Augustenburg, 7 Dec. 1847.
[2] L.A.S. Samwer 43, Samwer to duke of Augustenburg, 23 Nov. 1847.
[3] G. F. Jensen-Tusch, *Zur Lebens und Regierungsgeschichte Christian VIII Königs von Dänemark, Herzogs von Schleswig-Holstein und Lauenburg*, Altona, 1852, p. 394, Christian to Kapitän From-Moller, 27 Aug. 1847.

shows that it was far from being a desperate gamble doomed inevitably to failure. P. G. Bang was instructed to study the question and prepare a memorandum for consideration by the *Statsraad* in December. The memorandum was ready on time but the *Statsraad* meeting was postponed, for on 20 December, after a short illness, King Christian VIII laid down the burden of kingship for ever.

His death was not mourned like that of the *Herzensherzog* in 1839. There was general satisfaction in the duchies when the melancholy tidings were received. 'We have lost our ablest and most bitter opponent,' commented Samwer.[1] The duke of Augustenburg, while admitting that his brother-in-law had been an able and cultured ruler, attributed his 'failure' to a complete lack of political insight and to his obstinate and partisan support of the Hessians.[2] These were harsh words. King Christian was certainly no nearer a solution of the dynastic problem than he had been in 1840. In one sense he was worse off, for he could no longer rely on the loyalty of his German subjects, as King Frederik VI had been able to do in 1814 and 1830. But it would be unfair to suppose that King Christian was solely responsible for this deterioration, although he cannot escape some share of the blame. A conscientious and talented administrator, King Christian had done much to modernize the state and, although frequently misunderstood and attacked by nationalists on both sides of the Kongeaa, he genuinely desired to reconcile his German and Danish subjects and stand above party strife. He was indeed a tragic figure, born out of due season, who deserved a much better epitaph than that written by Samwer.

His son, the crown prince, a popular figure in Denmark, reputed to have liberal sympathies, but of lethargic habits and endowed by nature with no outstanding qualities, now ascended the throne as King Frederik VII. He at once announced his intention of continuing his late father's policies and confirmed Karl

[1] Liepmann, *op. cit.*, p. 224, Samwer to Prince Woldemar Charlottenburg, 30 Jan. 1848.

[2] Heils, *op. cit.*, p. 198, duke of Augustenburg to Professor Hjort, 29 Jan. 1848.

Moltke in office. In the first week of the reign the *Statsraad* approved Bang's draft and on 28 February a rescript was issued containing details of the proposed constitution. This was an historic moment in the history of the *Helstat*, for with a stroke of his pen the new king ended forever the absolute power of the crown established by King Frederik III in 1660.

The king proposed to create joint estates, meeting alternately in Copenhagen and Gottorp and possessing full financial and legislative powers, under the crown, in all matters affecting the *Helstat*. Provincial estates would still remain in being to deal with local matters. An assurance was given that there would be no alteration in the relations between Holstein and the German Confederation or between Schleswig and Holstein, and that the German and Danish languages would enjoy equal protection in Schleswig. A draft constitution based on these principles would be prepared shortly and submitted for approval to fifty-two *Erfahrene Männer*,[1] eighteen to be elected in the duchies, eighteen in the kingdom and sixteen to be nominated by the crown from the duchies and from Denmark.

The rescript aroused widespread interest throughout the *Helstat*. In Denmark it was welcomed by moderate opinion but received coldly by the Eiderdanes who were primarily interested in a common constitution for Schleswig and Denmark, with separate institutions for Holstein. In the duchies the reaction was by no means universally hostile. It seemed at first as if King Christian had been right after all for, when faced with the prospect of constitutional advance, the unity of the *Landespartei* melted away. Differences of opinion came into the open when those members of the Holstein estates who lived in Kiel met unofficially on 3 February to exchange views. Beseler, spokesman for the national liberals, characteristically denounced the rescript as a snare to entice the German duchies into an intimate relationship with a Danish national state. In any case the rescript failed completely to give recognition to the one essential point, namely, the right of Schleswig-Holstein to have its own constitution as befitted an independent state. Therefore Beseler advised against the election of

[1] Wise men.

the *Erfahrene Männer*, for it was surely pointless for them to discuss something that would obviously be unacceptable to the duchies. But the meeting was not convinced. Indeed a few members of radical persuasions like Olshausen and H. R. Claussen, 'fools who want to conquer freedom in Copenhagen' as Beseler called them,[1] were positively attracted by the prospect of constitutional advance in the immediate future. Close association with Germany was highly desirable; but did it follow that participation in a common constitution with the Danes would preclude association with Germany at a later date? It seemed to the radicals as if they could have the best of both worlds. Accordingly they supported the election of the *Erfahrene Männer*. The decisive factor, however, was that moderate opinion, represented by Falck, Wiese, Balemann and Bargum, was overwhelmingly in favour of election. Not that they were satisfied with the rescript. But these respectable law-abiding citizens of Kiel felt that no possibility of negotiation should be neglected, however remote the prospect of a common constitution for Schleswig-Holstein. It seemed the least they could do when the new king had done his best to allay their fears by recognizing the association between the duchies, and promising strict equality of treatment for both halves of the state under the new arrangements—a point which had already aroused critical comment from the numerically superior Danes. The *Ritterschaft* declaration on 4 February favouring election clinched the matter. The prudence and respect for legality displayed by the leaders of opinion in Holstein commended them in the eyes of the courts of Prussia and Hanover. Prince Woldemar warned Samwer that, although the King of Prussia had his heart in the right place, he was petrified by the thought of unlawful action and would only approve of passive resistance on the duchies' part.[2] Writing in similar vein, King Ernst August of Hanover counselled the duke of Augustenburg to restrain the radicals and avoid all precipitate action, temptations to which the duke was most unlikely to succumb.[3]

[1] L.A.S. 399, Lorentzen 4, W. Beseler to K. Lorentzen, 14 Feb. 1848.
[2] Liepmann, *op. cit.*, p. 227, 3 Feb. 1848.
[3] P.A. III, 29 Jan. 1848.

The national liberals were far from convinced that the immediate threat to the independence of the duchies had been removed by the prospect of lengthy negotiations in Copenhagen. Above all, the national liberals were concerned about the effect which news of impending negotiations between German and Dane might have on Germany. They feared that the docile collaboration of the people of Schleswig-Holstein with the Danes would alienate German opinion—perhaps with disastrous effects for the duchies if the rescript was intended to ensnare them as the national liberals supposed it was. To counteract this tendency the national liberals took steps to mobilize the German press, especially in Hamburg and Bremen, against the rescript. They were well placed to do this, for men like Karl Lorentzen had important contacts with papers in Cologne, Breslau and Augsburg. So successful were they that as early as 12 February the whole German press was referring to the rescript in unfavourable terms. Needless to say, this was a victory of considerable importance, for with the popular press on their side the national liberals could be certain that Germany would not forget the duchies in the hour of need. As strict censorship made all adverse comment on the rescript impossible in Schleswig-Holstein, Beseler and Droysen wrote pamphlets explaining the national liberal viewpoint, and through the good offices of Karl Lorentzen had them published anonymously in Bremen.

Droysen put the German case in uncompromising terms. A common constitution was quite unacceptable, simply because the inhabitants of Schleswig-Holstein were German, not Danish. 'In all the four centuries of personal union we have never learnt to look on Copenhagen as our capital city, as the focal point of our political, social or intellectual life.' [1] Why should the Germans begin to do so now when the days of dynasties were numbered and peoples were at last coming into their own? In bygone days the Germans had existed without Denmark and they were confident that those happy and honourable times would return. But

[1] *Die gemeinsame Verfassung für Dänemark und Schleswig-Holstein. Eine deutsche Frage*, Bremen, 1848. In *Kleine Schriften von J. G. Droysen*, Heft I, *Zur Schleswig-Holsteinischen Frage*, pp. 80–1.

if they accepted the common constitution what would happen? 'We would have to make Danish our mother tongue in order to understand and to be understood in the new estates . . . we would become German-Danes, political mongrels, a mulatto people. Never! We are not prepared, whatever the cost, to commit treason against ourselves and against Germany. Our roots are in Germany. We will hold fast to her with all our devotion, our strength and with unshakeable determination.'[1] There were other considerations. Schleswig-Holstein was the neck on the German body, the corner stone in the arch of German defence; but at present it was in the hands of the enemy, like a wedge driven down the line of the river Elbe into the very heart of North Germany. 'Is Schleswig-Holstein to remain under a foreign cabinet which can compel an English or Russian fleet to appear off Copenhagen at any time? Are the Danes to be allowed to dominate the mouth of the Elbe, and with it the greater part of the commerce of the North Sea, as they already control the trade of the Baltic Sea at the Sound?'[2] What were the duchies to do? Unlike Beseler, Droysen favoured the election of the *Erfahrene Männer*, recognizing the right of the king to call these men for consultation. But so that the election should not seem to imply approval of a common constitution, the men chosen by the duchies should, on arrival in Copenhagen, declare that this constitution was totally unacceptable. If the king recognized Schleswig-Holstein as an independent state and granted it a constitution, then, and then only, would it be possible for Denmark and Schleswig-Holstein to negotiate a northern union on terms of absolute equality, as envisaged by Lornsen a decade before. But if the Danes would not do this, one thing was certain; 'A great people and a great fatherland awaits us'. On that ominous note the pamphlet closed.

On 17 February sixty members from the Schleswig and Holstein estates assembled privately in Kiel, the first joint meeting of the estates in centuries, to decide whether or not to elect the *Erfahrene Männer*. It was significant that Balemann, an apostle of moderation held in high esteem by K. Moltke, was elected chairman. Beseler, with enthusiastic support from the Schleswig

[1] *Ibid.*, p. 81. [2] *Ibid.*, p. 82.

national liberals, led the attack, arguing that if they agreed to elect they were halfway towards accepting the constitution: he reiterated his conviction that election would be interpreted as weakness in Germany. He was opposed by a motley alliance of conservatives, led by Reventlow-Preetz, moderates, headed by Falck, and a few radicals like Olshausen and H. R. Claussen, all equally convinced that a conciliatory gesture could do no harm. They carried the day by thirty-nine votes to twenty-one. But this did not mean that a majority approved of a common constitution. Far from it; at a further meeting in the evening held to reconcile the opposing viewpoints, it was finally agreed that the members of the estates, in their capacity as electors of the *Erfahrene Männer*, should declare their intention of electing men who would promise to oppose a common constitution.

The position remained unchanged with moderate forces in the ascendancy almost to the end of February. Then suddenly the scene was transformed, when news arrived in Kiel on 28 February of the overthrow of Louis Philippe and the proclamation of a republic in Paris. This momentous event was quickly followed in the first few days of March by reports of unrest and disturbances in Italy, Germany and in the Habsburg dominions. These events had a catalytic effect on Schleswig-Holstein, activating the revolutionary potential inherent in the conflict between the duchies and Denmark. In February the unification of Germany still lay in the future; men of moderate and conservative persuasion were firmly in control, holding the national liberals at bay and enjoying the passive support of the people whilst carefully avoiding any intimate relationship with them. By March German unification had entered the realm of practical politics, the association of Schleswig-Holstein with a united Germany became an issue of immediate importance, the star of national liberalism was rising in the political firmament and, for the first time, the masses of the population were playing an active role in public affairs. This was a momentous development which threatened to wrest the political initiative from the educated minority whose preserve it had been for generations.

The political life of the towns underwent a profound change in these early March days; there was a sudden increase in the membership of the *Bürgervereine*. Kiel was typical in this respect; interest in the *Bürgerverein* had been extremely limited when it was founded by Olshausen; but in March 1848 membership quadrupled virtually overnight. In Kiel, as in other towns, the meetings of the *Bürgervereine* soon became focal points for political discussion. From these lively and genuinely popular gatherings, attended by people from all social classes, there emanated a spate of petitions, demanding a free constitution, freedom of the press —for which 900 Kiel citizens petitioned—the creation of a popular militia and full support for the cause of German unification. All eyes were now fixed on Germany. The red, white and blue favours of Schleswig-Holstein were rarely to be seen. These 'symbols of outworn particularism' had been replaced by the black, red and gold colours, worn openly by the students at Kiel university. It was symptomatic of the changing temperature of political life that Olshausen, who had enthused about constitutional freedom at the beginning of February, had now turned back to his first love, Germany, and that when the *Erfahrene Männer* were elected for Holstein on 13 March, radical candidates secured election in the towns and the nationalist professor, Ravit, replaced Falck for Kiel university.

As the days passed bringing news of the flight of Metternich to England and of revolt in Northern Italy, tension began to mount in the towns where the coercive power of the government melted away. In Kiel students were practising shooting supervised by the young nationalists, W. Ahlmann and L. Stein; the *Korrespondenz Blatt* grew daily more bold in its utterances and permission for public meetings was granted with alacrity by police authorities only too anxious to preserve some semblance of legality. In short, a revolutionary situation existed in the towns by the middle of March. To the national liberals it seemed that the tide of history was at last flowing in their favour. But the prospect of social disorder filled conservatives with dread and foreboding. Reventlow-Preetz, thoroughly frightened by the events in Paris, now exerted all his considerable influence to keep effective control of the situation in the hands of moderates. When Olshausen clamoured for a mass meeting in Itzehoe on 13 March, Reventlow-Preetz countered swiftly with a suggestion that the estates of both duchies meet in Rendsburg on 18 March to discuss an address urging the king to summon the *Erfahrene Männer* to Copenhagen without delay.

Reventlow-Preetz got his way. On 18 March seventy members of the estates assembled privately in Rendsburg. By now the town had assumed a revolutionary atmosphere hardly conducive to moderate counsels. The main buildings were decked with the German colours, the soldiers of the garrison were fraternizing with the townsfolk, a mass meeting had been planned for the same evening and some excited citizens even forced their way into the meeting of the estates, only to be ordered out by the chairman. It was a sign of the times that the intransigent Beseler had replaced the meek and mild Balemann in the chair. Soon Olshausen was on his feet, demanding immediate action to defend the independence of the duchies; he wanted the estates to draft an electoral law for a constituent assembly, to secure the entry of Schleswig into the Confederation, and to set up a permanent committee with a watching brief after the end of the meeting. Anxious to reassure the national liberals that his belated conversion to the German cause was genuine, Olshausen was now violently opposed to the election of the *Erfahrene Männer* and referred in disparaging terms to the Danes as 'idle and lazy folk' who no longer commanded the respect of Europe. Wild and intemperate language which, as will be seen presently, had an important bearing on the situation in Copenhagen. Again Reventlow-Preetz intervened to restrain members from provocative action. He succeeded in persuading them to keep their promise to send the *Erfahrene Männer* to Copenhagen—not that they expected much to come of this conciliatory gesture. He advised against the establishment of a permanent committee because this could easily be construed by the Danes as an attempt to set up a separate government. It was a tribute to Reventlow-Preetz's authority and persuasive powers that the estates finally agreed to empower Beseler, Bargum and himself to recall the estates only if they considered this warranted by events. The estates also turned down Olshausen's demand for a constituent assembly.

But this was March 1848. Popular pressure for some immediate action could not be resisted indefinitely as the estates soon realized. With reluctance and much to the discomfiture of Reventlow-Preetz, they finally decided not to wait until the king had summoned the *Erfahrene Männer*, but to submit five demands to the king at once. The estates demanded firstly, that a united estates be allowed to draw up a separate constitution for Schleswig-Holstein; secondly, that Schleswig be allowed to join the Confederation; thirdly, that a citizen's militia be formed at once; fourthly, that freedom of the press and of public meeting be guaranteed and, finally, that von Scheel, symbol of the old autocratic system, be removed from office. This was a decisive moment in the history of Schleswig-Holstein. Power was at last slipping through the fingers of the estates into the hands of the people. There was no mistaking the radical spirit inspiring most of the demands. The first demand, in fact, amounted to a clear rejection of the rescript which the *Erfahrene Männer* were supposed to be discussing in the near future. But by this time the *Erfahrene Männer* had faded completely into the background; contemporaries regarded the five demands as an ultimatum, certain to resolve their dispute with the Danes one way or another in the immediate future. Needless to say, Reventlow-Preetz did not accept the invitation to attend the mass meeting in the *Theatresaal* that evening. It was the more radical and nationalist-minded members of the estates who found their way to the packed meeting, which was attended by the younger citizens and by over four hundred soldiers from the garrison singing *Schleswig-Holstein stammverwandt, schmied de Dänen ut dat Land.*[1] The result was that national liberals, Gülich, Engel and L. Neergaard, together with Olshausen and H. R. Claussen, were entrusted by the mass meeting with the task of presenting the five demands to the king. Three days later this deputation set sail for Copenhagen.

Did the events of 18 March mark the beginning of a revolution in the duchies as some Danish historians maintain? There is no doubt that the civil and military authorities in Rendsburg were

[1] 'Schleswig-Holstein, united people, throw out the Danes'—a popular variant of the well-known song.

completely helpless; with the garrison firmly on the side of the people, resistance would have been out of the question had an uprising occurred. But even on 18 March the leaders of the people had not abandoned all hope of a peaceful solution. The deputation was sent with the genuine intention of resolving the dispute before irrevocable steps were taken. It is most significant that the committee of three set up by the estates did not remain in being after 18 March. Beseler returned to Schleswig, Reventlow-Preetz to Preetz and Bargum to Kiel—clear evidence that these leaders certainly did not anticipate an armed conflict in the immediate future. On the other hand, it was realized that there was a distinct possibility of the deputation returning empty-handed on 26 March, the day their ship was expected back from Copenhagen. Preparations were well-advanced to meet this eventuality; arms were being purchased in Hamburg and distributed throughout the duchies[1] and the prince of Noer was already deeply involved in negotiations for the establishment of a provisional government—negotiations fraught with great difficulty as Reventlow-Preetz was most reluctant to agree to this extreme measure. Had the deputation returned with a negative answer on 26 March, as anticipated, it is extremely probable that an armed uprising would have occurred at once.

The duke of Augustenburg had been a silent observer during these stirring events. Neither he nor his brother attended the Kiel and Rendsburg meetings, fearing that their presence would only add to the difficulties facing the government. But the duke was filled with grim foreboding by the trend of the times. The intemperate tones of the Rendsburg meeting alarmed him greatly. If the Danish reply to the deputation was couched in similar language, a conflict could hardly be avoided and the Danes would be able to place the onus for rebellion on the duchies. German and Danish radicals between them could easily endanger the *Helstat* which he had a vested interest in preserving. His sudden decision to visit Berlin was probably inspired by a desire to secure Prussian intervention in order to prevent a Danish invasion or—equally alarming prospect—social upheaval in the duchies. On 21 March

[1] F.O.33 133, Hodges to Palmerston, 14 March 1848.

he called at Noer and discussed the situation with his brother. The prince referred to a letter which he had written to the king two days before, advising him to make certain concessions in the interests of law and order—an ill-advised communication as will be evident later. The prince promised to take no precipitate action until the duke returned from Berlin. The latter, much relieved, continued his journey and arrived in Berlin on 23 March.

Excitement continued to mount in the duchies for on 20 March news of the momentous events in Berlin on 18 March had reached them; Prussia had ceased to be an absolutist state, the censorship had ended, a constitution had been promised and the king had declared that Prussia would play her rightful part in the unification of Germany. In honour of the Prussian king's proclamation Beseler ordered the illumination of Schleswig town, for national liberals were quick to realize that this was a decisive event, the salvation of the duchies and the pledge of future victory. They could now be reasonably certain of active Prussian intervention in an emergency. Without it, armed resistance to the Danes would have been an extremely hazardous operation.[1] They were fortified in their optimism by the dramatic news which followed. On 19 March there was serious fighting in Berlin, ending in the withdrawal of armed forces from the city and the victory of the insurgents. On 21 March the king rode through the streets of his capital, wearing the black, red and gold colours and declaring that Prussia would henceforth consider herself part of Germany; this was a notable victory for the national idea over the forces of particularism.

The spirit of 1848 affected Denmark as profoundly as Germany, creating a revolutionary situation in Copenhagen by the middle of March. When news of the events in Paris reached Copenhagen on 1 March, the masses of the Danish people emerged at last as an active force and introduced an urgent and increasingly radical note into political life. Heartened by this, the Eiderdanes launched a determined offensive against the rescript, which they had always

[1] The Danes also recognized the crucial importance of the proclamation, attributing to it major responsibility for the establishment of the provisional government in Kiel. F.O.22 162, Wynn to Palmerston, 27 March 1848.

regarded as a betrayal of Danish interests in Schleswig. Over two thousand people crowded into the first Casino meeting held on 11 March, to hear Tscherning assert that Schleswig would still belong to Denmark even if the people of Schleswig did not agree. If Schleswig tried to break away and join a foreign state, that would be an act of rebellion which the Danes must prevent by force if need be. But it was not so easy to turn the people of Copenhagen against the rescript. Eiderdanes, like German nationalists, discovered that many of their fellow citizens were still much more interested in the prospect of constitutional advance, afforded by the rescript, than in national questions. Olshausen, realizing this, cancelled a mass meeting to be held in Rendsburg on 18 March; the political isolation of the Eiderdanes seemed to render counter demonstrations superfluous.

The factor which transformed the situation in Copenhagen was the news, which arrived on 20 March, of the events in Rendsburg two days before. The authorities were gravely alarmed, all army leave was cancelled and orders given for the immediate transfer of the monetary reserves from Rendsburg and Altona. For the Eiderdanes this was the moment of decision. Did not the appointment of the committee of three imply that revolution in Schleswig-Holstein was imminent? Notices went up all over the city, proclaiming that the fatherland was in danger and that the duchies were in a state of rebellion. At midday the Eiderdane, L. N. Hvidt, summoned the *Borgerrepresentanterne*[1] and warned them that the latest news represented a grave challenge to the authority of the state in Schleswig. Action was imperative to forestall the establishment of a Schleswig-Holstein state and an *Anschluss* between Schleswig and Germany. When the deputation arrived it must be put firmly in its place, but the present ministers were not the men to do this. They must be replaced at once by men possessing the confidence of the people. A petition to this effect was drafted by Lehmann, submitted to the *Borgerrepresentanterne* by Hvidt, approved by them and subsequently by the *Magistrat*. In the evening 2,500 excited citizens crowded into the Casino to

[1] The *Borgerrepresentanterne* were elected by the citizens, unlike the members of the *Magistrat*, who were nominated.

listen to addresses by Eiderdane leaders. Lehmann put five resolutions to the meeting; firstly, the king must not abandon Schleswig to the Germans by agreeing to a separate constitution for Schleswig-Holstein; secondly, the Danish people would support the king in his efforts to defend the integrity of the sovereign 'Danish-Slesvig' state; thirdly, this state must have a common constitution; fourthly, Slesvig would be allowed to retain its provincial autonomy with its own estates and distinctive legal and administrative system and parity of esteem for both nationalities; finally, a new ministry must be appointed to implement this programme. A high official, C. P. Francke, intervened, to deny that an uprising had already occurred in the duchies and to plead with the meeting to avoid precipitate action before the arrival of the deputation. But to no avail. He was howled down. If an insurrection has not yet broken out, it soon will retorted Lehmann, and the resolutions were carried enthusiastically. Indeed the meeting would have marched on the royal palace there and then, had it not been restrained by the Eiderdane leaders. It was finally agreed by the Casino meeting, and by separate meetings of students and artisans, that the people should accompany the *Borgerrepresentanterne* and *Magistrat* when they went to the palace next day with their petition.

21 March was Denmark's day of revolution. The king was anxious to retain his popularity with the people and was to some extent in sympathy with their demands; therefore at 9 a.m. he announced to the *Statsraad* that he had finally decided to annex Schleswig. K. Moltke, H. Reventlow-Criminil, A. Ørsted and A. W. Moltke, all conservatives of the older generation, were quite out of sympathy with this radical proposal. They immediately tendered their resignations to the king and withdrew from the meeting. When the huge procession, 15,000 strong, arrived at the palace at midday, the king was able to announce to a deputation that the old ministry had already resigned; he assured them that he would defend Schleswig and appealed for their continued confidence. Satisfied that the king was on their side, the procession dispersed without incident about 1.0 p.m.

The new ministry was only formed after twenty-four hours of

protracted and arduous negotiations. The king sympathized with his people but he was not prepared to become the prisoner of the Eiderdanes. So C. E. Bardenfleth, a progressive conservative, was entrusted with the task of forming a cabinet with a mildly progressive flavour, including only one Eiderdane, D. G. Monrad, a man of moderate views. Difficulties arose with the conservatives. Francke refused to accept the presidency of the *Schleswig-holsteinische Kanzlei* unless the final decisions on the Schleswig problem were postponed until the *Erfahrene Männer* had met. The Dane, P. G. Bang, agreed with von Plessen, that a cabinet which did not include a representative of the duchies would antagonize the Germans unnecessarily. At the other end of the scale Monrad warned Bardenfleth that a Danish republic might be proclaimed if the wishes of the people in the Schleswig question were not respected. By the early hours of 22 March the king was in despair, talking of abdication and a new ministry was as far off as ever. Shortly afterwards he agreed that a cabinet must be formed on a provisional basis to give an answer to the Schleswig-Holstein deputation, newly arrived from Kiel that morning.

The steamship had also brought the prince of Noer's letter to the king. In his epistle the prince commended the five demands to be made by the deputation, and he suggested, as an interim precaution, that Reventlow-Preetz, Bargum and Beseler be given charge of the administration of the duchies while the prince take the *Statthalterschaft* and be responsible for law and order. If these requests were not complied with at once, the prince felt obliged to point out that the king could no longer rely on the obedience of his German subjects. The king was highly incensed by the tone of this letter. Throwing it aside, he remarked that the revolution had already broken out and the time had come for him to take charge of his people. It was a decisive moment. There now seemed no point in setting up a provisional cabinet. The king, although still undecided whether to include the Eiderdane leaders in his cabinet, now consented to receive them in audience. They arrived and at 3 p.m. on 22 March a ministry was formed. A. W. Moltke, a moderate conservative, had taken the decisive step by accepting the presidency of a cabinet. Other conservatives followed suit,

Bardenfleth, Knuth and von Plessen accepting the ministries of Justice, Foreign Affairs and the *Schleswig-holsteinische Kanzlei* respectively. The novel feature of the ministry was the inclusion of four prominent Eiderdanes, Tscherning as minister of War, Monrad as minister of Education and Hvidt and Lehmann as ministers without portfolio.

Excitement was mounting in Copenhagen. It was rumoured on the streets that the prince of Noer had actually taken command of the rebellious Schleswig-Holsteiner and appeals were made for volunteers to fight the Germans. Partly for their own protection the Schleswig-Holstein deputation had been accommodated at the home of consul Hage, Lehmann's uncle, while awaiting the reply to their petition. Lehmann visited them and listened with polite interest to suggestions from Olshausen and H. R. Claussen that the Schleswig question be settled by partition along a line running north of Flensburg and south of Tønder. It was curious that at the twelfth hour these ex-New Holsteiner should have abandoned national liberalism and reverted to the radicalism of long ago. Lehmann expressed agreement, perhaps out of respect for their radicalism, but he was hardly serious. Partition was quite incompatible with full-blooded Eiderdanism and would have evoked little popular support. It was significant that when *Faedrelandet* suggested partition in June[1]—for tactical reasons—its circulation fell by over a hundred within a few days. Similarly the Kiel provisional government on 31 March, in an attempt to curry favour in North Schleswig, offered to allow the Danes to opt for Denmark. But it soon changed its tune in May with Prussian support behind it, and nothing more was heard of partition. This is not surprising, for German and Danish national liberals alike were uninterested in partition as long as there was a prospect of obtaining the whole of Schleswig. The solution of 1920 was only possible because the Germans, defeated in a world war, were unable to retain the whole of Schleswig, and because the respect in which the principle of self-determination was held in 1919 made it impossible for the Danes to secure the Eider frontier.

The deputation was received in audience on 23 March by the

[1] *Faedrelandet*, 23 June 1848.

king, who promised a reply as soon as the *Statsraad* met. Von Plessen added hopefully that, as von Scheel had already resigned, one of their five requests had been complied with. But hope of a peaceful solution was fast fading. Inside the cabinet the lingering opposition of conservative members to the annexation of Schleswig had been overcome, and on the morning of 24 March the *Statsraad* reached its final decision. But by now the situation had deteriorated still further. When the deputation arrived at the palace, they were met by Monrad who handed them *Dannevirke's* report of the Rendsburg meeting, drawing attention to Olshausen's anti-Danish utterances. As the temper of the people was ugly, Monrad could no longer answer for Olshausen's personal safety and suggested he go aboard the warship *Hekla*. Eventually the entire deputation went on board where they were visited by Lehmann, who read out to them the official reply of the *Statsraad*; Holstein would be granted a constitution as befitted an independent state and member of the Confederation; but the king had no authority to allow Schleswig to enter the Confederation or be separated from Denmark; Schleswig was an integral part of Denmark and, while retaining provincial autonomy, would share in a common constitution with Denmark. This was pure Eiderdanism. No basis for discussion remained and in the afternoon the deputation sailed for home, accompanied by several German officials anxious to leave the capital while there was still time.

When the deputation arrived in Kiel in the early hours of 26 March, they discovered to their surprise that a provisional government had been set up two days before. Originally the intention was to await their return befoıe proceeding to any overt act of rebellion. But early on the morning of 23 March *Hardesvogt* Jacobsen called on his friend Beseler, bringing with him a copy of the conservative newspaper, *Berlinske Tidende*, which contained an account of the recent events in Copenhagen. The news of the Casino meeting, followed by the resignation of the old ministry and by negotiations for the formation of a new one likely to include Eiderdane leaders, was sufficient for Beseler. This was the moment of truth. Within the hour he was riding to Kiel, pausing at Eckernförde to leave a message for the prince of Noer, and on arrival in Kiel requested Reventlow-Preetz to meet him at once. The town was in a mood of tense expectancy following the news of the revolution in Copenhagen. Soldiers fraternized with the excited population; black, red and gold colours were much in evidence and crowds gathered on the hills looking out to sea, awaiting the arrival of the steamship from Copenhagen with news of the deputation. The fact that the ship was long overdue was considered evidence of political unrest in the capital.

On the evening of 23 March Reventlow-Preetz, Beseler and the prince assembled at Bargum's house in Kiel and, with some assistance from Samwer and Droysen at a later stage, reached their momentous decision. News of the imminent appointment of an Eiderdane ministry overcame all Reventlow-Preetz's scruples. '*Aut nunc aut nunquam*,' observed Beseler; '*Denn man los*,' replied Reventlow-Preetz, gripping his hand.[1] For the first time since January conservatives, radicals and national liberals were all united in the face of the old enemy, the Eiderdanes.

Reventlow-Preetz and the prince would have preferred to determine the detailed composition of the provisional government in the small select circle at Bargum's, undisturbed by popular pressure. But a mass meeting was being held that same evening in the *Rathaus*, organized by young radical supporters of Olshausen and H. R. Claussen. These young citizens were not prepared to leave the initiative in the hands of the older generation at Bargum's. In fact Beseler's original instinct was to transact all the important business at the *Rathaus* meeting. He only agreed later, after consultations with Droysen and Samwer, to abandon this plan and meet the others at Bargum's. Even so he was instrumental in persuading them to recognize, reluctantly, that effective power resided in the *Rathaus* meeting. It was agreed that no decisions would be taken without the approval of the *Rathaus*, and Beseler was authorized to go to the *Rathaus* meeting later with details of the new government. The names of Beseler and Reventlow-Preetz were accepted without question, but there were lively objections to the prince of Noer. His name was accepted only

[1] 'So be it.' Beseler, *op. cit.*, p. 52: 'The die is cast,' wrote Reventlow-Preetz to his wife. L.A.S. 399 Fr. v. Reventlow 48, 24 March 1848.

after Samwer explained that his military knowledge made him indispensable. Bargum's name was rejected and replaced by that of consul M. Schmidt, president of the *Rathaus* meeting and captain of the newly formed Kiel *Bürgerwehr*.[1] It was agreed that Olshausen and H. R. Claussen be invited to join the government on their return and J. Bremer, a Flensburg lawyer and staunch Schleswig-Holsteiner, was accepted as a representative of North Schleswig at Beseler's suggestion. The alterations were approved at Bargum's, Bargum himself readily withdrawing, and it was agreed to proceed later to the *Rathaus* for the formal installation of the government and the reading of the proclamation.

The proclamation was drafted by Reventlow-Preetz who scored a final victory by persuading his colleagues to accept his ingenious theory of the 'unfree duke' as an explanation of their act of rebellion. The king-duke had been constrained by a popular movement to dismiss his advisers and adopt a policy hostile to the duchies. As the will of their ruler was no longer free, it had been found necessary to form a provisional government to preserve law and order in the duke's name and defend the rights of the duchies. As soon as the duke regained his freedom these executive powers would be restored to him. This passage in the proclamation aroused indignation and contempt among many young people. Tiedemann, who wanted complete separation from Denmark, called it a piece of political hypocrisy.[2] But a realist like Beseler recognized its value, observing later that without the semblance of legality they would all have been seeking political asylum in Hamburg within three days.[3] The legal fiction of the 'unfree duke' undoubtedly secured a wide measure of support for the new government at the time of its inception by setting the minds of the officials at rest. They could have the best of both worlds, remaining faithful to their oath of allegiance and still obey the Kiel government. Once the officials and pastors had satisfied their consciences, the masses of the population would readily give their allegiance to the Kiel government.

Germany was very much in the thoughts of most members of

[1] Citizen's militia. [2] Tiedemann, *op. cit.*, p. 91.
[3] *A.D.B.*, vol. 46, p. 475.

the new government. Droysen was responsible for the references at the end of the proclamation to their determination not to surrender any German territory to the Danes. 'With all our might and main we associate ourselves with the German struggle for unity and freedom. We invite all men of good will in the duchy to join us. Let us show the German fatherland by our staunch demeanour and dignified bearing that the spirit of true patriotism fills the hearts of those who live in Schleswig-Holstein'.[1]

Their confidence in Germany was not misplaced. On the same day as the provisional government was proclaimed on the steps of the *Rathaus*, the king of Prussia issued a proclamation assuring the duchies of assistance in their fight against Denmark. This was the work of the duke of Augustenburg who arrived in Berlin on 23 March. Securing an interview with the king next day, Christian August urged him to issue a declaration in support of the duchies, primarily of course to avert that head-on conflict between German and Dane which could only be prejudicial to the duke's chances of securing the throne of the *Helstat*. King Friedrich Wilhelm finally consented and, fully supported by his new cabinet, issued a proclamation on 24 March in which he promised to defend the right of the duchies to remain in close association with each other and to form an independent state inherited by the male line. He was ready to use 'appropriate means' to protect the duchies against attack in accordance with the Federal Diet's decision of September 1846. He hoped that the nationality of the duchies was not in danger, but if it was he was sure that all members of the Confederation would help in the defence of Schleswig-Holstein. The duke hurried back to the duchies, arriving in Hamburg on 25 March. Here his banker informed him that a provisional government had been set up in Kiel; '*Der dumme Junge hat uns alles verdorben*,' he exclaimed in fury, for this was the failure of a mission.[2] Once the national conflict between German and Dane had broken out, his chances of securing the throne of the *Helstat* were remote. When he arrived in Rendsburg, where the provisional government

[1] D. von Liliencron, *op. cit.*, p. 27.

[2] 'The stupid fellow has ruined everything', i.e. the Prince of Noer, Gebauer, *op. cit.*, p. 218.

established itself, he suffered a further disappointment; he was not offered the post of regent as he had expected. The truth was that the duke was not a popular enough figure to attract much support in the duchies or in Germany once the German revolution had begun. The young volunteers who streamed into the duchies in March and April from all parts of Germany came not to uphold the dynastic claims of the Augustenburgs, but to strike a blow for German unification and to protect German soil against a foreign foe, as they saw it. '*Schleswig-Holstein meerumschlungen*' had now become a symbol of the national aspirations of the German people, and remained so for the next twenty years in good times and bad.

XIV

The epilogue
1848–64

All went well for Schleswig-Holstein in the spring of 1848. By the end of April the Danes had been defeated and driven out of Schleswig with the help of Prussia and the blessing of the Federal Diet. The provisional government quickly regained its self-confidence; it withdrew the offer of a plebiscite in North Schleswig and insisted on the entry of an undivided Schleswig into the German Confederation. On 18 May members from Schleswig-Holstein took their places in the Paulskirche in Frankfurt when the National Parliament opened.

Unfortunately for the duchies Prussia proved herself a most unreliable ally. King Friedrich Wilhelm IV very quickly repented of his precipitate promise to help the duchies. His innate conservatism reasserted itself and was reinforced by practical considerations; the Danish blockade of the northern coastline was beginning to have an adverse effect on Prussian commerce; it dawned on the king that prolonged activities were likely to strengthen the radicals, his enemies; finally, the Great Powers began to express their dissatisfaction with Prussian policy—Britain and France both supported Russia when she warned Prussia against an invasion of Denmark. The moral disapproval of these powers was quite sufficient to send King Friedrich Wilhelm IV hurrying off to Malmö to seek an armistice of the Danes.

The Malmö armistice—the first was signed in July, the second in August—was a turning-point in the 1848 revolution. The King of Prussia signed the armistice without the authorization of the Frankfurt government. Yet despite vehement protests from the Kiel government and bitter attacks from the radicals, the Frankfurt Parliament finally acquiesced in the situation, and approved the armistice on 14 September by a majority of twenty-one votes. The national cause suffered a grievous defeat and the pretensions of the Frankfurt government to pursue an independent foreign policy were exploded.

The armistice came as a great shock to the duchies. All the same, they did not fare too badly. The Danes were playing for time, confident that a spring campaign would restore the *status quo*. Meanwhile they were prepared to tolerate a provisional status for the duchies. The administration was entrusted to five commissioners ruling in King Frederik's name, two to be appointed by Denmark, two by Prussia with an agreed nominee as chairman. As the Danish nominees proved unacceptable in the duchies, Prussia eventually appointed all five. That their sympathies lay with the Germans is evident from the fact that the commissioners reintroduced many of the enactments of the provisional government, and that the latter handed over its powers to the commissioners early in October 1848.

The Danes were naturally displeased with this evidence of partiality. They denounced the commissioners and looked to their defences. When the armistice expired in March 1849 no progress had been made in the peace negotiations and hostilities were resumed. The presence of Prussian contingents with the federal forces involved that power, albeit reluctantly, in further military operations against the Danes. This time the military engagements were indecisive; the Danes were defeated at Kolding but they compelled General von Bonin to raise the siege of Fredericia. Once more the Great Powers expressed their disapproval of Prussian policy. Once more King Friedrich Wilhelm, intimidated by Russian threats, hastened to obey. In July 1849 Prussia and Denmark renewed the armistice and signed peace preliminaries, this time more favourable to Denmark. As a first step the administration of Schleswig was separated from that of Holstein and placed in the hands of three commissioners, one Danish and one Prussian with an Englishman acting as arbitrator. To facilitate this arrangement federal forces were withdrawn from the duchies, the Schleswig-Holstein army was withdrawn to Holstein, Swedish troops occupied North Schleswig and Prussian troops South

Schleswig. The *Statthalterschaft*[1] and the Frankfurt government protested vigorously against the separation of the duchies and 'the betrayal of the national cause' by Prussia. All in vain. There was still much sympathy for Schleswig-Holstein in German court circles but no hope of active assistance. The revolution had spent itself, the rulers of Austria and Prussia were rapidly regaining their old authority and by the summer of 1849 Prussian and Württemberg soldiers had chased the rump of the Frankfurt Parliament out of existence. The *Statthalter* were subjected to heavy pressure from Prussia and were finally obliged to recognize the armistice.

By the spring of 1850 King Friedrich Wilhelm was more anxious than ever to disengage himself completely from the affairs of the Elbe duchies. He was greatly alarmed by the attempts the radicals were making in the Holstein *Landesversammlung* to force the *Statthalter* into invading Schleswig and 'liberating' the Germans from 'Danish oppression'. This came at a most inopportune moment with civil war looming on the horizon in Germany, as Austria demanded the restoration of the Confederation and Prussia clung stubbornly to the Erfurt Parliament. As tension mounted between Austria and Prussia, the Tsar, fresh from his success in crushing the Hungarian revolt, offered to support whichever German power remained true to its treaty obligations, and urged Prussia to conclude a definitive peace with Denmark. Anxious to assure himself of Russian support, King Friedrich Wilhelm ordered the withdrawal of Prussian officers serving as volunteers with the Schleswig-Holstein army. Finally, on 2 July, acting on behalf of the Confederation, the king of Prussia signed a provisional peace with Denmark. Under the terms of the peace of Berlin Prussia promised to withdraw her forces from South Schleswig and, most ominous of all for the duchies, Prussia agreed that the king of Denmark, in his capacity as duke of Holstein, be invited to appeal to the Confederation to restore his lawful authority in Holstein.

Disowned by the Prussians, the duchies were left to their own

[1] The five commissioners resigned in April 1849 when hostilities were resumed. Reventlow-Preetz and Beseler were appointed *Statthalter* by the Frankfurt government to rule Holstein in the king-duke's name.

devices. The radicals got their way at last. The *Statthalter* ordered the Schleswig-Holstein army across the Eider—to be heavily defeated at the bloody battle of Idstedt on 24 July. This decisive engagement brought the First Slesvig War (or Three Years War) to an end. Only because the Danes had already signed the peace of Berlin, did they halt their advancing army on the line of the Dannevirke and allow the Schleswig-Holstein forces to retire into Holstein. Hope was rapidly fading for the duchies. It was finally extinguished in November 1850 when Prussia made up her quarrel with Austria. Under the terms of the Olmütz Punctation Prussia and Austria agreed to appoint a commission of pacification to bring about the submission of Holstein. Shortly afterwards Austrian forces entered Holstein with the approval of the Federal Diet. In January 1851 the Holstein *Landesversammlung* reluctantly bowed to the inevitable under the threat of federal execution; the *Statthalter*, Reventlow-Preetz, resigned and shortly afterwards the Schleswig-Holstein army was dissolved.

It was the object of Austria and Prussia to restore the *status quo* in northern Europe as quickly as possible. That they were not able to disengage themselves from the Elbe duchies for another twelve months, was not the fault of the Schleswig-Holsteiner but of the Danes. The Danish government was still committed to a modified form of Eiderdanism. It submitted draft proposals for a new constitution to an assembly of notables convened in Flensburg in May 1851. These proposals, whilst preserving the outward form of the *Helstat*, actually weakened the ties between the duchies, by making provision for separate consultation with Schleswig and Holstein-Lauenburg on matters of common concern to the whole monarchy. A majority of this nominated, Eiderdane-minded assembly was prepared to accept the constitution. The Holstein representatives refused and were supported in this by Austria and Prussia, who protested formally to Denmark and insisted on a return to the pre-1848 position. They did this not out of any concern for the national cause or affection for the duchies, but simply because as conservative powers they were suspicious of radical Eiderdanes and disliked the liberal nature of the new constitution.

Under pressure from Austria and Prussia and unable to secure assistance from other powers, the Danes weakened. At the end of 1851 conservative elements got the upper hand in Copenhagen. On 8 December the Danish government sent an important communication to the German powers in which it declared that it was the Danish intention to weld the component parts of the monarchy into an organic, constitutional and homogeneous union. Schleswig would not be incorporated in Denmark, as the Eiderdanes desired, but would enjoy provincial autonomy. All ties with Holstein, including the administrative and judicial ties dating from 1834, must be severed, for the king of Denmark could allow no closer union between Holstein and Schleswig than that which existed between the duchies and the kingdom. Austria and Prussia were satisfied with this formal abandonment of Eiderdanism and return to the traditional *Helstat* policy (or something very like it). On 28 January 1852 a new Danish government, headed by C. Bluhme, issued a formal declaration outlining the constitutional changes envisaged for the *Helstat*. The existing constitution of the Danish kingdom was to be preserved whilst in the duchies and in Lauenburg the estates were to be restored and given increased power over local affairs. Their government would be supervised by separate ministers directly responsible to the king. A common constitution for the whole monarchy would be prepared and submitted to the estates for their approval. Holstein would continue to be ruled by the king-duke according to its own laws which were not to be altered. In Schleswig the local constitution would include guarantees ensuring equality of treatment for German and Dane. The Federal Diet approved this declaration and federal forces were finally withdrawn from Holstein. At last, four years after the outbreak of the revolution in Kiel, the king of Denmark was master in his own house.

The return to normalcy was highly agreeable to the Great Powers. The *Helstat* was a familiar landmark, a reassuring symbol of the permanence of the old order of things. There was also the practical consideration that the Baltic Sea was still an area of some strategic importance even in the middle of the nineteenth century; on the whole the powers preferred that this sea be controlled by Denmark rather than dominated by a united Germany. In August 1850 Britain, France, Russia and Austria had expressed their desire, in the London Protocol, to see the integrity of the monarchy maintained, and had approved the efforts the king of Denmark was making to ensure this by preparing a new order of succession. King Frederik VII had much more success than his predecessor, Christian VIII, in this endeavour. One by one the obstacles to the succession of Christian of Schleswig-Holstein-Sonderburg-Glücksburg were removed. In June 1851 Tsar Nicholas, as head of the house of Oldenburg, renounced his claims on Holstein in favour of Christian. In July Friedrich of Hesse followed suit. Finally, after long and arduous negotiations, the duke of Augustenburg was prevailed upon by Prussia to renounce his claims and the claims of his family, and sell his estates in Schleswig for a considerable cash payment—this renunciation, incidentally, aroused little interest in the duchies where the duke's popularity had waned steadily since 1848. Finally, the Great Powers set their seal on this arrangement. Meeting in concert in May 1852, they placed on record, in the Treaty of London, their belief that the preservation of the *Helstat* was a European necessity and recognized that, in the event of the extinction of the agnate succession, Prince Christian of Glücksburg and his descendants would succeed to the *Helstat*. A year later, in July 1853, the king of Denmark promulgated this new order of succession as a law valid for the *Helstat*.

It was one thing for the Great Powers to guarantee the external fabric of the *Helstat*, but quite another matter to revitalize the monarchy by re-establishing the old amity between the German and Danish subjects of the crown. This was no easy task; the experiences of the Three Years War had exacerbated relations between the two peoples, especially in Schleswig, the sounding board for the monarchy in this respect. The provisional government in Kiel had not endeared itself to the Danish-speaking part of the population during its short term of office between March 1848 and July 1849. The economic dislocation caused by the war was blamed on the Germans. Increased taxation for military purposes was bitterly resented; when some pastors and teachers advised the people to withhold payment of taxes, the government ordered the military to act as tax gatherers, a departure which led to clashes with the population in some cases. The decision to seek admittance for Schleswig into the Confederation aroused bitter opposition, as witness the numerous petitions on this subject from North and even from Central Schleswig. Finally, there was opposition to the new military service law and widespread evasion of it by young men in North Schleswig. In the early months of 1849 feeling was running so high in this part of Schleswig that plans for a rising were being laid.

With the conclusion of the armistice in July 1850 and the appointment of commissioners to administer Schleswig, the tide turned in favour of the Danes. Count Eulenburg, the Prussian representative, and Colonel Hodges, the British representative and former *chargé d'affaires* in the Hansa towns, were both sympathetic to the Danes, and gave F. Tillisch, the Danish representative, a fairly free hand in Schleswig. The new administration set up by Tillisch in Flensburg took steps to reimpose the authority of the crown on Schleswig. Seditious pamphlets, meetings and songs—especially *Schleswig-Holstein meerumschlungen*—were forbidden together with the Schleswig-Holstein flag and the other insignia of the Schleswig-Holstein movement. Schleswig-Holstein currency issued by the provisional government was declared illegal. All enactments of the provisional government and of the *Statthalterschaft* were declared null and void. The court of appeal in Gottorp was dissolved and replaced by a commission sitting in Flensburg. Many German officials had already fled from Schleswig; other officials and pastors who refused to renounce their allegiance to the *Statthalterschaft* were removed from office and replaced by men from Copenhagen. In the spring of 1851 the requirement that all officials spend two *Semester* at Kiel university was cancelled—a heavy blow to the Schleswig-Holsteiner. Finally, the customs barrier was moved from the Kongeaa to the Eider, creating in effect an Eiderstate in the economic sphere.

These measures were understandable enough; on their own they might not have placed any undue strain on the relations between German and Dane. This cannot be said of the *Sprachrescripte* issued in the spring of 1851. This was undoubtedly a grave blunder seriously prejudicing the chances of reconciliation. Nominally the work of Tillisch, the *Sprachrescripte* were, in fact, the work of Theodore Regenburg, a native of Åbenraa and a one-time private secretary to Stemann. Regenburg was seconded to work under Tillisch and was given charge of education and religion in the new Schleswig administration in September 1850. A pupil at Sorø academy in the 1830's, Regenburg was deeply influenced by his history master, C. F. Wegener, a protagonist of the Danish way of life. Having attained high office, Regenburg determined to advance the cause in which he believed and with which King Frederik was known to sympathize. Regenburg's first step was to continue Tillisch's policy of eliminating German influence from church and school in North Schleswig. Danish was made the language of instruction in all North Schleswig schools with the sole exception of Christiansfeld, and the rescript of 1840, permitting private tuition in German in North Schleswig schools, was annulled. The Danish and German languages were at last accorded parity of esteem in the churches of Haderslev, Åbenraa and Sønderborg by wish of the inhabitants. At last German sermons disappeared from the area between Ladelund and Medelby where previously German and Danish had been used in church on alternate Sundays. The result of these measures was that, with the exception of Kristiansfeld, the whole of North Schleswig became as Danish, from an administrative point of view, as Nørrejylland or the islands.

The controversial *Sprachrescripte* were issued in February and March 1851. They applied to parts of Central Schleswig, an area where German had been used in church and school for generations despite the fact that some Danish was still spoken there. The *Sprachrescripte* made Danish the language of instruction in all schools, allowing only four hours a week instruction in German. Teachers who had no knowledge of Danish were either to be dismissed or appoint Danish-speaking assistants. In the churches Danish was to be used on alternate Sundays with the exception of Tønder where German and Danish was to be used every Sunday. A year later, in October 1852, the Danish government decided that German and Danish should enjoy parity of esteem in the so-called 'mixed districts', and the authorities were instructed to use whichever language the subject requested. The permission given by King Christian VIII to the lawyers of North Schleswig to use German in court was now withdrawn.

The *Sprachrescripte* did not apply to the whole of Central Schleswig. Practical difficulties obliged Regenburg to allow the use of German in churches and schools in the southern half of Angeln. Only in 1856 did the government extend the 'mixed district' to the mouth of the Schlei. Similarly along the west coast of Schleswig German was allowed to remain in church and school. C. F. Wegener, writing to his old pupil Regenburg in the autumn of 1850, had urged him to introduce Frisian in church and school to ease the transition to Danish. Regenburg realized that the absence of a Frisian literary language rendered this impossible. He preferred to await a more favourable moment for making a direct transition from German to Danish in this part of Schleswig. Finally, Flensburg was excluded from the 'mixed district' and allowed to keep German in church and school, curiously enough as a reward for the town's loyalty to the crown during the war.

Had the *Sprachrescripte* been restricted to those parts of Central Schleswig where Danish was still widely spoken—in Karr, Vis and Ugle *Harden* in the centre of the duchy—there would have been no grounds for complaint. But the inclusion of a large part of Angeln in the 'mixed district' was a disastrous blunder; for it was in Angeln that the German language had been making most rapid progress since 1800. In this part of Schleswig the *Sprachrescripte* were a completely artificial attempt to reverse what had become an almost irresistible forward movement of the German tongue. Officials whose loyalty to the crown could scarcely be doubted, like the *Amtmann* of Gottorp and the *Kirchenpropst* of Gottorp-Hütten, had warned against radical changes. Their worst fears were quickly realized. The people of Angeln bitterly resisted the attempt to impose Danish on them and clung all the more tenaciously to the German tongue. The result was that, far from increasing the use of Danish in Angeln, the *Sprachrescripte* decreased it; the last remnants of Danish, lingering on in North Angeln, were swept away, so that by the early 1850's the germanization of Angeln had been completed.

The *Sprachrescripte* had a wider significance for the *Helstat*. It is easy with hindsight to say that the collapse of the *Helstat* was inevitable in an age of triumphant nationalism. In the long run this was true—but it certainly did not seem inevitable in the 1850's. These were prosperous years for the *Helstat*. The rise in agrarian prices, which had begun in the 1830's, continued throughout the 1840's and 1850's; this was caused partly by the discovery of gold in Australia and California and partly by the repeal of the English Corn Laws in 1846 and the Navigation Act in 1849. The trade of the *Helstat* was growing and changing in pattern; economic ties with Germany were loosening and trade with Britain was increasing; Britain's share of the Danish export trade rose from under ten per cent in 1847 to over twenty-five per cent by 1856. Industrialization was beginning to affect the *Helstat* with a whole range of new industries springing up in the duchies, especially in Holstein, and finding markets for their products in Denmark. In short, the *Helstat* was becoming a more integrated and prosperous economy than ever before. This material prosperity, widely diffused throughout the *Helstat*, together with a certain sense of relief that the troubled times between 1848 and 1852 were finally over, might well have reconciled German and Dane and have delayed the break-up of the *Helstat* for a generation. That it did not do so was due largely to the *Sprachrescripte* which kept alive the flame of controversy between German and Dane in Schleswig.

This was quickly apparent when the Schleswig estates met in Flensburg in October 1853 to discuss the new constitution for Schleswig. The elections were held under the old law of 1834, so that although North Schleswig returned Danish members, twenty-four of the forty-three members were Schleswig-Holsteiner. In the main the constitution, which conferred increased powers on the estates in local matters, was approved.[1] But the Schleswig-

[1] There was much more lively opposition in the Holstein estates when they discussed the Holstein constitution. The members rejected the constitution and demanded the restoration of the old union between the duchies. Their representations were ignored by the government.

Holsteiner took this opportunity of expressing their discontent with government policy—in particular they attacked the *Sprachrescripte* which the government had incorporated in the constitution. One of the Schleswig-Holsteiner moved the suspension of the *Sprachrescripte* in those districts where German was spoken; he demanded that in those parishes where German and Danish was spoken, the people should be allowed to decide by plebiscite which language they wanted in church and school. The motion was supported by petitions from the 'mixed district', notably from Angeln, an area which had been most active in the Schleswig-Holstein movement before 1848; the town of Schleswig continued to exert a decisive influence on the surrounding districts after 1850, despite Danish efforts to reduce its importance by transferring administrative and judicial functions to Flensburg. The committee set up to examine this motion reported that the whole of the 'mixed district' was German-speaking with few exceptions. But the Schleswig-Holsteiner were on the defensive in 1853; they agreed to tolerate German and Danish on alternate Sundays in church and school and, whilst insisting that Danish be replaced by German in the schools, they were prepared to allow six hours a week instruction in Danish. Furthermore, they raised no objection to the use of Danish in the schools in the towns of North Schleswig—in effect they recognized that this part of Schleswig had been lost to the Germans. It was the Danish members who took the offensive on this occasion by demanding an extension of the 'mixed district'. Their motion was heavily defeated, but the other motion was carried by twenty-eight votes to fourteen. Not that it influenced the Danish government; the Schleswig constitution was promulgated in February 1854 unamended.

The *Sprachrescripte* were not the only cause of dissension between German and Dane. In October 1855 the long-awaited common constitution was announced; it was proposed to set up a *Rigsraad* of eighty members meeting every other year to discuss matters common to the whole monarchy including foreign policy, defence, trade and finance. Twenty members were to be nominated by the king, thirty by other bodies. The remaining thirty were to be elected by direct popular vote, seats being allocated according to the distribution of population. Of the king's nominees twelve would be from Denmark and eight from the duchies. Of the delegates of the representative bodies, eighteen would be from the Danish *Rigsdag* and twelve from the estates of the duchies. Of the directly elected members, seventeen would be from Denmark and thirteen from the duchies.

At the first meeting of the *Rigsraad* in Copenhagen early in 1856, eleven members, seven from Holstein, three from Schleswig and one from Lauenburg, drew up an address to the crown in which they challenged the validity of the constitution and of the electoral law on the grounds that it had not been submitted beforehand to the Schleswig and Holstein estates, as promised in the declaration of January 1852. The Danes disputed this interpretation of the declaration and in the end only fourteen members of the *Rigsraad* supported the address.

The eleven were not without powerful friends. Before the debate was concluded dispatches arrived from Berlin and Vienna supporting the views of the fourteen members, and threatening intervention by the Confederation on the grounds that the common constitution was incompatible with federal law, that the estates of the duchies had not been consulted, and that the electoral law did not give the Germans fair representation in the *Rigsraad*. The formal intervention of the German powers started a lengthy exchange of diplomatic notes which dragged on throughout the winter of 1856–7. As Austria and Prussia increased their pressure on the Danish government, the latter decided in the spring of 1857 to divert attention from the common constitution; C. Hall, the new Danish premier, recognizing that Holstein was the backbone of the opposition, offered that duchy a new constitution conferring additional powers on the estates. But the estates would not be appeased. They refused to discuss a revised constitution for Holstein unless the common constitution was also revised so as to preserve the independence and integrity of Holstein. They insisted that the component parts of the monarchy must be given equal representation in the *Rigsraad* regardless of the numerical superiority of the Danes—this touched the heart of the problem, for what the Germans really feared was integration in a unified *Helstat*. Integration conflicted with the essential tenet of Schleswig-Holsteinism, namely, that the duchies formed an independent state equal in all respects to the Danish kingdom and bound to Denmark only by dynastic ties. To give added weight to the objections of the Holstein estates, eighteen members of the *Rigsraad* resigned their seats.

These events did not fail to impress Schleswig. When the estates met in December 1856 a reinvigorated Schleswig-Holstein party emerged, no longer dominated by Kiel academicians but by landowners who were less liberal and a good deal more hostile to the *Helstat* than the academicians had been. The common constitution was an obvious target for attack; the Schleswig-Holsteiner demanded that it be revised and that the domain lands be excluded from the common finances. Their bitterest attacks were reserved for the *Sprachrescipte*, for hostility to the *Sprachrescripte* united the Schleswig-Holsteiner in the 1850's much as the language question had united the *Landespartei* in the 1840's. Ten members supported a motion for the cancellation of the *Sprachrescripte*, and again demanded that the people be allowed to decide for themselves which language they wanted in church and school. This motion was carried by twenty-seven to eleven votes in the face of bitter opposition from the Danish members led by L. Skau and H. Kryger. Their counter motion for an extension of the 'mixed district' was only supported by eight members. Tension between German and Dane increased still further when the estates debated the draft law dealing with Schleswig's contribution to the common finances; for the rejection of this measure by twenty-three votes to fifteen meant that the estates were, in effect, challenging the validity of the common constitution.

In the autumn of 1857 the *Ritterschaft* and estates of Lauenburg lodged a formal protest in Frankfurt against the common constitution on the grounds that the latter had been promulgated without the duchies' consent and in contravention of the Vienna treaties and the declaration of 1852. Early in 1858 Austria and Prussia invited the Diet to debate the situation in Holstein. In February 1858, despite Danish protests, the Diet declared the common constitution to be incompatible with federal law, and it requested the Danish government to ensure that Holstein and Lauenburg received that independent and equal status inside the *Helstat* promised them in 1852. A few days later the Diet requested the Danish government not to introduce any legislation into Holstein and Lauenburg in contravention of the Diet's previous resolution.

The Diet maintained its pressure on Denmark throughout 1858; in August it threatened Denmark with federal execution unless she complied promptly with the wishes of the Diet. In vain did Denmark turn to the Great Powers; Russia and Britain agreed with Austria and Prussia that Denmark must settle the dispute by negotiation. There was a further complication; the Eiderdanes had been growing steadily in strength in Denmark since 1856 and were urging Hall to loosen the ties between Denmark and Holstein. In November Hall announced the suspension of the common constitution in Holstein and Lauenburg. In this way Hall successfully averted the danger of federal execution, for in December the Diet agreed to suspend action against Denmark. Hall also placated the Eiderdanes by his manœuvre; it could be argued that, whilst preserving the outward form of the *Helstat*, he had taken the first step towards the establishment of an Eiderstate by allowing the common constitution to remain in force in Schleswig.

Early in 1859 the Holstein estates were summoned to discuss the implications of Hall's announcement. The government submitted an amended constitution for Holstein to the estates and also invited them to express their views on the common constitution and the electoral law. The estates were in no mood for compromise. They demanded the restoration of the administrative and legislative union between Schleswig and Holstein, and bitterly denounced the 'oppression' of the Germans in Schleswig. As for the common constitution, they proposed that the *Rigsraad* be replaced by four separate assemblies, one for Denmark and three for the duchies. Under this system all legislation on common matters and all amendments to existing legislation would require the consent of all four assemblies. By returning to the pre-1848 position and arming themselves with veto powers, the estates hoped to preserve the national identity of Holstein and reduce ties with Denmark to that minimum compatible with personal union; for, as von Scheel Plessen, president of the Holstein estates, remarked, the only national unity of interest to Holstein was that of Schleswig-Holstein.

The future of the Elbe duchies was now beginning to arouse great interest south of the Elbe, as liberalism and nationalism revived in Germany at the end of the 1850's. Throughout the years of political stagnation Germany had forged ahead economically; the German railway network was completed, her foreign trade trebled and her coal production rose so that by 1860 she had outstripped France and Belgium. As Germany grew powerful economically, the middle class became a considerable social and political force, desirous of liberal government and national unification. The 'New Era' in Prussia in the autumn heralded the liberal revival; with new faces in the Prussian cabinet and a liberal majority in the *Landtag*, the grip of reaction was loosened at last. This was followed by a national revival in the summer of 1859; the partial success of Italian nationalism in the war against Austria and the revelation of the military weakness of the Confederation stirred the German people profoundly. In September the *Nationalverein* was founded, working for unification under Prussian leadership, and in November the centenary of Schiller's birth was the occasion for a nation-wide demonstration. The practice of holding all-German congresses of professional men was reviving at this time; at these gatherings, and at numerous *Sängerfeste* and *Turnerfeste*, national unification was prominent on the agenda. As the national revival gathered momentum Schleswig-Holstein became the symbol of these popular aspirations as it had been in 1848; at every popular gathering there were fiery anti-Danish speeches and resolutions of sympathy for 'the gallant Schleswig-Holsteiner'.

Meanwhile Hall had rejected the proposals of the Holstein estates as totally unacceptable and destructive of the unity of the *Helstat*. However, for most of 1859 Austria and Prussia were too preoccupied with the Italian war to pay much attention to this latest development. Taking advantage of the relaxation of external pressure on Denmark, Hall issued in September an interim constitution for Holstein which slightly increased the financial powers of the Holstein estates, though falling far short of the equality of status they demanded. In November the Danish representative in Frankfurt announced that a commission to draft a new common constitution would be established with an equal number of representatives from the Holstein estates and from the *Rigsraad* (i.e. from Denmark and Schleswig). In March 1860 the Diet replied, expressing its displeasure at the rejection of the Holstein proposals. But it agreed not to invoke federal execution against Denmark, provided that no laws, especially on finance, were promulgated for the duchies without the consent of the estates. The Diet approved the procedure for drafting a common constitution on condition that Schleswig as well as Holstein was given representation separately, not as part of the *Rigsraad*.

The situation did not improve; on the contrary it had become much worse by the beginning of 1861. In July 1860 the Danes published a budget for the common monarchy making provision for a contribution from Holstein. Despite Prussian protests the Danes did not amend it. In February the Diet declared that the budget was invalid for Holstein, as it had been promulgated without the consent of the estates, and it threatened Denmark with federal execution unless she complied with the Diet's resolution of March 1860. The Danish *Rigsdag* retorted by collecting 71,000 signatures for an address to the crown indignantly rejecting interference by the Confederation in Danish affairs. It was indicative of the growing strength of Eiderdanism that the signatories declared themselves ready to make all the sacrifices necessary to preserve the union between Denmark and Schleswig and to protect the Danish nationality in Schleswig. The government was preparing for armed conflict with Germany; but it decided to make one last attempt to conciliate the Holstein estates by offering them further constitutional concessions. The attempt failed. Meeting in March 1861, the estates declared that peace was possible only when the old union between the duchies had been restored. They looked to Germany for deliverance. 'Germany has an obligation to defend our rights for they deprived us of the means of defending these rights,' observed the estates somewhat tartly. They added that Denmark would have to realize that she could not live in peace with Germany as long as she denied justice to the duchies.

As the storm clouds gathered, the Great Powers grew alarmed; Britain, France and Russia brought pressure to bear on Denmark to settle the dispute with Germany by negotiation. Hall gave way; at the end of July he announced a reduction for the current year in Holstein's contribution to the common budget, and declared that, for the time being, Denmark did not intend to introduce new legislation into Holstein. The concessions achieved their objective; in August the Diet suspended federal execution against Denmark. But Hall paid a price for his victory—to conciliate Danish public opinion he brought Orla Lehmann, the old *bête noire* of the Schleswig-Holsteiner, into his ministry in September. Not unnaturally this appointment strengthened German suspicions that Denmark was seeking to establish an Eiderstate.

One consideration weighing heavily with Hall when he made these concessions to Holstein, was his realization that the Great Powers were on Denmark's side. This was evident from proposals already put forward by certain powers as a basis for settlement between Denmark and Germany; Lord John Russell in May 1861 had proposed a close union between Denmark and Schleswig and a loosening of the ties with Holstein. Therefore Denmark made her concessions to Holstein conditional on formal negotiations with the German powers, and expressed the hope that those powers well-disposed towards Denmark would exert their influence on her behalf. In the summer of 1861 Austria and Prussia had rejected a British proposal for a meeting of the signatories of the London treaty on the grounds that the dispute concerned only the Confederation. Now, however, in the autumn, pressed by Britain, Prussia agreed to begin formal negotiations with Denmark.

The negotiations dragged on for twelve months without making any progress. They started in October 1861 with a Danish proposal that Holstein be given a provisional constitution. Austria and Prussia were not prepared to talk about Holstein in isolation. They insisted that Denmark fulfil the promises made in

1852 and cease her systematic 'oppression' of the Germans in Schleswig. Denmark retorted that Prussia had no business to interfere in Schleswig. Finally, in August 1862, Austria and Prussia demanded the abrogation of the 1855 constitution for Schleswig as well as for Holstein and Lauenburg. They proposed that it be replaced by a constitution acceptable to the estates, based not on the principle of representation according to population, but conferring on the various estates an equal voice in matters concerning the *Helstat* as a whole. There must be equality of treatment for both nationalities in Schleswig and legislation to guarantee this should be drawn up with the agreement of the Schleswig estates. The Danes were quite unable to accept these proposals, and curtly rejected all interference in Schleswig. It seemed as if complete deadlock had been reached.

Then in September 1862 Lord John Russell suddenly intervened in a last attempt to bridge the gulf between the German and Danish viewpoints and prevent the disruption of the *Helstat*. He proposed that Schleswig be given autonomous status with plenary powers in all local matters including the language question. Schleswig would not be represented in the *Rigsraad*, much less incorporated in Denmark. In as much as this arrangement implied a loosening of the ties between Schleswig and Holstein, it cut across the main tenet of Schleswig-Holsteinism. As for the common constitution, Russell accepted the German argument that the 1855 constitution was invalid because the estates had not been consulted. But he recognized that any arrangement conferring equal rights on four representative bodies—as the Holstein estates had proposed—was impracticable. As a compromise he proposed that the four assemblies agree on a budget every ten years and leave the detailed control to a council composed in equal parts of Germans and Danes. This was the Gotha dispatch, a document which aroused great displeasure in Denmark, although it met with the approval of Russia and of Prussia too, for Bismarck had just become minister-president.

Russell's plan remained an academic exercise, pleasing neither Germans nor Danes. The sad truth was that the time for compromise had passed. Nationalism was on the march in Denmark as well as in Germany; Eiderdanism was growing rapidly in 1861 and 1862 in Denmark and also in Schleswig—for after 1850 the duchy had been deeply influenced by Danish developments. Rødding *Højskole*, reopened in 1850, became a power house for the generation of Danish cultural values, whilst in the schools young Danish teachers captured the hearts of the young, keeping in touch with their pupils through *Sangforeninger*. The fruits of successful indoctrination were soon apparent. In 1860 the Danes gained three more seats in the elections to the estates. In February 1861 the Danish members, meeting in Flensburg, issued a public declaration in favour of Eiderdanism; Schleswig had decided at last that she wished to free herself from all ties with Holstein and become an integral part of Denmark. In January 1862 Kryger moved in the *Rigsraad* that Schleswig be given a common constitution with Denmark, though without success. In July there was a most impressive demonstration of the strength of Eiderdanism, when a memorial to Danish soldiers killed at the battle of Idstedt was dedicated in Flensburg churchyard in the presence of 5,000 visitors from Copenhagen, most of them members of the newly formed *Dannevirkeforeninger*.

In the 1840's the Eiderdanes were sustained by moral support from Swedes and Norwegians in what had been regarded by Scandinavians as a common struggle against the Germans. History repeated itself in this respect. In the early 1860's there was a renewed upsurge of Scandinavian feeling; students and professional men from the Scandinavian lands were coming together again at Pan-Scandinavian congresses; there was a spate of publications propagating the idea of a closer union of the Scandinavian countries; the kings of Sweden-Norway and Denmark exchanged visits. With the accession of King Karl XV in 1859, an ardent Scandinavian sat on the throne of Sweden-Norway. He gave vigorous diplomatic support to the Danes against Germany and proposed a formal alliance of the two kingdoms. Though nothing came of this project—an indication of the insubstantial basis of Pan-Scandinavianism—nevertheless, volunteers from Norway and Sweden fought with the Danes in the Second Slesvig War as they had done in the first.

1863 was a year of crisis for the *Helstat.* It started in January when the *Landsthing*, or lower house of the Danish parliament, voted an address to the king demanding a constitution for Denmark and Schleswig. Eiderdane pressure increased in the weeks that followed; in March a meeting was held at the Casino where, in an atmosphere reminiscent of the meeting fifteen years before, it was resolved that Schleswig be united with Denmark and all ties with Holstein be severed. The international situation seemed to favour a bold policy; the Great Powers were preoccupied with the Polish revolt and Austria and Prussia were divided over the reform of the Confederation. The Danes hesitated no longer. On 30 March a royal patent appeared offering Holstein a new constitution, conferring increased powers on the estates but practically excluding the duchy from representation in the *Rigsraad.* The patent was clearly intended as a first step towards the dissolution of all ties between Holstein and Denmark; speaking at the opening of the *Rigsdag* in April, the king reaffirmed that legislation approved by the crown and the *Rigsraad* was binding on Schleswig as well as Denmark.

Austria and Prussia immediately registered their protests against the patent. In July the Diet demanded the withdrawal of the patent within six months under pain of federal execution, and the opening of negotiations for a new common constitution in accordance with the declaration of 1852 or on the basis of the British mediatory proposals of September 1862. The Danes were unmoved. The international situation still looked encouraging; German opinion was sharply divided over the *Fürstentag*; Sweden had promised to come to Denmark's assistance in the event of war, and Palmerston had just reminded the House of Commons that those who tried to interfere with Denmark's independence 'would find, in the result, that it would not be Denmark alone with which they would have to contend'.[1] In August Denmark informed the Diet that the patent would not be withdrawn and that federal execution would be regarded as a *casus belli*. In the last days of September a common constitution for Schleswig and Denmark was submitted to the *Rigsraad.* The Diet, no longer dis-

[1] Parliamentary Debates, series III, 172, p. 1252.

tracted by the episode of the *Fürstentag*, acted promptly; brushing aside Russell's proposal for further negotiations, the Diet decided on 1 October to proceed with federal execution against the king of Denmark in his capacity as duke of Holstein. Austria, Prussia, Saxony and Hanover were ordered to take the necessary military steps on behalf of the Confederation.

The Danes were still not impressed. Austrian support for federal execution was discounted as a mere stratagem to regain the ground she had lost in Germany over the abortive *Fürstentag*. It was also noted in Copenhagen that Prussia, despite her support of federal execution, was still most conciliatory in her attitude, for Bismarck had no wish for a formal breach with Denmark. Finally, on 13 November, the new constitution was approved by the *Rigsraad*. Hall hurried off to Lyksborg to secure the king's signature. On arrival he found King Frederik dangerously ill and in his lucid moments unwilling to sign, preferring to leave the decision to his successor. On 15 November King Frederik died. As Prince Ferdinand had died a few months earlier, the agnate succession had now ended. In accordance with the succession law of 1853 and the provisions of the London treaty, Christian of Glücksburg, the 'protocol prince', ascended the throne of the *Helstat* as King Christian IX. On 18 November, under heavy pressure from the Eiderdanes and against his better judgement, the new sovereign put his signature to the constitution.

On 19 November Friedrich of Augustenburg, eldest son of the old Duke Christian August, proclaimed himself duke of Schleswig-Holstein, assuming the title of Friedrich VIII. In his proclamation to the people of Schleswig-Holstein he maintained that, as the agnate succession had ended with King Frederik VII's death, the connection with Denmark had ended and, the treaty of London notwithstanding, Schleswig-Holstein was now an independent state ruled by the Augustenburgs. When the German members of the Schleswig and Holstein estates met in Kiel, those from Holstein favoured recognition of the duke. The Schleswig members were hesitant, still hoping that the new king might resist Eiderdane pressure. News of the king's signature of the 'November constitution' swept away all remaining doubts. Schleswig joined with Holstein in refusing to send a deputation to swear allegiance to the new sovereign. Instead the estates appealed to the Confederation to give immediate recognition to Duke Friedrich VIII.

These events were the signal for a great outburst south of the Elbe. National feeling swept like a tidal wave over Germany; the Diet was inundated with addresses from *Landtage* and popular meetings, all demanding recognition of Friedrich VIII, separation of the duchies from Denmark and their inclusion in the Confederation; subscription lists were opened; volunteers enlisted for war against Denmark; historians and jurists vied with each other in demonstrating that the claims of nationality were higher than the clauses of the London treaty imposed on a reluctant and impotent Germany by foreign powers. Overnight the Augustenburg prince became a popular figure. Once again, as in 1848, the dynastic claims of the Augustenburgs happened to coincide with the national aspirations of the German people. The enthusiasm was inspired, as Virchow, the Prussian liberal, declared, by 'the desire for the unification of Germany, the desire to show the world that we are really a nation, that we can defend our own soil against foreign attack'.[1] On 28 November by fourteen votes to two the Diet refused admittance to King Christian IX's envoy and suspended, for the time being, the vote of Holstein and Lauenburg in that assembly.

This cautious decision did not satisfy the German liberals. They demanded that the Diet break completely with Denmark, order the occupation of the duchies and recognize Friedrich VIII as ruler of an independent Schleswig-Holstein. The Prussian liberals looked to the government to take the initiative in this matter; the new king, Wilhelm I, undoubtedly sympathized with the Augustenburg cause. But Prussia did not intervene to please the liberals as she had done in 1848. Her minister-president Otto von Bismarck, a confirmed enemy of political liberalism, had no desire to be swept into a popular war against Denmark. His yardstick was the national interest of the state he served; he believed these interests could best be served, not by creating another indepen-

[1] L. Hahn, *Fürst Bismarck. Sein Leben und Wirken*, Berlin, 1878, p. 196.

dent state in North Germany certain to be a centre of intrigue against Prussia, but by upholding treaty obligations. No doubt the thought of acquiring the duchies for Prussia crossed his mind—but that was a remote possibility. As far as the immediate future was concerned, Prussian policy was based on recognition of the fact that King Christian IX was indisputably king of Denmark and duke of Schleswig-Holstein in the eyes of the Great Powers, and that the Confederation had no right to interfere in Schleswig. It was a stroke of great good fortune for Bismarck that Austria was equally anxious to pursue a conservative policy in the Schleswig-Holstein question. With Austrian support Prussia urged the Diet to proceed at once with federal execution against Denmark, the reason being that although federal execution meant the occupation of Holstein, it also implied recognition of King Christian IX as duke of Holstein. In other words, federal execution was perfectly compatible with the treaty of London whereas the occupation of Schleswig by federal forces was not. Reluctantly the Diet agreed on 7 December by eight votes to seven to adopt the former course. This occasioned a great storm of protest in Germany. The liberals bitterly upbraided Bismarck for his 'treason' to the national cause; five hundred members from *Landtage* all over Germany met in Frankfurt and elected a committee of thirty-six to assume guidance of the Schleswig-Holstein movement and defend the rights of the duke. On 24 December Saxon and Hanoverian troops entered Holstein in the name of the Confederation, the Danish forces having withdrawn shortly before. Duke Friedrich appeared in the duchies, was acclaimed by the population and set up his court in Kiel.

As the excitement mounted in Germany, Bismarck grew apprehensive lest the pressure of public opinion force the Diet into precipitate action against Denmark. There were disturbing signs that the Diet was kicking over the traces; on 31 December an Austrian and Prussian motion ordering Duke Friedrich to leave Holstein had been rejected; on the same day Hesse-Darmstadt tabled a motion proposing that Schleswig be occupied by the Confederation. Drastic action of this kind might well lead to serious complications with the Great Powers. In any case there was nothing in it for Prussia, because a victory for the Confederation and the duke of Augustenburg implied the triumph of the liberal cause in Germany—this was an outcome worse than defeat in Bismarck's eyes. To forestall a liberal victory and to safeguard her vital interests, Prussia must act independently of the Confederation. She could do so as a signatory of the London treaty, her pretext for intervention being the fact that the November constitution was a violation of that treaty.

On 14 January the Diet debated an Austro-Prussian motion that Schleswig be occupied by the Confederation until Denmark fulfilled her obligations under the London treaty and withdrew the constitution—a motion which implied recognition of King Christian IX as ruler of Schleswig-Holstein, hence its rejection by the Diet. There were scenes of uproar when the Austrian and Prussian representatives announced that their governments would take whatever action they deemed appropriate without consulting the Diet. On 16 January Austria and Prussia signed a treaty of alliance reserving to themselves the right to decide the future of the duchies. The same day they sent an ultimatum to Denmark giving her forty-eight hours in which to withdraw the constitution. Bismarck's only concern was that Denmark might agree, thereby removing all justification for intervention by the German powers. However, although advised by the powers to comply with the ultimatum, Denmark stubbornly refused. She was isolated diplomatically; Britain, despite her bluster and sympathy for Denmark, was not prepared to fight without an ally; France would not become that ally because Napoleon III sympathized with the Germans and hoped to benefit by the general upheaval consequent upon war; Russia was far too concerned about Poland to risk a quarrel with Prussia over the Elbe duchies. So, on 1 February, Austrian and Prussian forces crossed the Eider and within a fortnight drove the Danes out of Schleswig. As the Danes retreated German opinion veered round in favour of Prussia. The liberals believed that Bismarck was hoist by his own petard and would be obliged to recognize the duke of Augustenburg in the near future. They were wrong. By 1867 Bismarck had annexed the duchies and united North Germany into the bargain without forfeiting the support of most liberals. It was a real turning-point in German history. As the *Preussische Jahrbücher* remarked in February 1867, 'if Germany is faced with the choice between unity and freedom, it must, in accordance with its history and its position, unconditionally choose the former'.[1] The choice had been made and its effects were never completely eradicated from the subsequent course of German history.

[1] Pinson, *op. cit.*, p. 152.

Appendix A

Language Statistics

	Geertz	*Koch*	*Jensen*	*Paulsen*	*Wimpfen*	*Biernatzki*
High German in church	212,920	204,587(*c*)	208,700(*c*)	—	—	217,112
Danish in church	104,751	110,213	110,610	109,200	—	120,653
Danish and German alternately in church	20,394	23,392	19,400	—	—	24,935
Dutch in church	121	—	—	—	—	—
German spoken	—	119,935	128,000	120,000(*c*)	142,000	133,700
Danish spoken	—	144,235	145,100	185,000	173,000	123,000
Frisian spoken	—	26,815	25,600	—	23,000	25,900
German and Danish spoken	—	47,207	60,000	—	—	75,000*
Total population	338,192	338,192	338,700	330,000	338,000	362,700

* Of these 45,000 spoke more German than Danish, 15,000 more Danish than German and 15,000 as much German as Danish.
(*c*) Calculated from available data.
— No figure is available.

Koch and Jensen's figures from P. Lauridsen, *op. cit, III*, p. 45 are based on the 1835 census. Geertz's figures from 1838 map and Biernatzki's from 1849 map. Paulsen's figures from the 1832 pamphlet, pp. 3–4, and Wimpfen's from his book, *Geschichte und Zustände des Herzogtums Schleswig oder Südjütland von den ältesten Zeiten bis auf die Gegenwart*, 1839, pp. 319–20. Neither Paulsen's nor Wimpfen's figures were used for calculations in Chapter IV as they give no estimates of those speaking both German and Danish.

Appendix B

The House of Holstein-Sonderburg

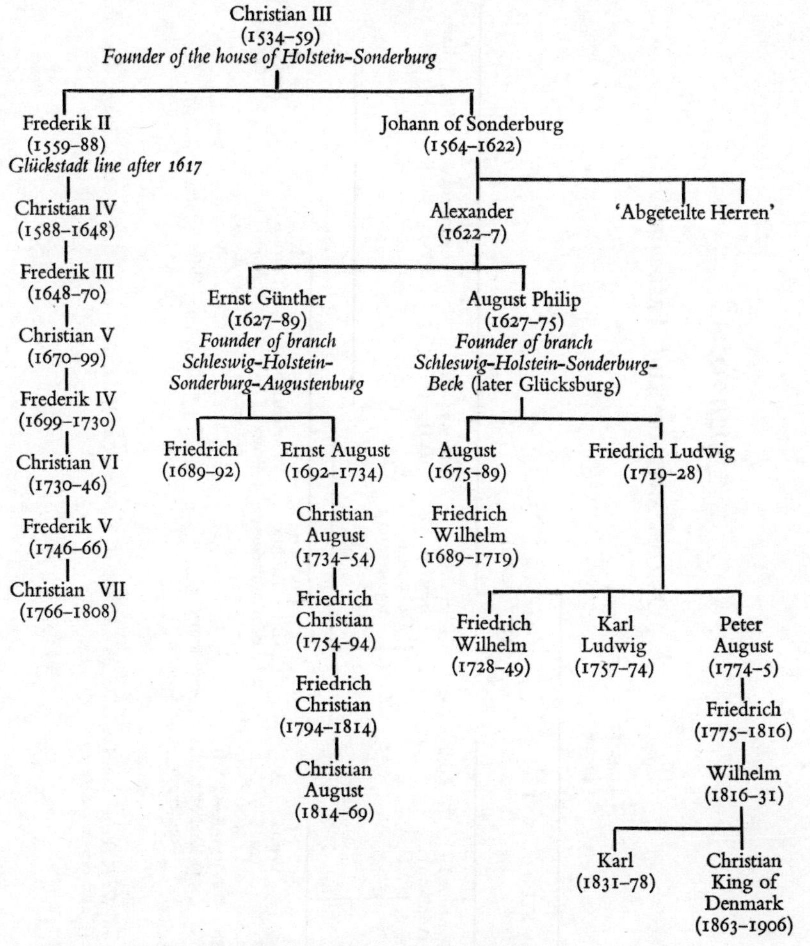

Based on W. K. Prinz von Isenburg, *Stammtafeln zur Geschichte der europäischen Staaten, Die ausserdeutschen Staaten*, Bd. I, Tafeln 89–90–91–92, Bd. II, Tafeln 72–73.

Dates refer to reigns of kings and dukes.

Appendix C

Descendants of King Frederik V

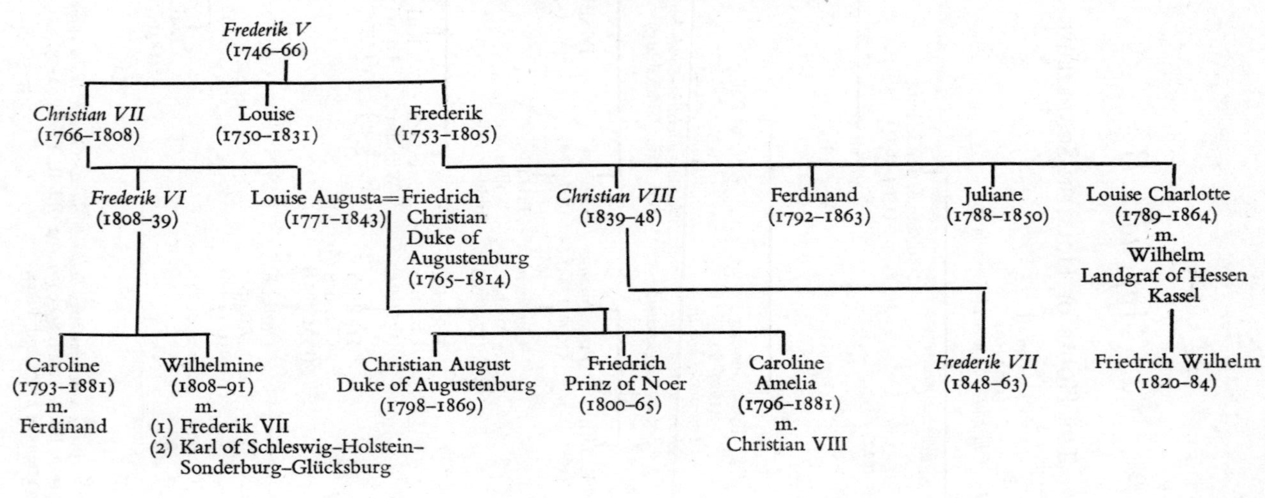

Based on W. K. Prinz von Isenburg, *op. cit.*, Bd. II, Tafel 73, and Bd. I, Tafel 100. In the case of kings, dates are of reigns; in all other cases dates of birth and death are given.

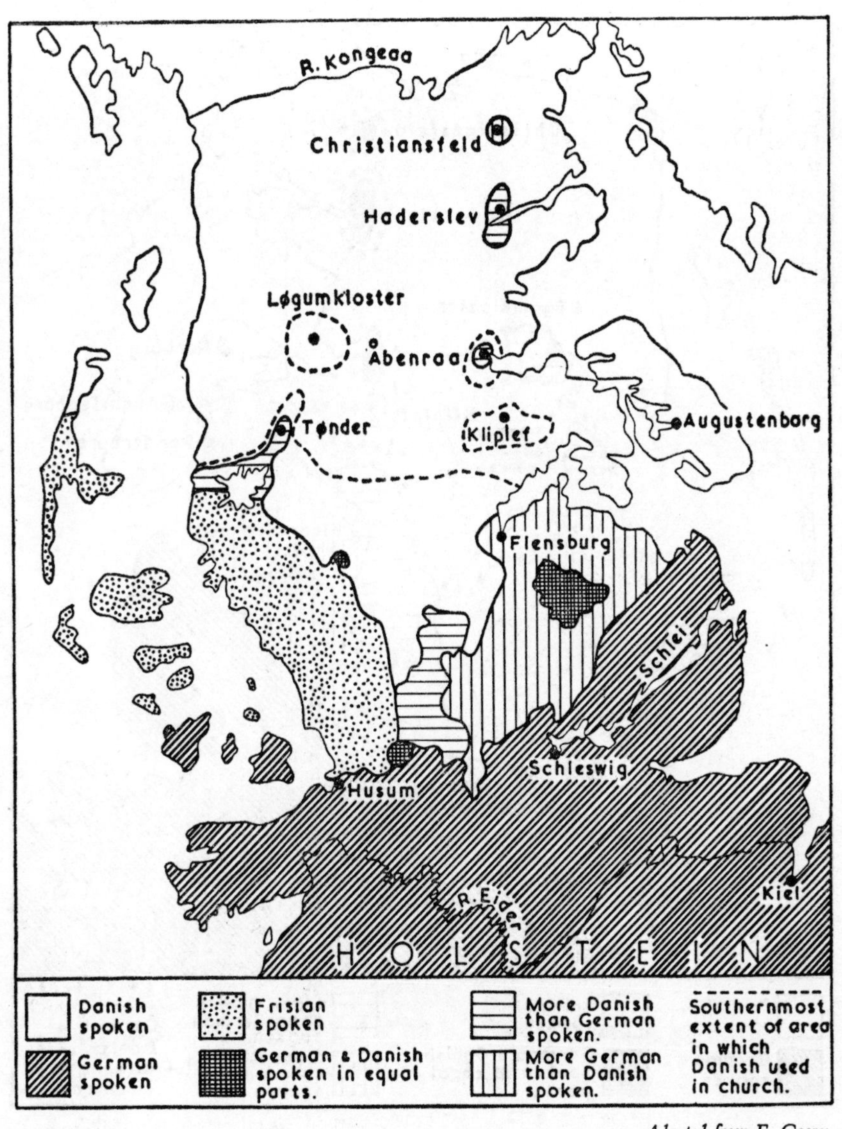

Adapted from F. Geerz

LANGUAGE MAP OF SCHLESWIG, 1838

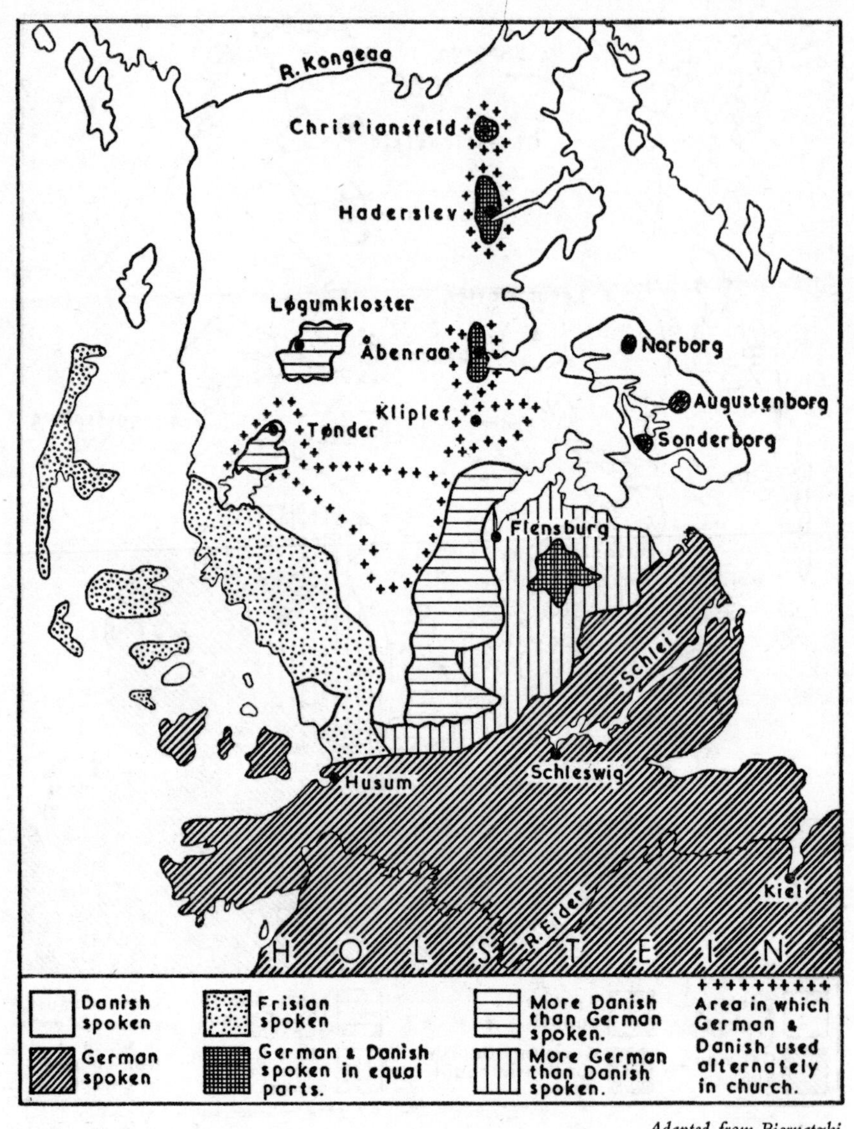

Adapted from Biernatzki

LANGUAGE MAP OF SCHLESWIG, 1849

Bibliography

THIS bibliography includes only the most important and useful sources used in this work. Sources of lesser importance, mainly articles and pamphlets, have been omitted. Where reference is made to these in the text full title, date and place of publication is given in the appropriate footnote.

PRIMARY SOURCES UNPRINTED

LANDESARCHIV SCHLESWIG

A major source housed at Schloss Gottorp. Originally *Landesarchiv Kiel.* Contains the papers of Samwer, Karl Lorentzen, Reventlow-Preetz, Reventlow-Farve, Jensen, Michelsen, etc.

PRIMKENAUER ARCHIV

A major source. Originally at Primkenau in Saxony, now in *Landesbibliothek Kiel.* The papers of the duke of Augustenburg include the correspondence between the Augustenburg brothers and letters from Samwer to the duke.

UNIVERSITÄTSBIBLIOTHEK KIEL

Schleiden papers mostly after 1848.

PUBLIC RECORDS OFFICE

F.O. 22 and 33. Dispatches of the British *chargé d'affaires* in the Hansa towns and the British ambassador to Denmark. Of minor importance.

PRIMARY SOURCES PRINTED

BAGGE, P., and ENGELSTOFT, P., *Danske politiske Breve fra 1830erne og 1840erne*, 4 vols., København, 1945–58. Letters from many Danish archives, mostly unpublished, illustrating political development mainly in Denmark.

BENZON, R. v. FISCHER, *Zur Geschichte der Jahre 1839–47*, Z 35 Kiel, 1905. Extracts from the correspondence between Baron Löwenstein and H. Reventlow-Criminil, mostly 1846–7.

BOYSEN, C., *Der offene Brief in seiner Auswirkung auf die Berliner Politik*, Z 67 Neumünster, 1939. Some letters from King Christian VIII to the king of Prussia.

DAHLMANN, F. C., *Urkundliche Darstellung des dem Schleswig-Holsteinischen Landtage, Kraft der Landesgrundverfassung zustehenden anerkannten Steuerbewilligungsrechtes*, Kiel, 1819. Explains the financial problems of the *Ritterschaft.*

— *Sammlung der wichtigsten Aktenstücke die gemeinsamen Angelegenheiten des Corps der Schleswig-Holsteinischen Prälaten und Ritterschaft und der übrigen Gutsbesitzer betreffend, 1815–1819*, Kiel, 1819. A useful collection.

DROYSEN, J. G., *Kleine Schriften Heft I. Zur Schleswig-Holsteinischen Frage*, Berlin, 1884. Includes the Kiel address of 1844 and his 1848 pamphlet.

FABRICIUS, K., AND LOMHOLT-THOMSEN, J., *Flensborgeren, Professor Christian Paulsens Dagbøger*, København, 1946.

FALCK, N., *Das Herzogtum Schleswig in seinem gegenwärtigen Verhältniss zu dem Königreich Dänemark und zu dem Herzogtum Holstein*, Kiel, 1816. One of the classic expositions of Schleswig-Holsteinism.

— *Sammlung der wichtigsten Urkunden welche auf das Staatsrecht der Herzogtümer Schleswig-Holstein Bezug haben*, Kiel, 1847. The most useful general collection of official documents.

FRIEDRICH AUGUST, *Aufzeichnungen des Prinz Friedrich von Schleswig-Holstein-Noer*, Zürich, 1861. Some interesting material in the early chapters.

GERHARD, D., AND NORVIN, W., *Die Briefe Barthold Georg Niebuhrs, 1776–1816*, 2 vols, Berlin, 1926. Correspondence of the young Frisian historian. Originally a staunch supporter of the *Helstat* he became conscious of his German nationality during the War of Liberation.

GUDME, A. C., *Die Bevölkerung der beiden Herzogtümer Schleswig und Holstein in früheren und späteren Zeiten*, Altona, 1819. Census report of 1803.

HANSEN, R., *Zur Geschichte der dänischen Politik 1840–1848*, Z 42 Leipzig, 1912. Correspondence between King Christian VIII and O. Blome, ambassador to Russia.

HEILS, A., *Augustenborgske Breve til I. G. Adler og P. Hjort*, D.M. r IV København, 1925. A major source. Letters from the P. Hjort papers which have profoundly modified the traditional view of the duke of Augustenburg as the leading figure behind the 1848 revolt (cf. Wegener).

HÜBNER, R., *Johann Gustav Droysen Briefwechsel Band I, 1829–1851*, Berlin and Leipzig, 1929.

IVERSEN, G., *Kniplingskraemer Jens Wulffs dagbøg*, S. A. Åbenraa, 1954–5.

JANSEN, K., *Zur Lornsenschen Bewegung*, Z 24 Kiel, 1894. Extracts from King Frederik's letters to Höpp, letters from Moltke to Höpp.

JESSEN, W., AND HOFFMANN, G., *Uwe Jens Lornsen Briefe an seinen Vater 1811–17*, Breslau, 1930. Some important letters supplementing Pauls' collection.

JØRGENSEN, H., *Aktstykker til den danske staenderforfatnings Forhistorie 1830–1831*, D.M. r. 7, Bd. 2, København, 1936. An important collection of letters.

LAURIDSEN, P., *Da Sønderjylland vaagnede*, 8 vols., København, 1908–22. A major source for the Danish movement. Correspondence between Flor, Koch, Fischer and P. Lorenzen, with a commentary by Lauridsen.

LIEPMANN, M., *Von Kieler Professoren. Briefe aus drei Jahrhunderten zur Geschichte der Universität Kiel*, Stuttgart and Berlin, 1916. Miscellaneous collection of letters from Dahlmann, Falck and Droysen.

LORNSEN, U. J., *Über das Verfassungswerk in Schleswig-Holstein*, Kiel, 1830.

— *Die Unionsverfassung Dänemarks und Schleswig-Holsteins. Eine geschichtliche, staatsrechtliche und politische Erörterung*, Jena, 1841.

MØLDRUP, A. E., *Breve fra Th. Olshausen til P. Hjort Lorenzen, 1831–39*, D.M. r 7, Bd. I, København, 1936. Correspondence from the P. H. Lorenzen papers illustrating liberalism in the 1830's.

OTTOSEN, J., *Niels Chr. Nissen*, S.A. 1892. A collection of letters from Nissen to Flor, 1837–9.

PAULSEN, P. D. C., *Für Dänemark und für Holstein*, Kiel, 1832.

— *Über Völkstümlichkeit und Staatsrecht des Herzogtums Schleswig; nebst Blicken auf den ganzen dänischen Staat*, Altona, 1836.

REGENSBURG, T. A. F., *Brevvexling fra 1846–47 mellem Graf Reventlow (Preetz) og Grev C. Moltke*, H.T. r. III, Bd. V, København, 1866–7.

SCHARFF, A., *Uwe Jens Lornsen. Politische Briefe*, Heide, 1938. A selection based on Pauls and Jessen.

— *Uwe Jens Lornsens Brief an Heinrich von Gagern von 16 September 1837*, Z 79.

SCHLEIDEN, R., *Erinnerungen eines Schleswig-Holsteiners. Neue Folge. 1841–48*, Wiesbaden, 1890. Memoirs of a young official in Copenhagen in the 1840's.

VARRENTRAPP, C., *Über die letzten Schicksale der deutschen Untertänen Dänemarks und die Hoffnungen von der Zukunft im März 1814*, Z 17 Kiel, 1887. Dahlmann's *Erstlingsschrift*.

— *F. C. Dahlmanns kleinere Schriften und Reden*, Stuttgart, 1886. Includes the 'Waterloo speech' and *Wort über Verfassung*.

Zeitung für die Verhandlungen der Provinzialstände des Herzogtums Holstein 1835–63, 16 vols., Itzehoe, 1835–63, and *des Herzogtums Schleswig 1836–54*, 14 vols., Schleswig Flensburg, 1836–54. A major source.

SECONDARY SOURCES

Allgemeine deutsche Bibliographie, 56 vols. Leipzig, 1875–1912. Useful biographical information but partisan and out of date. Being replaced by *Neue deutsche Bibliographie*.

Almanach de Gotha. Annuaire diplomatique et consulaire des etats des deux mondes, Gotha, 1830. Full genealogy of the house of Oldenburg in this number.

BESELER, O., *W. H. Beseler. Ein Lebensbild seiners Vaters. Als Handschrift gedruckt*, Braunschweig, 1914. Eulogy by his son.

BOYENS, J., *Politische Petitionen und Petitionsbewegung im Schleswig-holsteinischen Verfassungskampf. F. C. Dahlmann bis U. J. Lornsen 1815–1830*, Neumünster, 1944. The first detailed analysis of the petitions 1816–17 and 1818. Boyens sees in the constitutional agitation of Dahlmann and Lornsen a *Volksbewegung* to preserve *Deutschtum* in Schleswig. Strongly influenced by National Socialist theories.

BRANDT, O., *Geistesleben und Politik in Schleswig-Holstein um die Wende des achtzehnten Jahrhunderts*, Stuttgart, Berlin and Leipzig, 1927. His most important work based on the Bernstorff and Reventlow papers. Brandt seeks to prove that the Schleswig-Holstein movement originated at Emkendorf. Unconvincing but fascinating.

BRANDT, O., *Geschichte Schleswig-Holsteins, Ein Grundriss*, Kiel, 1949. Best outline account down to 1920. Available in Danish and favourably regarded by Danish scholars.

BROCK, J., *Die Vorgeschichte der Schleswig-Holsteinischen Erhebung von 1848*, Göttingen, 1925. Outstanding and penetrating analysis of the period. Indispensable reading. His death on the Russian front in 1915 was a great loss to historical studies.

CHRISTERN, H., *F. C.* 'Dahlmanns politische Entwicklung bis 1848. Ein Beitrag zur Geschichte des deutschen Liberalismus', Z 50 Leipzig, 1921. Useful.

Dansk Biografisk Leksikon, 26 vols. Kopenhagen, 1933–44. Excellent biographies based on the latest research.

DEGN, O., *Orla Lehmann und der nationale Gedanke. Eiderstaat und nordische Einheit*, Neumünster, 1936. A profound and stimulating analysis.

DONAT, W., *Die Anfänge der burschenschaftlichen Bewegung an der Universität Kiel, 1813–1833*, Berlin, 1934.

DROYSEN, G., *Johann Gustav Droysen*, Part I, Leipzig and Berlin, 1910. Standard biography.

DROYSEN, J. G., AND SAMWER, K., *Die Herzogtümer Schleswig-Holstein und das Königreich Dänemark, actenmässige Geschichte der dänischen Politik seit 1806*, Hamburg, 1850. Famous partisan vindication of the duke of Augustenburg. Useful letters in the appendices.

FABRICIUS, K., *Sønderjyllands Historie IV 1805–1864*, København, 1930–42. Indispensable for the Danish view. A mine of information.

FINK, T., AND HVIDFELDT, J., *Vegledning i studiet af Sønderjyllands Historie*, 1944. Useful critical bibliography of the main German and Danish works on Schleswig.

FRIIS, A., *Holstens Indlemmelse i Danmark i aaret 1806. En historisk Undersøgelse*, København, 1905. A standard work.

GEBAUER, J. H., *Christian August Herzog von Schleswig-Holstein. Ein Beitrag zur Geschichte der Befreiung Schleswig-Holsteins*, Stuttgart and Leipzig, 1910. Standard biography based on the Primkenau archives. Partisan but useful.

HAGENAH, H., *Revolution und Legitimität in der Geschichte der Erhebung Schleswig-Holsteins. Untersuchungen zur Entstehungsgeschichte und zur Politik der provisorischen Regierung*, Leipzig, 1916. Indispensable for the events of 1848. Recognized by Danish scholars as the first critical study on this subject.

HÄHNSEN, F., 'Tiedemann-Johannisberg. Ein Schleswig-Holsteinischer Führer', *Nord Schleswig Grenzdeutsche Monatsschrift für völkischen Aufgaben*, Tøndern, 1925. The only study. Very slight.

HECTOR, K., *Die politischen Ideen und Parteibildungen in den schleswigschen und holsteinischen Ständeversammlungen 1836 bis 1846*, I, Neumünster, 1938. Important analysis. Dr. Hector is unfortunately unable to complete a second part analysing national attitudes in the estates.

HEDEMANN-HEESPERN, P. VON, *Die Herzogtümer Schleswig-Holstein und die*

Neuzeit, Kiel, 1926. Erudite but unreadable study of the duchies since the sixteenth century by an ex-official, amateur historian, *Ritterschaft* secretary and anti-Prussian conservative.

HEINRICI, C. F., *D. A. Twesten nach Tagebüchern und Briefen*, Berlin, 1881. Some useful comments.

JANSEN, K., *Uwe Jens Lornsen. Ein Beitrag zur Wiedergeburt des deutschen Volkes*, Kiel, 1872. Still a standard work.

JENSEN, H., *De dansk Staenderforsamlingers Historie, 1830–1848*, 2 vols. København, 1931–4. Standard work on the origins of the estates and on proceedings in the Danish estates.

JENSEN, J., *Nordfriesland in den politischen und nationalen Entwicklungen des neunzehnten Jahrhunderts, 1797–1864*, Kiel dissertation, 1957. Useful on Lornsen's Frisian background. Draws attention to the conflict between Frisian particularism and Schleswig-Holsteinism in 1840's; only after the *Volksfest* of 1844 did the latter win through.

JØRGENSEN, A., 'Kong Kristian VIII og den danske Sag i Nordslesvig', S.A., 1894.

— 'Kristian VIII og Nordslesvig', *S.A.*, 1895. Both valuable articles based on the king's diaries at present in the possession of A. Linvald. Linvald, onetime archivist at *Rigsarchiv*, Copenhagen, is publishing the voluminous diaries—a major source for the 1840's—and intends to write a new life of King Christian VIII. So far diaries 1799–1814 have been published and two studies of Christian as a young prince.

— *Danmarks Riges Historie IV 1814–1864*, Kopenhagen, 1896. This work by a North Schleswiger can still be consulted with profit.

KLÜVER, W., *Franz Hermann Hegewisch. Ein Vertreter des älteren Liberalismus in Schleswig-Holstein*, Nordelbingen 4, Flensburg, 1925. The only study.

KOOPMANN, P., *Deutsch und Dänisch um die Wende des achtzehnten Jahrhunderts. Das volkliche Werden in den weltanschaulichen Spannungen des deutsch-dänischen Gesamtstaates 1770–1814*, Neumünster, 1939.

KRUMM, J., *Der Schleswig-Holsteinische dänische Gesamtstaat des achtzehnten Jahrhunderts 1721–1797*, Glückstadt, 1934.

LARSEN, SVEND, 'C. F. Heibergs politiske og nationale Anskuelser i Trediverne og Fyrrerne. En studie i den liberale Slesvigholsteinisme', *S.A.*, 1931. A useful analysis of the views of a typical German national liberal. Mostly before 1841.

LORENZEN, H. R. HJORT, 'Christian VIII og Slesvig Staender 1842', *S.A.*, 1891. Based on correspondence between the king and the royal commissioner.

MEETZ, A., *Johann Gustav Droysens politische Tätigkeit in der Schleswig-holsteinischen Frage*, Erlangen, 1930. Supplements the standard biography.

MEINECKE, F., *Weltbürgertum und Nationalstaat. Studien zur Genesis des deutschen Nationalstaates*, München and Berlin, 1928. A classic and indispensable study.

Neue deutsche Bibliographie, Historische Commission Berlin, 1952. This will replace the *A.D.B.*

OSTENFELD, J. M., *Studier over Stemninger og Tilstande i Holsten 1815–1830*, Kopenhagen, 1909. A valuable analysis of political attitudes and the cultural background.

OTTOSEN, J., *Peter Hjort Lorenzens historisk Gerning*, København, 1896. The most satisfactory life.

PAULS, V., 'Uwe Jens Lornsen und die Schleswig-holsteinische Bewegung', Z 60 Neumünster, 1931. Challenges the hitherto accepted view of Lornsen, but is rejected by Scharff, the latest worker in this field.

PAULS, V., AND SCHEEL, O., *Geschichte Schleswig-Holsteins*, Neumünster, 1940. For over a century attempts have been made to write a standard history of Schleswig-Holstein. Pauls and Scheel started work in 1933, but war intervened and for the 19th century only Hagenah's contribution, 1830–1844, appeared. Pauls was still working on the project when he died in 1954. A determined effort is now being made to complete the work. C. Degn has been commissioned to write on the period 1773–1830 and A. Scharff on 1830–64.

PAULSEN, H., 'Oplysningstiden i Hertugdømmerne 1773–1817, Studier over kirke og skoleforhold i Hertugdømmernes religiøse og nationale Brydningstid', 6 parts, *S.A.*, 1933–8. Only detailed study of a hitherto neglected aspect of the period.

PAULSEN, J., 'Tyske Embedsmaend i København i Tiden 1800–1840. En oversigt over deres Indflydelse paa Udvirklingen af den nationale modsaetning indenfor den danske Helstat', *S.A.*, 1936. Useful study.

PETERSEN, C., *Nikolaus Falck und die Entstehung des Schleswig-holsteinischen Gedankens*, Breslau, 1926. Useful study of his ideas.

—'Nikolaus Falcks politische Wandlung in den Jahren der Reaktion 1819–1834', Z 67 Neumünster, 1939. An important study showing that Falck considered preservation of the *Helstat* more important than a Schleswig-Holstein constitution.

RASCH, M., 'Thies Hansen Steenholdt 1784–1856 mit aufgefundenen Briefen', Z 80, 1956. The only study of the North Schleswig deputy who sided with the Schleswig-Holsteiner against the Danes in 1840.

RICHTER, P., 'Aus der Schleswig-Holsteinischen Verfassungs und Verwaltungsgeschichte von 1815–1835', Z 58 Kiel, 1929. Important article based on papers of J. F. Jensen, *Deputierte* in the *Deutsche Kanzlei* up to 1831 and a cousin of Dahlmann's. Reveals Lornsen's indebtedness to official circles for his ideas.

SACH, A., *Das Herzogtum Schleswig in seiner ethnographischen und nationalen Entwicklung*, III Abteilung, Halle, 1907. A standard work.

SCHARFF, A., 'Uwe Jens Lornsens Vermächtnis. Studien zu Lornsen und seinem Freundeskreis', Z 74/75, 1951.

—'Aus den Anfängen der Kämpfe um Sprache und Volkstum in Nord-Schleswig', in *Deutcher Volkskalender Nordschleswig Apenrade*, 1956. An examination of the petitions from North Schleswig on the language question, especially those from Norborg Amt opposing the introduction of Danish in court.

—'Zur Beurteilung der Petitionsbewegung 1816–1818', Z 81, 1957. Convincing refutation of Boyens.

—'Die Verfassungspetition der Stadt Flensburg vom Dec. 24 1816', Z 80, 1956. Based on the Flensburg archives and critical of Boyens' and Fabricius' interpretation.

SCHEEL, O., *Der junge Dahlmann*, Breslau, 1926. Important study, strongly critical of Brandt.

— 'Die Schleswiger Ständetagungen von 1838 und 1840 zur Einführung der dänischen Gerichts und Verwaltungssprache in Nordschleswig', in *200 Jahre Schleswig-Holsteinische Anzeigen*, Glückstadt, 1950. Scheel, a native of North Schleswig, is strongly critical of the Schleswig estates for rejecting Nis Lorenzen's *Sprachantrag*.

— 'Das Siebengestirn in der Schleswigschen Versammlung', in *Festschrift für Dr. F. Lammert*, Stuttgart, 1954. Brief study emphasizing the provincial outlook of North Schleswig members in 1838 and 1840.

— 'Eine Fehldeutung und Legende aus dem beginnenden Nationalitäten Kampf im Herzogtum Schleswig', in *Festschrift zum 65 Geburtstag von Otto Becker*, Wiesbaden, 1954. Defends his great grandfather, A. Petersen, North Schleswig member of the estates, against the Danish accusation that he sided with the Schleswig-Holsteiner.

SCHRÖDER, L., 'Christian Flor', S.A. Flensburg, 1892. An examination of his political activity in the 1830's.

SCHULTZ, J. H., *Danmarks Historie*, vol. IV, København, 1942. The most recent popular history.

SCHWEICKHARDT, G., *Wilhelm Beseler als Politiker*, Kiel, 1927. The only study. Useful analysis.

SKAU, L., *Peter Hjort Lorenzen. Et Bidrag til den dansk-slesvigske Sags Historie*, Kjøbenhavn, 1865. Partisan account by a prominent leader of the Danish movement.

SPRINGER, A., *Friedrich Christolph Dahlmann*, 2 vols., Leipzig, 1870–2. Standard biography.

THORSØE, A., *Den danske Stats Historie fra 1814–1848 eller fra Freden i Kiel til Kong Kristian den Ottendes Død*, København, 1879.

THURAU, H., *Die Anfänge eines deutschen nationalpolitischen Bewusstseins in Schleswig-Holstein*, Flensburg, 1939. Most useful for the period 1806–14.

TIEDEMANN, C. v., *Aus sieben Jahrzehnten Bd. I Schleswig-holsteinische Erinnerungen*, Leipzig, 1905. Written by his son.

WEGENER, C. F., *Über das wahre Verhältnis des Herzogs von Augustenburgs zum holsteinischen Aufruhre. Eine actenmässige Darstellung nebst Beilagen aus den Augustenburgischen Papieren*, Copenhagen, 1849. The duke's letters in P.A., captured by the Danes in 1848, are used to make him the villain of the piece. Highly partisan.

Contemporary Newspapers and Periodicals

Augsburger Allgemeine Zeitung
Numbers in 1840's.

Faedrelandet
Numbers in 1840's.

Itzehoer Wochenblatt
Numbers in 1840's.

Kieler Korrespondenz Blatt, 1830–47.
Especially numbers for 1839–40–41.

Kieler Blätter, Kiel, 1815–19.

Neuen Kieler Blätter.

Neues Staatsbürgerliches Magazin, 10 vols., Schleswig, 1833–41.

Proben Schleswig-Holsteinische Pressfreiheit, II, *Die deutsche Bewegung*, Leipzig, 1844. Collection of newspaper articles on the language question and the *Volksfeste.*

Staatsbürgerliches Magazin, 20 vols., Schleswig, 1821–41. Edited by Falck and Carstens in the 1820's and then by Falck alone.

Schleswig-Holsteinische Blätter, 9 vols., Schleswig, 1835–40. Edited by C. Heiberg.

Maps

Biernatzki, J., *Nationalitäten und Sprachenkarte des Herzogthums Schleswig der deutschen Nationalversammlung gewidmet*, 1849.

Geerz, F., *Karte zur Übersicht der Grenzen der Volks und Kirchensprachen im Herzogthume Schleswig*, Eutin and Kiel, 1838.

Index